SCENE FROM *DAYS OF THE TURBINS*

On the eve of battle, the Turbins and their friends, high-minded Tsarists, drink to the victory that never came, in the first act of Michael Bulgakov's drama as presented by the Moscow Art Theatre.

EDITED BY
EUGENE LYONS

Six Soviet Plays

TRANSLATED FROM THE RUSSIAN

WITH A PREFACE BY ELMER RICE

GREENWOOD PRESS, PUBLISHERS
NEW YORK   1968

PREFACE

To UNDERSTAND the contemporary Russian theatre, it is necessary to have some acquaintance with the essential facts of the Russian Revolution. But it is perhaps equally true that in order to understand the Russian Revolution, one must have some knowledge of the rôle which the theatre plays in the Soviet State. For not only does every post-revolutionary play deal with some phase of the gigantic social upheaval which, in less than two decades, has transformed half a continent, but — and this is much more important — the theatre itself has been made a pliant and potent arm of the State.

'Art is a weapon!' This is by no means the least familiar of the innumerable Communist slogans which bombard the eyes and ears of the visitor to the Soviet Union. And it is as a weapon that the Communists regard and use the theatre. Not as a medium of self-expression for the author or actor, not primarily as a means of re-creation for the spectator, but as a tool of the all-powerful and all-pervading State: an implement for disseminating the tenets of the Communist philosophy, for the graphic presentation of simple object lessons to an audience just emerged from illiteracy, and, in a more general sense, for the bringing to the masses of that 'culture' which is regarded as one of the essential perquisites of the citizen of a Socialist State.

Nevertheless, it must not be assumed — as it too frequently is — that the Soviet dramatists occupy themselves solely with problems of technology and industrial organization. These themes do figure prominently in the Soviet theatre — for the simple reason that they figure so prominently in the Soviet world — but the perusal of this volume should be convincing proof that they do not monopolize the Russian stage. Indeed, there is scarcely a theme that is not discussed by the Soviet dramatists: except the one that seems so important to us Westerners — the subjective problems of the individual!

For the Russian Revolution has not been content to overturn political and economic institutions. It has extended its challenge to every organized form of human life: religion, marriage, education, art. The plays in this volume present a good cross-section of this wide range of themes (although it is to be regretted that space limitations prevented the inclusion of an anti-religious play, to edify and startle the American reader). *Bread* deals effectively with the knotty problem of winning over the recalcitrant muzhiks to the all-important program of collective farming. In *Tempo* — a play which is particularly interesting to us because of its American hero — the muzhik is seen again, but this time in his efforts to transform himself from a feudal serf to a modern industrial worker: a subject which the author has enlivened by passages of broad humor. *Inga* is what would have been called twenty years ago a 'feminist' play. It deals with the woman who wishes to stand shoulder to shoulder with her man in the Soviet State. *Squaring the Circle* is a farcical quadrangle play — singularly reminiscent in spirit and in plot of Mr. Noel Coward's *Private Lives* — in which we are presented with some of those domestic complexities and infelicities which seem to have survived even the October Revolution. *Fear* — one of the outstanding successes of the Soviet theatre — treats of the subject so dear to the American liberal: the attempted adjustment of the individual-istic 'intellectual' to a mass civilization. Finally, the *Days of the Turbins* (a play distinguished by its deep humanity and the strength of its characterization) falls into the category of historical plays, which depict one or another of the momentous and tumultuous events of the Revolution itself. Taken together, the six plays should give the reader a fair sample of the Russian ferment.

From the point of view of the dramatist, there is nothing revolu-tionary about these plays. Technically, they are strictly orthodox. The *Days of the Turbins* is, more or less, in the Chekhov tradition. The others show a distinct reversion in form and treatment to the 'problem' play of Ibsen and of Brieux. But the Russian Revolution is young. Indeed, it is surprising that, in a time of turmoil and stress, so many interesting and provocative works have been produced. After all, the American Revolution (erudite readers will recall that there was one in 1776) produced little or nothing in the way of drama for nearly one hundred and fifty years.

The Soviet theatre is the most interesting in the world today. It is impossible to convey to anyone who has not seen it, a sense of the excitement which it arouses. The variety of production methods, the excellence of the acting, the ingenuity of the presentation and the scenic investiture, the attentiveness and enthusiasm of the audi-ences: these are unmatchable in any Western country. For theatre-lovers, a visit to the Soviet Union is indispensable.

ELMER RICE

CONTENTS

DAYS OF THE TURBINS

A Play in Four Acts and Seven Scenes

By MICHAEL BULGAKOV

Authorized translation from the Russian based upon the Moscow Art Theatre production

By Eugene Lyons

INTRODUCTION

IT IS not surprising that a large proportion of Soviet plays deals with the civil war and intervention period. It was the romantic epoch of the Revolution — an epoch of blood, grime, sacrifice, and tragedy, but all of it touched with heroism. Michael Bulgakov's *Days of the Turbins* is unquestionably the most outstanding of these plays.

The conventional pattern of the civil-war play matches heroic Reds against villainous Whites, with the Reds emerging triumphant. A variation of this simple theme can be found in almost every Soviet repertory. Bulgakov's play does not fit into this or any other standardized pattern. The actual fighting does not involve the Communists at all. It is between different reactionary military groups struggling for supremacy in the Ukraine. The Bolshevik Revolution rumbles and thunders under the very windows of the Turbin family. But there is not a single Bolshevik or near-Bolshevik character on the stage. The Turbin brothers and their comrades-in-arms are enlisted under the banner of Hetman Skoropatsky at a moment when the forces of Hetman Petliura are advancing upon Kiev. The tragedy of the Turbins is that they not only lose their war but lose their faith in the cause for which they are fighting.

Written in 1925 and first produced by the Moscow Art Theatre in October, 1926, *Days of the Turbins* has been an object of bitter controversy ever since. Because the Tsarist types which it portrays are presented in a sympathetic light, the play was attacked as politically harmful. Early in 1928 it was barred from the boards and it was not restored until four years later, in 1932. At present it is one of the most popular plays on the Moscow Art Theatre repertory and receives occasional production in Leningrad and other cities.

The initial performance in 1926 has become almost legendary in Soviet theatrical circles. The audience consisted in large part of just such Turbins as were depicted on the stage. The wounds of the expropriated classes were still fresh — there were brave Turbins on both sides of the footlights. Spectators wept and became hysterical. The play since then has remained unchanged, but the audience is no longer the same. The Turbins have been absorbed by the new society; or they are living corpses or literally dead. Events move so

3

fast that in eight years a play which was vibrantly contemporary has become almost historical. Bulgakov's fault, from the Communist viewpoint, was that he showed White Guards who were not black-guards; that he was more concerned with the nobility of his characters as individuals than with their villainy as a class. Time has dulled the edge of these objections. The play has taken its place as a true and profound picture of its time and its people.

Michael Bulgakov was born in Kiev, in 1891, the son of a professor at the Theological Academy of that old city. He was brought up among the kind of Russians, the 'intelligentsia,' whom he shows so accurately in this play and other works. At the age of twenty-five he received a degree in medicine, but he was already more interested in writing and practised medicine only a short time.

After the Revolution Bulgakov divided his time between acting and journalism, at the same time trying his hand at fiction. His first novel, *Deviltry*, appeared in 1924. It was followed the next year by *The White Guard*, upon which his *Days of the Turbins* is based. Shortly after the production of this play, the Vakhtangoff Theatre staged his comedy, *Zoika's Flat*, and in 1928 Tairov's Kamerny Theatre put on his satire on censorship, *The Purple Island*. An earlier play, *Flight*, has not yet been produced owing to objections by the censors. Bulgakov's dramatization of Gogol's classic, *Dead Souls*, under his own direction, is now on the Moscow Art Theatre repertory and another of his plays, *Molière*, is in rehearsal there. Since 1930 Bulgakov has been directing plays for the Moscow Art Theatre as well as writing them.

CHARACTERS

TURBIN, ALEXEI VASSILIEVICH: colonel of artillery; about thirty; an earnest, high-minded supporter of the old military traditions.

TURBIN, NIKOLAI VASSILIEVICH (NIKOLKA): his brother; about eighteen; a military student; life-loving, ardent.

TURBIN, ELENA VASSILIEVNA: their sister; about twenty-four; an attractive, intelligent woman.

LARIOSIK: their provincial cousin; aged twenty-one.

TALBERG, VLADIMIR ROBERTOVICH: Elena's husband; a colonel of the General Staff; some years older than his wife; a cold, self-centred type.

MISHLAYEVSKY, VICTOR VICTOROVICH: an artillery captain attached to the General Staff.

SHERVINSKY, LEONID YUREVICH: lieutenant; Personal Adjutant to the Ukrainian Hetman.

STUDZINSKY, ALEXANDER BRANISLAVOVICH: a captain of artillery.

HETMAN OF THE UKRAINE.

BOLBOTUN: commander of the First Cavalry Division of the Petliura forces.

GALANBA:
URAGAN: } officers under BOLBOTUN.
KIRPATY:

VON SCHRATT: a German general.

VON DUST: a German major.

MAXIM: watchman at the school building.

FYODOR: valet at the Hetman's headquarters.

A COSSACK DESERTER.

A BOOTMAKER.

A JEW.

OFFICERS, CADETS, SOLDIERS

Time: Winter of 1918.
Place: Kiev, capital of the Ukraine.

ACT I

SCENE I

SCENE: *The living-room of the Turbins, a cultured Russian family of the lower military aristocracy; a centre door opens into the library and another at the right leads into the kitchen; at the left, part of the vestibule is visible; a curtained window, centre, and a fireplace in the right wall. The room is simply and tastefully arranged, with a suggestion of family heirlooms in the solid mahogany furniture; a table stands in the centre, a piano in the corner, and an old-fashioned divan flanks the fireplace.*

As the curtain rises, the clock is striking nine, ending with a dulcet minuet. ALEXEI TURBIN *is sitting at the table, under a desk lamp, engrossed in official documents. His younger brother* NIKOLKA *is lounging on the divan, strumming a guitar. It is evening, the atmosphere is homey, a fire burns in the fireplace.*

ALEXEI *wears the uniform of a Russian Colonel of Artillery. He is a clean-cut young man, about thirty years old, pleasant, earnest, and likeable.* NIKOLKA, *eighteen, boyish, with more than a touch of mischief in his make-up, wears the uniform of a military cadet.*

NIKOLKA (*accompanying himself on the guitar, sings an anti-Petliura ballad popular at that time*).

> News is bad and growing worse,
> The Petliura gang's a curse;
> But our guns were helly-full
> And Petliura got a belly-full.
>
> Pulemyot-chiki-chiki
> Golubchiki-chiki —
>
> Saved us from a journey on a hearse.

ALEXEI. Devil knows what you're singing. A street-song! Do sing something decent.

NIKOLKA. A street-song? What do you mean? I composed it myself. Aliosha! (*Sings.*)

> You may sing or you may hum,
> All the same your voice is bum;
> There are voices beyond mend,
> Make your hair stand up on end.

ALEXEI. That's just what *your* voice is like.

NIKOLKA. Aliosha, really you are unfair. Of course my voice is not quite like Shervinsky's, but still it is pretty decent. It is something in the vicinity of a dramatic baritone. Lenochka, hey, Lenochka, what do you think? Have I got a voice, or not?

ELENA (*offstage*). Who? You? No, not in the least.

NIKOLKA. She is in a bad mood, that's why she answers that way. In fact, Aliosha, my singing-teacher told me, 'If not for the revolution, Nikolai Vassilievich, you could have been singing in the Opera.'

ALEXEI (*still trying to work*). Your teacher is an ass.

NIKOLKA. I knew it.... The whole house is in a state of nerves. No voice! Only yesterday my voice was all right.... But now the singing-teacher is an ass, and everything is pessimistic in general. But as far as I am concerned, I stick to optimism. (*Strums a pensive tune on the guitar.*) Still, do you know, Aliosha, even I am beginning to get uneasy. It's nine already and he said he'd be home early in the afternoon. I'm afraid that something might have happened to him.

ALEXEI (*with a gesture of warning*). Don't talk so loud.

(ELENA *comes in: she is a robust young woman of twenty-four, handsome rather than beautiful, modestly dressed; her abundant blonde hair is of a tint verging on red.*)

ELENA. What time is it? Look at the dining-room clock.

NIKOLKA. It's... er, yes... it's nine o'clock. But our clock is fast, you know, Lenochka.

ELENA. Don't tell me fibs, please.

NIKOLKA. Look how nervous she is... (*Sings.*)

> Gloomy, oh, how gloomy, is all hereabout...

ALEXEI. Don't tear my heart out. At least sing something cheerful.

NIKOLKA (*sings a military drinking-song with forced cheerfulness*).

> Come on, you good fellows,
> Here's wine, boys, that mellows,
> The season for swigging is getting on fine.
>
> Ring, song of mine — sing, song of mine,
> Gur-gur-gurgle bottle
> Of free and gratis wine.

Brimless hats askew,
Boots all shiny new,
We Cadets are marching and here's our White Guard line.

Ring, song of mine — sing, song of mine,
Gur-gur-gurgle bottle
Of free and gratis.

(*A rumble of music draws nearer: the electric light suddenly goes out; marching men can be heard singing as they swing by the house.*)

ALEXEI. Elena, have you got a candle?

ELENA. Yes... I think so... (*Goes out.*)

ALEXEI. God damn them. Every other minute the light goes out. I wonder what detachment that is.

(ELENA *returns with a burning candle.*)

ELENA. Keep quiet, listen...

(*A pause as all three listen. The electric light flares up again.* ELENA *blows out the candle. A cannon-shot in the distance.*)

NIKOLKA. How near it sounds. Sounds as if it were at Sviatoshin. Would be interesting to know what's happening there... Aliosha, maybe you'd send me to Headquarters to find out what's happening there. I'd like to go.

ALEXEI. Sure, only you are still wanted there! Just sit right here!

NIKOLKA. Yes, sir, Colonel. Do you know, it's this inactivity bothers me.... It's a bit vexatious... with people fighting over there. Wish our division were ready in a hurry.

ALEXEI. When I need your advice about preparing my division, I'll ask for it. Understand?

NIKOLKA. I understand. Beg your pardon, Colonel.

ELENA (*worried*). Aliosha, where can my husband be?

ALEXEI. He's coming, Lenochka, he's coming.

ELENA. But what can be the matter? He said he would come in the morning and here we are, nine in the evening, and no sign of him. Can it be that something happened...?

ALEXEI. But, Lenochka, of course nothing could have happened. You know well enough that the western railway line is guarded by the Germans.

ELENA. But why isn't he here yet?

ALEXEI. Well, I suppose they stopped at every station.

NIKOLKA (*reassuringly*). Revolutionary travel. An hour you ride, two hours you stop. (*Bell rings.*) You see, there he is, I told you. (*Rushes to open the door.*) Who's there?

MISHLAYEVSKY (*behind the scene*). Open the door, for God's sake, open quickly.

ALEXEI (*disappointed*). No, it isn't Talberg.

NIKOLKA (*admitting* MISHLAYEVSKY *into the vestibule*). Well! It's you, Vitenka.

(*Captain* MISHLAYEVSKY *is in a military greatcoat, a flat visored hat, leather boots; his face is frost-bitten.*)

MISHLAYEVSKY. Of course, it's me. Damn it... Nikolka, take my rifle, please.... Damn it to hell.

ALEXEI. Well, it's Mishlayevsky!

ELENA. Victor, where are you coming from?

MISHLAYEVSKY. Good evening, Lena. Just a second. (NIKOLKA *helps him out of coat and hat.*) Oh, oh! Go easy with my overcoat, Nikolka, there's a bottle of vodka in the pocket... don't you smash it. (*Walks, gingerly, in pain.*) Oh... I'm coming from the 'Red Inn.' Permit me, Lena, to remain here tonight. I won't be able to get home, I'm absolutely frozen. (*Throws his jacket over a chair; he, too, is in Russian army uniform; a year or two younger than* ALEXEI, *more rough-hewn in physique than the Colonel.*)

ELENA. Good Heavens! Of course. Come quickly to the fire. (*Helps him to the fireside.*)

MISHLAYEVSKY. Oh, oh, oh...

ALEXEI. Couldn't they give you felt boots, eh?

MISHLAYEVSKY. Felt boots! Those scoundrels... (*Throws himself on the rug before the fire.*)

ELENA. Listen, the bath's just being heated. Take his things off and meantime I'll prepare fresh linen for him. (*She leaves.*)

MISHLAYEVSKY (*to* NIKOLKA). My dear boy, pull 'em off, pull 'em off...

NIKOLKA. Just a minute, just a minute. (*Pulls off* MISHLAYEVSKY'S *boots.*)

MISHLAYEVSKY. Easy, boy, easy... There, that's better. Now let me have a drink... a bit of vodka, maybe.

ALEXEI. Right away. (*Pours a drink, which* MISHLAYEVSKY *swallows in one expert gulp.*)

MISHLAYEVSKY. My toes are going to the devil. Lost is lost. That's clear.

ALEXEI. Don't talk nonsense. They will thaw out in a jiffy. Nikolka, rub his feet with vodka.

MISHLAYEVSKY (*stops* NIKOLKA). Nothing doing. Not with vodka! I'm not going to waste the precious stuff to rub feet. Just rub with your hand, that'll do. (NIKOLKA *massages gently.*) Oh, oh, it hurts. Take it easy. (*Takes several gulps of vodka.*)

NIKOLKA. Oi, oi, oi... poor captain, how frozen he is!

(ELENA *enters carrying bathrobe and slippers.*)

ELENA. Now help him to the bath at once. There! Heavens, my poor boy! (*Gives him the things and goes out again.*)

MISHLAYEVSKY. God give you good health, Lenochka. Give me another sip of vodka, please. (*He throws down another glassful.*)

NIKOLKA. Well, Captain, are you a little warmer now?

MISHLAYEVSKY. I feel better.

NIKOLKA. Now tell us what is going on there near the 'Red Inn.'

MISHLAYEVSKY. A snowstorm. That's what's going on, and, Christ, I'd like to send this snowstorm, the frost, and the German rascals, Petliura and the whole lot of them to the...

ALEXEI. I can't understand why they've driven you like cattle to the Inn.

MISHLAYEVSKY. Because at the Inn there were supposed to be some moujiks, some of those same godly creatures, damn them, invented by Mr. Dostoievsky.

NIKOLKA. Is that so? But the papers say that the peasants are on the Hetman's side...

MISHLAYEVSKY. To hell with your papers, Cadet. I'd like to hang the whole newspaper crowd on one tree. I myself on a patrol ride this morning came across one old peasant. 'Where are your people?' I asked him. The village looked as if it were dead. But he must have been blinded by the snow. He didn't notice my shoulder-straps under the scarf and answered sweetly (*mimics the peasant*): 'All of 'em run over to Petliura'...

NIKOLKA. Oi, oi, oi...

MISHLAYEVSKY. Just so... oi, oi, oi... I grabbed the godly old bastard and said: 'So, all run over to Petliura! I'll shoot you, you old beast. I'll teach you to run over to Petliura! You'll run straight from me into Kingdom Come...'

ALEXEI. How did you get to town?

MISHLAYEVSKY. We've been relieved today, thank goodness.

They sent a detachment of infantry. I've kicked up a hell of a row at local Headquarters. It was terrible. There they were, sitting in a railway car and guzzling brandy. 'Yourselves you're lazying with the Hetman in the palace,' I told them, 'but you're chasing us artillery officers into the frost with nothing but light boots on us, to exchange shots with the village rabble.' They didn't know how to get rid of me. (*Mimics the officers.*) 'We'll give you a special command, Captain. Any kind you want,' they said. 'Go into town.' So here I am... An icicle... Aliosha, take me into your division.

ALEXEI. With pleasure. I myself wanted to commandeer you. I will give you the First Battery.

MISHLAYEVSKY. My benefactor...

NIKOLKA (*in rising spirits*). Hurrah! So we'll all be together. And Studzinsky will be the first officer. Gee, that's great.

MISHLAYEVSKY. Where are you stationed?

NIKOLKA. We took over the Alexander High School. (*Enthusiastically.*) We are almost set, Vitenka. Tomorrow or the day after, we can get to work.

MISHLAYEVSKY. I see, Cadet, you can't wait to give Petliura a chance to thrash you soundly.

NIKOLKA. It's still an open question, who'll thrash whom...

ELENA (*entering*). Well, Victor, go on, take your bath.

MISHLAYEVSKY. Lena, my soul, allow me to embrace you and kiss you for all this attention. (*Pauses at the door.*) What do you think, Lenochka, should I have some vodka now, or take it all at once later on, at supper?

ELENA. No, leave it until supper. Go ahead now, get along with you! You didn't happen to see my husband anywhere? He seems to have gotten lost.

MISHLAYEVSKY. He'll turn up, Lenochka. He'll be home soon, don't worry. (*Limps out.*)

(*Bell rings continuously.*)

NIKOLKA. Here we are. That's him. (*Runs into vestibule.*)

ALEXEI. Good gracious, what horrible noise!

(NIKOLKA *opens the vestibule door and admits* LARIOSIK, *bundled up to his eyes and laden with packages, baskets, a suitcase.* LARIOSIK *is a naïve, mamma's-boy provincial, aged twenty-one; not stupid but a little out-of-place in the world; the bell is still ringing raucously.*)

LARIOSIK (*awkwardly stumbles in*). Well, here I am... I must have done something to your bell...

NIKOLKA. You've pushed the button in. (*Runs to the front door.*)

LARIOSIK. Oh, my God, I'm awfully sorry. Please excuse me. (*Comes further in.*) Well, here I am. Good evening, most honored Elena Vassilievna (*bows*), I recognized you right away from your photo. Mamma sends you her warmest regards. (*The bell stops.* NIKOLKA *comes back.*) Also to Alexei Vassilievich! (*Bows again.*)

ALEXEI. How do you do!

LARIOSIK (*bows to* NIKOLKA). How do you do, Nikolai Vassilievich? I've heard so much about you. (*Looks around in growing confusion.*) You are surprised, I see... Allow me to hand you this letter. It will explain everything. Mamma told me to deliver the letter to you before even taking off my overcoat.

ELENA (*studies the letter*). A quite illegible handwriting.

LARIOSIK. Yes, horrible. If you permit, I'd better read you the letter myself. (*Takes it back.*) Mamma has such a handwriting — sometimes she can't make out what she's written herself. I have such a handwriting myself. It's in the family. (*Reads slowly and haltingly.*) 'My dear Lenochka...' (*points*) That's you! 'I am sending my little boy to you...' (*indicates himself*) That's me! '...to you, as to relatives. Take him to your bosom and be kind to him, you know so well how to do it. You have such a big apartment.' (*Interrupts himself.*) Mamma likes you and admires you very much, and you too, Alexei Vassilievich... (*Reads on.*) 'The boy will soon enter the Kiev University. With his abilities' (*coyly*) What nonsense, Mamma... 'it's no good for him to remain in Zhitomir and waste his time. I will send you payment for his board regularly. I should hate to think of him living with strangers. He's so used to family atmosphere. But I am in a hurry. The hospital train is soon leaving. He will tell you everything himself.' (*Notes their puzzled expressions.*) H'm, yes... that's all.

ALEXEI. May I ask whom I have the honor to meet?

LARIOSIK. Whom? How, whom? Don't you know me?

ALEXEI. I regret not to have the pleasure...

LARIOSIK. My God! And you, Elena Vassilievna?

ELENA. I don't know you either.

LARIOSIK. Good Lord, that's real witchery. I thought Mamma put everything in her telegram. Mamma sent you a telegram of sixty-three words...

NIKOLKA. Sixty-three words! That's a lot...

ELENA. We received no telegram.

LARIOSIK. Really, what a scandal! Excuse me, please... I thought I was expected and I came in just like that without even taking my things off. (*Begins to back out, knocks over a vase.*) Oh! I beg your pardon! I believe I smashed something. I'm so hard-lucky that way... (*Collapses in a chair.*)

ALEXEI. Won't you be kind enough to tell us your name?

LARIOSIK. You don't know my name? Larion Larionovich Shurzhansky.

ELENA. Ah, you're Lariosik, our cousin from Zhitomir?

LARIOSIK (*relieved*). Why, of course, that's me.

ELENA. Well, and... you've come to live with us?

LARIOSIK. Yes. You see I thought you'd expect me, after Mamma's telegram. But as it is... Excuse me please... I've left footprints on your carpet... (*Tries to erase them.*) I'll go to some hotel... (*Begins to gather his bundles.*)

ELENA. What hotels, in these days? Wait a while and take your things off.

ALEXEI. Nobody is sending you away. Take your coat off, please.

LARIOSIK. I thank you from the bottom of my heart.

NIKOLKA. Here, please. You hang your overcoat in the corridor.

LARIOSIK. I thank you from the bottom of my heart. How cozy it is in your house! (*Follows* NIKOLKA *back into the vestibule, where he begins to unbundle himself.*)

ELENA (*whispers to* ALEXEI). I suppose we'll have to keep him. What do you think, Aliosha? He's rather nice. You'll have no objections I suppose if we put him into the library? The room is empty anyway.

ALEXEI. Of course, tell him...

(LARIOSIK *re-enters, smiling nervously.*)

ELENA. First of all you must have a bath. There's somebody there already. Captain Mishlayevsky. After your railway trip, you know...

LARIOSIK. I thank you from the bottom of my heart. It took me fully eleven days from Zhitomir to Kiev.

NIKOLKA. Eleven days! What a haul!

LARIOSIK. Horrible, horrible... a real nightmare...

ELENA. Well, your bath is ready.

LARIOSIK. I thank you from the bot... But excuse me, Elena Vassilievna. I can't take a bath.

ALEXEI. Why not? What's wrong?

LARIOSIK. Excuse me, please. It's like this, some scoundrels in the train stole my suitcase with my linen... I am terribly hard-lucky, you know. They left me the suitcase with the books and manuscripts, but the linen is gone.

ELENA. Well, that can be remedied.

NIKOLKA. Never mind, I'll give you something.

LARIOSIK (*confidentially*, *to* NIKOLKA). I think I've got one shirt left. I wrapped Chekhov's complete works in it. (*Bashfully, in lowered voice.*) But won't you be so kind as to give me... well, a pair of drawers.

NIKOLKA. With pleasure. I'm afraid they'll be too large for you, but we can fix them all right with safety-pins.

LARIOSIK. I thank you from the bottom of my heart.

ELENA. We'll put you up in the library, Larion Larionovich. Nikolka, show him the way.

NIKOLKA. Come with me, please. (*They leave.*)

ALEXEI. There's a type for you! First of all I'd give him a hair-cut. I don't presume to guess what sort of person he really is. Well, Lenochka, I'm going to my room. I've got a lot more to do, and I'm being constantly interrupted here. (*Gathers his papers, takes the table lamp and leaves.*)

(*A pause; ELENA, alone, no longer conceals her agitation; she looks at the clock, paces the room and peers through the window. Suddenly the bell rings.*)

ELENA. Who is there?

TALBERG (*offstage*). It's me. Open the door.

(*Colonel* TALBERG *enters, impeccably uniformed. He is a tall, dry person, with a hard voice and choppy, exaggeratedly military manners; he wears pince-nez and carries a brief-case.*)

ELENA. Thank goodness! Where have you been so late? I was terribly upset. (*Approaches anxiously, as if to kiss him.*)

TALBERG. Don't kiss me. I'm frozen. You'll catch cold.

ELENA. Where have you been?

TALBERG. I was detained at German Headquarters. Some important affairs.

ELENA. Come on quick, get warmed. We'll have tea at once.

TALBERG. Wait a minute, Lena. I don't want tea. (*Inspects the room with his shifty eyes.*) Tell me, please, whose coat is that lying about?

ELENA. Mishlayevsky's. He just came from the front, absolutely frozen.

TALBERG (*grumpily*). All the same, it could be put in its place.

ELENA. I'll put it away directly. (*Hangs the coat behind the door.*) Well, do you know the news? Quite unexpectedly my cousin from Zhitomir arrived here, the famous Lariosik.

TALBERG. I knew he would.

ELENA. Alexei told him he could remain with us. He'll live in the library.

TALBERG. I knew he would! As if one Signor Mishlayevsky in the house were not enough... Some provincial cousins must show up from Heaven knows where! It's not a house we've got, but a country hotel. I just can't understand Alexei.

ELENA. Volodia, you are in a bad mood. I don't see what harm Mishlayevsky has done you. He is a very nice fellow.

TALBERG. Splendid fellow. A regular gadabout and drunkard.

ELENA. Volodia!

TALBERG. Anyhow, at this moment, I am not much concerned about Mishlayevsky. Listen, Lena, close the door, something important has happened.

ELENA (*closing the door*). What is it?

TALBERG. The Germans are abandoning the Hetman, letting him go to the Devil.

ELENA. What are you talking about, Volodia? How do you know?

TALBERG. I just heard it at German Headquarters, in strict confidence. Nobody knows it, not even the Hetman himself.

ELENA. And what will happen now?

TALBERG. What will happen?... H'm... (*Glances at wrist-watch.*) Half-past nine... so, so... (*Distracted.*) What will happen, Lena?

ELENA. What are you saying?

TALBERG. I say... Lena...

ELENA (*impatiently*). Well, 'Lena, Lena,' what is it?

TALBERG. Lena... I must run away, immediately.

ELENA. Run? Where to?

TALBERG. To Berlin. H'm... twenty-nine minutes to ten. My

dear, you know what faces me if the Russian army does not check Petliura and he gets into Kiev.

ELENA. You could be hidden here somewhere.

TALBERG. Darling, how can I be hidden? I'm not a pin. There is nobody in town who doesn't know Colonel Talberg. To hide the right hand of the Hetman's War Minister — a nice little job. I can't hang around in other people's houses without a jacket, like Signor Mishlayevsky. I would be found at once.

ELENA. Wait a bit. I can't understand how you mean to run away. It means we must both leave?

TALBERG (squirms). No, that's just what I was going to talk about. A terrible situation has developed. The town is surrounded by Petliura troops from all sides, and the only chance to get out is to leave on the train of the German Staff. But they don't take women. See? Thanks to my connections I've got one place promised for myself.

ELENA. In other words, you propose to leave alone?

TALBERG. My dear, I do not 'propose,' but I simply have no other way out... Twenty-five minutes to ten... You must understand — it's a catastrophe! The train leaves in an hour and a half. Decide, as quickly as possible.

ELENA. As quickly as possible! In an hour and a half! Well, in that case I have decided. Go!

TALBERG. You're a clever girl. (Kisses her hand formally.) I've always said so. (Nervously.) What was I going to say? (Busies himself with papers which he takes from the brief-case and from his pockets; some he destroys, others he conceals carefully as he talks.)... Yes, yes, you're a clever girl... but I've told you that already.

ELENA. For how long are you going?

TALBERG. Oh, about two months. I'll only wait in Berlin till this muddle is over and when the Hetman comes back...

ELENA. And if he shouldn't ever come back?

TALBERG. That can't happen. Even if the Germans leave the Ukraine, the Entente will take it and will restore the Hetman. Europe needs a Ukraine under a Hetman simply as a buffer against the Moscow Bolsheviks. You see, I've figured out everything.

ELENA. Yes, I see. But look here. The Hetman is still here. Our people are organizing armies. And you run away under everyone's eyes. Does it look decent?

TALBERG. Dear, you are a naïve girl. I tell you in secrecy that I

17

am running away because I know you would never say a word about it to anyone. Colonels of the General Staff never 'run away.' They are sent on missions. (*Taps his pocket.*) In my pocket I have an order from the Hetman's Staff sending me to Berlin. Not bad, is it?

ELENA (*bitterly*). Not bad at all. And what will happen to all the others now?

TALBERG. Permit me to thank you for lumping me with all the others. I am not all the others.

ELENA. You ought to warn my brothers.

TALBERG. Of course, of course. So everything is in order. Though it is hard on me to part with you for such a long time, I am glad in a way I am going away alone. With you here we won't lose our rooms.

ELENA (*in mounting anger*). Vladimir Robertovich, it's my brothers who are living here. Do you mean to imply that you are afraid that they will confiscate our rooms? You have no right to think such things.

TALBERG. No, no, of course not... But you know the proverb, my dear — Qui va à la chace perde sa place... And now one more thing... (*A softer, less business-like note in his voice; he sits on the divan and invites her to sit down beside him, which she does.*) In my absence... eh... (*takes her hand familiarly in his own and pats it*)... this fellow Shervinsky will be coming pretty often, no doubt...

ELENA. He comes when you're here too.

TALBERG. Unfortunately. You see, my dear, I don't like him.

ELENA. May I ask why?

TALBERG. His attentions to you are becoming... well, a little excessive and I should like... hm...

ELENA. Well, what would you like?

TALBERG. I can't give you a precise answer. You are a smart enough... you're an educated woman. You know yourself how to behave so as not to tarnish the name of Talberg.

ELENA. Very well... I won't tarnish the name of Talberg.

TALBERG. Why do you answer me so drily? I am not saying that I think you will deceive me. I know quite well such a thing couldn't happen.

ELENA. Why do you think, Vladimir Robertovich, that I could not deceive you?

TALBERG. Elena, Elena, I don't recognize you. This is the result of mixing with people like Mishlayevsky. A married woman deceiving her husband! Well, it's quarter to ten. I'll be late.

18

ELENA. I'll pack your things at once.

TALBERG. Darling, nothing more than a small suitcase with some linen. But for God's sake quickly. I give you one minute.

ELENA. Don't forget to say good-bye to my brothers.

TALBERG. Of course, only remember... I'm being sent on a mission.

ELENA. Aliosha, Aliosha! (*Runs out.*)

(ALEXEI *enters.*)

ALEXEI. Yes, yes, here I am. Ah, good evening, Volodia, how are you?

TALBERG. How do you do, Aliosha. (*They shake hands.*)

ALEXEI. What's all the excitement about?

TALBERG. Well, I must tell you some important news. The situation of the Hetman today became very serious.

ALEXEI. What do you mean?

TALBERG. Serious and very.

ALEXEI. What's wrong?

TALBERG. Altogether possible that the Germans won't help us and we'll have to fight off Petliura with our own forces.

ALEXEI. Is that so? Well, the business doesn't smell so good. Thank you so much for telling me.

TALBERG. Now the second thing. (*Clears his throat.*) I must leave immediately on an important mission.

ALEXEI. Where to, if you are not bound to secrecy?

TALBERG. To Berlin.

ALEXEI. Where? Berlin?

TALBERG. Yes, no matter how much I fought against it I couldn't get out of the thing. It's simply awful.

ALEXEI. For long, if I may be bold enough to ask?

TALBERG. For about two months.

ALEXEI (*frankly sceptical*). Ah, that's how it is.

TALBERG. And so... well... Allow me to give you my best wishes. Take care of Elena. (*Gives him his hand, but* ALEXEI *does not accept it.*) What's the meaning of this?

ALEXEI (*putting his hands behind his back*). This means that I don't like this mission of yours.

TALBERG. Colonel Turbin!

ALEXEI. At your service, Colonel Talberg.

TALBERG. You will have to answer for this, dear brother-in-law.

ALEXEI. Whenever you wish, Mr. Talberg.

TALBERG. When?... Oh, it's ten minutes to ten. When I get back.

ALEXEI. Well, God knows what will happen by that time.

TALBERG (*furious*). You... you! For a long time I have wanted to have it out with you.

ALEXEI. Quiet down... don't you dare to upset your wife, Mr. Talberg.

(ELENA *returns*.)

ELENA. What are you talking about?

ALEXEI. Nothing, nothing, Lenochka.

TALBERG. Nothing, nothing, my dear. Well, good-bye, Aliosha.

ALEXEI. Good-bye, Volodia. (*Forces himself to shake hands*.)

ELENA. Nikolka, Nikolka.

(NIKOLKA *runs in*.)

NIKOLKA. Well, here is me.

ELENA. Volodia is leaving on a mission. Say good-bye.

TALBERG. Good-bye, Nikolka.

NIKOLKA. Happy journey, Colonel.

TALBERG. Elena, here is some money for you. I'll send some more right away from Berlin. Good-bye, good-bye. (*Almost runs to the vestibule*.) Don't go with me, dear, you might catch cold.

ALEXEI (*in a disagreeable voice*). Elena, you'll catch cold.

(ELENA *and* TALBERG *go out; an embarrassing silence*.)

NIKOLKA. Aliosha, why did he leave that way? Where to?

ALEXEI. Berlin.

NIKOLKA. Berlin? Aha... at such a time... (*Looks through window*.) He's bargaining with the izvoschik. (*Philosophically*.) Aliosha, I noticed that he resembles a rat...

ALEXEI. And our house resembles a ship... Well, go to our guests. Go, go. (NIKOLKA *leaves*.) It seems our detachment is going straight to Heaven... Very serious, serious and very... The rat!

(ELENA *comes back and looks through the window*.)

ELENA. Gone!

CURTAIN

ACT I

SCENE 2

SCENE: *The same living-room about three hours later. The table has been moved farther to the left and is fully laid for supper.*

The curtain rises upon ELENA, *seated at the piano and absent-mindedly playing chords.*

ELENA (*sighs*). Gone! And now he's gone!

(*Lieutenant* SHERVINSKY *enters stealthily, unobserved. He's a handsome fellow and knows it; high-spirited, about twenty-seven; he is wearing a Caucasian burka, a great white cape, under which glitter boots and spurs.*)

SHERVINSKY (*looks at her affectionately, then blurts out*). Who has gone?

ELENA (*startled, swings around*). Good God! How you scared me. How did you get in without ringing?

SHERVINSKY. But your door is not even closed. Everything is open. Good evening, Elena Vassilievna. (*Kisses her hand.*) Allow me to present you... (*Draws an enormous bouquet from under the cape; kisses her hand again as she accepts the flowers.*)

ELENA. How often have I asked you, Leonid Yurevich, not to do such things? I don't like your throwing money away.

SHERVINSKY. Money exists to be thrown away, as Karl Marx said. Will you permit me to remove my burka?

ELENA. And if I should say that I don't permit it?

SHERVINSKY. Then I would remain seated at your feet the whole night wrapped in the cape.

ELENA. Oh, Shervinsky, that is an army compliment.

SHERVINSKY. I beg your pardon, it is a Guard's compliment. (*Removes the cape in the vestibule, disclosing a magnificent Circassian coat.*) I am so happy to see you! I haven't seen you for a long time. (*Kisses her hand again.*)

ELENA. If my memory does not fail me, you were here yesterday.

SHERVINSKY. Ekh, Elena Vassilievna, what does yesterday mean in these times? And anyhow, who has gone?

ELENA. Vladimir Robertovich.

SHERVINSKY. But wait a moment, he should have been returning today.

ELENA. Yes, he returned... and left again.

SHERVINSKY. Where to?

ELENA. What beautiful roses... To Berlin.

SHERVINSKY (*excited*). To Berlin? And for a long time, may I ask?

ELENA. For about two months.

SHERVINSKY. For two months? Is that so? (*Cannot conceal his joy.*) Sad, very sad... I am so upset, so upset. (*Kisses her hand too earnestly.*)

ELENA. Shervinsky, this is the fifth time you are kissing my hand.

SHERVINSKY. I might even say I'm crushed, simply crushed. My God! (*Executes a few dance steps.*) Hurrah, hurrah!

(NIKOLKA *enters.*)

NIKOLKA. Shervinsky, an aria from *The Demon*! (*He leaves again.*)

ELENA (*to* SHERVINSKY, *who is still cavorting*). What are you so noisily happy about?

SHERVINSKY. I am happy. Ekh, Elena Vassilievna, you can't understand...

ELENA. You are not a man of the world, Shervinsky.

SHERVINSKY. I am not a man of the world? Excuse me, but why ... No, I am a man of the world. It's simply that I am so upset, don't you know! And so he has gone and you have remained!

ELENA. As you see. How is your voice?

SHERVINSKY (*at the piano, tests his voice*). Ta-ra-ra-ram... (*Sings snatches from 'The Demon.'*) Voice rings pretty good, pretty good. Devil take it, coming here by droshky it seemed to me my voice was cracked, and here I am — I take one look at you, Elena Vassilievna, and the voice is in fine trim.

ELENA. Have you brought your music?

SHERVINSKY. You are a goddess of the first water.

ELENA. And the only thing worth while about you is your voice. Your appointed fate is a career in the Grand Opera.

SHERVINSKY (*modestly*). I admit there is something in me. You know, Elena Vassilievna, once in Zhmerinka I sang the epiphalamy of Nero. There as you know, is a high 'fa,' but I took a high 'la' and held it for nine bars.

ELENA (*dubiously*). How many?

SHERVINSKY. I held it for eight bars. Too bad you don't believe me. Good God, there was a Countess Hendrickov, a beauty, who fell in love with me immediately after that 'la.'

ELENA. And what happened afterwards?

SHERVINSKY. She poisoned herself with cyanide.

ELENA. Oh, Shervinsky! It's a disease with you, upon my word. (*Calls first into one door, then into the other.*) Gentlemen, gentlemen, come to the table.

(ALEXEI *comes in.*)

ALEXEI. Good evening, Leonid Yurevich. Please join us.

(MISHLAYEVSKY *enters from the right door, his head swathed in a towel turban-wise;* LARIOSIK *follows, rosy from the bath, his hair slicked down.*)

SHERVINSKY. Victor! Alive! Well, thank God! What's the idea of the turban?

MISHLAYEVSKY. Good evening, Adjutant.

SHERVINSKY. My respects, Captain.

(*Captain* STUDZINSKY *enters from the library; he is somewhat older than the other men; an erect military figure; precise and reserved in his manners. From the kitchen comes* NIKOLKA, *carrying a steaming samovar which he places on the table.*)

MISHLAYEVSKY. Permit me: Senior Officer of our Division, Captain Studzinsky. And this is Mr. Surzhansky. We took our bath together.

NIKOLKA. Our cousin from Zhitomir.

STUDZINSKY. Pleased to meet you.

LARIOSIK. Happy from the bottom of my heart. (*Shakes hands.*)

SHERVINSKY (*introducing himself*). Lieutenant Shervinsky of Her Imperial Majesty's Bodyguards, Uhlan Regiment and Personal Adjutant to His Highness.

LARIOSIK (*impressed*). Larion Surzhansky. Happy from the bottom of my heart... (*Shakes again.*)

MISHLAYEVSKY (*to* LARIOSIK). Don't get scared; ex-body, ex-guard and ex-regiment.

ELENA. Gentlemen, to the table.

ALEXEI. Midnight! Gentlemen, let's be seated. Remember we must rise early tomorrow morning.

SHERVINSKY (*surveys the table*). Oh, what splendor! May I ask what is the occasion?

NIKOLKA. It is the last supper of the Division. The day after tomorrow, we're off to war.

SHERVINSKY. Aha!

STUDZINSKY. Where do you permit me to sit, Colonel?

SHERVINSKY. Where am I permitted to sit?

(LARIOSIK *tries to sit near* ELENA, *but is gently eased out by* SHERVINSKY; *he ends up next to* MISHLAYEVSKY *on the opposite side of the table.*)

ALEXEI. Anywhere, anywhere. Please, gentlemen... Lenochka, we are all seated.

SHERVINSKY (*to* ELENA). And so... he is gone and you... have remained.

ELENA. Shervinsky, keep quiet.

MISHLAYEVKSY. Lenochka, won't you take some vodka?

ELENA. No, no, no.

MISHLAYEVSKY. Then some white wine?

STUDZINSKY. May I fill your glass, Colonel?

ALEXEI. *Merci*, help yourself.

MISHLAYEVSKY (*to* LARIOSIK). Your glass...

LARIOSIK. I, I... as a matter of fact I do not drink vodka.

MISHLAYEVSKY. I don't drink either. But just one little glass! How can you possibly eat herring without vodka? It just isn't done.

LARIOSIK. I thank you from the bottom of my heart. (*Chokes on his first drink.*)

MISHLAYEVSKY. It's a long, long time since I touched vodka...

SHERVINSKY. Gentlemen, to the health of Elena Vassilievna, hurrah!

(*All rise, clink glasses and drink, shouting* 'Hurrah! hurrah!')

ELENA. Quiet! Quiet, gentlemen, you will wake the whole street ... As it is, everybody thinks there are drunken parties at our house every day. Thanks, thanks.

MISHLAYEVSKY. Ekh, good! Vodka clears one's head. Isn't that so? (*Develops symptoms of tipsiness.*)

LARIOSIK (*uncertainly*). Yes, very.

MISHLAYEVSKY. I beg you, another glass, Colonel.

ALEXEI. Don't overdo it, Victor. Tomorrow, we take our place.

MISHLAYEVSKY. And take our place we shall.

ELENA. What news of the Hetman, tell me.

STUDZINSKY. Yes, yes, what about the Hetman?

SHERVINSKY. Everything is in order, Elena Vassilievna. It seems, gentlemen, that yesterday there was a supper for two hundred people at the Palace. Partridge... and the Hetman in national costume.

ELENA. Still, isn't it being said that the Germans are abandoning us to our fate?

SHERVINSKY. Don't believe... any rumors. Everything is in perfect order.

(MISHLAYEVSKY *is plying* LARIOSIK *with drink.*)

LARIOSIK. I thank you, most honored Victor Victorovich. As a matter of fact, I don't drink vodka.

MISHLAYEVSKY (*drinking*). Shame on you, Larion!

SHERVINSKY ⎱ Shame!
NIKOLKA ⎰

LARIOSIK (*gradually going under*). I thank you most humbly. (*Drinks more satisfactorily.*)

ALEXEI. Nikolka, you watch your step with this vodka.

NIKOLKA. At your service, Colonel. I'll switch to wine.

LARIOSIK (*admiringly*). How nicely you throw it down, Victor Victorovitch!

MISHLAYEVSKY. It comes with practice. (*Fills* ALEXEI's *glass.*) Aliosha...

ALEXEI. Thanks, Captain. Some salad?

STUDZINSKY. Many thanks.

MISHLAYEVSKY. Lena, darling, do drink some white wine. My joy! My red-headed Lena! I know why you are so upset. Forget it! Everything's for the best. (*Brings her a glass of wine, serving it on a plate.*)

SHERVINSKY (*enthusiastically*). Everything is for the best.

MISHLAYEVSKY. No, bottoms up, Lenochka, bottoms up.

NIKOLKA (*takes up guitar and sings a popular gypsy drinking-song*).

> Who's to drink this bowl?
> Who's to drink this bowl?
> Who's to get good health?
>
> Drink the bowl! Get good health!

ALL (*catch up the chorus, as* ELENA *begins to drink*).

> To our Elena Vassilievna!
>
> Lenochka, Lenochka, drink it, drink it...
> Lenochka, Lenochka, drink it, drink it...

(*Clap hands in rhythm, repeating the last line, until the glass is all drained;* ELENA *places it upside down on the plate.*)

ALL. Bravo! Bravo! (*Applaud her.*)

MISHLAYEVSKY (*to* ELENA). You look lovely today, I swear. And that wrap becomes you, 'pon my honor. Gentlemen, observe what a wrap, perfect green.

ELENA (*laughs gaily*). Vitenka, it's a dress and it's grey.

MISHLAYEVSKY. Well, so much the worse. It's all the same. Gentlemen, I call your attention: would anyone dare to say she is not a beautiful woman?

STUDZINSKY. Elena Vassilievna is very beautiful. To your health!

MISHLAYEVSKY. Radiant Lena! Permit me to embrace you and kiss you... (*Goes to her.*)

SHERVINSKY (*interferes*). Eh, there!

MISHLAYEVSKY. Leonid, you get away. Get away from another man's wife. (*Kisses* ELENA.)

SHERVINSKY. But listen...

MISHLAYEVSKY. I am allowed, I am a childhood friend.

SHERVINSKY. You're a swine, not a childhood friend.

NIKOLKA (*rises*). To the health of the Commander of the Division.

(STUDZINSKY, SHERVINSKY, *and* MISHLAYEVSKY *rise, clicking their heels.*)

LARIOSIK (*rises unsteadily*). Hurrah... excuse me, gentlemen, I am not a military man...

MISHLAYEVSKY. It's all right, Larion, quite all right.

LARIOSIK. Most honored Elena Vassilievna, I cannot express to you how nice I feel here at your house.

ELENA. I am very deeply touched.

LARIOSIK. Most honored Alexei Vassilievich...

ALEXEI. Very pleased.

LARIOSIK (*grows bibulously sentimental*). Gentlemen, these cream-colored curtains — behind them one's soul relaxes, you forget all the horrors of civil war... And our wounded souls are so famished for rest...

MISHLAYEVSKY. May I ask you, confidentially, do you indulge in poetry?

LARIOSIK. I... well, yes, I write...

MISHLAYEVSKY. So... pardon the interruption.

LARIOSIK. It's all right... cream-colored curtains, they cut you off from the whole world. But, by the way, I am not a military man. Ekh!... Fill another glass for me!

MISHLAYEVSKY. Bravo! Larion. Look at the rascal, and he says he doesn't drink. You are a good fellow, Larion, but you make speeches like a most honored cripple.

LARIOSIK. Don't say that, Victor Victorovich. I have made speeches, and pretty often... in Zhitomir... to the colleagues of my late Papa... at dinners. There were tax-collectors... and, you know, they too scolded me... and how!

MISHLAYEVSKY. It's a well-known fact that tax-collectors are swine...

SHERVINSKY. Drink, Lena, drink, darling.

ELENA. You want to make me drunk, do you? You bad boy!

MISHLAYEVSKY. Take the guitar, take the guitar, Nikolka!

NIKOLKA (*plays the guitar and sings a Tsarist military march*).

> Tell me, soothsayer, beloved of God,
> What does my future hold for me?
> Will I soon be buried and covered with sod,
> To bring joy to every enemy?

ALL (*take up the chorus*).

> So music louder sounds, play on the victory!
> We have conquered, and the enemy has fled, has fled, has fled,
> And so...

LARIOSIK (*naïvely blurts out the forbidden words*). To the Tsar!

ALEXEI (*alarmed*). Sh... what are you doing?

ALL (*sing the dangerous phrases without words*).

> Tra-la-la-la-la-la
> Tra-la-la-la-la-la...

(*Finish the last line of the chorus aloud.*)

> We shout a proud hurrah! hurrah! hurrah!

LARIOSIK. Ekh, how gay it is here! Elena Vassilievna, darling. Lights... curtains... hurrah!

SHERVINSKY (*stands up*). Gentlemen, to the health of His Highness, the Hetman of All Ukraine. Hurrah!

(*A sullen silence; all remain seated.*)

STUDZINSKY. Your pardon. Fight I shall tomorrow, but I refuse to drink this toast, and do not advise other officers to do so.

SHERVINSKY. Captain!

27

LARIOSIK (*bewildered*). A most unexpected development!

MISHLAYEVSKY (*drunk*). And for him, devil take him, I froze my feet. (*Drinks.*)

STUDZINSKY. Colonel, do you approve of this toast?

ALEXEI. No, I do not approve.

SHERVINSKY (*abashed*). Colonel, allow me to have a word.

STUDZINSKY. No, permit me to speak!

LARIOSIK. No, allow me, I shall speak! To the health of Elena Vassilievna and to her most honored husband who has departed for Berlin.

MISHLAYEVSKY (*jerks* LARIOSIK *down*). There! You hit it right in the bull's-eye, Larion. Couldn't have done better.

LARIOSIK. Excuse me, Elena Vassilievna...I am not a military man.

ELENA. Pay no attention to him, Lariosik. You are a man with a soul, my dear, a good man. Come to me!

LARIOSIK. Elena Vassilievna... (*Lurches forward and upsets a bottle.*) Oh, there I go, red wine!

NIKOLKA. Sprinkle it with salt... No matter...

STUDZINSKY. This Hetman of yours...

ALEXEI (*rises in agitation and speaks emotionally*). What the devil! Does he mean to make fun of us? If this Hetman of yours, instead of playing a damned comedy of Ukrainization, had begun to organize an officers' corps, there would be no trace of Petliura in Little Russia by now. Not only that — we would have crushed the Bolsheviks in Moscow like flies. And this is the proper moment. It is said they are reduced to eating cats over there. The scoundrel could have saved Russia!

SHERVINSKY. The Germans would not have permitted the organization of an army, Colonel. They are afraid of it.

(*The lights gradually grow dimmer as* ALEXEI *speaks and add to the growing melancholy of the scene; his voice is passionate, glowing against the gloom.*)

ALEXEI. Untrue! It should have been explained to the Germans that we are not dangerous to them. Finished. The war is lost. We now face something more terrible than war, than Germans, than anything on earth. We face the Bolsheviks! We should have told the Germans: 'What do you need? Ukrainian bread, sugar? Take it! Stuff yourselves, choke yourselves... Only help us to save our God-fearing population from catching this Moscow disease!' What in hell was the use of all this stupid business of Ukrainian uniforms!

And now it is too late. Now our officers have all become café-hounds. A café-army! Try and drag such an officer to war! You imagine you can make him fight! But the rascal has money in his pocket. He sits in the café on the Avenue. The same place where the Staff gang hangs out! Well, excellent! They gave Colonel Turbin a Division. Fly, hurry, organize — Petliura is coming. Splendid! I look it over, and I give you my word of honor, for the first time in my life my heart sank...

MISHLAYEVSKY. Aliosha, my dear little Commander. You have the heart of a cannonader. I drink to your health!

ALEXEI. It sank, because with my hundred cadets I have a hundred and twenty college-boys who handle a rifle like a shovel. And yesterday on the drill-ground... snow falling, fog-banks shrouding everything... it seemed to me, you know, like one grave...

ELENA. Aliosha, why do you say such depressing things? Don't, please.

NIKOLKA. Don't worry, Commander. We will hold out.

ALEXEI. There, gentlemen, I am sitting here in your midst, and there is one thought that haunts me. If we could only have foreseen all this! Do you know what this Petliura of yours is? Just a myth, a black ghost! He doesn't really exist. Look outside the windows and see what is there. A snowstorm and some shadows... Gentlemen, in Russia there are only two forces — the Bolsheviks and us. We will yet clash. I see more terrible times ahead. And even if we don't manage to hold Petliura back, he won't last long either. After him, will come the Bolsheviks. And that's why I will risk all. When we meet the Bolsheviks, things will begin to get more lively. Either we will finish them, or they'll finish us. I drink to that encounter, gentlemen!

(LARIOSIK *has stumbled to the piano; the lights are pale and throw ghastly shadows;* LARIOSIK *begins to hammer out a gypsy romance; everybody encourages him, as though to drown out forebodings.*)

LARIOSIK (*sings*).

> I thirst to meet you!
> Pledges, speeches,
> All was empty,
> All meant nought.

NIKOLKA. Well said, Lariosik.

> All was empty,
> All meant nought.

(*Everybody sings, mostly in different keys;* MISHLAYEVSKY *is no longer himself and grows every minute more sullen;* SHERVINSKY *tries to make* ELENA *dance; suddenly* LARIOSIK *stops playing and begins to sob.*)

ELENA. Lariosik, darling, what's the matter?

NIKOLKA. Lariosik!

MISHLAYEVSKY (*illogically angry*). What is it, Lariosik? Who has insulted you?

LARIOSIK. I was scared...

MISHLAYEVSKY. Of whom, the Bolsheviks? We'll soon show them. (*Draws out his revolver and flourishes it menacingly.*)

ELENA (*alarmed*). Victor, what are you doing?

MISHLAYEVSKY. I am going to shoot some commissars... (*Shouts at all of them.*) Any commissars among you?

SHERVINSKY. Stop him, boys, that gun is loaded!

STUDZINSKY. Captain, sit down at once.

ELENA. Take it away from him. Take it away!

(*The revolver is taken away after a struggle.*)

ALEXEI. What, are you mad? Sit down, gentlemen. It is my fault!

MISHLAYEVSKY (*disgusted, but suddenly calm*). In other words, I am in the company of Bolsheviks. That's nice. How do you do, comrades! How do you do. Let us drink to the health of the commissars. They are so gentle. (*Fills another glass.*)

ELENA. Victor, stop drinking.

MISHLAYEVSKY. Keep quiet, Madame Commissar...

SHERVINSKY. God, how tight he is!

ALEXEI. Gentlemen, it is my fault. Forget what I said. My nerves are a little on edge.

STUDZINSKY. Oh, no, Colonel. We understand, and believe me, we feel exactly the way you do. We shall always defend our Russian Empire.

SHERVINSKY. You misunderstood me, gentlemen. The Hetman will do just as you proposed. The Allies will help us to beat the Bolsheviks and the Hetman will bring the Ukraine to the feet of his Imperial Majesty the Emperor Nikolai Alexandrovich...

MISHLAYEVSKY. What Alexandrovich? And they dare say I am drunk!

NIKOLKA. The Emperor is dead...

SHERVINSKY. The news of the death of His Imperial Majesty...

MISHLAYEVSKY. ... Is somewhat exaggerated.

STUDZINSKY. Victor, don't forget you are an officer!

ELENA. Let him have his say, gentlemen!

SHERVINSKY. ... Is an invention of the Bolsheviks. You know what happened at Emperor Wilhelm's palace when the Hetman's retinue was presented to him? Emperor Wilhelm said: 'And future negotiations will be conducted by...' At those words the curtains parted and our Tsar appeared. He said: 'Go to the Ukraine, gentlemen, and form your divisions,' he said. 'When the time is ripe I will personally conduct you to the heart of Russia, to Moscow'... And there were tears in his eyes.

STUDZINSKY (*grimly*). He is dead!

ELENA. Shervinsky, is that true?

SHERVINSKY (*embarrassed*). ... Elena Vassilievna!

ALEXEI. Lieutenant, it's the same legend others have been spreading.

NIKOLKA. It doesn't matter. Even if the Emperor is dead, long live the Emperor. Hurrah! Sing the hymn... Shervinsky!

(NIKOLKA, *in a fervent voice, begins the Tsarist national hymn, 'God Save the Tsar!' The fervor draws the others into it;* SHERVINSKY, MISHLAYEVSKY, *and* STUDZINSKY *chime in, 'God Save the Tsar!'* LARIOSIK *stands up with difficulty and his drunken voice chimes in. Only* ALEXEI *and* ELENA, *still sober enough to realize the danger of singing this hated hymn, try unavailingly to stop them.*)

ALEXEI. Don't... don't, boys...

ELENA. Gentlemen! What are you doing!

(*The singers are too moved by patriotism and vodka to stop.* ALEXEI *and* ELENA *join in. The electric current is slowly returning and the lights grow gradually brighter as the scene proceeds.*)

MISHLAYEVSKY (*in tears*). Aliosha! But these Russians of ours are not people! They are brutes. A trade union of regicides! Take Peter the Third... And what harm had he done them? What, I ask? They yelled: 'War is unnecessary!' All right... he stopped fighting. And what then! His own noblemen hit him over the head with a bottle — Bang! Where is the Tsar? No more Tsar! Paul the First was killed by a wallop over the ear with a cigarette-case. And that other one... what's his name? With the side-breezers, a rather nice fellow, and he thought, 'I'll give the peasants a treat. I'll give the swines their freedom.' He got blown up with a bomb for

31

his pains! They ought to be flogged, the rascals, Aliosha! Oh, I feel so rotten, boys!

ELENA. He is sick.

NIKOLKA. The Captain is not well!

ALEXEI. Take him to the bathroom.

(STUDZINSKY, NIKOLKA, *and* ALEXEI *lift* MISHLAYEVSKY *and lead him out of the room.*)

ELENA (*follows*). I'll go and see what has happened to him.

SHERVINSKY (*obstructing her path*). Don't go, Lena! He'll be all right.

ELENA. But, Heavens, why do you men overdo it? And Lariosik too. (*Tries to wake* LARIOSIK, *who is sprawled at the table.*) Mess! Smoke! Lariosik!

SHERVINSKY. Don't wake him. Let him be! He'll sleep it off, that's all.

ELENA. You even make me tipsy. God, my legs won't walk. (*Sits on the divan.*)

SHERVINSKY. There, there! Let me sit beside you.

ELENA. Sit down... what will be the end of it all, Shervinsky? I had a bad dream. Everything of late seems to be getting worse and worse around us.

SHERVINSKY. Elena Vassilievna, everything will be all right. And pay no attention to the dreams. What was it you dreamt?

ELENA. No, no, my dream — was prophetic. As if we were all sailing on a ship bound for America and sitting down in the hold. A storm comes up. The wind howls. It is cold, cold... Mountainous waves... And we are down in the hold and the water licks our very feet. We climb onto benches, but the water keeps rising, rising... And worst of all, the rats!... Such horrible, immense rats! It was so terrifying that it woke me.

SHERVINSKY. And do you know, Elena Vassilievna, he won't come back?

ELENA. Who?

SHERVINSKY. Your husband.

ELENA. Leonid Yurevich, such cheek! What business is it of yours, whether he returns or not?

SHERVINSKY. It is very much my business. I love you!

ELENA. I've heard that before. You're just pretending.

SHERVINSKY. I swear I love you!

ELENA. Well, love and keep it to yourself!

SHERVINSKY. I won't. I'm tired of that!

ELENA. But hold on a minute. Why did you remind yourself of my husband when I spoke of rats?

SHERVINSKY. Because he looks like a rat.

ELENA. You're a swine, Leonid. In the first place, he doesn't resemble one in the least...

SHERVINSKY. Like two drops of water. With his pince-nez, his sharp little nose...

ELENA. Very, very pretty... to say such horrible things about a man in his absence, and in front of his wife...

SHERVINSKY. How are you his wife?

ELENA. What do you mean, how?

SHERVINSKY. Look at yourself in the mirror. You are beautiful, clever, intellectually developed, as one might say. In general, an A–1 woman! You accompany beautifully — and he beside you... a clothes-tree, a careerist, a General Staff clerk.

ELENA. Behind his back! Fine! (*Covers his mouth.*)

SHERVINSKY. I'd tell it to his face. I've wanted to a long time. I'll tell him and challenge him to a duel. You are unhappy with him.

ELENA. And with whom would I be happy?

SHERVINSKY. With me.

ELENA. You won't do.

SHERVINSKY. Why won't I do?... Oho!

ELENA. What's good about you?

SHERVINSKY. Take a good look at me.

ELENA. Adjutant's finery... a face like a cherub... and nothing more... except a voice.

SHERVINSKY. I knew it! What hard luck! Everybody says the same thing. Shervinsky the adjutant, Shervinsky the singer, but nothing else. But that Shervinsky has a soul, that nobody notices. Nobody! And so Shervinsky lives like a homeless cur and has nobody on whose breast he can rest his weary head. (*Leans his head against* ELENA.)

ELENA (*pushes his head away*). What an abominable Lovelace! I know all about your affairs. You say the same things to everybody ... even to that one... the long one... fui... with painted lips.

SHERVINSKY. She is not long. She's a mezzo-soprano. Elena Vassilievna, I swear I never told her and never could tell her any such things. It's not nice of you, darling. It's not nice of you at all, Lena.

ELENA. I'm not Lena to you.

SHERVINSKY. Well, it's not nice of you, Elena Vassilievna. It shows that you have no affection for me.

ELENA. Unfortunately, I like you very much.

SHERVINSKY. Aha! You like me and you don't love your husband.

ELENA. No, I love him.

SHERVINSKY. Don't lie. A woman who loves her husband does not have such eyes. Oh, feminine eyes, everything is visible in them.

ELENA. Well, of course, you're experienced.

SHERVINSKY. How did he leave?

ELENA. You would have done the same.

SHERVINSKY. I? Never! It's disgraceful. Admit yourself that you don't love him.

ELENA (*desperately*). Well, I don't love him and don't respect him. Are you satisfied? But don't jump to conclusions. Take away your hand.

SHERVINSKY (*pushing his advantage*). Why did you kiss me that time?

ELENA. You are lying. I never kissed you. You liar with shoulder-straps.

SHERVINSKY. I, lying? No... At the piano. I was singing 'God Almighty' and we were alone... I can even tell you when... On the eighth of November... We were alone, and you kissed me on the lips.

ELENA. I kissed you for your voice, you understand, for your voice. I kissed you maternally, because your voice is so marvellous. And that's all.

SHERVINSKY. That's all?

ELENA. This is torture. Upon my word. The dishes are dirty, everybody's drunk, my husband gone... the house all lit up...

SHERVINSKY. The light can be put out. (*Extinguishes upper lights.*) That's better. Listen, Lena. I love you very much. I won't release you anyhow. You will be my wife.

ELENA. Sticks like a leech, a leech...

SHERVINSKY. Why am I a leech?

ELENA. Takes advantage of every opportunity... and embarrasses me... and tempts me. It will get you nowhere, nowhere. He might be as bad as you say, but I will not destroy my life. Maybe you will turn out even worse.

SHERVINSKY. Lena, how lovely you are. (*Embraces her.*)

ELENA. Go away, I am drunk. You yourself purposely made me

drunk. You are a notorious rascal. All our life is crumbling. Everything is tumbling, falling...

SHERVINSKY. Elena, don't be afraid. I won't leave you at such a moment. I will be at your side, Lena.

ELENA. Let me go. I am afraid to tarnish the name of Talberg.

SHERVINSKY. Lena, leave him altogether and marry me, Lena. (*They kiss.*) Will you divorce him?

ELENA. Ekh... What will happen, will happen. (*They kiss again.*)

LARIOSIK (*awakes unexpectedly*). Don't kiss! It makes me vomit.

ELENA. Let me go! My God... (*Rushes out.*)

LARIOSIK (*groans*). Oh...

SHERVINSKY. Young man, you didn't see a thing!

LARIOSIK (*morosely*). No, I did see.

SHERVINSKY. What do you mean?

LARIOSIK. When you have a King, play the King and don't touch the Queen... Oi, oi...

SHERVINSKY. I didn't play with you.

LARIOSIK. Yes, you did.

SHERVINSKY. My God, how plastered!

LARIOSIK. Well, we will see what Mamma will tell you when I die. I said I'm not a military man. I can't drink so much vodka. I feel so lousy. (*Falls on* SHERVINSKY'S *breast.*)

(*The clock strikes three, plays its dulcet minuet.*)

SHERVINSKY. Lord, how soused!

CURTAIN

ACT II

Scene i

Scene: *The* Hetman's *study in the Palace, an immense and splendid chamber of marble and gilt; a huge map of Russia is painted on the back wall; a broad double door at the left opens into the corridor; another door at the right is hung with rich portières. A vast conference table is littered with documents, and on it two ordinary telephones. In the foreground, against the left wall, stands a field telephone.*

The scene is deserted when the curtain rises, but immediately the valet, Fyodor, *admits* Shervinsky. Fyodor *is a typical provincial menial, with puffy side-whiskers, servile manners and a regulation livery.*

Shervinsky. Good evening, Fyodor.

Valet. Good evening, Lieutenant.

Shervinsky. How's that, nobody here? Which of the adjutants is on duty at the telephone?

Valet. His Grace Prince Novozhiltzev.

Shervinsky. And where is he?

Valet. I cannot say. He left half an hour ago.

Shervinsky. How can that be? And the telephones have been abandoned just like that for half an hour?

Valet. But nobody rang. I was near the door all the time.

Shervinsky. No matter if nobody rang, but what if someone had rung! At such a moment. A hell of a business!

Valet. I would have taken the telephone messages. Those were His Grace's orders. Until you arrived, I was to take down messages.

Shervinsky. You! Take down military messages! He must have gone cuckoo. Ah, I understand, I understand. He got sick?

Valet. Not at all. His Grace has left the Palace for good.

Shervinsky. Left the Palace for good? You are joking, my dear Fyodor. Left the Palace without anyone on duty? It means he has left for an insane asylum?

Valet. I cannot say. But His Grace took his toothbrush, his towel and soap from the adjutants' toilet. I even gave His Grace some paper.

36

SHERVINSKY. What paper?

VALET. I'm just reporting, Lieutenant. His Grace wrapped the soap in yesterday's newspaper.

SHERVINSKY (*shrugs his shoulders in perplexity; discovers a sword*). But, wait a minute, there is his sword!

VALET. Yes, sir. His Grace left in civilian clothes.

SHERVINSKY. Either I'm crazy or you are. Did he at least leave me any reports? (*Searches on the desk.*) Did he leave any word for me?

VALET. His Grace ordered me to give you his regards.

SHERVINSKY. You may go, Fyodor.

VALET. Yes, sir. Allow me to report, sir.

SHERVINSKY. What else?

VALET. His Grace had received unpleasant news.

SHERVINSKY. From where, from home?

VALET. No, sir. On the field telephone. And immediately His Grace made haste to get away. And His Grace's face changed color.

SHERVINSKY. It seems to me, Fyodor, that the color of the faces of His Highness's adjutants does not concern you. You talk much too freely.

VALET. I beg your pardon, sir. (*Leaves.*)

SHERVINSKY (*emits a long whistle: then telephones from* HETMAN's *desk*). 1–4–2–3. *Merci.* Is this the home of Prince Novozhiltzev? Is Sergei Nikolayevich in? What? In the Palace? He's not in the Palace. (*Excited.*) But wait, Seriozha, that's your voice! Seriozha! What does it mean? (*The telephone is cut off.*) What gall! I'd swear that was his voice. Damn, damn, damn! (*A pause.*) Shervinsky, Shervinsky... (*Rings from field telephone.*) Is that Headquarters of the Svetozhinsk Division? Call the Officer in charge. What? He isn't there? What do you mean he isn't there? Then his assistant. You hear me? (*A pause.*) Devil take you! (*Drops the telephone; sits on the desk, rings for the valet, who enters:* SHERVINSKY *hastily writes a note.*) Fyodor, hand this at once to the courier. Tell him to go immediately to my house on Lvovsky Street, where he will receive a package for me. Let him bring it here, right away. Here are two rubles for a cab. And here is a note for the Commandant to pass him.

VALET. Yes, sir. (*Leaves.*)

SHERVINSKY (*caresses his sideburns thoughtfully*). Hell of a mess, upon my word. (*Desk telephone rings.*) Hello! Yes. The personal adjutant of His Highness, Lieutenant Shervinsky. Good evening, Your Excellency! What? (*A pause; obviously listening to alarming news.*) Bolbotun? How, with the whole Staff? Yes, sir. I will transmit it. Yes, Your Excellency, His Highness should be in at midnight. (*Hangs up receiver, the telephone rings off; a pause.*) I'm done for, gentlemen. (*Whistles meditatively.*)

(*From the corridor a muffled command is audible; 'Attention!' The* HETMAN *has arrived; the guards respond in chorus, 'Hail, Your Highness!'*)

VALET (*throws both halves of the door wide open*). His Highness!

(SHERVINSKY *jumps to rigid attention. The* HETMAN *comes in, a tall, impressive person in a gorgeous Circassian costume, raspberry-colored pantaloons, high Caucasian boots without spurs; brilliant General's epaulettes. His greying mustache is close-cropped; his head entirely shaven. The man is clearly haughty, self-centred and cruel.*)

HETMAN. How do you do, Lieutenant.

SHERVINSKY. Good evening, Your Highness.

HETMAN. Have they arrived?

SHERVINSKY. May I ask who?

HETMAN. I called a conference here for a quarter to twelve. The Commander of the Russian Army, the Commander of the Garrison, and representatives of the German Command should be here. Where are they?

SHERVINSKY. I don't know, sir. Nobody came.

HETMAN. Give me the reports of the last hour! Hurry.

SHERVINSKY. I take the liberty to report to Your Highness. I have just taken over duty. Prince Novozhiltzev was on duty before me.

HETMAN (*frowns*). For a long time I have wanted to emphasize to you and to the other adjutants that it is essential to talk in Ukrainian. It's shameful, after all. Not one of you speaks the language of our country. And on the Ukrainian forces this makes a most favorable impression.

SHERVINSKY (*mispronounces in a hopeless effort to speak Ukrainian*). Yes, sir. The adjutant on duty, Prince Novozhiltzev, temporarily acting as adjutant. I think...

HETMAN. Oh, speak Russian.

SHERVINSKY. Yes, sir, Your Highness. Prince Novozhiltzev unexpectedly left for home before my arrival. Apparently took ill...

HETMAN. What are you talking about? He abandoned his post? Are you in your senses? He left duty? What in the world is happening here? (*Calls on desk 'phone, angrily.*) Commandant! Let me have a small detachment... You ought to know by the voice who is talking! Send the detachment at once to the home of Adjutant Novozhiltzev. Arrest him and bring him to the Commandant's Office without delay. At once! Double quick!

SHERVINSKY (*aside*). That'll teach you to disguise your voice on the 'phone! Scoundrel!

HETMAN. Did he leave the tape?

SHERVINSKY. Yes, sir. But there is nothing on it.

HETMAN. What's the matter with him? Off his head? I shall have him shot at once. Right here, on the parapet of the Palace. I'll show you all! Connect me at once with the Commander's Office. Ask him to come here at once. The same applies to the Commander of the Garrison and all regiment Commanders. Look sharp!

SHERVINSKY. May I report to Your Highness some extremely important news?

HETMAN (*irritably*). What other news is there?

SHERVINSKY. Five minutes ago I had a call from the Commander's Headquarters and was told that the Commander of Your Highness's Volunteer Army has been taken seriously ill and left with his entire staff for Germany.

(*An awkward pause. The* HETMAN'S *dignity is ruffled.*)

HETMAN. What! Have you lost your senses? Your eyes are wild. Look here, do you understand the meaning of your report? What has happened? A catastrophe, or what? Have they run away? Why are you silent? Well...

SHERVINSKY. Yes, Your Highness, a catastrophe. At ten o'clock this evening Petliura's forces broke the front and Bolbotun's cavalry came through the breach.

HETMAN. Bolbotun? Where?

SHERVINSKY. Ten versts behind the Slobodka Suburb...

HETMAN. Hold on... hold, wait a minute. So... Um... (*Suddenly more friendly, pats him on the shoulder.*) In any event, you are a splendid, capable officer. I noticed that long ago. Well, now, listen. Get a connection at once with the German Command and ask them to send a representative to see me immediately.

SHERVINSKY. Yes, sir. (*At the telephone.*) Third line! Seien, Sie bitte, liebenswürdig, den Herren Major von Dust ans Telephon zu bitten. (*A knock at the door.*) Ja, ja...

HETMAN. Come in!

VALET. The representatives of the German Command, General von Schratt and Major von Dust, ask to be received by Your Highness.

HETMAN. Ask them to come in. (*To* SHERVINSKY.) Never mind 'phoning.

(VALET *admits* VON SCHRATT *and* VON DUST. *Both are in grey uniforms and gaiters.* SCHRATT *is long-faced, grey-haired and portly.* DUST *is cadaverous and has a purple-colored face. Both wear monocles.*)

SCHRATT. Wir haben die Ehre Ihr Hoheit zu begrüssen.

HETMAN. Ich freue mich hertzlich dass Sie, meine Herren, gekommen sind. Bitte nemen sie Platz. (*The Germans sit down.*) Ich habe eben die Nachricht von sehr schweren Zustande unserer Armee bekommen.

SCHRATT. Das haben wir ja schon lange gewusst.

HETMAN (*to* SHERVINSKY). Please keep minutes of this conference.

SHERVINSKY. Should I write in Russian, Your Highness? (*Prepares to write.*)

HETMAN. General, may I ask you to speak Russian?

SCHRATT (*with a strong German accent*). With pleasure.

HETMAN. I have just learned that Petliura's cavalry has broken through the front of the city. (SHERVINSKY *writes.*) In addition I have some quite incredible news from the Staff of the Russian Army Command. The Staff of the Russian Command has disgracefully deserted. Das ist ja unerhört! (*Pause.*) I wish to make through you the following appeal to the German Government. The Ukraine is in mortal danger. Petliura's bands threaten to capture the capital. If this happens, an orgy of anarchy is inevitable in the capital. I am therefore asking the German Command to send me immediately forces sufficient to repulse the bands of invaders and to restore order in the Ukraine which is a cordial friend of Germany.

SCHRATT. The German Command, unfortunately, is not in a position to do this.

HETMAN. But why? Will you be good enough to explain, General, why not?

SCHRATT. Physisch unmöglich. Physically impossible. Erstens, firstly, Petliura, according to our information has two hundred thousand splendidly armed troops. (*Decisively.*) Moreover, the German Command is now withdrawing its divisions and evacuating them to Germany.

SHERVINSKY (*aside*). The scoundrels!

SCHRATT. Therefore, we have not sufficient armed forces at our disposal. Secondly, it seems that all of the Ukraine is on Petliura's side.

HETMAN (*to* SHERVINSKY). Please underline this statement in the protocol.

SHERVINSKY. Yes, sir.

SCHRATT (*sarcastically*). I have no objections — underline it. Thus, it is impossible to offer resistance to Petliura.

HETMAN (*more and more agitated and struggling to maintain his haughty pose*). It means then that the German Army Command is suddenly abandoning me, and the army of the Government, to the mercy of fate.

SCHRATT. No, we have orders to take measures for your escape.

HETMAN. What measures does the Army Command suggest?

SCHRATT. Immediate evacuation of Your Highness. You must board the train at once and depart for Germany.

HETMAN. Excuse me, I don't quite understand. What does that mean? I beg your pardon. In that case was it the German Command that also evacuated Prince Belorukov?

SCHRATT. Quite right.

HETMAN. Without consulting me? (*Excited.*) I lodge a protest to the German Government against such procedure. I disagree with it. I can still concentrate my forces in the city and defend the capital with my own resources. But the responsibility for the destruction of the capital will fall on the German Army Command. And I think that the Governments of England and France...

SCHRATT. The German Government feels itself sufficiently strong to prevent the destruction of the capital.

HETMAN. Is this a threat, General?

SCHRATT. A warning, Your Highness. Your Highness has no forces at your disposal. The situation is catastrophic!

DUST (*whispers to* SCHRATT). Mein General, wir haben gar keine Zeit, wir mussen...

SCHRATT. Yes, yes... Well, Your Highness will permit me to

41

present the latest report. We have just been informed that the Petliura cavalry is eight versts from Kiev. Tomorrow morning it will enter the city.

HETMAN. And I am the last to hear of it?

SCHRATT. Your Highness is aware what will happen to you if you are captured? A sentence has already been passed against Your Highness in Petliura's camp. It is a very deplorable sentence.

HETMAN. What is the sentence?

SCHRATT. I must apologize to Your Highness (*Leans closer for emphasis.*)... Hanging!... Allow me, Your Highness, to ask for an immediate answer. I have only ten short minutes at my disposal. After that I reject all responsibility for Your Highness's life.

(*Long pause;* SCHRATT *calmly looks at his wrist-watch.*)

HETMAN. All right, I'm leaving.

SCHRATT (*to* DUST). Be good enough to act, Major, secretly and without any noise or excitement.

DUST. Of course, without noise. (*Fires his revolver twice into the ceiling.*)

(SHERVINSKY *is bewildered; the* HETMAN *grabs a revolver; a commotion among the guards in the corridor.*)

HETMAN. What is the meaning of this?

SCHRATT. Don't worry, Your Highness. (*Hides behind the portières. Offstage are sounds of excitement, footsteps and a cry,* 'To arms, guards!')

DUST (*opens the corridor door*). Ruhig! Quiet! General Schratt's revolver went off accidentally and hurt his head.

(*Voices offstage:* 'Where is the Hetman?')

DUST. The Hetman is well. Will Your Highness be kind enough to show yourself? Guards! Attention!

HETMAN (*in the doorway*). Everything's in order, no alarm!

DUST (*speaks through the door*). Please let the doctor with the instruments in.

(*The excitement outside subsides; German doctor enters, carrying a stretcher and a bag of medical appliances;* DUST *closes door and* SCHRATT *emerges from his hiding-place.*)

SCHRATT. Your Highness, please put on a German uniform as if you were me and I am wounded. We will thus remove you from here as if you were me and no one will know you have left and no excitement will be stirred up among the guards.

HETMAN. Do as you please.

DUST (*taking a German uniform from the instrument case*). Please, Your Highness, where do you wish to change?

HETMAN. Here to the right, in my bedroom.

(HETMAN *and* DUST *leave.*)

SHERVINSKY (*in the foreground, to himself*). Will Elena go with me or not? (*Turns resolutely to* SCHRATT.) Excellency, I beg you to take me along with the Hetman. I am his personal adjutant. I shall also have my fiancée with me.

SCHRATT. I'm sorry, Lieutenant, but I am not able to take either your fiancée or yourself. If you want to leave, our Staff train will be at the station. Only, bear in mind, there are no places free, there is already one personal adjutant.

SHERVINSKY. Who?

SCHRATT. What's his name... Prince Novozhiltzev.

SHERVINSKY. Novozhiltzev? Well, when did he manage to do it?

SCHRATT. In a catastrophe everybody becomes very adroit. He was just now at our Headquarters.

SHERVINSKY. And in Berlin will he also be in the Hetman's retinue?

SCHRATT. Oh, no. The Hetman will be alone, no retinue. We will take you only to the border. Whoever wants to save his head from your peasants... but after that everybody must look out for himself.

SHERVINSKY. Much obliged. I guess I'll try to save my neck here.

SCHRATT. Right, young man. One should never leave one's Fatherland.

(*Enter* HETMAN *and* DUST; *the* HETMAN *is in the uniform of the German General. He is rather nervous, puffs a cigarette.*)

HETMAN (*to* SHERVINSKY). All papers must be destroyed, Lieutenant.

DUST. Herr Doktor, seien Sie liebenswürdig. Your Highness, please be seated.

(*The* HETMAN *sits down. The doctor bandages his head and face completely.*)

DOCTOR. Fertig...

SCHRATT (*to* DUST). The car...

DUST. Sogleich.

SCHRATT. Your Highness, lie down on the sofa.

HETMAN. But it should be proclaimed to the people. Maybe a manifesto...

SCHRATT (*ironically*). A manifesto? Well, perhaps...

HETMAN (*dully, dictates*). Please write, Lieutenant. God did not grant me the forces...

DUST (*interrupts*). No time for manifestoes...

SCHRATT (*ironically*). You will do it by telegram from the train. Your Highness, lie down.

(*The* HETMAN *lies down; the telephone rings and* SHERVINSKY *answers, while the* HETMAN *sits up to listen.*)

SHERVINSKY (*on telephone*). Yes... yes... (*A pause.*) Hold on, I'll inquire. Your Highness, the officers of the outpost companies want to know what to do...

HETMAN. Tell them to defend the position, at least a half-hour... At least I must be able to get away... mustn't I?

(SHERVINSKY's *further conversation is drowned out by the* HETMAN's *departure; he is carried by* DUST *and the valet into the corridor;* SCHRATT *emerges from hiding as soon as the doors are closed.*)

SCHRATT. Everything in order. (*Glances at wrist-watch.*) One A.M. (*Puts on his cape and cap.*) Au revoir, Lieutenant. I advise you not to linger here too long. You still have a chance to retreat. Better remove those shoulder-straps. (*Listens; a rumble of firing in the distance.*) Do you hear?

SHERVINSKY. Rolling fire!

SCHRATT. Correct. Rolling fire! You'd better roll off yourself in a hurry. Have you a pass for the back door?

SHERVINSKY. Yes.

SCHRATT. Well, au revoir. Hurry up. (*Leaves through the portière.*)

SHERVINSKY (*crestfallen*). Clean German piece of work! (*Suddenly active.*) Well, then, out of here! No time, no time! (*At the table.*) Oh, a gold cigarette-case! The Hetman has forgotten it! To leave it here? Impossible, the valet will steal it. (*Tests it.*) Oho... weighs about a pound — of historical value. (*Lights a cigarette, and nonchalantly drops the case into his pocket.*) Now, as for these papers — I shall burn none of them except the list of adjutants. (*Searches among papers, burns one and puts a few others in his pocket.*) So... am I a swine or am I not a swine... No, I am not a swine. (*Rings telephone.*) 3-4-5-3. Is this the Division? Please call the Commander to the telephone at once. Wake him up. (*Pause.*) Colonel Turbin, Shervinsky talking. Alexei Vassilievich, listen carefully. The Hetman has sneaked off. Sneaked away, I tell you! No, we have time till dawn. Please tell Elena Vassilievna that under no circumstances should she leave the house tomorrow. I will come to hide at your house in the morning. (*Rings off.*) Now my conscience is clean and quiet. (*Rings for valet.*)

SHERVINSKY. Has the courier brought the package?

VALET. Yes, sir.

SHERVINSKY. Give it to me at once. (*Valet leaves, re-entering at once with a bundle.*) Thank you.

VALET (*bewildered*). May I ask what's wrong with His Highness?

SHERVINSKY. That's a funny question. You're a good fellow, Fyodor. There is something sympathetic, I might say something proletarian about your face. The Hetman is pleased to rest. Well, and in general you'd better not ask too many questions.

VALET. So...

SHERVINSKY. Fyodor, bring me my towel from the adjutant's lavatory, and my razor and soap.

VALET. Shall I bring some paper too?

SHERVINSKY. That's right, some paper too.

(*As soon as the valet leaves,* SHERVINSKY *opens the bundle, which contains a civilian overcoat and hat. He strips off the shoulder-straps, removes his spurs and puts on the civilian clothes. The hat, unfortunately, is large and awkward, but it must do. He makes a package of the things which he has removed. The valet re-enters, carrying the toilet articles.*)

SHERVINSKY. Does the hat fit me?

VALET. Of course. You'd better put the razor in your pocket.

SHERVINSKY. Razor in pocket, all right. Now, dear Fyodor, allow me to present you with fifty rubles as a souvenir. (*Gives him money.*)

VALET. My deepest thanks.

SHERVINSKY. Allow me also to shake your honest working hand. (*Does so.*) Don't be surprised. I am a democrat by nature and of course I've never been an adjutant.

VALET. Of course.

SHERVINSKY. I've never been in this Palace. You don't know me at all. As a matter of fact, I'm merely an opera singer.

VALET. Has he really beat it?

SHERVINSKY. Sneaked off!

VALET. Oh, the louse!

SHERVINSKY. Shameless bandit!

VALET. And left us all to our fate?

SHERVINSKY. It's not so bad for you, you see. Your proletarian face... But how about me? Well, dear Fyodor, charmed as I am to have a chat with you, but — you hear? (*Far-off cannonading; field telephone rings;* SHERVINSKY *disguises his voice.*) Hello! Ah, Captain! Send everything to hell and run away. It means that I know what I'm talking about. Shervinsky... Good-bye... So long. (*Drops the receiver; from the door to the valet.*) Do you know what? While I am still in power here — take this whole study for yourself. What are you staring at, fool... Think what blankets you can make out of these portières. (*Disappears.*)

(*First one telephone, then another rings insistently;* FYODOR *is perplexed, but finally answers in a humorously important voice.*)

VALET (*on telephone*). Yes... Yes... How can I help you? Send everything to hell and run away... Fyodor talking, Fyodor! (*Begins to yank down the portières as the curtain falls.*)

ACT II

Scene 2

Scene: *The curtain rises upon a pitch-black stage, the darkness pierced only by cigarette lights here and there, moving about like fireflies. An accordion plays slow Ukrainian folk-songs and rough voices take up the motif. From farther off other music, voices and movements can be heard dimly. The audience becomes aware that it is a makeshift army encampment on a dark night.*

Slowly the stage clarifies, but by the time it is entirely visible the scene has shifted to the interior of the temporary field headquarters of a Petliura division; a small, sinister peasant cottage, low-ceilinged with a door centre and a small window right; a kerosene lamp provides the only light; home-made peasant furniture; horse-collars and other farm paraphernalia lying around or hanging from the rafters. An inscription: 'Staff, 1st Cavalry Division' and a blue-yellow flag.

Bolbotun, Commander of this Petliura division, is seated at a table in the centre of the room, already rather far gone in liquor and taking swigs from a vodka bottle, lazily fussing over maps; like all the officers in this scene he is unshaven, in a greasy sheepskin coat, looking more like a bandit than a military leader. At the right an officer is tinkering with a field telephone, spitting and cursing in disgust. Several other officers and soldiers are disposed around the room, lounging on the floor.

Throughout the scene the life of the men encamped outside the headquarters penetrates in singing, cursing, noises, now dying down, then flaring up once more. Suddenly whistles and blows are heard offstage. The telephonist is shouting at his apparatus.

TELEPHONIST (*gestures as he yells*). It's me, Franko. 'Phone's working again. Working, I say! Do you hear me? Do you hear me? Damn your hide! This is the staff of the First Cavalry Division.
> (*Confused telephone signals that drive Franko nearly mad; the noise offstage approaches the door; enter Officers Uragan and Kirpaty, ruffians in appearance, with red tassels on their Circassian hats; they are dragging in a bearded Cossack in muddy uniform, his face blood-smeared.*)

47

BOLBOTUN. What happened? (*Takes a healthy swallow.*)

URAGAN. We've nabbed a deserter, Pan-Colonel.

BOLBOTUN (*to deserter*). What regiment? (*Silence.*) What regiment, I ask you! (*Silence.*)

TELEPHONIST. Hello, hello! (*Noises, the telephone is chronically misbehaving.*) It's me, Franko. Me! (*points to himself*), you dirty son-of-a-... Yes, First Division. 'Phone's connected again, I tell you, you God-damned...

BOLBOTUN (*approaches the Cossack, who has collapsed on the floor*). What, damn your soul! At a time when every decent Cossack is going into the field to defend the Ukrainian Republic against White Guards and sheeny Communists! When every peasant is enrolling in the Ukrainian army, you, you hide yourself in the bushes! Do you know what the Hetman's officers and the Communist commissars on the other side are doing to our peasants? They bury them in the ground alive. Do you understand me? I'll shove you, too, into the ground alive. Sotnik Galanba!

(*A voice offstage: 'Sotnik Galanba, to the Colonel.'*)

BOLBOTUN. Where did you catch him?

KIRPATY. The son-of-a-bitch was running behind the timber yards. Tried to hide.

BOLBOTUN. You dirty dog!

(*Enter* GALANBA: *cold, dark, savage-looking, though a little more suave than his disreputable superiors.*)

BOLBOTUN (*to* GALANBA). Pan-Sotnik, examine the deserter!

GALANBA (*with an expressionless face takes a ramrod from the table and calmly hits the deserter over the face; the latter remains silent*). What regiment? (*Silence; another blow.*)

DESERTER. I'm not a deserter. Have pity, Pan-Sotnik. I was creeping to the hospital. My feet are entirely frozen.

TELEPHONIST (*yells into 'phone*). Give me the dispositions, please. The Commander of the Cavalry Division asks for your dispositions. Do you hear me? God-damned...

GALANBA. Your feet are frozen? Why haven't you a certificate of leave from your regiment? Dog! From what regiment? (*Threatens with the ramrod.*)

(*Offstage the tramping of horses over a wooden bridge is audible.*)

DESERTER. Second Cossack Regiment.

GALANBA. We know you damn Cossacks. You're all scoundrels,

traitors, Bolsheviks. Take off your boots. Off with them! And if we find your feet are not frozen and that you are lying, I will shoot you on the spot. Boys, a lantern!

TELEPHONIST. Send a courier to keep liaison. To the Slobodka Suburb... Yes, yes, I hear you all right!

(*The deserter is being searched by lantern light.*)

GALANBA (*revolver in hand*). These are my terms: if your feet are healthy, you'll be despatched to the next world at once. (*Gestures with the revolver.*) Get out of the way, boys. I might hit the wrong one.

(*The deserter painfully removes his boots.*)

BOLBOTUN (*enjoys the sport*). That's the idea. It'll be a good example for the others.

KIRPATY (*sighs regretfully*). Yes, they're frozen all right. He told the truth.

GALANBA. But you should have got a certificate! A certificate, you swine. And not run away from your regiment.

DESERTER. But there was nobody to give me a certificate. There's no doctor in our regiment. Nobody was there.

GALANBA. Put him under arrest and send him to the hospital under guard. After the doctor has attended to his feet, bring him back here to the Staff and give him fifteen strokes with the ramrod. That'll teach him to run away from the regiment without a certificate of leave.

URAGAN (*pushes him out*). Off with you, go! (*Follows him.*)

(*Offstage an accordion plays 'Yablotchka,' a Ukrainian folk-song, and a voice sings soulfully: 'Whither sweet apple...' Suddenly agitated voices are audible: 'Catch 'em! Catch 'em! They're near the bridge! Running on the ice!'*)

GALANBA (*through the window*). Boys, what's the matter there?

VOICE (*offstage*). Some sheenies, Pan-Sotnik, running away from Slobodka to town. They passed under the bridge across the ice!

GALANBA. Boys! Patrol! Take horses! Kirpaty! Chase 'em! But take 'em alive, that's the main thing, alive!

(*Screams, laughter, rifle-shots offstage, then heavy footsteps; enter* URAGAN *leading a man with a large wicker basket.*)

MAN. Dear, kind people! I didn't do anything wrong! What do you want from me? I'm a simple artisan.

GALANBA. What's he got in his basket?

Man. Please! Comrade Soldier...

Galanba (*as if stung*). What! Comrade! Who are you comrading here?

Man. Pardon, Sir Soldier!

Galanba. I'm not a sir either. The sirs are all in the city with the Hetman. We'll tear the guts out of your sirs! Boys, bring him nearer. Give this sir a good punch in the jaw! (*It is done.*) Now you see what sirs there are here!

Man. Yes, yes, I see.

Galanba. Boys, put some light on him! It seems to me he's a dirty Communist.

Man. No, no, what an idea, have mercy! I'm just a cobbler.

Galanba. Well, you talk with a damn good Moscow accent.

Man. We're from Kaluga Province, Your Grace, from Kaluga. We'll be sorry for the rest of our lives that we ever came to the Ukraine. I'm a shoemaker.

Galanba. Your documents?

Man. My passport? Just a moment. My passport, I can tell you is as clean as water, as it were.

Galanba (*inspects passport, hands it back*). What's in your basket? Where are you going?

Man. In the basket... boots, Your Grace, just boots. We are shoemakers, working for a shoe-store. We live in Slobodka and bring the boots to the city.

Galanba. Why are you carrying on your business at night?

Man. If I start now I'll get to town just in the morning.

Uragan. Boots, oh — oh — oh. That's fine!

(Uragan *investigates the basket, draws out shining new boots. The soldiers are greedily excited by the vision.*)

Man (*almost hysterical with fright and despair*). Excuse me, honored citizen, the shoes are not ours, they belong to the shop-keeper.

Bolbotun. To the shopkeeper? So much the better. Shopkeeper's stuff is good stuff. Boys, everybody help himself to a pair of the shopkeeper's boots.

(*Soldiers and officers eagerly grab a pair of boots each.*)

Man. Citizen, War Minister! I'll be ruined. Nothing remains but to throw myself into a grave. There's two thousand rubles' worth of goods and it all belongs to the shopkeeper.

Bolbotun (*laughing*). We'll give you a receipt.

MAN. Oh, have pity on me. What good will the receipt do? (*Rushes to* BOLBOTUN, *who merely slaps his face; whereupon he rushes to* GALANBA.) Mister, Cavalry Officer, General, two thousand rubles' worth. If I were a bourgeois, or a Bolshevik. (GALANBA *also hits him; he squats on the floor in stupefied despair.*) What's happening? Well, take them for your army! Let everything go to hell. (*Has an inspiration.*) But at least allow me to take a pair, too. (*Begins to take off his old boots.*)

BOLBOTUN. How dare you? Are you making fun of us? You wretch! Get away from the basket. How long will you be crawling under our feet here? I've got no more patience. Boys, get out of the way. (*Takes aim with his revolver.*)

MAN. What... What are you going to do?

BOLBOTUN. Out with you!

MAN (*dashes to the door and bumps into* KIRPATY, *who is dragging in a blood-covered Jew*). Take what you want. Take everything! (*Flees.*)

GALANBA. Well, look what he's got... you're welcome!

KIRPATY. We shot two of them, Pan-Sotnik, but this one we managed to catch alive as you ordered.

JEW (*deadly frightened*). Pan-Sotnik...

TELEPHONIST (*into 'phone*). Yes, boots, brand-new boots. On my word! (*Places boots near telephone receiver.*) Look, here they are!

GALANBA (*to the Jew*). Shut up, no shouting here!

JEW. Mister General, what will you do with me?

GALANBA. We'll do what we find necessary! (*Pause.*) Why did you try to cross the ice?

JEW. May my eyes rot in my face, may I never see the sun again if I wasn't going to visit my children in the city. Pan-Sotnik, I swear I have little children in the city.

BOLBOTUN. You have to go over the bridge to reach your children — over the bridge.

JEW. Mister General, all-powerful commander, on the bridge there are guards, your people — excellent people, heroic people — but they don't like us Jews. This morning I tried and they beat me and wouldn't let me cross.

BOLBOTUN. Well, it's clear they didn't beat you enough.

JEW. His Honor the Colonel is joking. His Honor is very witty, may God be good to you.

BOLBOTUN. Yes, I'm witty. Don't be scared of us. (*Ironically.*)

We like Jews. We love the Jews. (*Accordion plays softly offstage.*) Cross yourself, cross yourself.

JEW. With pleasure, most honored sir. (*Crosses himself amid hilarious laughter.*)

BOLBOTUN. And now shout, 'Long Live Free Ukraine!'

JEW. Long Live Free Ukraine! (*Laughter.*)

GALANBA. You're a patriot all right. (*Silence;* GALANBA *suddenly strikes the Jew with the ramrod.*) Boys, search him!

JEW. Most honored...

GALANBA. What did you want in Kiev?

JEW. I swear to you I was going to my children.

GALANBA. I'll tell you what you are, you're a lousy spy, that's what.

BOLBOTUN. That's right, a goddam lousy spy.

JEW. I'm not, I swear to God, I'm not.

GALANBA. Own up what you've been doing behind our back! (*Strikes him again.*)

JEW. No, no. I've done nothing, nothing at all, Pan-Sotnik. I'm a tailor here at Slobodka, with my wife and my mother.

BOLBOTUN. His wife is here, his children in town. His family lives all over the blooming globe.

GALANBA. Well, I see there's no use talking sense to you. Boys, open the lantern and hold his hands.

> (*Two soldiers hold the Jew while a third burns his face with the kerosene flame.*)

JEW (*shrieking*). Officer, officer! I call on God... What are you doing... Oi, oi, oi... I can't stand any more, have pity!

GALANBA. Now will you own up, you dirty dog?

JEW. Yes, yes, I'll confess.

GALANBA. You're a spy.

JEW. Yes, yes, yes... (*The torture is stopped.*) No, no, no... I have nothing to confess. I couldn't stand the pain. Mister, my wife and children. I'm a tailor. Let me go... let me...

GALANBA. So you haven't had enough? Boys! Give him some more.

JEW. Better kill me, I confess... kill me....

GALANBA. Now what have you been doing behind our front?

> (*The soldiers, relishing the sport, open the lantern again.*)

JEW. Officer, officer! Your Highness! Take away the lantern and I'll tell everything. Yes, yes, oh, my God.

GALANBA. Are you a Communist?

JEW. Yes, I'm a Communist, yes.

BOLBOTUN. Every Jew in the world is a damn Communist, Communist sheeny.

JEW. No, no, what do you want me to say, Officer? What can I say? Only don't torture me. Scoundrels, scoundrels! (*Tears himself loose in a rage and rushes to the window.*) I'm not a spy!

GALANBA. Grab him boys, hold on to him.

URAGAN. He'll jump into the ice-hole there.

(GALANBA *shoots the Jew in the back.*)

JEW (*topples backward*). Curses on you!

BOLBOTUN. Too bad, eh, too bad.

GALANBA. Why didn't you hold on to him?

KIRPATY. Too bad, he died an easy death, the dog! (*They empty the Jew's pockets.*)

TELEPHONIST (*still shouting*). Hallo, hallo! I hear you! Hooray, hooray! Pan-Colonel!

BOLBOTUN (*takes the 'phone*). This is the Commander of the First Cavalry Division, Colonel Bolbotun. I'm listening!... Yes... Yes... That's right. We're coming at once. (*To* GALANBA.) Pan-Sotnik! Order all four regiments to mount right away! The approaches to the city are in our hands! Hooray! Hooray!

URAGAN } Hooray! Now we'll charge.
KIRPATY }

(*Excited preparations for departure.*)

GALANBA (*through the window*). Mount horses!

(*Great bustle and shouts of 'Hurrah' behind the scenes;* GALANBA *departs hurriedly.*)

BOLBOTUN. Take the telephone apparatus. My horse.

URAGAN (*through the window*). The Colonel's horse!

(*Voices outside: 'First Squadron, in trot! Second Squadron, in trot!' Stamping of horses, shouts, whistling offstage. Everybody runs from stage. Strains of the accordion ever dimmer in the distance as the curtain falls.*)

ACT III

SCENE I

SCENE: *The main lobby of a High School, now headquarters of Colonel* TURBIN'S *division. A broad marble staircase is at the right, with a huge portrait of Alexander I over the upper landing, which extends to the left in a sort of balcony with a decorative railing, all the way across the stage; the balcony leads into the upstairs corridors and classrooms; on the right the upper landing is cut off by a large window. On the lower level, the lobby merges at both ends into corridors, the one at the left leading into the interior of the school, the one on the right to the main exit. In the centre back, almost under the stairway, a low door opens into the basement.*

An old-fashioned wood-burning stove stands somewhat in front of the cellar door. Rifles are stacked here and there, several cases of ammunition are in evidence, as well as a machine-gun or two. A few school closets stand against the back wall.

The rhythmic tread of marching men can be heard offstage, where drill is in progress, as the curtain rises. Pale dawn-light filters through the upper window. NIKOLKA'S *voice can be heard somewhere behind the scene, singing a popular military air, other voices chime in, humming and whistling softly.*

The marchers enter from the left, Captain STUDZINSKY *in the lead. About a score of them in military formation come on the stage, the rest being audible offstage. The soldiers, in cadet uniforms, are all young men, some of them mere boys.*

STUDZINSKY. Division — halt! (*Division halts sharply.*) At ease! Captain!

MISHLAYEVSKY (*appears on the upper landing*). First Battalion, mark time! Forward march!

       (*His men are offstage, only their marching can be heard.*)

STUDZINSKY. In place! Left, right! Left, right!

MISHLAYEVSKY. 'At! 'At! Battalion — Halt!

FIRST OFFICER. Second Battalion, halt!

MISHLAYEVSKY. The Battalion may smoke. At ease!

       (*The young men break ranks.*)

FIRST OFFICER (*to* MISHLAYEVSKY). Captain, there are twenty-

54

two missing in my battalion. It seems they took to their heels. College-boys!

SECOND OFFICER. It's all a stupid business! I'm in a rotten muddle!

FIRST OFFICER. What! The Commander isn't here! At six we were supposed to get started and now it's a quarter to seven.

MISHLAYEVSKY. Hold your tongue, Lieutenant! He was summoned to the Palace by 'phone. There is some news. He will come at once! (*To cadets.*) Are you frozen?

ONE CADET. Yes, sir, Captain, it's rather chilly.

MISHLAYEVSKY. Then why are you standing around blue as cadavers? Stamp your feet, move around, stretch yourselves. After the command 'at ease' you are no longer monuments. Every man is his own stove! Get a move on. Hey! First Squad! Go to the nearest classroom and break up a few desks to heat the stove. Be quick about it.

CADETS (*shouting*). Boys, come on, smash up the desks. Into the stove with them! (*Noise and activity.*)

(MAXIM, *a grizzled old watchman, appears from the basement, horrified.*)

MAXIM. Your Excellencies, what are you doing there? Heating the stove with desks! What an outrage! His Excellency the Rector told me himself...

FIRST OFFICER (*amused*). Scene 14!

MISHLAYEVSKY. And with what, old fellow, could we heat the stoves?

MAXIM. With firewood, little father, with firewood. Only we have no firewood.

MISHLAYEVSKY. Thanks for the information. (*Sternly.*) Get the hell out of here, you old fool. (*To the soldiers.*) More action! Hey! Second Squad, devil take you!

MAXIM. God Almighty and Holy Saints, what is happening here? Tartars! Real Tartars! Vandals! Many soldiers have been through here... (*Hobbles out.*)

(*Offstage* MAXIM *can still be heard remonstrating: 'Gentlemen, officers, what are you doing?' The cadets noisily dismember desks, saw them and heat the stove, singing the plaintive folk-song:*

Storm veils sky with darkness,
And whirls the snowflakes mild,
Oft whining like some wild beast,
Oft weeping like some child...

Others strike out on a more cheerful tune:

> Here you girls, lovely girls, honey mine —
> Change these bills, brand-new bills, money mine —
> All these bills, crispy new,
> Twenty-ruble bills for you...

(MAXIM's *hysterical voice is still pleading, 'Lord save us, for the last time!' Suddenly a cannon-shot booms near-by. A few continue to sing half-heartedly, but soon they all lapse into tense silence.*)

CADET. I think it's intended for us, Captain.

MISHLAYEVSKY. Oh, it's nothing, Petliura's spitting.

(Singing has expired.)

FIRST OFFICER. I think, we'll have the pleasure of meeting him face to face. It's interesting to see what he looks like.

THIRD OFFICER (*glumly*). You'll recognize him, all right. Don't hurry!

MISHLAYEVSKY. Our job is a small one, but a sure one. When we're ordered we'll meet him. (*To the cadets.*) Cadets, what the hell? Why so down in the mouth? Cheer up!

(*The men resume singing but without much spirit. A cadet rushes in and announces to* STUDZINSKY.)

CADET. The Division Commander is here!

STUDZINSKY. Division, attention! Officers! Officers!

(ALEXEI *enters.*)

ALEXEI (*to* STUDZINSKY). The list. How many missing?

STUDZINSKY (*in a low voice*). Twenty-two.

ALEXEI. Let me see.

STUDZINSKY. Yes, sir.

ALEXEI (*tears the list*). Is our advance patrol at Demeyevka?

STUDZINSKY. Yes, sir.

ALEXEI. Recall it at once.

STUDZINSKY (*to a cadet*). Recall the advance patrol.

CADET. Yes, sir. (*Runs off.*)

ALEXEI. I order the Division to listen attentively to what I have to say. (*Mounts staircase about halfway.*) Keep silence. During the night our situation, the situation of the whole Russian army... I should say, the position of the Government of Ukraine... has undergone a sharp and unexpected change... I am therefore informing you that I am disbanding the whole division. (*Silence.*) The campaign against Petliura is ended. I command everybody, including the officers, to remove all shoulder-straps and insignia, to get away quietly and hide in their houses. (*Pause.*) I have finished. The order must be obeyed!

STUDZINSKY (*breaks the electric silence*). Colonel! Alexei Vassilievich!

ALEXEI. Silence! No back talk!

THIRD OFFICER. What is this! It is treachery.

(*Commotion and rumble of voices.*)

CADETS. He ought to be arrested... Arrest him... We don't understand anything... What do you mean, arrest him? Are you crazy?... Petliura has crashed into Kiev... There's a business for you... I knew it... Keep quiet...

FIRST OFFICER. Colonel, what is the meaning of this?

THIRD OFFICER. First detachment, follow me!

(*Bewildered cadets seize rifles and run after him.* NIKOLKA *and* MISHLAYEVSKY *jump between the angered men and* ALEXEI.)

NIKOLKA. Gentlemen, what are you doing?

SECOND OFFICER. Arrest him! He has gone over to Petliura!

THIRD OFFICER. Colonel, you are under arrest!

MISHLAYEVSKY (*holding back the* THIRD OFFICER). Hold on, Lieutenant.

THIRD OFFICER (*almost hysterical*). Let me alone, Captain. Hands off! Cadets, seize him!

MISHLAYEVSKY. Cadets, back with you!

STUDZINSKY. Alexei, look what is happening!

NIKOLKA. Back!

STUDZINSKY. Back, I tell you. Don't listen to an inferior officer.

FIRST OFFICER. Gentlemen, what is this?

THIRD OFFICER. Gentlemen, gentlemen! (*Excitement, noise; the officers draw revolvers.*) An agent of Petliura! Don't obey the orders of the higher officers!

A CADET. Insurrection in the Division...

FIRST OFFICER. What are you doing?

STUDZINSKY. Quiet! At attention!

THIRD OFFICER. Take him!

ALEXEI. Quiet! I have more to say to you. (*His expression is grim, touched with bitter irony; he speaks down from the balcony, pacing in agitation.*)

57

(*The cadets are crowding the stairway and the lobby, utterly bewildered; above the confusion and shouting a phrase emerges now and then.*)

CADETS. There's nothing to talk about... We don't want to listen to you... Obey the Commander of the Second Battalion... Oh, God! Oh, God!... Arrest him!

NIKOLKA. Let him talk!

THIRD OFFICER. Quiet, cadets, let him have his say. We won't let him out of here.

MISHLAYEVSKY. Put your cadets back in their places immediately.

FIRST OFFICER. Attention! To your places!

CADETS. Attention! Attention! 'Tenshun!

ALEXEI. Yes... I should be in a fine position if I had to fight with the kind of material God has sent me in your persons. But, gentlemen! What can be excused in a college-boy volunteer cannot be excused... (*to* THIRD OFFICER) in you, Lieutenant! I thought all of you would understand that a great misfortune has overtaken us. That your Commander cannot utter the disgraceful news. But you are not discerning enough to guess it. Whom do you want to defend? Answer me! (*Silence.*) You must answer when the Commander asks you! Whom?

THIRD OFFICER. We have promised to defend the Hetman.

ALEXEI. The Hetman! Excellent. At three this morning the Hetman left his army to its fate and ran away, disguised in a German uniform, in a German train to Germany. And thus, gentlemen, while the lieutenant is about to defend him, he has long ago departed.

CADETS. To Berlin? What is he saying? We don't want to listen!

(*A far-off rumble; the light grows clearer in the window.*)

ALEXEI. And that is not all. Together with this canaille, another canaille, His Grace the Commander of the Army, Prince Belorukov, ran away in the same direction. And so, my friends, there is not only no one to defend but even no one to command us, because the Prince's Staff ran off together with him. (*Commotion; voices: 'It can't be, can't be! It's a lie!'*) Who said 'a lie'? Who said 'a lie'? I'm just back from Headquarters. I have verified all this news. I take responsibility for every word I've said. Well... here we are... two hundred of us. And there is Petliura. What am I saying — there. Here! My friends, his cavalry is on the outskirts of the city. He has an army of two hundred thousand and we have with us four infantry detachments and three batteries. Understand? Somebody aimed a revolver at me. He frightened me terribly. Silly schoolboy!

THIRD OFFICER. Colonel!

ALEXEI. Quiet. Well, there you are. If under these conditions you would even all insist on remaining to defend... whom? what? in a word, to fight... I could not lead you, because I don't take part in puppet-shows, especially as this puppet-show would be paid for in blood — by you — and all to no purpose.

NIKOLKA. Bastards of the Staff!   (*Commotion and shouting.*)

CADETS. What are we to do now? Lie down in the grave? Disgrace! Go to hell! Are you at a meeting? Stand at attention! We're trapped!...

ONE CADET (*bursts into tears*). They yelled, 'Forward, forward!' and now it's 'Back!' If I find the Hetman I'll murder him.

FIRST OFFICER. Send this old woman to the Devil. Cadets, listen! If the news which the Colonel brought us is true, do as I tell you. On to the Don! We'll organize transports and join Denikin.

CADETS. To the Don! To Denikin! As if that were so simple! To the Don! To the Don!

STUDZINSKY. Alexei Vassilievich, that's right. Drop everything. We'll take the Division to the Don.

ALEXEI. Captain Studzinsky, silence! I'm still commanding the Division! Quiet! To the Don? Listen to me, you who want to go to the Don. Even if you ever reach it, you will find the same mess there! You'll find the same generals, and the same Staff gang!

NIKOLKA. The same swine!

ALEXEI. Right you are! They will set you to fighting against your own people. And when your people have broken your necks, your generals will run away abroad. I know that on the Don things are the same as in Kiev. There, too, the divisions are without munitions; the cadets are barefooted while their officers lounge in cafés. Listen, my friends! To me, as a fighting officer, has been entrusted the task of throwing you into battle. If only there were something to fight for ... but there isn't. I declare before the world that I will neither lead you nor let you be led... I tell you that the White cause in the Ukraine has collapsed. It has fallen to pieces in the east, on the Don... everywhere. Dead... buried! And here am I, a professional officer, Alexei Turbin, who has gone through the whole war against Germany, as Captains Studzinsky and Mishlayevsky can attest. I take everything on my own conscience and responsibility. Everything. I take everything on myself. And I send you home because I love you! (*Commotion of voices; outside, a cannon-shot.*) Tear off your shoulder-straps. Throw away your rifles and run home... at once.

> (*Cadets tear off shoulder-straps, throw away rifles and begin to leave, some reluctantly, others in a hurry.*)

MISHLAYEVSKY (*shouting*). Quiet! Colonel, may we set the school on fire?

ALEXEI. I don't permit it.

> (*Another cannon-shot, nearer; windows rattle.*)

MISHLAYEVSKY. Machine-gun!

STUDZINSKY. Cadets, home!

MISHLAYEVSKY. Cadets, sound the retreat! Run home.

> (*Offstage a bugle-call is heard; cadets disperse.* NIKOLKA *smashes the electric switchboard with the butt-end of his rifle; darkness blots out everything; curtain falls for one minute.*
>
> *When curtain rises again the same scene is lit up by pale morning light; rifles and papers are strewn chaotically on the floor. A fire burns in the stove;* ALEXEI *squats in front of it tearing papers and burning them;* MAXIM *hovers over him.*)

ALEXEI. Who are you?

MAXIM. I am the watchman here.

ALEXEI. Get out of here, old man. They'll riddle you with bullets.

MAXIM. Your Honor... where shall I go? I can't abandon government property. They've broken the desks in two classes. They've done so much damage I can't find words to tell you. And the lights... what can I do now? It's a real pogrom! Many soldiers have been through here, but this kind... you will excuse me...

ALEXEI. Old man, let me alone!

MAXIM. You can cut me to pieces with your sword... I can't go away... His Grace the Rector himself told me...

ALEXEI. Well, what did His Grace the Rector tell you?

MAXIM. Maxim, he said, you are remaining alone. Maxim, he said, watch carefully...

ALEXEI. Listen, old man... Do you understand Russian? I'm telling you straight. They'll kill you! Go somewhere... to the cellar, anywhere, hide yourself so that no trace of you remains...

MAXIM. And who will have to answer for all this? Maxim will have to answer for everything. All kinds of reckless soldiers were here — for the Tsar, against the Tsar... but this, breaking the desks and smashing the lights. Oh, Queen of Heaven!

ALEXEI. Where the devil can the list be? (*Smashes in the door of another closet with his foot.*)

MAXIM (*horrified*). Your Excellency, there is a key for it. The closet belongs to the school and Your Honor breaks it with his feet. (*Backs up, crossing himself; another cannon-shot.*)

ALEXEI. That's right! Damn it, give 'em more. Concert, music! Well, Pan-Hetman, if ever I can lay my hands on you, dirty dog! Dirty dog! Swine!

(MISHLAYEVSKY *appears on upper landing; reflections of flames play on window.*)

MAXIM (*mounting stairway, to* MISHLAYEVSKY). Maybe Your Excellency will order him not to! He's broken in the closet with his feet.

MISHLAYEVSKY. Old man, out of here!

MAXIM. Tartars, Tartars! (*Goes out.*)

MISHLAYEVSKY (*speaks down from the landing*). Aliosha, I've set fire to the military warehouse. Petliura will find a fig instead of equipment!

ALEXEI. For God's sake, don't hang around here!

MISHLAYEVSKY. Just a little more business! I'll simply deposit a couple of bombs in the hay and I'll be off! What are you sticking around here for?

ALEXEI. Until the patrol returns, I can't leave.

MISHLAYEVSKY. Aliosha, must you really!

ALEXEI. What a question, Captain!

MISHLAYEVSKY. Then I'll remain with you.

ALEXEI. But I don't need you, Victor. I command you. Go to Elena at once. Guard her! I'll follow you right away. (MISHLAYEVSKY *lingers.*) Have you all gone mad? Will you listen to me or not?

MISHLAYEVSKY. All right, Aliosha. I'll be off to Lenochka.

ALEXEI. Nikolka, see that he really goes and clear out yourself. Go with him. For God's sake, Victor, make him go.

MISHLAYEVSKY. All right, Aliosha. I'll go, but don't take any chances.

ALEXEI. Don't teach the teacher! (MISHLAYEVSKY *leaves.*) Very serious, serious and very! (*Hums a military tune.*)... Damn it, if only the patrol keeps out of Petliura's clutches! (NIKOLKA *appears on the upper landing, on tiptoes.*) Good God! You still here! Are you joking with me? Go home this minute! Remove your straps. Out with you!

NIKOLKA (*grimly, taking a few steps down the stairway*). Without you, Colonel, I will not budge.

ALEXEI. What's that? (*Draws revolver and walks toward* NIKOLKA.)

NIKOLKA. All right, shoot your own brother.

ALEXEI. Idiot! (*Puts away the revolver.*)

NIKOLKA. Insult your own brother! I know why you are lingering here! I know why! You are waiting for death because of this terrible disgrace. That's it! All right, then, I'll watch you. Otherwise Lenochka will kill me!

ALEXEI. Ekh... Is anyone still here? Mishlayevsky, place Cadet Turbin under arrest.

NIKOLKA. Everybody's gone!

ALEXEI. All right, I'll talk it out with you at home.

(*Noise and trampling; cadets of the advance patrol rush in, excitedly.*)

CADETS. Petliura's cavalry is here! They're chasing us! Get out, get out!

ALEXEI. Cadets, listen to my command! Run through the basement passages and get away. Tear off your shoulder-straps on the way. (*Cadets run out, Petliura's forces are approaching; whistling and wild accordion playing can be heard; a Ukrainian ballad is being sung in raucous voices.*) Run! Run! I'll cover you. (*Rushes to upstairs window, smashes the panes and hurls his last grenade;* NIKOLKA *also hurls one.*)

ALEXEI (*to* NIKOLKA). Run! For pity's sake! Have mercy on Lenochka!

(*A shot through the window;* ALEXEI *is hit and falls.*)

NIKOLKA. Colonel, Aliosha! What have you done!

ALEXEI. Corporal Turbin, to hell with heroism... (*Collapses, dead.*)

NIKOLKA. Colonel! It can't be! Aliosha, Aliosha! Get up!

(*Lifts him and tries to carry him down the stairway. The noise, tramping and drunken music is quite near.* URAGAN, KIRPATY, *and a few other Petliura men enter.* NIKOLKA, *trapped, lays* ALEXEI *down on the stairs, but still hovers over him.*)

URAGAN (*pointing with drawn sword to* NIKOLKA). Get him, boys! Get him! (KIRPATY *shoots at* NIKOLKA, *who runs away.*)

GALANBA (*rushing in*). Alive! Take him alive, boys!

(NIKOLKA, *wounded, crawls up the steps, gnashing his teeth in pain and fury.*)

KIRPATY. Look at the wolf-cub! The puppy of a bitch!

URAGAN (*chasing upstairs*). You won't get away from us. We'll catch you.

> (*Petliura's band, noisy and drunken, rush in from all directions. Some of them are already on the upper landing.*)

NIKOLKA. Hangmen! I won't give up! Bandits! I won't give up!

> (*Vaults over the railing and disappears in the confusion.*)

KIRPATY (*reaching the landing, slaps his thighs*). Damn you, look at the puppy! The acrobat! (*Shoots after* NIKOLKA.)

GALANBA. Why did you let him wriggle out, boys! Ekh!

> (*The accordion plays wildly above the noise and excitement; off-stage cries of 'Hail, hail!' Bugles sound.* BOLBOTUN, *gloriously drunk, enters, followed by standard-bearers; the standards are carried upstairs to the tune of a deafening victory march.*)

CURTAIN

ACT III

Scene 2

SCENE: *The* TURBIN *living-room at dawn; a candle burns on the table.* ELENA *and* LARIOSIK *are on the stage when the curtain rises.*

LARIOSIK. Elena Vassilievna, dear, I am entirely at your disposal. I'll dress and go to look for them.

ELENA. Oh, no, no. It's no use, Lariosik. You will be killed on the street. Let's wait. (*The window flares up with the blood-red reflection of a distant fire.*) God! Another fire somewhere. What a horrible dawn! I wonder what's happening there? If only I knew where they were... (*Paces the room, wringing her hands.*)

LARIOSIK. Yes, God, what an awful thing civil war is!

ELENA. You know what, I'm a woman. They won't touch me. I'll go and see what's going on in the streets.

LARIOSIK (*blocks the doorway*). Elena Vassilievna, I won't permit you to leave the house. What an idea! I simply won't let you! What will Alexei Vassilievich say! He gave me strict orders not to let you out under any circumstances and I gave him my word.

ELENA. I'll remain close to the house!

LARIOSIK. Elena Vassilievna...

ELENA. Just to see what's happening.

LARIOSIK (*frightened*). No, I'll go.

ELENA. Never mind. Let's wait.

LARIOSIK. Your husband has done very well to leave. It was clever of him. Now he will wait in Berlin, out of danger, until this whole terrible chaos is over and then he'll come home.

ELENA. My husband... my husband. Larion, never mention my husband again in this house. Do you understand?

LARIOSIK. Very well, Elena Vassilievna. I always manage to put my foot in it... Shall I make you some tea? I could prepare the samovar.

ELENA. No, thank you. I don't want any tea.

(*A knock at the door.*)

LARIOSIK. Ah, somebody is coming... (*Clearly scared.*) But wait a bit, don't open at once, Elena Vassilievna. (*Timidly.*) Who's there?

64

SHERVINSKY'S VOICE. It's me, me, Shervinsky.

ELENA. Thank God! (*Opens the door;* SHERVINSKY *enters in his civilian disguise.*) What's wrong! A catastrophe?

SHERVINSKY. Petliura has taken the city.

LARIOSIK. Taken! How dreadful, Heavens!

ELENA. Where are our boys? Perished? What do you mean, taken the city?

SHERVINSKY. Don't get upset, Lena... Elena Vassilievna. Everything is in perfect order.

ELENA. What do you mean in order?

SHERVINSKY. Don't be alarmed, Elena Vassilievna. They'll all be back here soon.

ELENA. But where are they? Fighting?

SHERVINSKY. Quiet yourself, Elena Vassilievna. They will manage to get out of the high school in time. I've warned them.

ELENA. And the Hetman's troops?

SHERVINSKY. The Hetman ran away last night.

ELENA. Ran away? Abandoned the army?

SHERVINSKY. That's right. And Prince Belorukov, too. (*Takes off his overcoat.*)

ELENA. Scoundrels, traitors.

SHERVINSKY. Impossible swine.

LARIOSIK. And why is there no light?

SHERVINSKY. The electric station is being bombarded.

LARIOSIK. Oi, oi, oi...

SHERVINSKY. Elena Vassilievna, may I hide in your house? Now they will be hunting for officers. (*Tears various papers and throws the pieces into the fire.*)

ELENA. Certainly you may.

SHERVINSKY. I'm so happy that you at least are alive and well.

ELENA. And what are you going to do now?

SHERVINSKY. I'll join the opera. (*A knock at the door; to* LARIOSIK.) Ask who's there.

LARIOSIK (*in a frightened voice*). Who's there?

MISHLAYEVSKY'S VOICE. Friends, friends.

(LARIOSIK *opens the door;* MISHLAYEVSKY *and* STUDZINSKY *come in.*)

ELENA. Thank God! And where are Aliosha and Nikolka?

MISHLAYEVSKY. Be calm, Elena. Be calm! They'll be here right away. Don't be afraid. The streets are still clear. (*Notices* SHER-

65

VINSKY.) Ah, he's here already! In that case you know the whole story.

ELENA. Thanks, everything. Well, those Germans, those Germans!

STUDZINSKY. Never mind, never mind. Some day we'll remind them of everything, never mind.

MISHLAYEVSKY. Hello, Larion!

LARIOSIK. Ah, Vitenka, what horrible things are happening. Oi, oi, oi...

MISHLAYEVSKY. Yes, first-class events.

ELENA. My God, what you look like! Go to the fireside. I'll make the samovar immediately.

SHERVINSKY (*near the fireplace*). Shall I help you, Lena?

ELENA. No, don't bother, stay where you are. (*Goes to the kitchen.*)

MISHLAYEVSKY (*to* SHERVINSKY, *sarcastically*). Well, how are you, Pan-Personal Adjutant? Where are your insignia? (*Mockingly.*) 'Officers, go to the Ukraine and organize your divisions.' And he shed tears, you say? Damn your low-down hide.

SHERVINSKY. Why this farcical tone?

MISHLAYEVSKY. Because the whole damn business has degenerated into a bloody farce! Well, you promised us the Tsar and you drank the health of His Highness the Hetman. By the way, where is His Highness at present?

SHERVINSKY. Why do you want to know?

MISHLAYEVSKY. I'll tell you why! If I could lay my hands on this Highness, right now, I'd grab him by his ankles and bang his head on the pavement until my feelings would be fully relieved. As for your whole gang of the General Staff, they all ought to be drowned in the toilet. And I'd gladly pull the chain!

SHERVINSKY. Mr. Mishlayevsky, please don't forget yourself.

MISHLAYEVSKY. Scoundrels!

SHERVINSKY. What!

LARIOSIK. Why quarrel?

STUDZINSKY. As your superior officer, I ask you to stop this talk immediately. It's absolutely nonsensical and purposeless. (*To* MISHLAYEVSKY.) Why do you pick on him, Captain? (*To* SHERVINSKY.) Lieutenant, keep cool.

LARIOSIK (*like the voice of conscience*). Good gracious, but why quarrel?

SHERVINSKY. And above all, the swinishness of it! Is the catastrophe my fault? On the contrary, it was I who warned you all. If not for me, it is a question if he would still be sitting here alive or not.

STUDZINSKY. Quite right, Lieutenant, and we are all very grateful to you.

(ELENA *enters*.)

ELENA. What's the matter?

STUDZINSKY. Don't upset yourself, Elena Vassilievna, everything will be quiet, I guarantee it. Go to your room. (ELENA *exits; to* MISHLAYEVSKY.) Apologize to him. You had no right to...

MISHLAYEVSKY. Well, forget it, Leonid. I was a bit excited. It is such a disgrace.

SHERVINSKY. But why pick on me, of all...

STUDZINSKY. Forget it, we have plenty of other worries. (*Sits down near the fireplace and removes his spurs.*)

(*A pause.*)

MISHLAYEVSKY. But really, where can Aliosha and Nikolai be?

STUDZINSKY. I am anxious about them myself. I'll wait another five minutes and then I'll go to meet them.

(*Another pause.*)

MISHLAYEVSKY. Of course. (*Again anxious silence; to* SHERVIN-SKY.) So you were there when he made his get-away?

SHERVINSKY. I was there — till the last moment.

MISHLAYEVSKY. It must have been a remarkable sight, on my word! I'd give a lot to have witnessed it. Why didn't you kill him like a dog?

SHERVINSKY. Thanks. You ought to have gone and killed him yourself.

MISHLAYEVSKY. You may be sure I would have, believe me. Well, at least what did he say by way of farewell?

SHERVINSKY. What did he say? Well, he embraced me, thanked me for my loyal service...

MISHLAYEVSKY. And shed some tears?

SHERVINSKY. Yes, he shed some tears!

LARIOSIK (*naïvely*). Oh, so he shed tears? Think of that!

MISHLAYEVSKY. Didn't he give you some present for remembrance? (*Again cannot resist mocking him.*) For instance, a gold cigarette-case with his monogram?

SHERVINSKY. Yes, he gave me his cigarette-case as a present.

MISHLAYEVSKY. Oh, the devil...! Excuse me, Leonid. I am

afraid you will be in a rage with me again. You are not really a bad fellow, but you do have... shall I say... some peculiarities...

SHERVINSKY. What do you mean by that?

MISHLAYEVSKY. Well, how shall I put it... You ought to have been a novelist... You have a very rich imagination... (*Mimics.*) 'He shed tears'... I don't want to put you to any trouble but if I said to you now, 'Show me the cigarette-case?'

(SHERVINSKY *silently exhibits the cigarette-case.*)

MISHLAYEVSKY. Oh... hell! I'm staggered. Really his monogram? (*Examines it.*)

SHERVINSKY. Captain Mishlayevsky, what have you to say now? (*Offstage someone is throwing snow at the window to attract attention.*)

MISHLAYEVSKY. Gentlemen, in your presence, I apologize.

LARIOSIK (*inspecting the cigarette-case*). What a beauty! I've never seen such a beauty in my life. It weighs a pound at least.

SHERVINSKY. 422½ grams. (*Again the window is pelted with snow; they notice it.*) Wait a minute, gentlemen. (*They all rise wonderingly.*)

MISHLAYEVSKY. I don't like tricks... Why not through the door? And where can Aliosha be? (*Draws his revolver.*)

STUDZINSKY. Damn it... and all this junk lying around here. (*Hurriedly gathers up military equipment and throws it under the sofa.*)

SHERVINSKY. Gentlemen, be more careful with your revolvers. Better hide them. (*Conceals the cigarette-case behind the curtain. All approach the window, peep out cautiously and recognize someone.*)

STUDZINSKY. I can't forgive myself...

MISHLAYEVSKY. What a hell of a business...

LARIOSIK. My goodness! (*Rushes to inform* ELENA.) Elena, Elena!

MISHLAYEVSKY (*stops him*). Where are you running, damn you, are you mad? How can you! (*Closes* LARIOSIK'S *mouth. All run out; soon they re-enter carrying* NIKOLKA.)

STUDZINSKY. Easy...

MISHLAYEVSKY. Gently, gently! Get Lena out of the way, under some pretext. My God! Where is Aliosha? Killing is too good for me. Put him here, here, on the floor. Get snow, someone.

STUDZINSKY. Better put him on the sofa. Let's find the wound.

SHERVINSKY. His head is beaten up.

STUDZINSKY. There is blood in his boot. Take off his boots.

SHERVINSKY. Let's take him over there, on the sofa. We can't leave him on the floor.

MISHLAYEVSKY. All right, let's put him on the sofa, but gently gently. We mustn't scare Lenochka.

STUDZINSKY. Cut the boot, cut the boot.

MISHLAYEVSKY. There are some bandages in Aliosha's study. Bring them here, someone, quickly. (SHERVINSKY *and* LARIOSIK *rush out.*) Some iodine, too! God, how did he get so mangled? What does it mean? Where is Aliosha? (SHERVINSKY *and* LARIOSIK *return with iodine and bandages.*)

STUDZINSKY. Bandage his head, his head. Carefully.

LARIOSIK (*panicky*). Good God, he's dying!

NIKOLKA (*regaining consciousness, groans*). Oh, oh...

MISHLAYEVSKY. I'm going crazy. Tell us only one word. Where is Aliosha!

STUDZINSKY. Where is Alexei Vassilievich?

NIKOLKA. Oh, oh....

(ELENA *dashes in.*)

MISHLAYEVSKY. Lenochka, don't get excited. He fell down and hurt his head. There's nothing terrible about it.

ELENA. But he's wounded, what are you telling me?

NIKOLKA. No, Lenochka, no...

ELENA. And where is Aliosha. (*Insistently.*) Where is Alexei? You were with him. Answer only one word.

MISHLAYEVSKY. What's to be done now?

STUDZINSKY (*to* MISHLAYEVSKY). It cannot be. It cannot...

ELENA (*to* NIKOLKA). Why don't you answer?

NIKOLKA. Lenochka... right away...

ELENA. Only don't lie to me.

(MISHLAYEVSKY *signals* NIKOLKA *to keep quiet.*)

STUDZINSKY. Elena Vassilievna.

SHERVINSKY. Lena, why are you...

ELENA. Now I understand, now... Alexei is dead. They killed him.

MISHLAYEVSKY. Don't, Lena, don't. Calm yourself! Why must you think such things?

ELENA. Just look at his face, look at it! I felt it when he left, I knew it would end this way.

STUDZINSKY (*to* NIKOLKA). Tell us what happened to him.

SHERVINSKY. Lena, stop it... bring some water...

ELENA. Larion, they've killed Aliosha, they've killed Aliosha.

The day before yesterday you sat with him at this table. Do you remember? And now he is dead.

LARIOSIK. Elena Vassilievna, darling.

SHERVINSKY. Lena, Lena.

ELENA. And you, senior officers, senior officers, you are all back here and the Commander is dead.

MISHLAYEVSKY. Lena, have pity on us, what are you saying? We all obeyed his command, all of us. You must understand he ordered us to escort the cadres.

STUDZINSKY (*in a sudden determination*). No, she is perfectly right. I am guilty. We should not have left him. Well, I am the senior officer here and I will make good my mistake. (*Attempts to leave.*)

MISHLAYEVSKY. Where to? No! You remain here. (*Detains him forcibly.*)

STUDZINSKY. Let me go!

MISHLAYEVSKY. But no! You think I'll remain here alone? I alone! You are not the least bit guilty. Not the least bit! I was the last to see him. I warned him and obeyed his command. Lena, Lena!

STUDZINSKY. Captain Mishlayevsky, let me go, this moment!

MISHLAYEVSKY. Give up your revolver... Shervinsky!

SHERVINSKY (*to* STUDZINSKY). You have no right! You want to make the mess still worse. You have no right. (*Holds* STUDZINSKY.)

MISHLAYEVSKY. Lena, order him. It's all on account of what you said. Take his revolver away.

ELENA. I spoke out of grief. My head is bursting. (*To* STUDZINSKY.) Give me your revolver, please——

STUDZINSKY (*hysterically*). Nobody has the right to reproach me. Nobody! Nobody! I carried out all Colonel Turbin's orders.

ELENA. Nobody. Nobody. I was insane. (*Throws away the revolver.*)

MISHLAYEVSKY. Nikolka, have your say. Lena, be brave. We'll find him. Tell the whole truth.

NIKOLKA. The Commander is dead. (*Weeps hysterically.*)

(ELENA *swoons.*)

CURTAIN

ACT IV

SCENE: *The* TURBIN *living-room two months later, on Christmas Eve. The piano has been removed; the house is festively lit up;* ELENA *and* LARIOSIK *are decorating a Christmas tree;* LARIOSIK *stands aloft on a stepladder, attaching the trinkets which* ELENA *hands him; the months have taken a little of the provincial out of* LARIOSIK, *who seems now slightly more urbane in appearance.*

LARIOSIK (*on the ladder*). I think this star goes here... (*Listens.*) No, it only seemed to me... Most respected and dear Elena Vassilievna, I assure you that it's the end. They have taken the city.

ELENA. Don't hurry, Larion, nothing is known yet.

LARIOSIK. Well, there's one sure sign — no shooting going on. I must confess to you quite frankly, Elena Vassilievna, that I've grown terribly tired of shooting these months. I don't like it.

ELENA. I share your taste. (*Listening.*) Yes... No...

LARIOSIK. I think the star will fit in exactly right here. (*Too absorbed in admiring* ELENA *to tend to business.*) My God, I dropped the candle.

ELENA. Climb down, Lariosik. I'm afraid you'll break your neck. Never mind, there's another box of candles.

LARIOSIK. Well, here's an A–1 Christmas tree, as Vitenka would say. I'd like to see anyone who wouldn't call this tree perfectly beautiful. Dear Elena Vassilievna, if you only knew... The Christmas tree reminds me of those indelible days of my childhood in Zhitomir. Lights, green Christmas trees... (*Sighs.*) Though here I am better off than in my childhood. I don't feel like going anywhere. I should like to sit here for ever under the Christmas tree, at your feet, and never stir...

ELENA. You would get bored, I'm afraid. You are quite a poet, Larion.

LARIOSIK. Oh, no, what sort of a poet am I? What has it to do with poetry? What in hell... I beg your pardon, Elena Vassilievna.

ELENA. Recite something new for me, Larion. Please, do. I like your poems very much. You are very gifted, Lariosik.

LARIOSIK. Are you serious?

ELENA. Absolutely.

LARIOSIK. Well, then, all right. I will recite something... (*Holds a dreamy posture on his ladder perch.*) It is even dedicated... dedicated to... No, I'd better not read you that one.

ELENA. Why not?

LARIOSIK. No, better not.

ELENA. And to whom is it dedicated?

LARIOSIK. To a lady.

ELENA. Is it a secret?

LARIOSIK. A secret... (*suddenly, grimly*) to you!

ELENA. Thank you, my dear.

LARIOSIK. What's the use of your thanking me? Ekh! You can't make an overcoat out of thank-yous! But excuse me. I've caught it from Mishlayevsky. He always uses such language.

ELENA. I see. I am beginning to think you are in love with Mishlayevsky.

LARIOSIK. No. (*It escapes him.*) I'm in love with you.

ELENA. You mustn't be in love with me, you really mustn't.

LARIOSIK (*descends, speaks earnestly*). Do you know what, marry me!

ELENA (*seriously*). I am touched, Larion, but it cannot be.

LARIOSIK. He won't come back and what will become of you alone? Alone, what a terrible word! Without support, without sympathy. Of course, I'm not much of a support but I would love you so much all my life. You are my ideal. He won't ever come back, especially now when the Bolsheviks are advancing. He won't come back.

ELENA. I know he won't come back, but that is not the point. Even if he did come back, my life with him is finished.

LARIOSIK. He has been cut off. And how my heart bled when I saw you left alone... It was terrible to look at you, I tell you.

ELENA (*coquettes a little*). Did I look so bad?

LARIOSIK. Terrible. A nightmare! Your face was quite yellow, like a lemon!

ELENA. It's all your imagination, Larion.

LARIOSIK. Oh, I suppose I don't know how to talk properly to beautiful women... Only now you look better, a lot better. You are rosy, rosy as can be.

ELENA. Lariosik, you are priceless! Come over here, I will kiss you on the forehead.

LARIOSIK. Oh, my forehead...? Well, let it be my forehead. My hard luck! (*Approaches.*) Sure, how can anyone fall in love with me...

ELENA. Of course one can, and easily. (*Kisses him on the lips.*) But I have a love affair of my own.

LARIOSIK. What! Who? A love affair! You? Impossible! It can't be!

ELENA. Excuse me. Am I not worthy of one?

LARIOSIK. You! Not you! Who is it? Do I know him?

ELENA. You know him very well.

LARIOSIK (*racking his brains*). Wait, wait... (*Sits down, recalls.*) 'Young man, you have seen nothing.' And I thought it was all my dream. Oh, damn the lucky rogue.

ELENA. Larion, is that nice?

LARIOSIK. I'm going, I'm going.

ELENA. Where to, where to?

LARIOSIK. To the Armenians, to buy some vodka. I'll get drunk as a log.

ELENA. I won't let you take it like that. Larion, I'll always remain your friend.

LARIOSIK (*in the vestibule, putting on his overcoat*). I've read it, I've read it in novels. The moment she says: 'I'll remain your friend,' well, then everything is finished, done for.

ELENA. Larion, come back quickly.

(*In the doorway,* LARIOSIK *meets* SHERVINSKY *who enters in a sort of disguise, wearing a threadbare hat and coat and blue spectacles.*)

LARIOSIK. Who's that?

SHERVINSKY. Good evening.

LARIOSIK (*doesn't recognize him*). Good evening... yes, a very good evening. (*Goes.*)

ELENA. My God, what you look like! How are you?

SHERVINSKY. Thank you, Elena Vassilievna. Now I've tried it. Today I was riding in a droshky and some proletarians on the sidewalk were loitering on the pavement and one of them says to me: 'Look at that Ukrainian gentleman. You wait until tomorrow, tomorrow we'll kick you out of your droshky.' *Merci!* I have an experienced eye. I took one look at him and realized at once that I must go home and change my clothes. I congratulate you! Petliura is finished — out! Tonight the Reds will be here, which means we are going to have a Socialist Soviet Republic and all the rest of it.

ELENA. Why are you so pleased? One might think you have turned Bolshevik yourself.

SHERVINSKY. I am a sympathizer. This overcoat I rented from the janitor. A non-party rag.

ELENA. Remove the horrible stuff at once!

SHERVINSKY. At your service! (*Removes overcoat, hat, goloshes and spectacles and remains impeccable in a splendid full-dress suit.*) Well, congratulate me, I've just come from my début. I sang and I have been accepted. (*Sings.*) 'O Mama mia!'

ELENA. I congratulate you!

SHERVINSKY. Oh, Lena... and how's Nikolka?

ELENA. He got up today. I think he's resting now

SHERVINSKY. Lena, Lena! (*Embraces her.*)

ELENA. Let me go! Just a minute, why have you shaved off your sideburns!

SHERVINSKY. It's easier to put on make-up.

ELENA. Yes, it's easier to put on Bolshevik make-up. Don't be afraid, nobody will touch you. Oh, you sly little coward.

SHERVINSKY. Who would dare touch a man whose larynx contains two full octaves and even two notes higher? (*Sings.*) 'O Mama mia!' Elena, as nobody is here yet, I've come to explain myself.

ELENA. All right, explain yourself.

SHERVINSKY. Now everything is over... Nikolka is getting well. Petliura is being driven out. I have had a début. In general, a new life is beginning. Everything will straighten out.... It is impossible to live like this any more... He isn't coming back. He's cut off. Divorce him and marry me, Elena. I'm not a bad fellow, really. I'm not bad. And like this it is torture. You are lonely yourself.

ELENA. Will you improve?

SHERVINSKY. But in what way do you want me to improve, Lenochka?

ELENA. Leonid, I will become your wife when you have reformed yourself. In the first place, you must stop lying. It's a shame! You saw the Tsar behind the curtain and he shed tears... and not a word of it is true. And that long mezzo-soprano... and now it turns out she's just a waitress in a café.

SHERVINSKY. Lenochka, she was at the café only a short time, between engagements at the Opera.

ELENA. I recall you said she actually was working at the Opera.

SHERVINSKY. Lena, I swear by the memory of my dead mamma,

and papa too. There was nothing between us, not a thing. Besides, I am an orphan.

ELENA. It's all the same to me. Your dirty little secrets don't interest me. The important thing is that you must stop boasting and lying. The only time in your life you told the truth was about the cigarette-case, and then no one believed you. You had to show proofs.

SHERVINSKY (*dolefully*). Just about that cigarette-case... it was all a pack of lies. The Hetman didn't give it to me as a present. He didn't embrace me and he shed no tears. He just left it on the table and I helped myself.

ELENA. You filched it from the table! My God, only that was lacking! Give it to me.

SHERVINSKY (*hands it over*). Lenochka, but at least, let me keep my cigarettes.

ELENA. Keep quiet. A good thing for you that you confessed yourself. If I had found out!

SHERVINSKY. And how could you ever find out?

ELENA. You're a savage!

SHERVINSKY. Nothing of the kind. Lenochka, do you know, I have reformed an awful lot during these two months. I don't recognize myself, upon my word of honor. The catastrophe had a great effect on me, and the death of Aliosha too... Yes... I am a new man now. And about the material side, don't you worry, Lena. I am, oho-ho... Today I sang at my début and the director told me: 'For you,' he told me, 'Leonid Yurevitch, I hold out the greatest hopes.' He says, 'You ought to go to the Moscow Opera House, to the Bolshoi Theatre.' He embraced me... and...

ELENA (*incredulously*). And what...?

SHERVINSKY (*catches himself*). And nothing... went out into the corridor.

ELENA. You are incorrigible.

SHERVINSKY. Lenochka.

ELENA. What shall we do with Talberg?

SHERVINSKY. Divorce him, divorce him. Do you know his address? Send him a wire and a letter that everything is over for good.

ELENA. Well, then... It is sad and dull. And lonely too... All right. I agree.

SHERVINSKY. 'Thou didst conquer, Galilean.' Lena (*points to*

Talberg's photo), I demand that you clear him out right away. It's insulting to me. I can't look at it.

ELENA. Oh-ho, what a tone!

SHERVINSKY (*tenderly*). Lenochka, I can't look at him. (*Removes the photo from the frame, tears it and throws the pieces into the fire and the frame on the divan.*) The rat! Now my conscience is clear. Lena, play something for me. Let's go to your room. For two months now we haven't been able to say a word between ourselves. There are always so many other people.

ELENA. People are coming soon... Well, let's go.

(*They leave, closing the door behind them: sounds of a piano are heard;* SHERVINSKY *is singing beautifully the Epitholamy from 'Nero.'* NIKOLKA *comes in, moving slowly on crutches, looking pale and weak; he carries a flagon of wine.*)

NIKOLKA. Elena, Elena? Where are you? Ah, rehearsing... (*Notices the empty frame.*) So! Torn out! I understand! I guessed it a long time ago! All right, go on rehearsing! (*Lies on the divan.*)

(LARIOSIK *enters from the vestibule; carefully places a bottle of vodka on the table.*)

LARIOSIK. Nikolka, you got the wine? Why did you go for it yourself? Wait a minute, I'll bring you a cushion. (*Adjusts a cushion under* NIKOLKA'S *head.*)

NIKOLKA. Don't bother, Larion. It looks, Larion, as if I'll remain a cripple.

LARIOSIK. What are you talking about, Nikolasha. You ought to be ashamed of yourself. What nonsense!

NIKOLKA. Haven't they arrived yet?

LARIOSIK. They are coming right away. There's a lot of military equipment being moved through the streets and the Petliura fellows with it. Moving fast, too. Looks as if the Reds have given them a sound beating.

NIKOLKA. Serves them right. They deserve it.

LARIOSIK. All the same, despite this chaos, I managed to get some vodka. The first time in my life I've had any luck. I thought I'd never get any. I'm that kind of a person. When I went out the weather was marvellous. The stars were shining, the guns stopped barking... Well, I thought, the sky is clear, nature is in good order, but no sooner will I step onto the sidewalk than it will probably begin to snow. And sure enough, it started snowing, and the snow

76

blinded me. The weather was just like on that night when I first came to you, Nikolashka. All the same, here's the vodka, I've got it. Let Mishlayevsky see what I'm capable of. Twice I slipped, hit the back of my head, but never let the bottle out of my hands.

(SHERVINSKY *can be heard singing his aria from 'Nero.'*)

NIKOLKA (*picks up the frame*). Look, look, no picture! Just a frame! Alarming news! It means Elena is getting divorced and my heart tells me she's marrying Shervinsky!

LARIOSIK (*shocked by the news, leans against the table and upsets the bottle which falls to the floor and breaks*). What, already?

NIKOLKA. Ekh, Lariosik, ekh!

LARIOSIK. Already!

NIKOLKA. What's the matter with you, Larion? What's the matter? So, you too fell for her?

LARIOSIK. Nikolai, when talking about Elena Vassilievna, such expressions as 'fell for her' are out of place. She is a golden woman, you understand?

NIKOLKA. She's just a red-head, Larion. It's a real misfortune. That's why everybody loves her, because she's a red-head. Everybody makes love to her. Just one look at her, and they start bringing her bouquets. Our house always had a couple of bouquets standing around like feather-dusters. Talberg was in a rage about it. Well, Lariosik (*points to broken bottle*), you'd better clear up this mess. Mishlayevsky is coming in a minute and he'll murder you for it.

LARIOSIK. Don't tell him anything about it. (*Gathers the pieces and mops the floor.*)

(*Bell rings;* LARIOSIK *admits* MISHLAYEVSKY *and* STUDZINSKY, *both in civilian clothes and carrying parcels.*)

MISHLAYEVSKY. Good evening, Lariosik. Good evening, boys. Petliura is leaving the city.

STUDZINSKY. The Reds are in the Slobodka Suburb and will be here in half an hour.

MISHLAYEVSKY. Which means that tomorrow at this rate we'll have a Soviet Republic here. Wait a minute (*sniffs*), I smell something. By Jove, vodka! 'Fess up, who's been drinking vodka before time? What's going on in this benighted house? (*Notices stain on the floor.*) Do you wash your floors with vodka here? I know whose work this is. (*To* LARIOSIK.) Why do you smash everything? You certainly have hands of gold. Anything you touch is splintered at once. If you must break something, why not pick on the dishes? But vodka —— (*Offstage the piano is again audible.*)

LARIOSIK (*suddenly angry*). What right have you to bawl me out? I won't tolerate it!

MISHLAYEVSKY. Why does everybody shout at me? Soon they will begin to beat me up? Nevertheless, I don't know why, but I'm in a good mood today. Peace, Larion. I'm no longer angry with you.

NIKOLKA. Why is there no sound of shooting?

STUDZINSKY. They are advancing quietly, politely, and without any fighting at all.

LARIOSIK. And the strangest part of it is that everybody is glad, even the bourgeois who managed to survive. Everybody is so sick and fed up with Petliura.

NIKOLKA. I wonder what Trotsky looks like?

MISHLAYEVSKY. You'll see him, you'll see him.

LARIOSIK (*to* STUDZINSKY). Captain, your opinion?

STUDZINSKY. I don't know... I don't understand anything these days. The best thing for us would be to get up and follow Petliura. How can we, White Guards, live among these Bolsheviks? I can't imagine it.

MISHLAYEVSKY. Follow Petliura, but where to?

STUDZINSKY. Out into Europe somewhere.

MISHLAYEVSKY. And after that?

STUDZINSKY. Later on, get to the Don somehow and join Denikin and fight the Bolsheviks.

MISHLAYEVSKY. You mean again to place ourselves under the command of these rotten generals? A very clever plan! It's a great pity that Aliosha is in his grave. He could tell us a lot of interesting things about your generals.

STUDZINSKY. Don't torture my soul. Don't remind me of it.

MISHLAYEVSKY. No, excuse me. He is no longer with us, so it's up to me to speak. In the army, again? Fight again...! And he shed tears! No, thank you, I've had a bellyful. Especially when I saw Aliosha in the morgue. (NIKOLKA *weeps silently.*)

LARIOSIK. Nikolka, don't, Nikolashka!

MISHLAYEVSKY. Enough is enough! I've been fighting since 1914. What for? For my Fatherland. All right. But after these Excellencies abandoned us so shamefully, shall I go back to those Excellencies? No. That's enough! (*Twists his thumb into a scornful 'fig.'*) Here it is, a fig to them!

78

STUDZINSKY. We would request the speaker to confine himself to words.

MISHLAYEVSKY. I'm going to say what I have to say plainly enough, rest assured. Do you think I am an idiot? No. I, Victor Mishlayevsky, announce that I have no further dealings with scoundrelly generals. I'm through!

NIKOLKA. Captain Mishlayevsky has turned Bolshevik!

MISHLAYEVSKY. Well, if you insist, I'm for the Bolsheviks — but against the Communists.

LARIOSIK. Allow me to inform you that it is the same thing — Bolsheviks and Communists.

MISHLAYEVSKY (*mocking him*). Bolsheviks and Communists. In that case I'm for the Communists too.

STUDZINSKY. Look here, Captain. You used the word Fatherland. What Fatherland remains when the Bolsheviks are in control? Russia is ended. You remember what our Commander said, and he was right — the Bolsheviks are here with us.

MISHLAYEVSKY. Bolsheviks... Fine. I'm very glad.

STUDZINSKY. They'll proceed to mobilize you.

MISHLAYEVSKY. All right, I'll go and fight for them.

STUDZINSKY *and* NIKOLKA. Why?

MISHLAYEVSKY. Here's why! Because... Because Petliura, how many did you say he had — two hundred thousand men? Well, those two hundred thousand men, as soon as they heard the word Bolsheviks took to their heels as fast as they could. Did you see it? Clean work! Because behind the Bolsheviks our godly peasants follow like a cloud of glory. And with what can I resist them? With military riding-breeches! They simply can't bear the sight of these breeches and immediately answer with machine-guns. Would you like that? In front of us the Red Guards like a solid wall. Behind us, speculators and all the rubbish of the Hetman's bands, and me in the middle. Thank you very kindly. I'm sick of being used like manure to fill all the holes. Let them mobilize me. At least I'll know I am serving a Russian army.

STUDZINSKY. They've finished up Russia. They'll shoot us anyhow.

MISHLAYEVSKY. And they'll be doing well. They will take us to the Cheka, investigate us to a cinder and give us our reckoning. They will be quiet and we too — very quiet.

STUDZINSKY. As for me, I'll fight them.

MISHLAYEVSKY. You're welcome. Put on your uniform. Go ahead! Run to the Bolsheviks, yell at them, 'I won't let you in.' You saw Nikolka's head that time? Yours will be smashed in altogether. And right too; keep out of the way. The day of the simple people has come.

LARIOSIK. I'm against the horrors of civil war. Why all the bloodshed!

MISHLAYEVSKY. Have you been to the war?

LARIOSIK. No. I was exempted. Delicate lungs. And besides I'm mamma's only son.

MISHLAYEVSKY. Right you are, exempted comrade.

STUDZINSKY (*sadly*). Once there was a Russia, a great Empire.

MISHLAYEVSKY. And it will be again, it will be.

STUDZINSKY. Oh, yes, it will be... wait for it.

MISHLAYEVSKY. Not the kind there was in the past, but a new empire. Tell me this. When you will be beaten on the Don — and beaten you will be I prophesy — and when your Denikin will sneak off abroad — and that I prophesy also — where will you go then?

STUDZINSKY. Also abroad.

MISHLAYEVSKY. You're needed there, like the third wheel on a cannon. Wherever you'll come they'll just spit in your face. I'm not going. I'll remain here in Russia. Come what may. And that's all. Enough. I close the meeting.

STUDZINSKY. I see that I stand alone.

(SHERVINSKY *enters, followed by* ELENA.)

SHERVINSKY. Excuse me, gentlemen. Don't close the meeting. I have a special announcement to make. Here's what! Elena Vassilievna Talberg divorces her husband, the former Colonel of the General Staff and marries...

LARIOSIK (*groaning*). ...Oh!

MISHLAYEVSKY. Never mind, Larion. Where do you and I come in with these mugs of ours? Lena, my glorious one, allow me to embrace you and kiss you.

(LARIOSIK *begins to slink off to the vestibule.*)

STUDZINSKY. I congratulate you, Elena Vassilievna.

MISHLAYEVSKY (*drags* LARIOSIK *back*). Lariosik, congratulate them, go on.

LARIOSIK (*slowly and glumly*). I congratulate you and wish you all happiness.

MISHLAYEVSKY. Lena, darling (*to* SHERVINSKY). Well, you're a smart one! Such a woman! Talks English, plays the piano, and at the same time knows how to make the samovar... I myself, Lena, would gladly have married you.

ELENA. But I, Vitenka, would never have married you.

MISHLAYEVSKY. Well, you don't have to. I love you all the same. I am by nature a bachelor and a military man. I like a house to be comfortable, without women and children, like in the barracks.

NIKOLKA. With dirty puttees hanging around — cheerful-like.

MISHLAYEVSKY. Please, no jokes. Lariosik, serve the wine, please.

SHERVINSKY. Wait, gentlemen. Not that wine. I've got champaigne for you. (*Produces a few bottles.*) You know what this is? Oh-ho-ho! (*Glances at* ELENA *and is deflated.*)... Just ordinary champaigne. The bottle costs only three and a half rubles. Average sort of stuff, you know.

MISHLAYEVSKY. This is Lena's work. Lena, you red-haired angel, you are a great girl. (*To* SHERVINSKY.) You can get married, you are completely cured. Well, I congratulate you both and I wish you...

(*Door of the vestibule opens; enter* TALBERG *in civilian clothes, snow-covered and carrying a suitcase.*)

TALBERG (*grumpily*). The door is not closed for some reason.

(*Pause; an electric silence.*)

MISHLAYEVSKY. A nice how-do-ye-do.

TALBERG. Good evening, Lena. I beg your pardon. My appearance seems to have surprised this honorable company. Good evening, Lena. (*Silence.*) Rather strange, strange. I should think there's more reason for me to be astonished at finding such a gay crowd in my house in these hard times. Good evening, Lena. What's the meaning of this? (*Silence; shrugs his shoulders.*) What does it all mean?

SHERVINSKY. It means...

ELENA. Wait, Leonid. I must ask you gentlemen to leave me alone with Vladimir Robertovitch for a moment.

SHERVINSKY. I don't want to...

MISHLAYEVSKY. Wait, wait, everything will be cleared up. No excitement. (*To* SHERVINSKY.) You listen to her. Shall we disappear, Lenochka?

ELENA. Yes, go.

MISHLAYEVSKY. I know. You are a clever girl. If you need me, call. For me personally... Well, gentlemen, let's go and have a smoke in Larion's room.

SHERVINSKY (*to* ELENA). I beg you...

MISHLAYEVSKY. I take all responsibility. Please, gentlemen.

SHERVINSKY. Wait a minute...

MISHLAYEVSKY. I ask you...   (*All leave the room.*)

TALBERG. Please explain what all this means? What's all this tomfoolery? Where's Alexei?

ELENA. Alexei is dead.

TALBERG. It cannot be. When?

ELENA. Two months ago. Two days after your departure.

TALBERG. Oh, my God! Of course, that's dreadful. But I warned him, you remember.

ELENA. And Nikolka is crippled.

TALBERG. But you must admit that all this does not justify this stupid business; surely I'm not to blame for his death.

ELENA. Tell me, how did you get back? The Bolsheviks will be here right away.

TALBERG. I am very well informed. The whole Hetman business turned out a silly farce. The Germans deceived us. In Berlin I succeeded in obtaining a mission to General Krasnov on the Don. We've got to leave Kiev for good. I came to fetch you.

ELENA. A little late. You see, I am going to divorce you. As a matter of fact, I am marrying Shervinsky.

TALBERG. Very nice. Very nice... Ah-ha... Very nice indeed. You took advantage of my absence to indulge in a cheap little love affair. You...

ELENA. Victor!...

MISHLAYEVSKY (*rushes in*). Elena, do you give me full authority to have things out with this gentleman?

ELENA. Yes.

MISHLAYEVSKY. All right. (ELENA *leaves;* MISHLAYEVSKY *seizes* TALBERG *by the throat, draws out revolver.*) Out with you! (TALBERG *grabs his overcoat, suitcase and runs out.*)

MISHLAYEVSKY. Elena! Personally!

(ELENA *returns.*)

ELENA. Well?

MISHLAYEVSKY. He's gone. He'll give you a divorce. We had a pleasant conference.

82

ELENA. Thanks, Victor. (*Runs out.*)

MISHLAYEVSKY. At your service. (*Salutes.*) Larion!

(LARIOSIK *enters.*)

LARIOSIK. Has he gone already?

MISHLAYEVSKY. Gone! Gone!

LARIOSIK. You are a genius, Victor.

MISHLAYEVSKY. I'm a genius all right. Turn out the lights and light up the Christmas tree.

(LARIOSIK *turns off the house lights; presses a button and the tree lights up.*)

(*Enter* SHERVINSKY, STUDZINSKY *and* ELENA.)

STUDZINSKY. How pretty! And how homey one feels.

MISHLAYEVSKY. Larion's work. Bravo! Bravo! Well, Lariosik, play us the march.

(LARIOSIK *runs out and immediately a heroic march is heard on the piano offstage;* NIKOLKA *enters and lies on the sofa.*)

MISHLAYEVSKY. Everything is in full order. Now permit us to congratulate you properly. (*Yells.*) Larion, that's enough!

(LARIOSIK *re-enters with the guitar which he hands to* NIKOLKA.)

LARIOSIK. I congratulate you, Lena darling, once and for all. Forget everything, and, in general... to your health! (*Drinks.*)

(NIKOLKA *softly strums the guitar.*)

LARIOSIK (*dreamily*). Lights, lights...

NIKOLKA (*plays and sings the same military march he played that night before the catastrophe*).

> Tell me, soothsayer, beloved of God,
> What does my future hold for me?
> Will I soon be buried and covered with sod,
> To bring joy to every enemy?

(STUDZINSKY *stands glumly aside, but all the rest pick up the chorus.*)

ALL (*sing*).

> So music louder sounds, play on to victory.
> We have conquered and the enemy has fled, has fled, has fled.
> And so ——

MISHLAYEVSKY (*shouts the next line, which previously was, 'To the Tsar!'*).

> To the Soviet of People's Commissars!

83

ALL (*follow his lead, some sadly, others gaily*).

> To the Soviet of People's Commissars,
> We shout a proud hurrah! hurrah! hurrah!

MISHLAYEVSKY. Larion, now you make a speech. You are an expert!

LARIOSIK. Gentlemen, I really can't, and besides I am very bashful.

MISHLAYEVSKY. Larion is making his speech.

LARIOSIK. Well, if the company insists, I will say something. Only please excuse me, I haven't prepared for it... We met in the most difficult and most terrible times and have lived through so much, so very much... and I too. I, too, have lived through a great human drama. But, never mind that... And my rudderless vessel has been tossed on the waves of the civil war.

MISHLAYEVSKY. Very good, that about the vessel, very good...

LARIOSIK. Yes, the ship... until the storm brought it to this haven with cream-colored curtains... to people whom I love so much... Here too, I met a drama... but let's forget these sad events. Times have changed and Petliura is no more, and we are alive. We are all together again and even more than that... Elena Vassilievna... she has also suffered very much and she deserves her happiness, because she is... a wonderful woman, and I want to say in the words of our national poet: We rest, we rest!

> (*Cannonading in the distance.*)

MISHLAYEVSKY. Yes, we rest... (*Counts the cannon-shots.*)... Five, six, nine...

ELENA. Is there fighting again?

SHERVINSKY. No, you know what it is? A salute!

MISHLAYEVSKY. Right you are! That's the truth. Six-inch battery saluting. (*Music is heard in the distance.*) The Bolsheviks are coming!

> (*All except* STUDZINSKY *rush to the window; the sound of the 'Internationale' draws ever nearer.*)

NIKOLKA. Gentlemen, do you know this evening is a great prologue to a great historical play.

STUDZINSKY (*glumly*). For some a prologue — for me, an epilogue.

CURTAIN

SQUARING THE CIRCLE

A JEST IN THREE ACTS

By VALENTINE KATAYEV

Translated from the Russian

By CHARLES MALAMUTH *and* EUGENE LYONS

INTRODUCTION

SINCE its first production in 1928, Valentine Katayev's comedy *Squaring the Circle* has become the unchallenged favorite of the mass of Soviet theatre-goers. Its amiable exaggeration of the search by Communist youth for a new code of love, romance, and morality — and of the crowded housing conditions under which the search proceeds — touched Soviet risibilities as nothing behind the footlights before or since. The characters and lines of the play are familiar even to millions who have never seen it performed. The Moscow Art Theatre alone has already played it more than seven hundred times, scores of provincial theatres have put it on and it is still going strong.

In the new Russia even broad farce has its social purpose. In this case it is twofold. The play pokes fun at petit-bourgeois notions of marriage and the family. At the same time it caricatures no less gently silly attempts to discount love as a mere bourgeois prejudice. The scrambled loves and marriages and their facile unscrambling in *Squaring the Circle* are in no sense a realistic picture of domestic relations in the Soviet Union. While either husband or wife may end a marriage at will, there are social and ethical limits to this freedom prescribed by no law but none the less binding.

Written in 1927–28, the action of *Squaring the Circle* transpires in the last years of the NEP (New Economic Policy) epoch. The leading characters are all 'Komsomols,' members of the Communist Youth League. The play stands as hilarious proof that these earnest young followers of Marx and Lenin are utterly human and no more immune to the thrills and thrusts of love than youth under any other social system.

Katayev was born in Odessa in 1897, the son of a school teacher. At the age of nine he began writing poetry and by sixteen had achieved publication of his poetry in the Odessa press. His first book, however, did not appear until 1923, six years after the Revolution. It was a volume of short stories. In the revolutionary and civil-war years he worked as journalist and literary propagandist. It was in the latter capacity, as he recounts himself, that Katayev developed the satirical touch evident in this play and in most of his other works.

INTRODUCTION

His first play, produced by the Moscow Art Theatre, was a dramatization of his novel *The Embezzlers*, which had considerable vogue some years ago in the English version. This was followed by *Vanguard*, staged by the Vakhtangoff Theatre in Moscow. Late in 1928 the 'Small Stage' of the Moscow Art Theatre — an experimental offshoot of the famous theatre — put on *Squaring the Circle*. Later the play was transferred to the Moscow Art Theatre proper.

Since then Katayev has published, besides a great deal of short fiction, sketches and political articles, the play *A Million Torments*, the novel *Time — Forward!* and a dramatization of it under the same name, and the play *The Flowered Path* which was recently produced by the Vakhtangoff Theatre. Several of his plays, and *Squaring the Circle* in particular, have been staged successfully in foreign languages.

CHARACTERS

VASYA: a member of the League of Communist Youth; a serious-minded young worker, simple and abrupt in manner, sincere and without frills.

ABRAM: also of the Communist Youth; roommate and closest pal of Vasya but with frivolous mundane appetites that contrast with Vasya's genuine seriousness.

TONYA (whose full name is ANTONIA KUZNETZOVA): a serious-minded member of the Communist Youth who disdains feminine frivolities and is determined to be as hard and useful in the world as any man; unaware of, and disinterested in her good looks.

LUDMILLA: a real she-girl, not belonging to the Communist Youth, chiefly interested in her own pretty face, domestic comforts and boy-friends.

COMRADE FLAVIUS: an older Bolshevik, wiser and more experienced than these four young people but chummy with them all.

EMILIAN: a poet of the masses; a tall, blond, lumbering giant of a man who looks more like a longshoreman than a poet.

Also: boys and girls of the Communist Youth, who take their fun where they find it and manage to mix Karl Marx and vodka with heady effects.

Time: The present.
Place: Moscow.

ACT I

A typical room in an overcrowded noisy municipalized tenement in Moscow, barnlike, dusty and neglected. A battered door on the right, rear.

In one corner lies a dilapidated striped spring mattress propped on four bricks, which is a bed at night and a sofa during the day. On it lies a grimy pillow in a mildewed ticking and without a pillow-case. Beside the improvised couch stands a decrepit stool. A pair of old trousers against one wall and a crude home-made radio are the only embellishments of this corner, which is VASYA'S.

ABRAM'S *corner on the other side of the room contains only a pile of books, papers and booklets, and a few nails in the walls for clothes.*

In the foreground on one side is an untidy iron sink. From the middle of the ceiling hangs a lone, unshaded electric bulb, which glares at the room and brings out sharply its chaotic poverty.

Directly under the lamp stands a heavy wooden park bench which must have been dragged here by heroic efforts; initials and a large pierced heart betray its earlier career. On the bench lies a preposterously thick volume of Lenin, useful to bewilder poor ABRAM'S *head in daytime and to support it as a pillow at night.*

The one window in the room, with a broken window-pane, stuffed with a rag and decorated with the pendent remnant of a thick sausage, is in the foreground, left, facing the audience.

The room is entirely dark when the curtain rises, except for the dribble of light through the window from a flickering street-lamp.

LUDMILLA'S *saccharine voice and* VASYA'S *anxious one are heard offstage, from the corridor behind the door.*

VASYA. This way, Ludmillochka, this way. Don't get lost in the corridor.

LUDMILLA. Hell! I caught my skirt on something.

VASYA. Oh, it's only the bicycle. Here, hold on to me!

LUDMILLA. Darn! What a shame, pussykin. Your corridor's two miles long and not a single lamp in it.

VASYA. It burned out last week.

LUDMILLA. On ninety rubles a month couldn't you afford a new one?

VASYA. Didn't think of it. Look out there for the cupboard.

Somehow I didn't find the time for it. I work in the daytime, study at night... Walk right in.

(*Enter* Vasya, *followed by* Ludmilla. Vasya's *costume, much to his discomfort, jars with his natural serious inclinations. His gaudy butterfly tie, shiny puttees, plastered, well-parted hair, semi-military cap, and well-pressed coat are obviously* Ludmilla's *doing. The young lady's own femininely provocative clothes, however, are part of her personality.* Ludmilla *is kittenishly pretty.*)

Ludmilla. No one's had the time to spank you properly, darling. Just you wait, my dear husband, now I'll get after you.

Vasya. That's right. Get after me. Put me to work. That's why we signed up in the Marriage Registry Bureau. Watch your step. Wait. I'll turn the light on right away. The room is just what we need, only there really isn't too much furniture, you know.

(*He gropes stumblingly and nervously for the pendent lamp.*)

Ludmilla. I'm dying to see how you live.

Vasya. Damn it, I can't find the blasted light. Abram, are you home?

Ludmilla. Wait a minute — don't you live here alone?

Vasya. Eh... eh... I forgot to warn you. But Abramchik's a regular guy. Don't you worry, Ludmilla, darling.

Ludmilla. So you have a roommate! H'm — that's a nice wedding present! And I suppose the roommate is married!

Vasya. Who? Abram married? No — he's a confirmed bachelor.

Ludmilla. And does he know that we're married?

Vasya. Wait... he doesn't know yet. But it doesn't matter. He will be very glad. My word of honor. You'll see. He'll just dance with joy.

Ludmilla (*reproachfully*). Oh, Vasya...

Vasya. Really now... he'll be here right away and I'll tell him everything immediately: thus and so... got married... there's nothing to be afraid of. The main thing is don't you worry your little head, Ludmilla, darling. As a matter of fact, he's hardly ever at home. Where in thunder is this devilish light! He only sleeps here, see? Don't worry, we'll manage somehow. Well, see, here it is. (*He turns on the light revealing the neglected room, in contrast with their dressed-up tidiness.*) Of course one can't claim that this is any too elegant. The chief trouble, you see, there's not really too much furniture. Well, how about it, Ludmilla, darling?

LUDMILLA. As clean as a pigsty! What a frost!

VASYA. That's because the windows haven't been puttied. The cold gets in. But listen, Ludmillochka, the main thing is not to — not to get panicky. We'll fix it all up all right. Wait a while, we'll get things little by little. We'll have the windows puttied, we'll buy a lamp for the corridor, we'll sweep the floor. Everything will be swell.

LUDMILLA. So you and your roommate actually live in this... stable?

VASYA (*without enthusiasm*). Uhu...

LUDMILLA. What do you sleep on?

VASYA. I? I sleep on this... eh... couch. And he sleeps on the bench. And, believe it or not, it's really a very comfortable bench. It comes from Clean Pond Park. Don't you worry, Ludmillochka. If you like, I'll turn on the radio. I made it myself. It gets long distance... very long... I can get Berlin on it and everything. Ludmillochka... Why don't you say something? Don't you want to talk to me?

LUDMILLA. You go and talk to your radio. I'm no loud-speaker. Joking aside, it seems to me that on ninety rubles a month we could buy a few things. Where's your quilt?

VASYA. There isn't any.

LUDMILLA. What do you cover yourself with?

VASYA. I cover myself with the overcoat. Don't worry, it's padded with cotton.

LUDMILLA. Your head is padded with cotton. I wish I'd never seen this place. Ludmillochka, Ludmillochka! And all he has is one pillow for the two of us! And what a pillow — (*lifts it as if it were a dead rat*) — the kind you hate to touch. How in the world do you and your roommate manage to sleep here?

VASYA. We manage it all right. We take turns. One day I sleep on the pillow and he sleeps on Lenin. And the next day he sleeps on the pillow and I sleep on Lenin.

LUDMILLA. And there's filth everywhere. Filth! filth! filth! A regular pigsty. Just look at the dirt here! I bet you haven't swept this room for a whole year.

VASYA (*offended*). Why, I swept the room myself only two weeks ago.

LUDMILLA. Have you a primus stove?

VASYA. There isn't any...

LUDMILLA. Awfully pleased to hear that. Just you wait, my dear

93

husband. (*Paces the room indignantly and behaves like a general disposing his forces.*) I'll put the bed there! The table here! The chair there! And the other chair here! So! A runner here! The shelf here!

VASYA. That's right. There's a real housewife for you. A life's partner. Just what I need!

LUDMILLA. The plates here, and over here the curtains.

VASYA. Well, as for curtains, that seems to me a bit too much. After all that's petty bourgeois, middle-class...

LUDMILLA. What! Well, if that's petty bourgeois, then you had no business signing up with me. You'd better keep quiet. (*Goes back to generalling.*) And here we'll put the china closet. So! Ah-ha... You wait here and I'll run down to my sister's and bring a few things — after all, you don't expect me to sleep in this stable. Is there a broom?

VASYA. No.

LUDMILLA. Get one! Understand? And while I'm gone you sweep up the place.

VASYA. Yes.

LUDMILLA. Pussy... do you love me?

VASYA. One hundred per cent.

LUDMILLA. Then kiss me on my teeny-weeny nose.

VASYA. Ludmillochka! (*Seizes her in his arms.*)

LUDMILLA. Tsss... Have you gone mad! Let go of me! (*Struggles coyly.*)

VASYA. Ludmillochka... wait! Why not?

LUDMILLA. Because! Good-bye, spouse. Remember, the floor must be spotless! (LUDMILLA *departs.*)

VASYA. Spouse! So that's what I've turned into! Nice being married, Devil take it! (*Pounds the wall and shouts.*) Nikonorov... have you got a broom? Are you home? A broo-oom? Too bad!

(TONYA *enters, pretty despite her attempt to conceal her charms under negligent mannish attire: a boy's cap over close-cropped hair, a loose overlong skirt, sweater and sheepskin mackintosh. She carries bundles of books, a toothbrush, tin cup, and other paraphernalia wrapped in a towel.*)

TONYA (*in the doorway*). Abram, are you here?

VASYA. Hasn't come yet. Well, well... (*Astonished.*) Is that you, Kuznetzova? Haven't seen you in ages.

TONYA. Vasya! How are you?

VASYA. Tonya... (*Somewhat agitated.*) You've come to see Abram?

TONYA. Yes, to Abram. Hasn't he told you anything?

VASYA. No, I haven't seen him since yesterday. Let's have a look at you. Come on, let's have a good look at you.

TONYA. I'm just the same. Just as ordinary as I always was. And you, what are you doing here?

VASYA. What am I doing here? Nothing, I just live here.

TONYA. You live here? In this room?

VASYA. Yes, in this room.

TONYA. You mean... together with Abram?

VASYA. Yes... yes... together with Abram... But now...

TONYA. He didn't tell me a thing about it!

VASYA. And if he had, you would have come sooner? Is that right?

TONYA. Yes, that is, not altogether... h'm... Is this Abram's corner? (*She points to the corner where the books are piled.*)

VASYA. That's Abram's.

TONYA. So... not bad... the quarters are fairly large. Where does Abram sleep?

VASYA. On the bench. This is his half and that's mine... Yes... That's how things go, Tonyechka.

TONYA. I'll sit here meanwhile.

VASYA. Yes, yes. You sit here meanwhile. Abram will be coming any minute. He always comes about this time. I also have something to tell him... But you know it's such a ticklish matter... (*Puts his head out into the corridor.*) Rabinovich! Have you a broom? No? Too bad. Who has one? In the ninth apartment? Good. (*To* TONYA.) Here, you see, we have to sweep a bit... otherwise it's not especially... And no one seems to have a broom... Now, look here... I haven't seen you in ages... Don't you go away now.

TONYA. I don't intend to.

VASYA. I'll be back right away. In two shakes. (*He runs off in a business-like manner.*)

TONYA (*alone*). Nothing to be done about it. Good.

(*She unrolls the towel, takes out the toothbrush, tin cup, etc., and disposes them on a shelf; takes off her cap and puts on a red head-kerchief; in a word, she has moved in.*)

(*Enter* ABRAM, *simply dressed in a blue high-necked Russian blouse, unshaved, his pompadour unkempt. Laboriously he carries on his back a crude work-table, more like a carpenter's bench, and some books under his arm.*)

ABRAM. Kuznetzova, are you here already? Did you get the Plotnikov book?

TONYA. We can keep it only until Tuesday at the outside. I had to give my word of honor to get it.

ABRAM. We'll have to read it together. Look, here I've finally got the famous table. And by the way, damn it all, because of the lousy Marriage Registry I was late to a Communist Youth meeting. Were you late, too? I ask you now, why was the damn ceremony necessary? As if we couldn't live together without registering! Who gets any good out of it anyhow?

TONYA. It's a concession to the petty bourgeoisie and to the prosperous peasantry.

ABRAM. Yes... Where shall I put the blamed table?

TONYA. I think the best place is probably under the lamp so that we'll be able to read. Here, let me help you. Like this. That's right. Thank you. (*She takes off her mackintosh, spreads it on the table like a blanket, lies down, supporting herself on her elbows to read.*) By the way, I think there is another comrade living in this room. You haven't told me about it.

ABRAM. Oy! I clean forgot about it. What did you say? But don't worry, Kuznetzova, it's just a trifle. He's a regular guy. It's only Vaska.

TONYA. I hope he's not married.

ABRAM. Who? Vaska married! He's a confirmed bachelor.

TONYA. Yes, I know him.

ABRAM. Has he been here already?

TONYA. He ran off to find a broom. He'll be back right away.

ABRAM. Listen, Kuznetzova, have you told him already that we've registered?

TONYA. No. But he's been looking at me all the time in such a funny way... that I think he has guessed...

ABRAM. You think he's guessed? Oy, that's too bad. And say, have you had any dinner today? (TONYA *shakes her head negatively.*) Gee, how I want to eat! Maybe Vaska has something. (*He explores.*) Sausage! Kuznetzova, what do you think, if I were to take some of his sausage, would it be ethical or unethical?

TONYA. Unethical.

ABRAM. But he's a regular guy.

TONYA. Is that so! And I thought quite the contrary. I thought that I had noticed symptoms of unhealthy bourgeois degeneration: a striped bow-tie, Nepman boots, and in general he looks like a bridegroom from the Sukharev Market.

ABRAM. Does he really look like a bridegroom? As a matter of fact, come to think of it, I have noticed for a long time that Vaska has been degenerating. All the same, we must come to some agreement with him in this matter of our marriage. I think that he can only welcome it. (*Sighs.*) So I mustn't take Vaska's sausage? Or may I take it, perhaps? Well, Kuznetzova, what do you *really* think? Or is it altogether unethical?

TONYA. I think we can probably get together enough money to buy four hundred grams of our own sausage. Have you any money?

ABRAM. After buying the table, I have only twelve kopecks and I need eight for tomorrow's car-fare.

TONYA. I have a little bit too. Wait... five, ten, and here's some more... thirty-nine kopecks. Let me have your money. I think there's a stand around the corner. I'll run down right away.

ABRAM. Why should you run down and not I? After all, I'm your husband.

TONYA. Husband! Abram, I beg you, no bourgeois tricks, please. You bought and dragged the table — I shall go for the food.

ABRAM. Mutual understanding, equitable division of labor, and workers' solidarity.

TONYA. Precisely.

ABRAM. In that case I don't object. (TONYA *goes out.*) What is needed for a durable marriage? (*Counts on his fingers.*) Class consciousness, a common political platform, labor solidarity... Is there character similarity? There is. Is there mutual understanding? There is. Is there membership in the same class? There certainly is. Is there a common political platform? How could it be otherwise? Is there labor solidarity? And how! Then what is lacking? Love, perhaps? Why, that's a social prejudice! A lot of banana oil, rotten idealism... and by the way... (*Sniffing hungrily.*) Ugh! The room reeks of sausage. Should I? Or is it unethical?... Is it?

(VASYA *enters with a broom; is embarrassed when he sees his roommate.*)

VASYA. Oh, so you're here already. (*He begins to sweep, more and more embarrassed. To himself.*) I must tell him at once.

97

ABRAM (*to himself*). I must inform him. (*To* VASYA.) Hello, there.

VASYA. Hello! Listen, Abram. (*To himself*.) How awkward! (*To* ABRAM.) You see, Abram, it's like this... By the way, Kuznetzova has been waiting. Have you seen her yet?

ABRAM (*disturbed*). Well, what of it? Well, she was waiting and is not waiting any longer. What of it?

VASYA. But no, I said it just so, by the way.

ABRAM. By the way!

VASYA. By the way... Abram...

ABRAM. Well, hasn't she told you anything?

VASYA. Nothing, why?

ABRAM. Nothing. I said it just so, by the way.

VASYA. By the way? Aha... Abram, I see you have bought yourself a funny table.

ABRAM. Well, it's a mere trifle. (*To himself*.) I must tell him. (*To* VASYA.) By the way, about the table... I must ask you one question that involves a matter of principle.

VASYA. Well? (*To himself*.) I think he's guessed.

ABRAM (*desperately, with gloomy resolution*). Vaska... Would you admit that three people can live in this room?

VASYA (*equally desperately*). What's the point?

ABRAM. I'm asking you, would it be ethical or unethical?

VASYA. Of course it would be ethical. What else could be done about it? I've always considered you a regular guy. You understand...

ABRAM (*overjoyed*). That's right, Vaska. That's just why I like you so much. Thanks, old man, I knew you wouldn't fail me. I give you my honest word as a Communist Youth that I shall try not to crowd you.

VASYA (*with tears of tender emotion*). Thanks, pal; thanks, Abram. I've always said that you were one hundred per cent a regular guy. I certainly hope that I will not crowd you.

ABRAM. Nonsense! Trifles! You can never crowd me. What worries me is that I may...

VASYA. Still, you know, there'll be all kinds of curtains, canary birds in cages, this and that... Although, of course, she's a pretty good kid.

ABRAM. Shake, comrade. I'm so glad that you approve of her.

VASYA. Thanks, thanks. I was certain that you would be frightfully glad.

ABRAM. Why, of course, my dear fellow, why, of course. I should think so. How could it be otherwise? How could it be otherwise?

VASYA. Still, you know, she likes to dance a bit, and to cut capers ... To a certain extent, you know, she is sort of... shall I say... petty bourgeois.

ABRAM. Who's bourgeois?

VASYA. She.

ABRAM. Kuznetzova?

VASYA. What has Kuznetzova to do with it?

ABRAM (*losing courage*). Quite right, quite right. She has absolutely nothing to do with it. I said it just so, by the way. You know, one word leads to another, but please don't think of it. It's only that Kuznetzova has gone to the store to buy some sausage and there's nothing...

VASYA. For sausage? Kuznetzova?

ABRAM. Well, yes. And why shouldn't she go for sausage? There she is; ask her yourself. (*Enter* TONYA.) We've just been arguing about you. Vaska said that you hadn't gone for the sausage. And I said that you did go for sausage... Hi, hi... Such a silly misunderstanding. (*Desperately, winking to* TONYA.) Incidentally, are you acquainted with Vaska?

TONYA. Sure, we're acquainted.

VASYA (*sweeping altogether too industriously and dustily*). We have met.

TONYA (*sotto voce, to* ABRAM). Have you told him?

ABRAM (*also under his breath*). It just won't come out. My tongue won't move. Kuznetzova, please do me a real favor — you tell him.

TONYA. I?

ABRAM. Oh, yes. It's too embarrassing for me.

TONYA. I don't understand this futile delicacy. This is a very simple matter. There's nothing terrible about it. Just walk right up and explain everything.

ABRAM. It's easy to say, explain everything. Go yourself and explain everything.

TONYA. Why should I? You're the husband, aren't you?,

ABRAM. Kuznetzova, no bourgeois tricks.

TONYA. If you want to know, here's how the matter stands: I went for the sausage — you must tell him.

ABRAM. Equitable division of labor?

TONYA. Precisely.

ABRAM. It means that I must walk straight up and explain honestly.

TONYA. Walk straight up and explain honestly.

ABRAM. Or is it unethical?

TONYA. It's ethical.

ABRAM. Ugh! I'll go straight up and explain honestly. Ugh! (*He approaches* VASYA.) Listen, old man, it's like this. I'd like to talk seriously to you about something... M'm... By the way... Why did you get all dressed up today? You look like a bridegroom.

VASYA. I! A bridegroom? How do you make that out?

ABRAM. Well, well. I'm joking. I know very well that you're a confirmed bachelor. And incidentally, talking about bachelors... that is, I mean about bridegrooms... that is, by the way, about marriage in general...

VASYA (*very embarrassed and sullen*). What do you mean, marriage?

ABRAM. Wait, wait, old man. The main thing is, don't get angry ... Well, two of us have lived together, and now three of us will live together. (*Disparagingly.*) Think of it, what a tragedy! If I were you, for example, I'd be mighty glad of it.

VASYA. You'd be glad?

ABRAM. Why not? It will be much jollier.

VASYA. Abram, are you saying this seriously?

ABRAM. Most seriously.

VASYA. Shake, comrade! (*Very vigorous handshaking.*)

ABRAM. One might say, seriously and for a long time. Even signed up in the Marriage Registry.

VASYA. Registered! Registered! Of course, according to form! You know there was a funny man there sitting at a marriage table, you understand, the fellow with the mustache. He made a speech.

ABRAM. Right, right. He made a speech. Wait a minute, wait... And how do you know about it?

VASYA. What do you mean, how do I know about it? And who do you think registered today if it wasn't I?

ABRAM. *You* registered? Wait a while — it is I who have registered.

VASYA. You? You also registered?

ABRAM. What do you mean, I also? Not also, but in the first place.

VASYA. Abram, then that means that both of us... today... re...

100

ABRAM. Registered. Tss...

VASYA. ... gistered.

ABRAM. Kuznetzova, the most awful smash-up has occurred. Have you heard?

(TONYA *has long been standing with a petrified face, buried in a book, as if completely absorbed in it.*)

TONYA. Yes... no... what is it? Have you told him?

ABRAM. I've told him all right. And how!

TONYA. Does he object?

ABRAM. Object! What do you mean object? It's worse; he doesn't object. And what's more, he is solidly with us to the extent of a hundred and twenty per cent...

TONYA. Why do you complain, then? What are you excited about? I don't understand. If he is solid with us, so much the better. If there are three of us, then there will be three of us. And the three of us will make the best of it.

ABRAM (*almost shouting*). Three of us! She says three of us! Kuznetzova...

TONYA. What is it? Have you anything against the three of us living together?

ABRAM. Three of us living together... Kuznetzova, throw the book away. Think of what's happened.

TONYA. I don't understand a thing.

ABRAM. She doesn't understand! Tonka, understand!

TONYA. Well.

ABRAM. He...

TONYA. Yes?

ABRAM. My tongue won't move. Let me have my share of the sausage. I want to stuff myself, Kuznetzova. Well, do you understand?

TONYA. Don't understand a thing. Please don't bother me; I'm reading.

ABRAM. At such a time, she reads! Kuznetzova!

TONYA. Drink a glass of water.

ABRAM. I'll guzzle the whole water system. Even two water systems. (*He's exhausted with excitement.*)

(*The clatter of a bicycle crashing in the corridor.*)

LUDMILLA (*from the corridor*). Vasya! Vasyuk! We've lost our way here. I ripped my skirt on something here. Well, where in the world are you?

VASYA (*in terror*). Ludmillochka! (*To* ABRAM *and* TONYA.) Comrades, she'll eat me up. The Devil take you all! (*Shouting towards the corridor.*) Oh, that's only the bicycle. (*To* ABRAM *in a sibilant whisper.*) You should have thought of it before getting registered. (*Shouting into the doorway.*) Right away, Ludmillochka. (*To* ABRAM.) I wish you'd croak! Rrr... (*He goes out.*)

TONYA. What's all the noise about? Who has come?

ABRAM. That's for Vaska. Some responsible Communist Youth has come... to call on him.

(*Enter* LUDMILLA, *half-smothered by pillows, blankets, other household goods which she is carrying; followed by her young nephew* SASHA, *a Red Pioneer, khaki-clad and with the red neckerchief of this children's organization;* SASHA *too is laden with a birdcage, cheap framed pictures and other staples of domestic bliss; behind them the distracted* VASYA *with odds and ends of bundles.*)

LUDMILLA. I nearly ripped my skirt to pieces. You simply must have the lamp by tomorrow. Sasha, don't break the lampshade! Don't crawl all over my feet. Oh, my God, what an impossible child! Put the things here and don't upset the darling canary.

TONYA (*to Abram*). So this is the responsible organizer?

ABRAM. Well, yes... That is, she is not yet altogether responsible. Why do you look at me like that?

TONYA. Why has she come with all those bundles?

ABRAM. What a strange person you are, Kuznetzova. Must you know everything? Why? That's her own affair. Maybe she's moving to the country and on the way she's dropping in to say good-bye to a comrade.

TONYA. Going to the country — in January?

ABRAM. Well, in two weeks it will be February. But that's not the point. Oh, Kuznetzova, you better read and not pay attention to anybody.

TONYA (*looks at* LUDMILLA *and shrugs her shoulders*). H'm... So that's that.

ABRAM. Complete smash-up.

LUDMILLA (*peremptorily, to* VASYA). And who are these?

VASYA. This, my dear little Ludmilla, is Abram. Haven't you ever met him before? Abram, come here and I shall introduce you to Ludmilla.

ABRAM. Well, how do you do? I am Abram. (*They shake hands.*)

102

LUDMILLA. And who is that one?

ABRAM. That...

VASYA. Tss... This, my dear little Ludmilla... so to say... a very good old acquaintance of Abramchik's... She's come here to visit... to have a little talk... to take tea... Never mind her... Isn't that right, Abram? (*Making desperate signs to him.*)

ABRAM. Well, yes... a very good acquaintance... That's clear... Don't you disturb yourself...

LUDMILLA. But why the funny table? How did it get here?

VASYA. How did it get here... Abram... Why the funny table? (*Desperately winking.*)

ABRAM. Why the funny table? She brought it with her, of course. Such a queer girl she is. *Such* a queer girl. It's January and she insists on moving to the country. Such a queer girl. She ran in to say good-bye.

TONYA (*hearing him*). Abram, what does all this mean?

ABRAM. Ah... it means... Kuznetzova... it means that the most stupendous smash-up has occurred. (*In a hoarse whisper.*) They also registered today.

TONYA (*slightly stunned*). Where?

ABRAM. In the Marriage Registry Bureau.

TONYA (*not yet recovered*). What for?

ABRAM. Just another concession to the petty bourgeoisie and to the prosperous peasantry. Do you think that only you and I are such smart-alecks? Kuznetzova, do you understand what has happened?

TONYA. I begin to understand.

LUDMILLA (*pointing disgustedly to* TONYA). Vasya, why is she spread out here in the middle of the room? She's in my way. I have to straighten things out. Tell her so.

VASYA. Oh, let her alone, Ludmilla. Let her alone. There you are... Let her lie and don't pay any attention to her.

LUDMILLA. What do you mean, don't pay any attention! If I don't pay any attention and let things go, then she'll move in on us. Why, she's occupying most of our living-space already. Impudent creature! I'll tell her myself right away. Let her come and call on us tomorrow, not today.

VASYA. Ludmillochka, for God's sake...

LUDMILLA. And I'll do it too.

VASYA. Ludmillochka, I beg you... I must tell you... But don't be angry, please. Of course you won't get angry... You see, the thing is that Abram also got married today... to her.

LUDMILLA. What! Wha-at! (*Thunder and lightning. She drops a bundle of bedding and collapses on it.*)

VASYA. That's life for you...

LUDMILLA. You shameless deceiver! Don't you dare touch me!

VASYA. Ludmillochka, my precious one.

LUDMILLA. Go away! I hate you!

VASYA. My sugar...

LUDMILLA. Go away, go away, go away, go away, go away!!! (*She stamps her feet and weeps buckets.*)

VASYA. Ludmillochka! Ludichka! Milichka! Ah... I wish you'd all sink in the mud — may you croak... My sugar, my pussy-cat...

ABRAM. Kuznetzova, here before your face you see a smash-up.

TONYA. Trifles. There's room for all of us here. Nothing terrible.

ABRAM. Four in one room?

TONYA. I can go away if you wish.

ABRAM. Where to? What do you mean, you can go away? Have you a place where you can spend the night? Why, it's Siberian weather outside. I can't let you go.

TONYA. I should like to see you stop me from going.

ABRAM. Cut out the nonsense. After all, I *am* your husband.

TONYA. Now, now — none of those bourgeois tricks.

ABRAM. Kuznetzova, I beg of you. After all, you know, we do have labor solidarity, and where in thunder will I get the Plotnikov book if you desert me?

TONYA (*persuaded by this incontrovertible logic*). Very well...

VASYA. On my word of honor I don't know what in hell to do. Kuznetzova, maybe you can exert some influence on her.

TONYA (*goes up to* LUDMILLA, *assumes the attitude of an earnest soap-boxer about to exhort a hostile mob, one foot forward, hands behind back; clears her throat and begins to orate*). Comrade, what is to be done? What is to be done now that this unprecedented and annoying situation has arisen? Are you a member of the All-Union League of Communist Youth? Are you...

VASYA (*in desperation*). She's not a member so far.

ABRAM. I've always said that our agitation among the non-members isn't worth a damn.

LUDMILLA (*through tears*). This is not to the point... My grandfather is a hero of labor.

ABRAM. All the more reason not to weep.

LUDMILLA (*begins to unburden her soul*). Yesterday evening, as soon as we met, comrades, he began to tell me all sorts of things until my head turned around — now don't interrupt, Vasya — and of course in the end he made me altogether dizzy. He says to me — keep quiet! (*Poor* VASYA *hasn't the least intention of interrupting.*) — Dear little Ludmilla, he says, let's live together; let's keep house. You, he says, come over and move into my room. I have, he says, a lot of living-space and a loud-speaker of my own construction, and a gas range — shut up, Vasya, you know you said it — He says, I have this and that and I listened to him, listened and then, fool that I am, went off with him like an idiot to get registered. And now it's a nice mess! Now I see that he shares his living-space with someone else, that there is no electric bulb in the corridor, that the someone else is married, and as for the gas range, if there is one I haven't seen it. Maybe he meant his bicycle.

VASYA. I'll show you the kitchen...

LUDMILLA. Yeh... I'll bet there are a thousand families in the kitchen.

VASYA (*softly*). No, only twelve. (*Tries to caress her.*)

LUDMILLA. Go away!

VASYA. Oh, let's make up, Ludmillochka.

LUDMILLA. Go away, go away. Let go of me. I'm going away... I'm going away this minute. (*But doesn't budge.*)

VASYA. Ludmillochka, after all, I'm your husband.

LUDMILLA. My husband! You're my calamity, my first big mistake!

VASYA. So that means you're going to stay?

LUDMILLA. And where am I to go? My sister has four people in one room. Of course, I must stay. What else can I do? But don't you dare look at me — or touch me! (*Nevertheless they clinch affectionately.*)

ABRAM. And what can you do with a girl like that?

VASYA. Never mind...

ABRAM. Well, I guess we'll have to live together. As they say, we're four in a boat. Now, let's do something about it.

LUDMILLA (*brightening after the storm*). Yes — we'll have to put up a partition. Right from the door. We can divide it into equal halves.

VASYA. Gee! You're a smart one, Ludmillochka. That's a corking idea!

ABRAM. That's right. I'm with you. Kuznetzova, have you heard it?

TONYA (*engrossed in her book*). Heard what?

VASYA. It has been proposed to put up a partition.

TONYA. No objections on my part.

ABRAM. Passed unanimously.

LUDMILLA. For the time being, we can mark it with chalk. Vaska, have you any chalk?

VASYA. Yes, here it is.

LUDMILLA. Draw the border-line. From there right to here, and you shove over a little. (*This is for the benefit of* TONYA.)

TONYA. With pleasure. (*She moves the table to* ABRAM'S *side of the room.*)

VASYA. In two shakes, sugar. Drafting is the first thing they taught us at the Institute. So, and so, and so. (*He's drafting on the floor.*)

ABRAM. This is a rare experiment in building socialism in one room.

VASYA. Look what came out of this. Just look. It's a beauty. Simply marvellous. Five minutes — and presto! A two-room apartment. There's American tempo for you.

LUDMILLA. Look, Vasyuk, we'll have a wonderful room. Isn't that so?

VASYA. You see, there was no sense in grumbling.

LUDMILLA. Comrades, neighbors, this is our half — and that is your half. Vasya, push the bench into their room. (*He does.*) That's right. Now come here. Here we'll have our bed, here the table, and here the two chairs. Do you like that, pussykin?

VASYA (*who, much relieved, is busying himself with the radio*). Very nice, and do you like it?

LUDMILLA. I like it awfully! (*Interfering with his beloved radio; whispers.*) And do you love me? I love you awfully, awfully. And you me?

VASYA. Sure. (*Glances longingly at the radio.*)

LUDMILLA. Then kiss your wifie on her teeny-weeny nose. (*Whispering.*) They don't see us. (VASYA *kisses her. Little* SASHA *is not even shocked.*) There, Sashka, time for you to go home.

(VASYA *fusses with the radio while* LUDMILLA, *humming happily, begins to turn her half of the barnlike room into a home; nonchalantly she tosses old papers, rags, etc., into* TONYA'S *half as if it were infinite space.* TONYA, *lifting eyes from her book, notices this procedure; first she shrugs, but finally registers her protest; demonstratively she climbs down from her table, takes the mackintosh and shakes its dust into* LUDMILLA'S *half. The women glare at each other;* TONYA *replaces the coat and goes back to education.* ABRAM *meanwhile divides his admiring glances between* LUDMILLA'S *domestic talents and the tempting sausage.* VASYA *has some difficulty finding his radio station, which gives the audience bits from programs from many Soviet stations, with plenty of static whining in between.* SASHA *is fascinated by the radio.*)

VOICES ON THE RADIO. Hello! Hello! Hello! Workers, peasants and Red Army men... (*A snatch of 'Stenka Razin,' switching abruptly to 'Volga Boatmen Song' played by balalaikas.*)... Religion is the opiate of the people. Science instead of superstition. The unbroken work-week and abolition of Sunday. Comrades... Whizzzz ... (*Too many stations at once: a jumble of words scrambled with music.*)... President Goovyer and fat American exploiters... Poincaré — war.... C.A.T. — cat... R.A.... Workers, peasants and Red Army men... American combines... Diapers should be washed immediately and... down with sabotage and intervention... and the prevention of venereal diseases. (*A blast of confused noises that eventually clarifies into 'Budenny's March.'*)... Socialist competition ... results in... Brrr... Whizzz.

VASYA (*has finally got what he's looking for*). There it is.

VOICE ON THE RADIO. Hello! Hello! Hello! Moscow speaking. Comintern Station transmitting on a wave-length of ten hundred and fifty metres. Broadcasting from the Great Academic Theatre the opera Eugene Onyegin. Hello! hello! You may now listen to the audience. (*Sounds of the orchestra tuning in; hubbub of muffled voices. Then everything quiets down.*) It hasn't begun yet, comrade radio listeners. It will begin in five or ten minutes. Stand by your radios. Please send your comments to the Radio Broadcasting Trust. For the time being we are signing off...

LUDMILLA. Vasya, shut off the radio or the kid'll never leave. Go, go! Tell mother that everything is all right. That she needn't worry. Everything is all right. (SASHA, *wrapped in coats, scarfs and sweaters like a mummy, is pushed through the door.* VASYA *disposes himself on the mattress, picks up a guitar, strums and sings a doleful Russian love song. As he sings, his eyes keep travelling to* TONYA, *still buried in her book.* LUDMILLA *suspects it.*) Terrible light. I'll fix it right away. (*She mounts a chair and covers the bulb with a colored handkerchief.*) Isn't this better, pussykin? (*Sits down and reclines over him.*) Do you love me, darling? They can't see us.

TONYA. Now, please, comrade, I wish you would open our half of the light; otherwise it's impossible to read.

LUDMILLA (*acidly polite*). Excuse me. (*She uncovers one half.*) Can you see now?

TONYA. I can see very well, thank you. (*She continues to read.*)

(ABRAM *is ostensibly reading, but following* LUDMILLA'S *every move.* VASYA *continues his strumming.* LUDMILLA *goes back to the couch and in a cattish whisper, with gesture toward* TONYA.)

LUDMILLA. Vasya, she's not bad-looking, but she dresses so shabbily.

VASYA. M'm...

LUDMILLA. Have you known her very long?

VASYA. M'm... two years.

LUDMILLA. And you haven't fallen in love with her?

VASYA. M'm...

LUDMILLA. Tell your little pussy 'Meow.' (*She imitates a cat to perfection.*)

VASYA (*perfunctorily*). Meow!

LUDMILLA. Come on, kiss pussykin. They can't see us.

ABRAM. I'm frightfully hungry. Vaska! Haven't you anything a fellow can munch?

VASYA. I have some sausage.

ABRAM. Let's have the sausage.

LUDMILLA. Wait a minute, comrades. That's not proper. Let's do it respectably. I brought something from sister's. Here are some rolls and we can make tea. Would you like to have some tea? (*She revels in the rôle of generous hostess.*)

ABRAM. Oh-ho, oh-ho, and how! Kuznetzova, have you heard? The motion has been made and seconded that we drink tea with rolls.

TONYA. I really don't know about that.

LUDMILLA. Please don't be bashful.

TONYA. Thanks, of course. But we have none of these things. We've no cups... spoons... forks...

LUDMILLA. Never mind! Never mind! Until you get your own, you may use ours. Isn't that right, pussykin? You don't object to their using ours do you, pussykin?

VASYA. Of course not.

ABRAM. Motion unanimously carried.

LUDMILLA (*taking the kerosene primus stove*). Where is the kitchen here?

VASYA. Let me take it. I'll go down with it.

ABRAM. Comrades, this is not the correct procedure. Perhaps I too desire to participate in this building of socialism in two halves of one room. Let me have the primus. Equitable division of labor. (*To* LUDMILLA.) You will instruct me a bit how to use it. Kuznetzova, you must also assume your share of civic responsibility.

LUDMILLA (*giggling*). What a funny fellow you are! You're holding the stove upside down. You mustn't hold the stove like this — but like that. (*Fixes it for him, bursting with laughter.* ABRAM *basks in her attentions.*)

ABRAM. And how do you light it?

LUDMILLA. This is how you light it. Do you see this little saucer? You pump a little kerosene into it. And do you see this little screw? You turn it. Then you take a wire and clean the top. Do you understand?

ABRAM. I understand. You take the pump. Then you clean the saucer and then you buy the kerosene...

LUDMILLA. Oh — you don't understand anything. Come on, I'll show you everything. (*To* VASYA.) Pussykin, you won't be jealous, will you? (*To* TONYA.) Would you mind getting the dishes ready meanwhile?

TONYA. Yes, but I don't know where and how.

LUDMILLA. Vasya, you help her. (*To* ABRAM.) Come on, show me that kitchen of yours. (*Takes his hand.*) I'm going to hold on to you because there's that bicycle out there.

ABRAM (*swinging the primus*). You hold on. Pump... then the pumping... the screw... in one word, super-industrialization. (*They go out.*)

VOICE OVER THE RADIO. Hello! Hello! This is the Grand Opera. (*During the beginning of the following scene, the radio transmits a soft romantic overture.*)

TONYA. Well, show me where you keep things here.

VASYA. Take the basket. The glasses are there. Get them out. Careful!

TONYA. Don't worry.

VASYA. That's how things go, Tonyechka Kuznetzova. (*Contemplatively.*) How many summers? How many winters?

TONYA (*avoids looking at him*). About a year. Where shall I put the rolls?

VASYA. About... Oh, you can put the rolls on a plate. It was a wonderful winter, wasn't it?

TONYA. What shall I do with the teapot?

VASYA. Put tea in it. Do you ever still go to the Clean Pond skating-rink?

TONYA. No, no — I haven't even thought about such things.

VASYA. You haven't thought of it? Stop, what are you doing? Why, you've poured out all the tea. Let me show you — like this... (*Wistfully.*) And do you remember, Tonka, how you and I nearly got killed on that sleigh gliding down Sparrow Hill?

TONYA (*making a brave effort to be indifferent*). Why do you look at me like that?

VASYA. A year... only one year. I have a wife, you have a husband. Do you love Abram very much?

TONYA. It seems to me that this is my personal affair. Where shall I put the sugar?

VASYA. Why do you blush, then?

TONYA. I ask you, where shall I put the sugar?

VASYA. Put it... anywhere...

TONYA. Please stop looking at me!

VASYA (*sighs*). That's how things go, Tonyechka. And do you remember that tree at the park? The tenth one from the end, counting from the side of the ash-can? Do you know, Tonyechka, after that I spent the whole night long... you know... and the next day I wandered through the streets of Moscow like a lunatic... I remember how the snow fell. It just plastered my chest... and the eyelashes, you know, with such little needles... Ekh, a whole year... Easy to say... And you, you're the same as you've always been... Yes, yes, don't turn away... The same strand of hair over the ear peeking from under your head-kerchief. (TONYA *quickly tucks away this strand of hair.*) Where have you been all this time?

TONYA. I was working in the country.

VASYA. What a lovely lock of hair!

TONYA. Let's go. Stop this nonsense. I'm asking you, where shall I put the sugar?

VASYA. To hell with the sugar! Put it where you like. Bygones are bygones... Tonyechka... wonder what will happen next?

TONYA. I'm putting it in a little jar.

(LUDMILLA *and* ABRAM *return with the primus and tea-kettle; both of them are in gay spirits and a little flushed.*)

ABRAM. It's finally boiled but after great difficulties. She's been instructing me so well, comrades, that now I could set fire not only to one primus, but to a whole factory of primuses.

LUDMILLA (*laughing*). Oh — I can't stand it any longer. He's a scream, this Abramchik. You can simply die laughing with him.

TONYA (*firmly, to* VASYA). I've put it in a little jar...

LUDMILLA. Well, how are things with you folks? Is everything done?

VASYA. Everything. But where shall we put the sugar?

LUDMILLA. Why, you haven't done a thing. Is this the way to prepare tea? You haven't cut the sausage. You haven't even opened the bag of rolls. You haven't even taken out the bread. You're a perfectly useless little pair. Let me do it! I'll fix everything right away! Comrade Abram, you sit right here. You deserve a rest, dear boy.

ABRAM. After toiling in the sweat of my brow.

LUDMILLA. And you, Comrade Tonya, sit down beside your husband. And I shall sit beside *my* darling husband. Like this. Now we shall all drink tea.

(*Enter* EMILIAN, *the hulking athletic poet; his long arms swinging like an ape's.*)

EMILIAN. Listen, brethren, can I spend the night here? (*Noticing the company.*) Oh-ho! So you're having a regular banquet here, with a couple of girls. (*Comes up to* LUDMILLA, *and then to* TONYA *and peers at them brazenly.*) Not so bad, not so bad! They'll do in a pinch! I have the pleasure to introduce myself. (*To* TONYA.) Have you heard of Pushkin?

TONYA. I have.

EMILIAN (*to* LUDMILLA). Have you heard of Tolstoy?

LUDMILLA. I have.

EMILIAN (*to* TONYA). Have you heard of Dostoievsky?

TONYA. I have.

EMILIAN (*to* LUDMILLA). Have you heard of Shakespeare?

LUDMILLA. I have.

EMILIAN (*to* TONYA). Have you heard of Maxim Gorki?

TONYA. I have.

EMILIAN (*to both of them, throwing out his chest*). Have you heard of Emilian Chernoziomny?

TONYA *and* LUDMILLA. No — I haven't.

EMILIAN. Well, look at me, then. In me you behold Emilian, the poet of the masses. Now you understand? I can beat anybody at verse-writing. Have you heard my latest poem? Everybody listen: It's called 'The Izvostchik.' (*Recites in bellowing voice.*)

> Ekh, the city has gnawed me to pieces
> I will not see my native moon
> I will tear my collar wide-open
> That I may hang myself soon.
>
> I was a gay tempestuous fellow,
> In golden curls my head,
> But now I am perishing, master,
> Because Moscow has nibbled me dead.

And if you dare me I'll show you how st-r-rong I am. (*Doubles his arm and presents it to* TONYA *who touches it gingerly.*) Here, feel this. Don't be bashful. (*Generously offers it also to* LUDMILLA, *who is not so gingerly and shows admiration.*) And look at this chest! (*Bangs it.*) I can beat anybody at physical culture as well as poetry. Think I'm lying?

ABRAM. Now, he's at it — we'll never stop him.

EMILIAN. Well, brethren and sistren, can I spend the night here?

VASYA. That's a bad guess, old man. You see, it's like this: we all got married!

EMILIAN. Who-o-o-?

VASYA. Both of us. Abram and I. So that, comrade, the car is full-up.

EMILIAN. No! Are you serious?

ABRAM. It's a fact.

EMILIAN. When did you do it?

VASYA. I married her, that is Ludmilla, and Abram married Kuznetzova — her over there. So that...

EMILIAN. Wait, boys and girls. Here are extemporaneous verses. Listen! H'mm... (*Recites.*)

> The kids are spliced, they've lost their head — O!
> And frisk like calves in fertile meadow;
> Only Emilian, the masses' poet
> Lacks a bride but doesn't know it.

ABRAM. Pretty rotten...

EMILIAN. Let's see you do it better, wiseacre. Well, good-bye.

VASYA. Where are you bound for? Have some tea!

EMILIAN. Forget it! I'm hastening to draw the appropriate organizational conclusions. (*He rushes out.*)

ABRAM. Have you ever seen anybody as crazy as that? He has run away to spread the news. He'll spread it everywhere too. Well, the meeting will continue.

TONYA. It's evident that he's one of the decadent school of poets. (*Pause.*)

LUDMILLA. The radio plays so beautifully. (*Pause.*)

ABRAM. Quiet family happiness. (*Pause.*)

(VASYA *and* TONYA *begin a Communist student song;* VASYA *accompanies with guitar;* LUDMILLA *and* ABRAM *are chiefly engaged with their food and covert glances at each other; but they join the choruses with full mouths.*)

VASYA *and* TONYA.

> If in studies he surpasses
> Tsimla-la, tsimla-la,
> Then he's from the working classes,
> Tsimla-la, tsimla-la.

ALTOGETHER.

> Tsimla, tsimla, tsimla-la,
> Tsimla-la, tsimla-la,
> Tsimla, tsimla, tsimla-la,
> Tsimla-la, tsimla-la.

VASYA.

> If the girl is very pretty
> Tsimla-la, tsimla-la,
> I am bound to sing this ditty
> Tsimla-la, tsimla-la.

ALTOGETHER (LUDMILLA *casts suspicious glances at* VASYA *and* TONYA *as they repeat the same chorus*).

TONYA.

> A red communistic fellow
> Tsimla-la, tsimla-la,
> Should not wed a girl that's yellow
> Tsimla-la, tsimla-la.

ALTOGETHER (*sing same chorus.* LUDMILLA, *by now really jealous and insulted, withers* TONYA *with a glance and goes up to* VASYA, *caressing his hair — claiming her property, as it were.*)
VASYA (*continuing to look at* TONYA).

> If she looks at him intensely,
> Tsimla-la, tsimla-la,
> Then she loves the boy immensely
> Tsimla-la, tsimla-la.

LUDMILLA (*interrupts the singing, attempting to draw* VASYA *from the risky flirtation with* TONYA). Vasyuk, darling, tell your pussykin 'Meow'! Right away, say 'Meow'!
VASYA (*barks out in annoyance*). Meow!

CURTAIN

ACT II

The room is now split into two distinct 'apartments.' The dividing line is formed — reckoning from the rear of the stage — by a rose-colored screen, one panel of which serves as a door between the two apartments; then the massive brown Russian cupboard, nearly ceiling-high, then a small table, the space above which is filled in with a flimsy canary-colored curtain. The two apartments are sharply contrasted. The left half, under LUDMILLA's control, is garishly 'bourgeois'; it has flowered wallpaper, a strip of rug, decorations on the walls, the couch gaudily covered and stacked with cushions, a little table with a potted plant, the canary cage hanging where once hung a lowly sausage, etc.; the cupboard faces this paradise of LUDMILLA's and is obviously well provisioned; an artificial rose in a drinking-glass adorns the ledge of the cupboard; everything here is spic and span and excessively homey. The right half, TONYA's apartment, is as bleak as before; in fact, bleaker by contrast; the garden bench has been shoved against the wall; the floor and walls are bare and not too clean; the table is well to the fore, with the old stool near it; piles of books and papers on the floor and on the bench; the only decoration is the toothbrush sticking out of a tin cup on the wall-shelf; the ugly back of the cupboard faces this half.

The curtain, however, opens only on the left 'apartment,' leaving the other half as yet concealed from the audience. LUDMILLA is putting finishing touches on her proud housecleaning, then — as she talks — busies herself with hanging large homely portraits of an old man and an old woman on the flowered wall, stepping back to admire her handiwork. VASYA, evidently bored, lounges among the cushions and strums his guitar. He notices the portraits.

VASYA (*pointing*). Who is this?
LUDMILLA. This is my grandma — a housewife by trade.
VASYA. Grandma?
LUDMILLA. Grandma.
VASYA. Grandma!
LUDMILLA. Grandma. And this is grandpa, hero of labor, a promoted worker.
VASYA. Promoted worker?

LUDMILLA. Promoted worker. Pussykin! You've put your dirty boots on the clean bed-spread. Aren't you ashamed of yourself? Do take your feet off.

VASYA (*reluctantly takes his feet off*). Grandma and grandpa. H'm...

LUDMILLA. Pussykin, do you love me?

VASYA. And you me?

LUDMILLA. I love you, and you?

VASYA. I love you too.

LUDMILLA. Very much?

VASYA. Very much.

LUDMILLA. Very, *very* much?

VASYA. Very, very much.

LUDMILLA. Very, very, *very* much?

VASYA (*somewhat irritated*). Very, very, very, very much.

LUDMILLA. Well, then show me how much you love me. So much? (*Indicates with her hands.*)

VASYA. So much. (*Indicates a little more.*)

LUDMILLA. And I love you this much. (*Goes him one better with her hands.*) How much do you love me?

VASYA (*suppressing a growl with difficulty and stretching his hands full length*). Yes, I love you this much.

LUDMILLA. Well, then, kiss me on my teeny-weeny nose. (*He does, obediently.*) And now I shall kiss *you* on *your* teeny-weeny nose. (*She pecks him and gazes admiringly.*) Will you have some warm milk, pussykin? Don't you want some warm milk?

VASYA. Don't want it.

LUDMILLA. But I think you ought to have some, pussykin. I want you to have some nice warm milk and grow up to be your wifie's roly-poly little boy.

VASYA. I don't want to be roly-poly, roly-poly!

LUDMILLA. Fie on you! Shame on you! You'll be thin as a rail, thin as a rail. Please drink some nice warm milk. For my sake, pussykin.

VASYA. M... m... m... (*Shakes his head negatively.* LUDMILLA *brings milk on a tray, with the artificial rose beside it, and coaxes him to take it. His annoyance grows apace.*) M... m... m...

LUDMILLA. Drink it, pussykin.

VASYA. I don't want any milk!

LUDMILLA. And I want you to drink it.

VASYA (*sharply*). And I don't want to.

LUDMILLA. And I want you to.

VASYA. Once for all ——

LUDMILLA. Once for all ——

VASYA. Once for all — no!

LUDMILLA. Once for all — yes!

VASYA. Once for all — I won't drink it!

LUDMILLA. Then you don't love me.

VASYA (*angrily*). I love you.

LUDMILLA. Once for all — you don't love me.

VASYA. Once for all — I do love you.

LUDMILLA. This is not how people love.

VASYA (*growling*). And how do people love?

LUDMILLA. Anyhow, they don't love like this.

VASYA (*almost yelling*). Well, how do they then? Well, how?

LUDMILLA. Don't yell at me! I'm not your dog. Keep your shirt on. (*Decides to make the best of a bad bargain.*) All right, let's make up. Kiss me on my teeny-weeny nose, darling. Don't you want to? Fine! All right, then I'll kiss your teeny-weeny nose! Pussykin, tell your little pussy 'Meow'!

VASYA (*with a disgusted bark*). Meow!

LUDMILLA (*offended*). Oh!

VASYA. I can do it again. (*Barks it out.*) Meow! (*Flies into a passion.*) Come on, you pussy, I'll bite your teeny-weeny nose off! Meow! Drink some nice warm milk. I don't want any milk! Meow! I'm sick of it all! I can't live any longer with grandma who was a housewife by trade and grandpa who is a promoted worker. Meow! I can't stand them. I'm beginning to rot. And whose fault is it? It's your fault. Meow!

LUDMILLA (*frightened*). Why am I to blame?

VASYA. Whose grandpa is it? Your grandpa! Whose grandma is it? Your grandma!

LUDMILLA. Think of it!

VASYA (*paces distractedly*). Shut up! Whose curtains are these? Your curtains. Whose milk is it? Your milk. And who's drowning in this petty bourgeois swamp? I'm drowning. I'm drowning in this swamp.

LUDMILLA. Think of it! He's drowning in the bourgeois swamp! And don't you think I'm drowning too? Who promised me everything one time and is now singing a new tune? (*Mockingly.*) 'And we shall build a new life together, Ludmillochka, and I will read books to you, Ludmillochka. And I shall take you to the different clubs, Ludmillochka, and you will be a model exemplary life mate, Ludmillochka, the pal of my life,' and this and that and the other thing. And what's become of it all now?

VASYA. Just think of it!

LUDMILLA (*her turn to be angry*). Shut up! Where is all that you promised me, I'm asking you? There's none of it. Forget it. ' (*Mocking him.*) 'Ludmillochka, sew a button on for pussykin. Ludmillochka, give pussykin a little milk. Pussykin wants bye-bye. Meow! Pussykin wants yum-yum. Meow! Kiss pussykin on his teenyweeny nose. Meow!...' This is all you know and you can't teach me anything cultured and nice.

VASYA (*pulling his coat off the hanger*). Oh, what a mess!

LUDMILLA. Where are you going, pussykin?

VASYA (*going*). I'm not asking your permission.

LUDMILLA. Pussykin, wait, wait! Let's make up! Pussykin, kiss my teeny-weeny nose!

VASYA. Devil take your nose. Let your grandpa, the promoted worker, kiss your damned nose! (*He goes out, banging the door.*)

> (*The other half of the curtain opens, revealing the right side of the dividing line, in all its spartan simplicity.*)

LUDMILLA. Well, what do you think of that? He doesn't like my grandpa! (*Suddenly weeps.*) And why do I deserve this unhappiness? (*Huddles into the cushions, pulls blankets over her, so that she is completely hidden and only an occasional sob is heard.*)

(*The clatter of a falling bicycle comes from the corridor;* ABRAM *and* TONYA *enter, carrying books.*)

ABRAM. Damn this bicycle! Just look, Tonka, look how large this hole is. (*Points to a rent in his trousers.*) It wouldn't hurt to regulate it a bit. Do you happen to have a needle and thread?

TONYA. No.

ABRAM. Model wife!

TONYA. Abram, I ask you, please, none of these bourgeois tricks.

ABRAM. When the husband tears his last pair of pants, that's a bourgeois trick! A fine thesis. Well, shall we read?

TONYA. Let's.

ABRAM (*points to the book*). Let's have it.

TONYA. Abram, wouldn't you like to eat something?

ABRAM. And you?

TONYA. I really would.

ABRAM. You really would — and wouldn't I? Oh, boy! My bowels cry for sausage! Only yesterday I gobbled up a pound of it and now I want some more. Really, it's an inexplicable fact... (*Resignedly.*) Well, let's read.

TONYA. Let's. (*She lies on the table, face down, and props herself on her elbows to listen.*)

ABRAM. Let's. (*Reading.*) 'First lecture: introduction. The significance of science. Human society. Studying the history of mankind, we observe how people in the struggle for existence, step by step, created and perfected their tools. With the latter they subjugated nature, they increased the quantity and improved the quality of the means necessary for their physical survival...'

TONYA (*conscience-stricken*). Abram, don't you think there's a tiny bit of yesterday's sausage left?

ABRAM. That's an idea. I'll have a look. (*Gropes on the shelf.*)

TONYA. Well, is there anything left?

ABRAM. Yes, there's something left. Two pages from a lousy bourgeois romance. (*Shows her the two pages in which sausage once was wrapped.*) We can have a nice healthy bite of that. (*Making a wry face.*) Ah...

TONYA. You're a fine husband.

ABRAM. Kuznetzova, none of those bourgeois tricks.

TONYA. Bourgeois tricks have nothing to do with this.

ABRAM. And who is to blame for this? Are you saying that I am to blame for this?

TONYA. Let's not go into that. Read! Where did we stop? (*Takes the book and searches for the place.*)

ABRAM. We stopped at the point where we'd like to gorge ourselves...

TONYA (*severely*). Abram, don't forget that we have the book only until Tuesday. Read!

ABRAM. I don't want to.

TONYA. What's happened to you, Abram? Read!

ABRAM. But I don't want to.

TONYA. But I want you to read.

ABRAM. Once for all — no!

TONYA. Once for all — yes!

ABRAM. Once for all — I will not read!

TONYA. Then you don't... eh... respect me. And you don't... eh ... love me. That is, there's no workers' solidarity between us.

ABRAM. There is workers' solidarity.

TONYA. Once for all — there is no workers' solidarity.

ABRAM. Once for all — there is solidarity.

TONYA. When there is solidarity, one does not behave like this.

ABRAM. And how does one behave?

TONYA. Anyhow, not like this.

ABRAM (*ferociously*). But how does one? Well, tell me!

TONYA. Abram, don't forget that just because I'm your wife I'm not your slave, but a free woman, your life partner, and your comrade in toil.

ABRAM. Bah — she thinks she's discovered America!

TONYA. Well, all right, then, let's quit this discussion and go on reading. (*Reading.*) 'The economic epochs of history. We are far, as yet, from having attained unanimity of opinion on an adequate scheme of economic development of humanity...'

ABRAM (*sighing, aside*). Uh... I could eat an ox!

TONYA. What?

ABRAM. Nothing, nothing.

TONYA (*continues to read*). 'Without stopping to analyze former endeavors, we shall pass at once to one of the latest, the work of the famous German economist, Carl Buecher.'

ABRAM. Kuznetzova... I'm sick of this. I don't want any more of Carl Buecher. What I want is a large chunk of bread and a large hunk of meat. I want a gigantic omelette made of at least six or seven eggs. I want bacon, I want butter, I want milk, I want fats, I want vitamins, I want cucumbers... Tonka, after all you *are* my wife, and let me announce it quite categorically: I want to stuff myself.

TONYA. Abram, don't shout. You have a mediæval concept of marriage.

ABRAM. Mediæval concept... She dares to teach me the political ABC!

TONYA. Sh... Shshsh... What will the neighbors think?

ABRAM. The neighbors! And isn't that a mediæval concept? And when the husband's last trousers are torn and there is no one to sew them up, isn't that a mediæval concept?

TONYA. So that's it! (*She jumps from the table, yanks her mackintosh off the table and puts it on.*) Reproaches!

ABRAM. Where are you going, Kuznetzova? (*Tries to bar her way.*)

TONYA. I'm not obliged to report all my actions to you. (*Departing.*)

ABRAM. Tonka, Tonyechka, come on let's read, come on...

TONYA. Let me alone. Let me quiet myself. (*She goes.*)

ABRAM (*picks up an accordion, sits on the edge of the table, and accompanies himself softly during the soliloquy*). It's self-evident, damn it. Facts are facts. A real hundred per cent mediæval family scene. And the main thing, what's wrong? Let's consider all the prerequisites. Is there compatability of characters? There is. Is there workers' solidarity? There is. Is there the common political background? There is. And in spite of it all, here's some horrible misunderstanding. And on top of it all, I'm beastly hungry. (*He sniffs the air.*) Oh-ho. Vaska's half smells divinely. M'mm... (*He sniffs, struggling with temptation.*) Cutlets, I think. Possibly cutlets. But no — let's see — I almost venture to say it smells more like an onion omelette. (*Knocks hesitantly on the partition and weakly, almost in a whisper.*) May I? Nobody there... (*Sniffs.*) Really, this is a mediæval odor. Or is it unethical? (*Tiptoes into* VASKA'S *half of the room and does not see* LUDMILLA *bundled up in the farthest corner.*) Oy, this is the life! And how much of it! Is it ethical or isn't it? I think it's cutlets... or isn't it... I wonder if it would be all right — just to find out. (*He bites into a cutlet and swallows it guiltily; puts down the accordion on* LUDMILLA'S *table, then mounts a chair and begins to rummage in the upper reaches of the cupboard. Suddenly, dishes and containers come down with a crash, covering him with flour.*) Wow!

LUDMILLA (*aroused by the crash, disentangles herself, at first horror-stricken, but then bursting into shrieks of laughter*). Oh, you're such a sight! I can't stand it any more, can't stand it any more!

ABRAM (*shaking off the flour, and terribly flustered*). Excuse me, but a great misunderstanding has occurred.

LUDMILLA. Misunderstanding! Oh, I can't stand it! Just look at him! God has punished you!

ABRAM. God is a purely mediæval concept.

LUDMILLA. And to crawl around in other people's shelves. Isn't that me... me... whatever you called it? Oh, I can't even say it!

ABRAM (*continues to stand on the chair, doleful under his flour*). What is private property anyhow?

LUDMILLA. You poor boy! Just look at yourself in the mirror. Oh, I can't... can't... You're just too funny! (*Inspects him.*) The poor boy's hungry, and his trouser leg is torn. I'd like to know what your wife is doing for you.

ABRAM. I regret to say that my wife devotes herself exclusively to the *History of Social Forms*, by Plotnikov.

LUDMILLA. Oh, my poor little Abramchik. What a hard-lucky fellow you are! Why do you stand on the chair like a statue? Come on down and I'll fix you up.

ABRAM (*brightens up*). Oh-ho, Kuznetzova, do you hear? The non-partisan comrades are beginning to be kind to your husband!

LUDMILLA. Stand still, silly.

ABRAM. What's going to happen?

LUDMILLA. I'm going to sew up your trouser leg.

ABRAM. At your service, always. (*He bows, with mock ceremony.*)

LUDMILLA (*sewing*). Stand still, you silly. Now that's that. Like this. Some hole this is! As if dogs have pulled it about.

ABRAM. It's that mediæval bicycle, devil take it!

LUDMILLA. Well, well! Don't turn around, or I'll stick you. I'm serious about it. Like this! Like this!

ABRAM. Who's this hanging there?

LUDMILLA. That's my grandma, a housewife by trade.

ABRAM. What a likeable old lady; and who's this?

LUDMILLA. My grandpa.

ABRAM. Also a first-class old man.

LUDMILLA. A promoted worker, a hero of labor.

ABRAM. Who would have thought it? So young and already a hero of labor! And how nice it must be to have such a lovely grandma and such a distinguished grandpa.

LUDMILLA. Now you're kidding me.

ABRAM. How could I be kidding you when I am ready right now to embrace both of your remarkable ancestors? (*He moves and is pricked by the needle.*) Ouch!

LUDMILLA. I told you to stand still. Now you got it. Now will you stand still? (*She bites the thread.*) Finished!

ABRAM. There was a hole — and now there is no hole. Really remarkable! Astounding! The wonders of science and of technology!

LUDMILLA. Well...

ABRAM. Well...

LUDMILLA. Well!

ABRAM. Well, what?

LUDMILLA. Well, what shall we do now?

ABRAM. How should I know?

LUDMILLA. And who should know? Don't you know that you ought to thank me now?

ABRAM. Yes, I'm very grateful.

LUDMILLA. Is this how to thank a lady? That's not the way to do it. You're a fine gentleman!

ABRAM. Perhaps you want me to say 'merci.' Well, then, 'merci.'

LUDMILLA. Why, no. That's not it. (*Stretching out her hand.*) Well?

ABRAM. Well, what?

LUDMILLA. You must kiss my hand. Do you understand?

ABRAM. Kiss... your hand!

LUDMILLA. Well, what's the matter with you? Hurry up!

ABRAM (*kisses her hand, in a stupor*). Oy! (*He runs into his half of the room and begins frantically to pore over his books.*)

LUDMILLA (*laughing*). Oh, I can't stand it any more! Oh, I'm dying! What a funny fellow he is! Why did you run away, Abramchik? Wait! (*She runs after him.*) And the other hand. You must kiss the other hand too!

ABRAM. Wait a minute, wait! (*He leafs quickly through a book.*)

LUDMILLA. What are you looking for?

ABRAM. I'm looking for the book on Communist Ethics. Wait! The most terrible crash has happened. Someone swiped my Communist Ethics.

LUDMILLA. Well, what of it?

ABRAM. And who will tell me now whether it's ethical or unethical for a member of the All-Union League of Communist Youth to kiss the hand of a non-partisan comrade?

LUDMILLA. A non-partisan comrade! You are a scream! Come on and kiss my hand.

ABRAM. Do you think it's ethical?

LUDMILLA. Never mind — kiss it! Kiss it!

ABRAM. But perhaps it is not ethical!

LUDMILLA. Stop this nonsense, really. If it's ethical for the little hands to sew up your trousers, then why isn't it ethical for you to kiss the little hands? Well, come on, kiss the hand.

ABRAM (*confused*). Is it ethical? What? Is it unethical? Isn't it? What?

LUDMILLA. Kiss it!

ABRAM (*does so*). Or is it?

LUDMILLA. Now this one. (*Abram kisses it.*) And now again this one... and this one...

ABRAM. And now this one again? Yes? (*Kisses with increasing fervor.*)

LUDMILLA. That's enough. Don't! Stop! (*She laughs and pulls her hands away.*) That'll do!

ABRAM. Altogether ethical.

LUDMILLA. I should think so! Oh, my darling! Oh, my poor little boy! Nobody to look after him. Oh, how thin he is... Thin as a rail. He must drink milk. Would you like some nice warm milk?

ABRAM. And how! And bread too!

> (LUDMILLA *bustlingly fetches the tray, with the milk and artificial flower, sets them out on the table in her room and settles him down to the feast.* ABRAM *digs in without ceremony.*)

LUDMILLA. Drink, Abramchik. Drink the nice warm milk, darling Abramchik. (*She pours the milk.*) I'm afraid it's a little cold...

ABRAM (*with a full mouth*). It's fine, Ludmillochka, swell!

LUDMILLA. Would you like one of my nice little cutlets, pussykin? (*She goes to fetch it.*)

ABRAM. Do I!

LUDMILLA (*bringing it, looks at the plate*). You've tried it, haven't you?

ABRAM (*mumbles, embarrassed*). U — hu...

LUDMILLA. There's a smart boy. Eat, darling, and get well. You'll get roly-poly...

ABRAM. Always at your service.

LUDMILLA. Eat hearty. I'll make you my own little roly-poly.

ABRAM (*with mouth full*). And it wouldn't hurt me at all to be roly-poly. I don't understand why I have such a healthy appetite today.

LUDMILLA. Well, that's good, Abramchik. Don't be bashful. By the way, do you know that all night I dreamt about you? (*Giggles.*) It was very funny. I dreamt that you and I were skating on the railroad track, and such a terrible night around us. Ter — rible, ter- rible! And suddenly, on the rails behind us the primus stove was running. Like an engine with head lights... toot, toot, toot!... Run- ning after us — Ooh — ooh — ooh...

ABRAM. Sounds like a bad accident in the transportation depart- ment.

LUDMILLA (*more enthusiastic*). And suddenly, do you know what you did? You embraced me!

ABRAM. You don't say!

LUDMILLA. So help me God! And then suddenly I embraced *you*. (*Spontaneously they embrace each other, scarcely aware of what they are doing.*) And suddenly both of us together... (*They kiss.*)

ABRAM. Oh-ho!

LUDMILLA. Yes! And suddenly we wake up... I mean I wake up.

ABRAM. And don't I wake up?

LUDMILLA. You... also... wake up.

ABRAM (*remembers his conscience*). These are fine tricks. And kissing too!

LUDMILLA. What about kissing?

ABRAM. Kissing my comrade's wife... Is it ethical or unethical?

LUDMILLA. But that was in a dream.

ABRAM. Oh, in a dream?

LUDMILLA. In a dream.

ABRAM. Well, if it was in a dream, then I think it is ethical rather than unethical. (*Pause.*)

LUDMILLA (*sighing*). Abramchik, I swear to God I'm conscience-stricken. I must admit I don't know what ethical and unethical mean.

ABRAM. She doesn't know what ethical means! Well, I would like to know what your most respected husband Vaska is doing about this! It's his duty to see to it that you should develop.

LUDMILLA. He only sees to it that I should make love to him.

ABRAM. What a scoundrel!

LUDMILLA. And there's no one to take care of me, and no one to develop me. (*She weeps.*) And no one to read books to me, and no one to take me to the zoo!

ABRAM. Poor, poor, little girl! Why haven't you told me all this time? Come on now, I'll take care of you. I'll develop you and I'll read books to you and take you to the zoo. (*He runs off and brings a book.*) Only please don't cry. When a woman cries there's something beastly mediæval about it. Come on, let's read. We can begin with the simplest thing, at the very beginning. (*He reads.*) 'The electromagnetic theory of light. We are living in an era of unusually profound changes which bear the character of revolutionary cataclysms in all phases of life. The future historian of our epoch will be obliged to explain that intrinsic relation which unites into one historical law all the social and political changes that we are experiencing and all the profound differentiations which...' Are you following me?

LUDMILLA. Why, yes, what is there to understand here? Very simple.

ABRAM. '... all the profound differentiations which are the determining factor in creating new forms, new...'

LUDMILLA. Abram, will you really take me to the zoo?

ABRAM. Always at your service. Have you got the cash?

LUDMILLA. You're a fine gentleman! Of course I have.

ABRAM. Why hesitate, then?

LUDMILLA. And Vasya? What will Vasya think?

ABRAM. And Tonya? What will Tonya say?

LUDMILLA. Akh! But it is so interesting! Help me on with my coat. Be a gentleman! Well, let's go. (*She leads the way into the corridor.*)

ABRAM. Right away, Ludmillochka, right away. (*He helps himself to* VASYA'S *necktie, puts it on and attempts to plaster down his hair with spittle on both palms.*) Right away, right away! Can't hurt to wear a lousy little necktie, even if it is Vaska's. Is it ethical or unethical? What is a necktie anyhow, and what's ethics? Ethics is a mediæval concept anyhow. (LUDMILLA'S *voice: 'Abram!'*) Right away! I just want to put a little powder on. Have you any toothpaste? Let me have some toothpaste. Right away, right away! Like this. (*Inspects himself in the mirror.*) Is it ethical or unethical? I should say it's ethical! I'm coming. (*He runs into his half of the room and is about to put on his scarf, coat and hat when he notices* TONYA'S *red kerchief.*) Poor Tonya! I can't do it.

LUDMILLA (*comes back*). Hurry up, Abram. Hurry up!

ABRAM. I can't go, Ludmilla. What will Tonya think of it? It would break her heart.

LUDMILLA. But going to the zoo will develop me. Don't forget that you must educate the non-party comrades.

ABRAM. In that case it's ethical.

> (LUDMILLA *goes out;* ABRAM *puts on his hat and coat and follows, but at the door bumps into* TONYA *who is just entering.*)

TONYA. Abram, what does this mean?

ABRAM. It's a concession to the petty bourgeoisie and to the wealthy peasantry. Adieu!

TONYA. Where are you going, Abram?

ABRAM (*proudly*). I'm not obliged to report all my actions to you.

126

TONYA. Abram!

ABRAM. Let me alone! Let me quiet myself. (*He runs out.*)

TONYA. So that's it! Very well. (*Lies down on the table and reads aloud.*) 'Marxism in its contemporary form, dialectic materialism...' (*She suppresses sobs and continues to read.*) 'This is a priceless weapon the use of which insures immeasurable superiority of the proletarian revolutionist over the bourgeois politician.' (*Her voice becomes fuller and fuller of stifled sobs.*) 'The latter is limited by the necessities of the present, by the coarse practicality... prac... tic... ality... (*Her head sinks on the book and she sobs freely.*)

VASYA (*enters quickly into his half of the room; with determination, looking straight before him, stops at the table and begins to orate; he doesn't look at the corner where he had left* LUDMILLA.) Ludmilla, I have something important to tell you. This can't go on any longer. Ludmilla! (*He looks around and doesn't see her.*) Are you home, Ludmilla? Her coat is gone! She's gone! So much the better. (*Looks at the portraits of the grandmother and grandfather.*) Grandma, a promoted worker and hero of labor! Grandpa, housewife by trade! Meow! Enough of it! This cannot continue any longer! Her damned necktie... (*Tears it off.*) To hell with the necktie! (*Musses his hair.*) To hell with sleek hair! (*Hears* TONYA's *sobs.*) Kuznetzova, are you home?

TONYA (*lifts her head*). Vasya? Wait a minute. (*She gets off the table, sits down in a chair, adjusts her hair, puts on the red head-kerchief, wipes her face and pretends to be absorbed in a book.*)

VASYA. May I come in?

TONYA. Right away. Just a minute. (*She finishes adjusting herself.*) All right, come in.

VASYA (*steps into her apartment*). Isn't Abram home? Are you alone?

TONYA. Alone.

VASYA. That's good. I must talk to you seriously about something. (*Brief pause.*) Tonya...

TONYA. Yes?

VASYA (*peering at her*). What's the matter, Tonya? You have been crying.

TONYA. Nonsense!

VASYA. Tonya...

TONYA. Yes?

VASYA. Have you had anything to eat today? Would you like

some milk? (TONYA *shakes her head negatively*.) Kuznetzova, please do me a favor and drink some milk.

TONYA. Thanks, I don't want any... milk.

VASYA. Kuznetzova, aren't you ashamed of yourself? Why these bourgeois pretenses? I know very well that you haven't had anything to eat since this morning. (*He goes to fetch the milk*.) There's a whole pitcher of it. (*He notes with surprise that the pitcher is empty*.) Empty! Who could have lapped it all up, I wonder? Tonyechka, there happens to be no milk. But wait, I'll get you some cutlets right away. We had half a dozen of them. (*He finds no cutlets on the plate*.) H'mm... none left... disappeared... very, very strange... (*Picks up* ABRAM's *accordion from the table*.) I'm beginning to guess whose work this is. Well, all right. Ah-ha, there's some sausage left and half a roll. (*He brings it to her*.) Please eat some of this sausage.

TONYA (*eating*). Thank you, Vaska.

VASYA. That's right; there's a good fellow. (*A brief pause; regards her earnestly*.) Tonya...

TONYA (*with full mouth*). Yes?

VASYA. Tonya, this can't go on any more. Tonya, look at me!

TONYA. Why should I?

VASYA. Look at me, right straight into my eyes.

TONYA. Well... (*Looks into his eyes*.)

VASYA. Do you love Abram?

TONYA. That's none of your business.

VASYA. Yes, it is! Do you love him or don't you? Tell me honestly.

TONYA. I don't understand why you place the questions so ideologically. Do I love, or don't I love. I don't understand. It's not correctly formulated.

VASYA. Tonya, it is very important to me. Do you love him or don't you love him?

TONYA. Well, now, really, I don't understand you. I respect Abram very much... Abram respects me... Abram and I have workers' solidarity... compatibility of interests... a common political background. It seems to me that this is sufficient for people to live together.

VASYA. Stop! Not another word! You don't love him! On my word of honor, you don't love him! (*Happily*.) You don't love him, you don't love him! Kuznetzova, why do you turn red like this?

Hurrah! Tonka! I cannot live without you any longer, do you understand?

TONYA. You're crazy!

VASYA. That's right, I'm crazy! I'm crazy about *you*. I should worry. Tonka, Tonyechka, do you love me? Do you? (*He embraces her*.)

TONYA. Hold on! Wait a minute! (*Struggles*.)

VASYA. You love me. By God, you love me! I can see it in your eyes. Hurrah! Now everything will be different. We'll all be happy. We'll read together, work together, love together, have a good time together.

TONYA. You're crazy!

VASYA. Hurrah!

TONYA (*severely*). Wait a minute, Vasya. Wait! Sit down! Let us discuss the new situation objectively and calmly. Very well, let us suppose that you should leave Comrade Ludmilla and I should leave Comrade Abram, and that you and I should come together on the basis of... eh... (*Indecisively*.) Will it be the right thing to do from the point of view of Communist family morality?

VASYA. Absolutely right.

TONYA. Absolutely wrong. Today I register with one man. Tomorrow I divorce him; the next day I register with another man! What kind of an example are we setting to our other party comrades, and to the most active elements among the non-partisan youth and the poorer peasantry?

VASYA (*embraces her violently*). And perhaps the poor peasantry will not even notice it!

TONYA (*recovering for a moment*). This is pure and simple opportunism.

VASYA. What's the difference!

TONYA (*tearing herself away*). Moreover, we have no right to build our individual well-being, and if you please, our happiness, on the unhappiness of other party and non-partisan comrades. I'm thinking of Comrades Ludmilla and Abram. I have no access to data concerning Comrade Ludmilla, but as for Comrade Abram, his life will be shattered by this.

VASYA (*sobering*). And Ludmilla's life will be shattered too.

TONYA. Comrade Abram, if I must use the antiquated sentimental terminology, is madly in love with me. He will not survive this.

VASYA. Neither will Ludmilla survive this. She's in love with me like a little kitten. That's a definite fact. All day long she tells me tales about her grandma and grandpa, and forces me to lap milk.

TONYA. There you are!

VASYA. What is to be done then? Tonka...

TONYA. We shall have to surrender our personal well-being in the interest of general social well-being.

VASYA. How unpleasant.

TONYA. Be a man, Vasya, be a man! You see, it is equally difficult for me. Let us be friends. Here's my hand on it. (*She offers her hand which* VASYA *presses and does not release.*)

VASYA. How unpleasant... And only today, at night, I dreamed of you. You and I were setting the table, and all around us plates were falling and breaking, and all around us such a dark night... and the wind moaned... and the plates were falling and breaking... whooo...

TONYA. Ideologically the dream was incorrect.

VASYA. And suddenly you embraced me!

TONYA. What are you saying!

VASYA. So help me God! And then suddenly I embrace you! (*Spontaneously they embrace.*) And suddenly both of us together... Tonyechka... (*They kiss.*)

TONYA. Wait a minute. Wait... My precious pussykin... what are we doing?

VASYA. And suddenly once again... (*They kiss again.*)

(*In the midst of the prolonged kiss enters Comrade* FLAVIUS, *the party organizer.*)

FLAVIUS. Kiss, my children, kiss!

TONYA. Oh!

VASYA. Oh!

TONYA. Comrade Flavius!

VASYA. Flavius!

FLAVIUS. That's all right. Go on, don't mind me. It won't hurt the Revolution any.

VASYA (*worried stiff*). That's a fine mess.

TONYA. Comrade Flavius, the Devil knows what you may think ... My word of honor, this is a pure misunderstanding.

FLAVIUS. Ho-ho! Vaska, how do you like that? She calls a Soviet marriage a pure misunderstanding. And you as a husband, don't you protest?

TONYA. Believe me that he... that I...

130

FLAVIUS. No, my children, no joking. But tell me, how did you do it so quickly? Just like the work of the shock-brigades. Our famous poet of the masses, Comrade Emilian, comes along and presto, without any warning, comes right out and says, 'Comrades, the latest news! Vaska got married; Abramchik got married; they're all sitting around and drinking tea with rolls; in a word, complete degeneration.' Wait! we cry. Who got married? When did they get married? Whom did they marry? Why did they marry? But do you think you can get any sense out of that ape? All he says is, 'I must run along to draw the proper organizational conclusions, arrange for a little celebration, call the gang together,' and there you are. And I didn't see him any more. So you kids had better expect some guests. Get a move on! Have the tea ready, light the primus.

TONYA. Primus! (*Sinks into a chair, exhausted by worry.*)

FLAVIUS. Now, kids, seriously, I congratulate you! Live together happily, my children. Don't quarrel, work together! But you know, the one who surprised me most was our little Abramchik. Who would have thought it? Abram getting married. Ho-ho! That's a subject for our poet laureate, Demian Biedny. By the way, where is Abram?

TONYA. Yes, indeed, where is Abram?

VASYA. Abram, what you may call it... there.

TONYA. Went for a walk... with his wife.

VASYA. You know, it really is fine weather... the snow is falling...

TONYA. Yes, the snow is falling... it's a wonderful... I think they'll be back soon.

FLAVIUS. Whom did Abram marry?

VASYA. Yes, indeed, whom did he marry? That is to say, that girl... Kuznetzova, whom did Abram marry?

TONYA. Abram... he married... why, Comrade Ludmilla!

VASYA. Ludmilla! That's a fine one! That is, I mean to say... precisely, that is, Comrade Ludmilla. You know, when you take her all in all, she's not so bad...

TONYA. I don't think there's anything nice about her. Just an ordinary girl with typical petty bourgeois ideology... oof... But perhaps it would be better not to discuss this.

FLAVIUS. Well, well, my children. Show me your geography. Demonstrate your technical attainments. In brief, where do you live?

VASYA. Well, in general, here... like this, you know...

FLAVIUS. And Abram and his family?

TONYA. Abram, also... he's living here... in general...

VASYA. Here. Right here... like this... over there.

FLAVIUS. Ah-ha... hmm... very nice, very nice... (*He enters the other half and they follow meekly.*) And who is this? (*He points to the portrait of grandma.*)

TONYA. This? Oh, that's just so... an old intellectual.

VASYA. That's grandmother.

FLAVIUS. Whose grandmother?

VASYA. Her grandma... a housewife... And that's grandpa... my grandpa... a promoted worker... a hero of labor...

FLAVIUS. You're doing well, kids. And this, so to speak, are your technological accessories. (*He examines the cupboard and the primus.*) Oh-ho! It's a good primus. And just look at the pots! And what do you know, four glasses... and a mirror! Well, well, the kids are growing rich.

TONYA (*aside, to* VASYA *while* FLAVIUS *is busy investigating the household*). Vasya, well!

VASYA. A complete mix-up! As clear as mud!

(*Both go to the couch, where they sit down and whisper.*)

TONYA. What a shame! What a disgrace! I cannot continue to take part in this low, petty bourgeois farce. This lie is unworthy of us, and we must root it out!

VASYA. What do you want to do?

TONYA. I'll tell Flavius at once that this was a joke.

VASYA. Tonka, are you crazy? Why, he saw us kissing.

TONYA. All the same...

VASYA. Kuznetzova!

(*Enter Communist Youth boys and girls, ten or twelve of them, high-spirited, laden with bundles for the party.*)

FIRST BOY. Ho! Flavius is here already. Hello, Flavius.

SECOND BOY. He's always first at the scene of the crime.

FIRST GIRL. That's what I call a real organizer, a real organizer.

SECOND GIRL. He's hardly a man. He's right on the spot like an ambulance.

FLAVIUS. That's right. I always respond without delay and answer to the first call.

FIRST BOY. Well, now, let's see, who are the chief victims of this careless love? Let's have a look at you!

FIRST GIRL. Vaska! Just look at him. Ho-ho! That's a nice thing to do.

SECOND BOY. Tonka Kuznetzova! Couldn't hold out any longer and got burned.

FIRST BOY. Comrades, let's get organized. Not all at once. Attention! One, two, three...

EVERYBODY IN CHORUS. Long live the Red newlyweds! (*They force them to kiss again and again.*)

VASYA (*aside*). That's a fine pickle, a fine pickle.

TONYA (*aside*). I can't bear this disgrace!

SECOND BOY. And where's Abram with his wife? I don't see Abram here.

FLAVIUS. Abram will be here presently.

FIRST BOY. And I don't see any tea, nor anything to chew on. That's even worse.

FIRST GIRL. Well, now, family unit, demonstrate your economic situation.

SECOND GIRL. Yes, yes. And it wouldn't hurt to have some tea. Kuznetzova, why don't you say something? Here you've called guests together and you don't do anything about it.

SECOND BOY. That's a nice thing. We want tea. Comrades, let's protest.

FIRST BOY. Attention! One, two, three...

ALL TOGETHER IN A CHORUS. We—de—mand—tea! We—de—mand—grub!

SECOND GIRL. Really, I think it's outrageous. Where's the good time we were promised by Comrade Emilian?

FLAVIUS. Now, kids, let there be peace and quiet. Don't disturb the young turtledoves. Everything will come in time.

FIRST GIRL. Just look how cleverly they've divided the room!

SECOND BOY. Well, what do you think of that!

FIRST BOY. Come on, comrades. Down with the petty bourgeois fences, or we shall have no place for our revelry. Come on, down with it! (*Riotously they push back the cupboard, and the rest of the artificial wall.*)

VOICES. Here! Push it this way! Pull the partition! Like this. Now there's more room. Once again! Once again! (*Break into the 'Volga Boatmen Song' as they clear the middle of the room.*)

TONYA. Vasya... what will happen? What will Abram think?

VASYA. Abram! And what will Ludmilla think?

TONYA. This is terrible... He'll never survive this!

VASYA. And she will never survive this either.

TONYA. What is to be done?

FLAVIUS. Children, attention! Abram and his wife are coming.

VASYA (*groans*). That's the end. The funeral. Darkness. Complete mess.

FIRST BOY. Hide, kids!

VOICES. Hide, hide! Why are you standing there? Right here behind the books! Turn out the lights! (*Someone switches off the light and the room is completely dark.*)

SECOND GIRL. Vaska, hide yourself quickly, right here.

FLAVIUS. Everybody quiet! Imagine Abramchik playing the husband!

TONYA. Comrades, this is all a mistake. We...

FIRST BOY. Shsh... Quiet! Not a sound! Shh!

(LUDMILLA'S *laughter is heard from the corridor. She runs in laughing, followed by* ABRAM. *They come into foreground where they can be seen by the audience.*)

LUDMILLA. Pussykin, kiss my teeny-weeny nose.

TONYA (*whispers*). The viper!

ABRAM. But is it ethical? (*He kisses her.*) Or perhaps it is unethical. (*Kisses her again.*)

VASYA (*whispers*). The lousy, rotten renegade! And he has my necktie on too!

LUDMILLA. Pussykin, say 'Meow'!

FLAVIUS (*whispers*). Just look! Little Abramchik has become a pussykin!

LUDMILLA. Well, will you say 'Meow'?

ABRAM (*sweetly*). Meow!

VASYA (*barks out angrily, aloud*). Meow! (*Everybody jumps up.*)

EVERYBODY IN CHORUS. Meow! Meow! Meow! (*The light goes on.*)

LUDMILLA. Oh, Vasya!

ABRAM. Oh, Kuznetzova! A terrible smash-up! I'm like a fish out of water.

EVERYBODY IN CHORUS. Lo... ng... li... ive... the... Re... ed... new... ly... we... ds!

TONYA (*throws herself into* VASYA'S *arms*). I can't stand this any longer. Take me away from here.

ABRAM. Ludmilla, hold me. I think I'm fainting. (*He falls into her arms.*)

FLAVIUS. Go on kissing, kids, go on kissing. This can't hurt the Revolution.

(*The thunder of a falling bicycle and the poet* EMILIAN *lumbers in.*)

EMILIAN (*puts first one foot, then the other on the table and massages his bruised shins*). The Devil take you and your bourgeois bicycle! I almost tore my trousers to pieces, not to mention my shins.

FLAVIUS. Emilian! You're the only thing we needed to complete our celebration.

EMILIAN. Hello, kids. (*Suddenly dumbfounded, seeing* ABRAM *in* LUDMILLA's *arms and* TONYA *in* VASYA's *arms*.) Wait! What do I see here? Vaska and Tonka! Abramchik and Ludmillka! Surprising! Astounding! Sh! Listen to an impromptu verse:

> To marry in such manner, really
> Is not so good, is rather silly
> And who has married whom right now
> No one can tell, I must avow.

FLAVIUS. What are you jabbering about? Seems perfectly clear who's married to whom. Abram married Ludmilla and Vasya married Tonya. Why, you yourself were the first to tell us about it. What's the matter? Are you drunk?

EMILIAN. No, boys. Wait a minute. Perhaps somebody here is drunk, but it's not me. Smell me! (*Blows his breath into the face of a boy who shakes his head negatively.*) I'm not drunk. I'm perfectly sober, but I must say I've seen with my own eyes who has married whom.

VASYA (*in a desperate whisper*). Sh! Shut up!

ABRAM (*also whispering, making signs to him*). Shut up! It isn't ethical.

FLAVIUS. Comrades, can you make him out? It's a couple of marriages in a mad-house!

EMILIAN. You yourself belong in a mad-house. Thank God, I still have my senses about me, my memory, and I can beat anybody at writing verses. Do you know my latest, 'The Izvostchik'? Listen:

> Ekh, the city has gnawed me to pieces...

FLAVIUS. Choke up, genius! I'm sick of your 'Izvostchik.' I can't listen to it any more.

EMILIAN. And as for these pairs of lovebirds... (*He points to the couples who are making desperate signs to him.*) Ah, forget about it, you! And as for them, I saw with my own eyes that Vaska is married to Ludmilla and here they are pulling your legs.

ABRAM. Sure, sure, of course, it's a fact. Of course we're just pulling your legs. That's right, Ludmilla, isn't it?

VASYA (*laughing unnaturally*). Why of course, we're just fooling! Ha-ha! What did you think! He-he! Why, of course, Flavius, Kuznetzova and I played a fine joke on you, didn't we? Tonka, you back me up! What do you say?

TONYA. Comrades, this was all a joke. And Comrade Ludmilla can confirm this.

LUDMILLA. Oh, what funny people you are! Why, you can't even understand a joke. Fie! (*Reluctantly pulls* VASYA's *sleeve.*) This is my lawful, duly registered husband. We can even show you the document from the Marriage Registry.

ABRAM (*reluctantly going to* TONYA). This is the lawful, duly registered comrade of my life... life's companion. Eh, what, Kuznetzova? Is there workers' solidarity? There is. Is there compatibility of interest? There is. Is there a common political background? There is.

TONYA (*sadly*). There is.

ABRAM. What's the matter, then?

EMILIAN. Sh! Sh! Four lines! Listen. Extemporaneously...

> You've all been played for foolish lambs
> Except Emilian the poet
> Because Emilian is wiser than the lot of you
> He is not — eh...

Anyhow, he's not... not a foolish lamb.

FIRST GIRL. Pretty rotten for a genius!

EMILIAN. Well, why don't you say it better then, wiseacre?

FLAVIUS. Well, what do you know about this! Why you certainly tripped us up. But what surprises me most is our Tonyechka Kuznetzova. Who would have thought that such a serious-minded girl with such an excellent social political record would be capable of such silly jokes! Well, what do you say, kids? Well done, Kuznetzova. I'm sincerely glad for you. You can't be chewing rocks all the time. Have to have a good time once in a while. Isn't that right?

FIRST BOY. Well, what's the matter, then? Comrades, the session is not yet over. Pull out the grub. (*The guests noisily open the parcels.*)

SECOND BOY. Half a kilo of sausage.

FIRST GIRL. Four rolls. Four eggs.

FIRST BOY. Smoked sturgeon.

SECOND GIRL. A quarter of a pound of butter and two herrings.

EMILIAN (*pulls out of his overcoat pocket three bottles of beer*).

Ekh, the city has gnawed me to pieces...

TONYA. Comrades, I categorically protest against the use of alcohol by members of the All-Union League of Communist Youth.

EMILIAN. Think of it! Alcohol! Why, this is nothing but lousy beer! Flavius, we're asking you to decide. Is it all right to have three bottles of beer?

FLAVIUS. For such an occasion... three bottles! Go to it, kids. This can't hurt the Revolution.

EMILIAN. You said a mouthful, Flavius. (*Opens the bottles.*)

FIRST BOY. Comrades, attention. All together: (*They sing a drinking song.*)

ABRAM. Good-bye, Ludmilla.

VASYA. Good-bye, Tonya.

LUDMILLA. Good-bye, Abramchik.

TONYA. Good-bye, Vasya.

CURTAIN

ACT III

The same setting as in preceding act — the bourgeois and proletarian 'apartments' distinct — but both in chaotic condition as a result of the late celebration. The curtain opens upon LUDMILLA *and* ABRAM *in their respective homes, eavesdropping upon each other. As soon as they are convinced that they are quite alone, they rush towards each other, clinching in a passionate embrace in the middle of the stage, tangled and concealed by the pesky canary-colored curtain. Their fervor, however, is apparent to the audience even through the curtain. Then they come up for air, flustered and conscience-stricken.*

LUDMILLA. What are we doing?

ABRAM. How should I know what we're doing?

LUDMILLA. No, no, you mustn't kiss me any more. I have a husband.

ABRAM. It's easy to say a husband and it's easy to say don't kiss me.

LUDMILLA. Don't kiss me, pussykin. Don't torture me. I'll go mad. Don't! No!

ABRAM. All right, then, you'll have to put a muzzle on me, or —— (*He grabs her once more, and the three of them —* ABRAM, LUDMILLA, *and the curtain — are again tangled.*)

LUDMILLA. I cannot live without you.

ABRAM. And do you think I can live without you?

LUDMILLA. What shall we do about it, then?

ABRAM. Let's get registered.

LUDMILLA. I'm going cuckoo.

ABRAM. Or is it unethical? What do you say?

LUDMILLA. But how about Vaska?

ABRAM. Don't talk to me about Vaska. Whenever Vaska is mentioned, I want to knock his block off. What about Vaska?

LUDMILLA. He won't bear it. He'll kill himself. I'm sure he will.

ABRAM. Does he love you so much?

LUDMILLA. Oh, Abramchik, that's the tragedy. Love me? He simply worships me. I don't know what to do about it.

ABRAM. All the same, you must choose. Either Vaska or me. Shall we go to the Registry Bureau? Nu? Ludmillochka? Come on, be a serious grown-up comrade. Well?

138

LUDMILLA. But how can we, pussykin? Today I register with one man, tomorrow I un-register, the day after I register again with another man. It's not right! What will people say?

ABRAM. Ludmilla, none of these bourgeois tricks. What have other people to do with it when we can't live without each other? And the main thing, what's the matter? Is there compatibility of characters? There is. Is there mutual understanding? There is. Is there labor solidarity? There is. Nu, Ludmilla, what's to stop us, then?

LUDMILLA. Oh, you're making my head swim.

ABRAM. Well, Ludmilla, decide in two shakes.

LUDMILLA. I'm going cuckoo, I tell you.

ABRAM. We'll lead such a wonderful life! Such a wonderful life!

LUDMILLA. Oh, it's all the same to me. My happiness! (*She throws herself into his arms.*) Let's go!

ABRAM. Let's go!

LUDMILLA. My treasure! (*Takes him by the hand.*) My precious husband. (*Coquettishly.*) And aren't you even a little bit sorry for Tonya?

ABRAM. Wait! As a matter of fact, I haven't even thought of Tonya. That's a nice thing to do! Here Tonya will come home from a meeting of her Communist Youth cell, all tired out, and suddenly she'll discover that her husband is no longer her husband, but somebody else's husband. Is it ethical or is it unethical?

LUDMILLA. Come on, pussykin, let's go.

ABRAM. But Tonya!

LUDMILLA. What about Tonya?

ABRAM. She'll never survive it.

LUDMILLA. Does she love you?

ABRAM. Love me? She worships me!

LUDMILLA. All the same, you must choose — either Tonya or me. Put on your coat, or the Marriage Registry will be closed. Be a serious grown-up comrade. Well?

ABRAM. Today I register. Tomorrow I un-register. The day after I register again. Moral and ethical laxity. Downright sexual delinquency. What will the comrades of the district committee think of it? What will Comrade Flavius say to it?

LUDMILLA (*weeping*). Fla-vi-us! Is it unethical?

ABRAM. Decidedly.

LUDMILLA (*still weeping*). My treasure, my little treasure... or perhaps... it is eth-ic-al.

ABRAM. No doubt. It is wrong in principle to build personal family happiness on a foundation of the domestic unhappiness of other comrades.

LUDMILLA (*suppressing sobs*). Tha-at me-ans tha-at we mu-st not...

ABRAM. We must not...

LUDMILLA. But I thou-ght, but Abram, but I — so...

ABRAM. But, Ludmillochka, darling, can't you see that I'm also suffering? But I control myself. Can't you also control yourself? Be a man!

LUDMILLA. It means then... good-bye, Abram.

ABRAM. Good-bye, Ludmilla.

LUDMILLA. Very well. Now I know. (*In a quavering voice.*) Good-bye, pussykin. (*They embrace, both weepy.*) Tell me, tell your pussykin 'Meow'!

ABRAM (*through his tears*). Meow!

LUDMILLA. Abramchik...

ABRAM. Yes...

LUDMILLA. Good-bye, good-bye. (*They embrace again.*)

ABRAM. Good-bye. (*They embrace and then part.*) Why does everything come out so unethical when everything really feels so ethical? I must take a long walk and figure it all out. (*Departs.*)

LUDMILLA. Very well, now I know. I can't stand it any longer. (*She begins to gather her gaudy belongings but suddenly exhausted, collapses to the floor and drops her head on the bundle, sobbing.*) I can't stand it any more, I can't stand it any more!

(*The crash of the bicycle in the corridor, and* VASYA *stalks in, purposefully.*)

VASYA. The Devil take him and his damned bicycle! Family happiness, eh? Meow! Down with it! There! I've forgotten all the things I wanted to say... Ludmilla, I must talk to you seriously... This can't go on any longer in this way... The fact of the matter is that we... The fact of the matter is that our relations... the very foundation... but the main thing is that you mustn't get angry and you must try to understand me... I wish I knew how to explain it to you... You see, in regard to you, I want to remain to the very end a decent man. Perhaps you will find it unpleasant and even painful... but it is best to speak right out and to speak honestly... Sew up my pants, I mean... (*Aside.*) What am I saying?

LUDMILLA (*indignant*). None of your bourgeois tricks!

VASYA (*astounded*). What? What?

LUDMILLA. No bourgeois tricks. It is not ethical.

VASYA. Well, what do you know about that! (*Looks her up and down in astonishment; whistles his surprise, guessing where she has caught the lingo.*) No, no, Ludmillochka. You're wrong in saying it is not ethical. If I were to deceive you, to lie to you, to pretend... do you understand me?... Then of course it would be rotten and not ethical. But I want to speak to you frankly, honestly, like a true Communist Youth, like a real comrade.

LUDMILLA. I am not a female slave but a free companion. You tore the pants yourself, now sew them up yourself.

VASYA. What! What have the pants to do with it? We're not speaking about pants.

LUDMILLA. Then what *are* you belly-aching about?

VASYA (*irritably*). About something altogether different. You see... (*Aside.*) My tongue simply won't move... she'll never survive this... She'll kill herself, I'm sure of it. Oh! (*With exaggerated sharpness.*) We're speaking about you and... well, of course... well, and about Abram... about your...

LUDMILLA. Oh, my God! He knows everything. I'm going cuckoo!

VASYA. Don't interrupt me. I'm speaking... about your... that is, about your... Do you understand me?

LUDMILLA. Oh, pussykin. I don't understand a thing! You can crucify me, but I don't understand a thing! (*To herself.*) I realize now that he'll never be able to survive this. He will kill himself. Gee! his eyes are wild already... (*To him.*) I don't know a thing, pussykin, I don't understand a thing... and I beg you, pussykin, only not to worry yourself... and don't torture my poor heart. As it is... (*She drops her head on a bundle for a new instalment of sobs.*)

VASYA. Look here, Ludmilla... (*Turns away in despair.*) My tongue just won't move. She can't stand it! She'll kill herself! That's a fact. She worships me so that I'm scared stiff! Eh! (*Waves his hand, dejected.*) What's the use...

LUDMILLA (*lifts her head and notices* VASYA's *stooped figure*). Poor boy! How he's suffering! But all the same, let him... (*Again begins to pack her bundles.*) All the same... all the same...

VASYA. What are you doing?

LUDMILLA. Don't ask me, Vasya.

VASYA. You're not going away, are you!

LUDMILLA. Yes, I'm going away.

VASYA (*with ill-concealed joy*). But why all of a sudden?

LUDMILLA. I'm going away. Don't ask me.

VASYA (*hypocritically*). But... Ludmillochka...

LUDMILLA. No, no... Don't you remember what we agreed upon? Don't tell me anything... don't try to hold me by force... let me go...

VASYA. But my dear Ludmillochka... how can I keep you from going, pussykin? Well, what do you know about that...! On the other hand, ours isn't some sort of mediæval marriage... for God's sake... please... do you think that I... I merely asked as a matter of curiosity... Of course, love can't be forced...

LUDMILLA. Well, in that case... then I... (*Lifts the bundles.*) I'm going... good-bye...

VASYA. Well... (*Wants to bid her good-bye, but can't make up his mind how to behave.*)

LUDMILLA (*to avoid a difficult scene*). No, no, never mind... I'll come again.

VASYA (*frightened*). You're coming back?

LUDMILLA. Just to get some things... I can't take everything with me at once.

VASYA. Good-bye... Ludmillochka... (*She goes. VASYA, scarcely able to contain his joy over this fortunate turn of events, follows her, muttering indecisively.*) And yet, perhaps... after all... somehow... you would remain... Word of honor... really, Ludmillochka... be careful and don't stumble over the bicycle. (*Begins to caper happily.*) She's gone! She's gone! He-he... ho-ho... without any melodrama ... gee, I'm lucky... Tonka, my little cabbage, where are you? I'll bet she's at the Communist Youth cell. I must tell her the happy news. (*Departs.*)

> (*Crash of bicycle. ABRAM enters, both trouser legs tattered, but too absorbed in sad thoughts to notice; sits down.*)

ABRAM (*meditatively*). Is there compatibility of character? There is. Is there mutual understanding? There is. Is there common class background? There is. Is there labor solidarity? There is. There is everything — and at the same time such an awful smash-up! Why? Why? I don't understand... Compatibility of character? Yes. Labor solidarity? Yes. Everything is there, but altogether — a grand smash-up. Shall I tell Tonka everything? Straight out? Or would it

be unethical? No, she'll never survive it. Is it ethical? Or isn't it?
My head's in a whirl.

(EMILIAN *enters, in high spirits, none the better for vodka.*)

EMILIAN. Hello, old man.

ABRAM. Hello.

EMILIAN. Dance!

ABRAM. Why must I dance?

EMILIAN. Because you must. Dance!

ABRAM. To hell with you!

EMILIAN. Dance, I tell you!

ABRAM. What's the matter with you? Are you drunk or crazy?

EMILIAN. Dance, dance! Well? (*Sings a dance song, stamping his
feet to the beat of the music.*)

> Why are you so gloomy...
> Just because you're pa—ale...

Well?

ABRAM. Have you ever seen a crazy cuckoo? That's him.

EMILIAN. You're a cuckoo yourself. Dance, I say!

ABRAM. But why should I dance? Of all the lunatics!

EMILIAN. Because you don't understand the regulations. There's
a rule among us: whoever receives a letter is obliged to dance according to instructions and without objections. (*Exhibits a letter.*)
Here! A letter. Dance! (*Sings again.*)

ABRAM. For whom is this letter?

EMILIAN. For you, for you... Dance! (*Continues to sing, beating
time with hands and feet.*)

ABRAM. A letter for me? This is a rare historical occasion. I
haven't received a letter since 1917. I've even forgotten how it's
done. Let me have it!

EMILIAN. Dance!

ABRAM. All jokes aside, let me have it. (EMILIAN *holds the letter
tantalizingly over* ABRAM's *head but does not give it to him.*) Come on,
quit playing the fool.

EMILIAN. Dance, or I'll teach you a few tricks. (*Doubles up his
arm and displays his muscular prowess.*) Just feel this!

ABRAM. Did you ever see such a crazy loon? From whom is it?

EMILIAN. From your life's companion. From your beloved
wife.

ABRAM. From whose wife?

EMILIAN. What do you mean whose — how many wives have you got? From Tonka.

ABRAM. From Kuznetzova? Has anything happened to her?

EMILIAN. Nothing happened. We just ran into each other and she asked me to give it to you. Dance!

ABRAM. Stop your fooling. Let's have it.

EMILIAN. Stop your fooling. Dance!

ABRAM. Oh, for God's sake! Did you ever see such a fool? Here I'm facing a terrible domestic smash-up, and he's forcing me to dance! I don't know how to dance. Haven't the slightest idea. Come on, let's have it.

EMILIAN. Dance!

ABRAM. But I'm telling you I don't know how. I can't dance. Oh, what a rotten egg you are... Well, to hell with you! (*He begins to dance clumsily to the accompaniment of* EMILIAN'S *song and beating of time.*) Well, let's have it. (*Disgusted with himself; stops dancing.*)

EMILIAN. Come on, a little more. (*Continues to sing and beat time.*)

ABRAM. But I have danced!

EMILIAN (*threateningly*). Dance! (ABRAM *resumes foolishly, with a sad mien until even the implacable* EMILIAN *is satisfied.*) You're a hell of a dancer, you are! You dance like an elephant on bottles. There! (*Gives him the letter.*)

ABRAM (*fingers the envelope*). Ugh! I can feel it already — these mediæval tricks are already beginning. (*In his excitement he can't tear the envelope open.*)

EMILIAN. Wait, let me have the letter. Your hands are trembling. (*He snatches the letter, opens it, gives* ABRAM *the envelope but retains the letter.*) Here, read this meanwhile.

ABRAM. Oh, for crying out loud! Have a heart! (*He snatches the letter and reads aloud in a quavering voice while* EMILIAN *peeks over his shoulder.*) 'Comrade Abram! I have been thinking this over a long time, and I have come to the conclusion that things cannot continue thus any longer. Under the newly arisen objective conditions...' I might have guessed that she would come to the objective conditions...

EMILIAN. Why, I said the very thing. Don't you remember when we were going to the bath-house? I told you so.

ABRAM (*vexed*). Emilian, have a heart. This is no time for joking. (*Reads again.*) 'Under the newly arisen objective conditions, our living together is inadmissible. You understand, of course, to what I am referring.' Ugh! I'm facing a smash-up... (*Reads.*) 'I consider

144

it indispensable to draw the appropriate organizational conclusions...' Oh, my God! I'm afraid she'll poison herself.

EMILIAN. No, she'll drown herself, my dear boy, she'll drown herself. (*Strokes* ABRAM'S *head*.)

ABRAM (*in a rage*). Let me alone, Emilian! (*Reads.*) '... I must go away. Gather all of your manliness, like a true Communist Youth, and do not attempt to hold me back... It must be so...' Complete smash-up — I knew it.

EMILIAN. Horrors, horrors!

ABRAM (*reads*). 'By the time you will be reading this letter, I shall probably be...' Oh, my God! Only not in a crematorium! Not in a crematorium!

EMILIAN. No, in the Moscow River. It's cooler there.

ABRAM (*jumps up, furious, shouts*). Emilian, cut it out! (EMILIAN *quiets down. Reads.*) '... I shall probably be... rushing by train...'

EMILIAN (*correcting him*). Crushed by the train...

ABRAM (*yielding to him in fright*). '... crushed by the train... to the village.'

EMILIAN (*reading over his shoulder*). ... crushed by the train to the village — no, there's something wrong here.

ABRAM (*joyfully*). '... rushing by train to the village. I have been sent there by the management at my own request. Try to forget me and return the book to Sonya Ogurtsova. With Communist greetings, Antonia Kuznetzova.' (*Quite revived.*) Oh, Tonka, Tonka. There's a fine girl for you. And I expected something horribly mediæval. Ha — no melodrama. Ludmillka, do you hear? 'With Communist greetings, Kuznetzova. With Communist greetings, Kuznetzova.' (*He begins a wild dance to his own accompaniment on the accordion.*)

(VASYA *enters his own half, in excellent mood, takes up his guitar and does a jig to his own accompaniment.*)

EMILIAN (*admiring* ABRAM'S *outburst*). Just look at the big fraud. Only a moment ago he was crying on my shoulder and insisting he doesn't know how to dance. Well, I'll be jiggered...

ABRAM (*still playing and dancing*). 'With Communist greetings, Kuznetzova. With Communist greetings, Kuznetzova.' She's gone! She's gone!

(EMILIAN *is attracted by the music in the other half; dumbfounded, stares from one side to the other, as the two happy dancers meet in the foreground.*)

145

VASYA. She's gone, she's gone, she's gone, she's gone.

ABRAM. She's gone, she's gone, she's gone, she's gone. 'With Communist greetings, Kuznetzova. With Communist greetings, Kuznetzova.'

EMILIAN. Have you ever seen such idiots?

VASYA (*stops abruptly and stares at* ABRAM). She's gone! Ha-ha! She's gone!

ABRAM (*stops and stares at* VASYA). She's gone. Fact.

VASYA (*laughs and winks*). She's gone.

ABRAM (*laughs and winks*). She's gone.

VASYA. Wait, who's gone?

EMILIAN (*echoes their words, in mounting bewilderment, jerking his head from one to the other and back*). Wait, who's gone?

ABRAM. Yes, who's gone?

EMILIAN. Yes, who's gone?

VASYA. What do you mean who? Ludmillka.

EMILIAN. What do you mean who? Ludmillka.

ABRAM. Wha-at... Ludmillka's gone! You're crazy. Kuznetzova is gone.

EMILIAN. You're crazy. Kuznetzova is gone.

VASYA. Wha-at, you're crazy yourself. Tonka — gone? Are you joking?

EMILIAN. Are you joking?

ABRAM. Wait! (*He's dumbfounded.*)

VASYA. Wait! (*He's dumbfounded.*)

EMILIAN. Wait! Don't wait! Listen, boys, the case is perfectly clear. Both chickens have flown the coop. That's as clear as day.

VASYA. Wai-ait... she... entirely... gone...

EMILIAN. Entirely gone?

ABRAM. Entirely. Why?

EMILIAN. Entirely. Why?

VASYA. Where to?

EMILIAN. Where to?

ABRAM. She went to work in a village. Why?

EMILIAN. She went to work in a village. Why?

VASYA. To the village... what do you mean... wait...

EMILIAN. What do you mean? Wait!

ABRAM. Wait... Ludmilla... entirely...

EMILIAN. Entirely?

VASYA. Entirely. Why?

EMILIAN. Why?

ABRAM. Where to, where to? Tell me.

VASYA. Just so. I don't know. Why?

ABRAM (*in despair*). Why didn't you look after her?

EMILIAN. Why didn't you look after her?

VASYA. Well, why blame me? Why didn't you? How could you let her go?

EMILIAN. How could you let her go?

ABRAM. No, but why didn't he look after her?

EMILIAN. No, but why didn't you look after her?

VASYA. Why didn't I look after her? Wait. What business is it of yours, after all?

EMILIAN. What business is it of yours, after all?

ABRAM (*vehemently*). I'd like to know whose business it is? Do you think it concerns you more than it concerns me?

EMILIAN. Do you think it concerns you more than it concerns him?

VASYA. Shut up! You brought Tonyechka to the point where she would go to the Devil rather than see your disgusting mug. Where can I look for her now?

EMILIAN. Where can he look for her now?

ABRAM. I brought the girl to that point! And you? What have you done? And to what have you brought Ludmilla? (*Mocking him.*) Pussykin, kiss my teeny-weeny nose. Pussykin, say 'Meow.'

VASYA. And what business is it of yours?

EMILIAN. And what business is it of yours?

ABRAM. And what business is it of yours?

VASYA. I can't bear to look at you, you lousy little bourgeois!

ABRAM. You're a bourgeois yourself!

VASYA. Whom are you calling a bourgeois? Am I a bourgeois?

ABRAM. You're worse. You're a renegade and an opportunist!

EMILIAN (*in rapture*). If I were you, Vaska, I'd sock him one for calling me a renegade.

VASYA. Whom did you call a renegade? (*Advances, swinging his arms.*)

EMILIAN (*happy at the prospect of a scrap*). That's right, boys; fight it out, but don't damage the musical instruments.

VASYA. Who's a renegade?

EMILIAN. Yes — whom did you call a renegade?

ABRAM. Throw down your guitar and fight like a man. (*They rush into the corridor.*)

EMILIAN (*peering into the corridor*). That's right. Sock him! Don't hit below the belt! Sock him! Ho-ho! Not bad for an extemporaneous fight!

VASYA'S VOICE. Who's a renegade? (*All voices are drowned for a moment by the crash of the bicycle.*)

EMILIAN (*shouting into the door*). Boys, that won't do at all. You'll break the guitar. If you want to fight, fight according to all the rules of the novel. On the second floor, in apartment 18, Volodya has a pair of Denikin swords. Sock him! (*Noise.*) A haymaker! Let's have a fight according to rules. I won't permit it otherwise. (*But despite the poet's enthusiasm,* ABRAM *and* VASYA *can't get really started; Russian fashion, they shout more than they fight.*)

ABRAM'S VOICE. Drop the guitar!

VASYA'S VOICE. Who's a renegade?

ABRAM'S VOICE. Drop the guitar or I won't be responsible for anything I do to you... Let go of me!

VASYA'S VOICE. Wait!

EMILIAN Come on, get the swords. Ho-ho-ho. Now we'll have a real fight. (EMILIAN *goes out; noises in the corridor which gradually die down.* EMILIAN *returns, wiping his brow as if after a strenuous battle.*) That's what I call dancing! Oh, boy! What fun! (*Whistles.*) Even I got hot. Well, now that the hens have flown the coop, I'll have a chance to sleep here, and I'll even get a bite to eat now and then. (*He pulls up the spring mattress, props it against the table so that it is in an inclined position.*) Now I must compose a new poem. But first it is necessary to create the proper environment and the right mood for inspiration. (*He knocks the furniture about, gathers all the available food, sprawls on the mattress at princely ease, and composes aloud with a full mouth.*) Well now, I have an order for a poem on bottled mineral water — 'Narzan.' Here goes:

> If you must drink merely water,
> Then it's Narzan that you oughter!

Even I admit, it doesn't sound so extra.

(*Enter* FLAVIUS, *regards the deserted rooms and the sprawling* EMILIAN *in puzzlement.*)

EMILIAN. Hello, Flavius. Do you want a bite?

FLAVIUS. Hello. What in thunder are you doing here disturbing the domestic peace of two homes?

EMILIAN. Yes, the homes *have* been here, but they're both out now.

FLAVIUS. What's going on here?

EMILIAN. A melodrama in six acts. The chicks have flown the coop and the boys have gone up to apartment 18 for the swords.

FLAVIUS. What's the matter with you? Are you drunk? Talk sense.

EMILIAN. I'm talking sense, and I'm telling you that Tonka has, all of a sudden, made up her mind that Vaska is her soul-mate. Ludmilla has lost her head over Abramchik. Vaska, like the braying ass he is, has lost his heart to Tonka, while Abramchik has thrown himself on the soft bosom of Ludmillka and is pining away for her. And they were all ashamed of themselves and scared to look each other in the eyes, but finally the whole business went into bankruptcy. Tonka couldn't stand it and disappeared. Ludmillka couldn't stand it and disappeared. Vaska and Abramchik have run upstairs to apartment 18 to hack each other to pieces. And in the meantime I'm seriously thinking of moving in here.

FLAVIUS. A duel?

EMILIAN. According to all the rules, like Pushkin fought with Gogol. A blow with a sword over the head and yours truly is gone. They're so hot under the collar that something terrible is bound to happen. Grrr...

FLAVIUS. Then why do you lie here braying like an ass? Two damn fools have run off to fight an idiotic duel, are disgracing the All-Union League of Communist Youth, and the third fool is lying with his dirty shoes on a strange bed, and... grr... Come on. Get a move on you! Show your athletic prowess. Bring the duellers here, dead or alive! And damn quick!

EMILIAN. Ee-ekh! (*Departs.*)

FLAVIUS. This is the most scandalous thing that has ever happened in our district. (*Whistling significantly.*) That's a fine state of affairs. (*Pause.*) What do you think of these Soviet hussars? (TONYA *arrives, tearfully begins to gather her toothbrush, tin cup, towel, which she stuffs into the pocket of her mackintosh.* FLAVIUS *notices her.*) Where are you bound for, Tonya?

TONYA. I'm going away, Flavius.

FLAVIUS. Where are you going?

TONYA. I'm going to work. In the village.

FLAVIUS. What new-fangled idea is this? Suddenly, out of a clear sky, you're burning with desire to work in the village. What's the big idea?

TONYA. Don't ask me, Flavius. It's very difficult for me, but it can't be helped. Good-bye, Flavius.

FLAVIUS. Oh, no, you don't! Wait! You tell me sensibly, has anything happened?

TONYA. Yes... no... nothing has happened. Well, good-bye.

FLAVIUS. Kuznetzova, don't try to put anything over on me. You tell me right out what's happened here.

TONYA. Nothing.

FLAVIUS. So — nothing?

TONYA. Nothing. I don't know.

> (*Meanwhile,* LUDMILLA, *in tears, has returned with her bundle, evidently not having been welcomed at her old home.*)

LUDMILLA (*suppressing sobs and blowing her nose*). I've forgotten ... grandma and grandpa. (*She removes the portraits and, hearing* FLAVIUS *and* TONYA *in the other half, comes close to the partition.*)

FLAVIUS. You don't know, eh? Well, I know. You're in love with Vaska. Well, little girl, look me straight in the eye.

TONYA. I love him.

FLAVIUS. And does Vaska love you? Look me straight in the eye.

TONYA. He loves me.

FLAVIUS. Then why in thunder are you trying to put something over on me and trying to make a psychological melodrama out of the business? If you love each other, what's to stop you? Rush down to the Marriage Registry. You can't hurt the Revolution that way and there's no sense in running away to the village.

TONYA. And what about Abram?

FLAVIUS. You should have thought of this before you went down to register.

TONYA. I thought... we thought... compatibility of character... workers' solidarity... common political background... (*Sobbing.*) And so... and so... no, no! Comrade Abram will not be able to survive it... Can't you see that Comrade Ludmilla will not be able to survive it... Don't you see, Flavius, that we must not build our own happiness upon the unhappiness of other comrades.... (*She cannot control her sobs.*)

> (LUDMILLA, *while peeping into their part of the room, suddenly drops the grandparents' portraits with a bang, and stands there, bundle in hand, bawling like a child and on the verge of running away.* FLAVIUS *jerks the curtain, revealing her thus.*)

FLAVIUS. Where to?

LUDMILLA (*indecisive for a moment, then impulsively runs to the weeping* TONYA *and embraces her*). Oh, Tonyechka, oh, my little treasure!

TONYA. Comrade Ludmilla...

LUDMILLA. Oh, my pussykin! I heard everything... Don't weep, darling, you mustn't weep... Take Vaska if you want him, but for God's sake, don't worry yourself, because as far as I'm concerned it's all the same to me... without Abramchik... what's life worth? (*Both of them now shed tears of joy over the bundle.*)

TONYA. My dear, my little baby, my little sister!

FLAVIUS (*soothing them*). Well, there, there you are! Now they've set to bawling! Oh, you dear little monkeys! On the other hand, it can't do any harm. Sometimes weeping helps. Go on, cry it out. It can't hurt the Revolution.

   (*Behind the scene are heard shouts, noise, ringing of bells, horrible commotion, cries, climaxed by the familiar crash of the bicycle.*)

TONYA. What has happened?

LUDMILLA. Oh, what is it? A fire?

FLAVIUS. Quiet down, girls. Nothing terrible. That's our two little roosters, the black one and the white one, settling their little domestic quarrels.

   (VASYA *and* ABRAM *fall into the room, fighting clumsily.* VASYA *has found a ludicrous old sword, while* ABRAM *holds a scabbard and is trying desperately to pull the sword out. Somehow they have held on to their guitar and accordion throughout the scuffle. Behind them, yelling loudest of all, is* EMILIAN.)

EMILIAN (*clumsily running around the duellists*). Where you going? Where you going? Stop! Take it easy! Take it easy! You've both gone crazy, upon my word! You'll damage the musical instruments ... Vaska! Abramchik!

VASYA. Where is Tonka, I'm asking you?

ABRAM. What did you do with Ludmilla?

VASYA. And what business is it of yours?

ABRAM. And what business is it of yours?

VASYA. You lousy little bourgeois!

ABRAM (*to* EMILIAN). Let go of me! I'll knock his block off!

   (*He finally pulls the sword out of the scabbard, tumbling over from the exertion. The sword proves to be broken, and he holds only a hilt in his hand.* VASYA, *retreating, stumbles against the partition, which falls on* TONYA, LUDMILLA, *and* FLAVIUS. *General confusion.*)

VASYA. Tonka, Ludmillka!

ABRAM. Ludmillka! Tonka!

(*The boys do not know what to do, nor how to behave.*)

VASYA. Flavius...

ABRAM. Flavius...

FLAVIUS. That's a pip. Perfectly scrumptious! Tonka, Ludmillka, what have you to say to this? Two perfect idiots are duelling with musical instruments. It's a picture worthy of a painter.

ABRAM (*pretending joy*). Kuznetzova! You're not in the village yet? (*He is about to run to her, but* TONYA *stops him with a proud gesture and points to* LUDMILLA.)

VASYA (*hypocritically*). Ludmillochka, have you come back? I'm frightfully happy. (LUDMILLA *echoes* TONYA'S *gesture.*)

ABRAM. What's the trouble, Tonyechka?

FLAVIUS. Now, listen, kids. Cut out the fooling. Don't twist the bull's tail. Everything is clear. We all understand the situation and we know everything.

EMILIAN. And what's more, everything has been investigated.

FLAVIUS. Tonka, do you love Vaska?

TONYA. I love him.

FLAVIUS. Ludmillochka, do you love Abramchik?

LUDMILLA. I love him.

ABRAM. Comrades, this isn't ethical. What? Or is it ethical?

FLAVIUS. Abramchik, don't be an over-clever parrot. Now, kids, what are you standing around for?

EMILIAN. Indeed, why? (*He sits down on the bench. They all understand everything.*)

FLAVIUS. You got married, all of you, as if you had been running away from a fire, without thinking of consequences, and then turn your rooms into an art theatre, and in the meanwhile you put me to all the trouble of divorcing and remarrying you properly. I must remind you, comrades, that I have other business to attend to. Well!

(LUDMILLA *throws herself into* ABRAM'S *arms,* ·*and* TONYA *into* VASYA'S.)

TONYA. Vasyuk!

LUDMILLA. Abramchik, my little treasure!

VASYA. Tonka!

ABRAM. Ludmillochka! (*The couples embrace.*)

FLAVIUS (*to* EMILIAN). Pull up anchor, my boy. You're not going to sleep here tonight. Roll on!

EMILIAN. Can't I even recite an extemporaneous poem before I go?

FLAVIUS. Roll on, roll on! Get a move on!

EMILIAN. Ee-ekh!

> The city has gnawed me to pieces —
> I will not see my native moon.
> I will tear my collar wide-open
> That I may hang myself soon.

Ee-ekh! They see a poor prodigy perishing and yet nobody will do anything for him. I guess I'll have to sleep in apartment 18.

(Departs.)

FLAVIUS. All right. All right. The trouble is that he may come back. He turns up like a bad poem. (*He picks up the portraits from the floor, gives the grandpa to one couple and the grandma to the other.*) Well, on the basis of the marital code, all property must be equally divided. Here's a grandpa for you and a grandma for you. (*They accept the portraits.*) And so it seems that everything is in order. Good-night.

VASYA (*humorously, to* ABRAM). Pussykin, tell your little pussy, 'Meow'!

ABRAM (*brightly*). Meow!

FLAVIUS. Never mind, kids. Don't be bashful. Go to it. Love one another and don't play the fool. It can't hurt the Revolution.

(*The confusion of stations on the radio suddenly erupts once more. It continues its medley of Soviet music, slogans and speeches even after the curtain goes down. At one point,* EMILIAN *suddenly appears astride the famous battered bicycle bellowing, 'The city has gnawed me to pieces... I have not a place to sleep...'*)

VOICES ON THE RADIO. Workers of the world, unite! You have nothing to lose but your chains... (*A gay voice singing.*) 'By radio we met, and by radio we wed and by radio we got a pretty baby Red...' (*In horribly mispronounced English.*) '... begin tonight's lesson in advanced course of ze English langvidge. My oncle's hat is small, but your aunt's garden is beeg...' (*The gay voice emerges again, singing the following words to the same tune.*) 'Now Kalinin is my beau, and I'll surely let him know, that I fell for him last night — on the radio!'... Workers, peasants and Red Army men, the toiling masses... (*Snatches from the doleful 'Volga Boatmen Song,' broken abruptly by a balalaika orchestra strumming a wild Caucasian*

153

tune.)... Shock-brigades and more shock-brigades... the world's biggest steel foundry, the world's tallest building... Love, superstition and other bourgeois prejudices... As Karl Marx said... the K.V.Zhe.D.... the V.K.P.B. and V.S.N.X.... Komsomol... Mostorg... Narkompochtel... R.S.F.S.R.... Workers of the world...

(*The blare of a Red Army song.*)

CURTAIN

TEMPO

A Play in Four Acts and Nine Scenes

By NIKOLAI POGODIN

Authorized translation from the Russian
By Irving Talmadg

INTRODUCTION

THE arduous period of the first Five-Year Plan in the Soviet Union produced a large crop of plays glorifying machinery and industrial construction. The theatre, like every other branch of national life, was regimented for the tasks of the great undertaking. Machines, tractors, building projects, rather than flesh-and-blood characters, came to dominate the stage. Most of these plays, it must be said, were lifeless and as mechanical as the objects which they glorified. The Soviet drama in a measure still suffers the blight of that epoch and is now deliberately humanizing its repertory.

Tempo, by Nikolai Pogodin, was one of the few exceptions. In many ways typical of the Five-Year Plan crop of plays, it differed in the decisive fact that it did succeed in coming alive. In its portrayal of the peasants involved for the first time in the industrial process, Pogodin was especially successful. It is a pity, indeed, that the rich tang of their peasant speech, peasant humor and bewilderment cannot possibly be translated into English; it can only be roughly suggested, as in the present translation.

For foreign readers the character of the American engineer, Mr. Carter, is especially interesting. To Americans he may seem a juiceless creature, but for the Russians he is a symbol of that implacable American efficiency, Fordism, Taylorism, for which they seem to strive the more desperately because it is so alien to their natures. It is an open secret that Jack Calder, an American who did an outstanding job in building the Stalingrad tractor plant and other factories, is the original of Pogodin's Mr. Carter — quite as high-minded and capable but a lot more human than the symbolic character in the play.

The fight for higher industrial 'tempos' is the foundation theme of the play. The Bolshevik director, class-conscious workers and engineers, the non-political American specialist are ranged on one side; the sabotaging engineers, old-régime left-overs and shiftless workers on the other. Victory, of course, is on the side of the loyal proponents of higher tempos — the 'happy ending' is as inevitable in Soviet Russian drama as the tragic ending was in pre-revolutionary Russian plays.

INTRODUCTION

This was Pogodin's first play. It was written in 1929, as the by-product of a newspaper assignment. He had been sent by the Moscow *Pravda* to Stalingrad to describe the work on the American-style tractor plant then under construction. Remembering the slow, conservative building methods of pre-revolutionary years, observing the peasant men and women under the discipline of American 'tempos,' Pogodin was deeply impressed. Westerners accustomed to modern industrial processes can scarcely understand how romantic, how heroic it all appeared to a sensitive Russian observer. Pogodin's reaction, expressed in *Tempo*, is in a sense all of Russia's reaction.

The author was born in a Cossack town on the Don, in 1900, of poor parents. He had no formal education whatsoever. At the age of twenty he joined the staff of *Pravda*, first as its correspondent in Rostov-on-the-Don, then in its Moscow editorial offices. He remained with this newspaper for nearly ten years, until he switched to playwrighting.

After *Tempo*, he wrote five other plays, the last of them based on the construction of the White Sea–Baltic Canal by several hundred thousand prisoners.

SCENE FROM *TEMPO*

Fresh from their fields, peasants are being turned into proletarians. A group of construction workers puzzling over a political article in Act III, Scene 7, of Nikolai Pogodin's play, as presented by the Vakhtangoff Theatre in Moscow.

CHARACTERS

BOLDYREV, STEPAN SEMIONICH: Director of the construction project; although still a young man he is a veteran Communist; of peasant-worker origin and therefore close to the workers around him; a native of the Kostroma Province.

VALKA: his sister, about nineteen; a medical student; an earnest and pretty product of the revolution.

MAKSIMKA: a Young Communist of twenty-two; manager of the Bureau of Rationalization on the construction project; typical of the new enthusiastic youth.

LAGUTIN: Secretary of the Communist Party Committee at the construction; a middle-aged, level-headed Party functionary.

GONCHAROV, URI NIKOLAYEVICH: chief engineer; a technician of the pre-revolutionary stamp who resents the new order; despite his obvious hostility he is tolerated for his technical knowledge; in his early thirties.

CARTER: an American engineer; he is the dry, close-mouthed, pipe-smoking, super-efficient American as visualized by Russians; devoted to his job and oblivious to the political drama around him.

GRUZDEV: a mechanical engineer of the old type, who has adjusted himself to the new régime.

KASTORKIN: engineer in charge of transportation; a happy-go-lucky young man, of non-proletarian origin, with a taste for gaiety.

DANILO DANILOVICH: an old engineer.

KALUGIN: an old engineer; an old-régime type, but too timid to oppose the new ways.

TATIANA LVOVNA: his frivolous young wife.

RYBKIN: secretary to the Director.

WOMAN INTERPRETER.

KOSTROMA PEASANTS: Yermolay Laptev, Mikhalka, Artamon, Sumatokhinov, Zotov, Tusha, and others; they are typical 'muzhiks,' drawn into an industrial job for the first time, the human raw material of the Five-Year Plan; like the director, they are from Kostroma, whose peasants are reputedly shrewd, salty individuals.

CHARACTERS

THREE WOMEN WORKERS: constituting the Production Committee of the brick factory; boisterous, aggressive peasants.

KRALICHKIN: a class-conscious metal worker; city-bred.

Physician, Nurse, Chairman of Production Meeting, Kitchen Maid, Chauffeur, Drunkard, Bricklayers, Hodcarriers, etc.

Time: First year of the Five-Year Plan, 1928–29.

Place: A remote section of the U.S.S.R. which is being newly industrialized.

ACT I

SCENE I

Site of the construction project, at twilight. Far in the background, behind a thicket, a portion of the barracks is visible; workers are in the barracks noisily eating their evening meal. In the foreground are signs of construction in the earliest stages; the first excavation work is under way; crude machinery, tools and materials are scattered around chaotically. Several felled trees and patches of green indicate that the site is freshly and as yet incompletely cleared.

VALKA and GONCHAROV are on the scene as the curtain rises. The pretty VALKA is roughly dressed, but not without feminine charm. GONCHAROV's personality and attire are faintly European — he tries to cling to the old ways.

VALKA (*indignantly*). Do you know they have discovered the eighth case of typhoid on our project here?

GONCHAROV. Supposing I do?

VALKA. Well, if you know, you ought to be reprimanded for it. Your high-brow specialists, damn them, seem to have forgotten to purify the water supply. Think what it means: five thousand workers drinking water from that river, and your crowd doing nothing about it... someone should be brought to responsibility for such neglect.

GONCHAROV (*contemptuously*). Brought to responsibility...

VALKA. Do you realize what this neglect may lead to? I'm a medical student, and I know. I certainly intend to protest and bring this matter up. There is an epidemic here, and you — you, Comrade Goncharov, pass it off so lightly. (*Pause.*) Where is barrack number six? Is that it?

GONCHAROV. Over there... (VALKA *goes off in the direction of the barrack.*) Reprimanded for it... Her kind attacking me... to hell with them! She sure is sharp-tongued...

(LAPTEV, *a bearded peasant, one of the construction workers, rushes in excitedly from beyond the thicket. He is without trousers, in white drawers, his shirt unbuttoned.*)

LAPTEV. Comrade chief, allow me to ask you, what is all this...?

GONCHAROV. Speak.

LAPTEV. What is this business? The upstart! She comes to me with an order to take off my drawers — there, before everyone. The brazen hussy. I, who have lived with my old woman for thirty years and never removed my underwear in front of her... and now, in front of all these women, and the kitchen maids, she tries to rob me of my shame! You can't do it! There is no such law...

GONCHAROV. What are you talking about? What girl? What shame?

(*A group of construction workers and the* KITCHEN MAID *enter, all angry and upset. In the group are* MIKHALKA, *an outspoken, quarrelsome peasant lad; and* ARTAMON, SUMATOKHINOV, *and* ZOTOV, *older men. They are all in peasant working clothes, their faces and garments crusted with cement dust.*)

LAPTEV. You don't understand, eh? A brazen hussy makes us remove our drawers, and he doesn't understand. Here, these good men will tell you. I never complain. If there is work to be done, I'll do it. I'll whistle, I'll run, but I'll be damned if I'll let anyone take my drawers off.

GONCHAROV (*to the workers*). Explain — what has happened?

MIKHALKA (*self-importantly*). What has happened? The muzhik is talking sense. Why should we be mocked like this, and forced against our will? He is one of our brigade, and we'll stick by him. (*Making his way back into the crowd.*) What's more, we know the water's been poisoned.

GONCHAROV. The water poisoned! What nonsense is that from you?

KITCHEN MAID. Comrade architect, you can't blow dust in our eyes. We in the kitchen have noticed it, too.

GONCHAROV. Noticed what?

KITCHEN MAID. Our men are being poisoned.

LAPTEV (*noticing* VALKA *approaching*). Here comes that she-devil again. What does she want from me? I won't... I won't give up my drawers... Let her call the militia... let her... there is no such law.

VALKA (*kindly*). You queer uncle... why did you run away?

MIKHALKA. Yes, we're all queer. (*Sneers.*) Only you are clever.

VALKA. You — you're young and literate. You should know better. Why play the fool?

MIKHALKA. Fools tie mares' tails, but we are working people. We're not devil's dolls. (*To* ARTAMON.) She inspects... struts... gives orders. (GONCHAROV *leaves*.) And who is she? Why should she be here?

ARTAMON. See here, sister, what are you up to? What are these new-fangled ideas? From where are you a representative? Show us the papers that give you the right to undress us men.

LAPTEV (*encouraged by this support*). Are you trying to draw our last drop of blood? What am I to you: Yermolay Yerofeyev, or just an animal? I have never been so shamed. Taking advantage of simple folks, you are. You're an assassin, that's what you are!... Oh, I'm fainting. (*Drops to the bench.*) My insides are burning, burning like fire.

VALKA. Comrades, is it possible you don't understand?

KITCHEN MAID (*sneeringly*). We understand...

VALKA. Don't you understand the man has typhoid and he must be taken to the hospital immediately?

ARTAMON. And what if he doesn't want to go; have you the right to compel him?

MIKHALKA. Don't let anyone be taken away from our brigade.

SUMATOKHINOV. Comrade lady, don't you go upsetting us people, we are all upset enough as it is.

VALKA. Why all this babbling, just like a crowd of old women? Your comrade is sick and he must be taken to the hospital. That's all there is to it. Help me carry him to the ambulance. If you don't want to do it, you don't have to. I'll call the chauffeur. (*Leaves.*)

LAPTEV. Brothers... Mikhal, hey, Mikhal, take me to my place. I'm unable to get there myself. (*Rises.*) Brothers, keep that little wench out of the barrack. (*Staggers out.*)

MIKHALKA. What is this, fellows? Are we going to stand for it?

ARTAMON. We must elect a deputation.

SUMATOKHINOV (*sceptically*). Deputations... they'll spit on your deputations.

ARTAMON. But we must have deputations; without deputations we are no power.

MIKHALKA. What are you talking about, we are no power? Why, we are the very first of the first class, first-rate prime power... yes, that's what we are! Under the Tsars there never was such blaspheming of the working class. They poison the water, the sons-of-bitches.

ZOTOV. Now, you shut up, you sow's-ear. Let wiser men talk. Yearlings shouldn't bawl so loud.

ARTAMON. Yes, youngsters should not put spoons into their mouths until their elders have come to table.

(*Enter* VALKA *and* CHAUFFEUR.)

VALKA. We have to take the man to the hospital. (*Looking about.*) Where is he?

MIKHALKA. He's gone to the toilet, lady. He asked you to wait for him a while.

VALKA. Well, if that's where he's gone, we'll wait for him.

ARTAMON. No matter where he's gone, *you* won't see him again... so there.

MIKHALKA. Our brigade has decided not to give up our comrades.

CHAUFFEUR (*to* MIKHALKA). What the hell are you yelling about?

ARTAMON. Our men have decided that all curing should be done here, in front of us.

CHAUFFEUR (*to* ARTAMON). And why are *you* yelling? Hey — not so loud!

MIKHALKA (*shoving the* CHAUFFEUR). And what kind of trump are you?

CHAUFFEUR. Now be careful, youngster, or I'll clout you so hard you'll see devils.

MIKHALKA. Brothers, he's threatening me.

KITCHEN MAID. What a leather commissar he is!

VALKA. Quiet, everybody, let me say a few words.

MIKHALKA. There is nothing you can tell us.

SUMATOKHINOV. Don't plague us any more, we have trouble enough.

VALKA. You are talking nonsense, comrade!

KITCHEN MAID. What a wise one you are!

VALKA. You're being foolish, aunty.

KITCHEN MAID. And you — you're a hussy...

VALKA. I see there is nothing I can say. Comrade chauffeur, let's go and get the patient.

CHAUFFEUR. All right, let's go.

ARTAMON. No, you're not going!

CHAUFFEUR. Let's go.

ARTAMON. And I say you won't go. (*Tries to hold him back.*)

CHAUFFEUR. Let loose!

VALKA (*to all*). Clear out of here, all of you.

MIKHALKA. If you use force, we'll use force. (*Grabs* VALKA.)

SUMATOKHINOV. Let her have it, so she remembers how to disturb folks.

ZOTOV. Muzhiks, I warn you, this will end badly for us.

ARTAMON. I'll fix you!

CHAUFFEUR. Try it!

ARTAMON. I'll...

CHAUFFEUR. Go ahead, do it!

SUMATOKHINOV. Muzhiks, they're beating us.

KITCHEN MAID (*picks up brick and aims it at* VALKA). I'll treat you, you bitch.

(BOLDYREV *enters, rushes toward the* KITCHEN MAID *and seizes the brick.*)

BOLDYREV. Here, woman, you can go to jail for this.

KITCHEN MAID. Mother of God... It's Boldyrev!

ALL. The director... Boldyrev... (*Pause.*)

ZOTOV. Mikhalka, you can give the report.

BOLDYREV. What's all the fighting about, Valka?

SUMATOKHINOV. That's just it, Stepan Semionich...

BOLDYREV. Hold on. (*To the* CHAUFFEUR.) Rubtzov, what's the matter?

CHAUFFEUR. They've gone crazy. They won't let us move a typhoid patient.

BOLDYREV. What! A fight over a typhoid patient!

VALKA. If not for you, Comrade Director, they would have settled us.

BOLDYREV (*looking at the brick*). I see they would have. You better calm down now, all of you.

KITCHEN MAID (*in a whisper*). She must be none other than the director's wife.

ZOTOV. Not his wife, his sister.

KITCHEN MAID (*startled*). Queen of Heaven!

ZOTOV. Huh, the Queen can't help you.

BOLDYREV. Let's talk it over, boys. But not all at once, not all at once... (*To* MIKHALKA.) Maybe, you want to speak, I see your nose is scratched.

MIKHALKA. Why pick on me? I'm not the only one, we all...

ZOTOV. All? No, not all...

BOLDYREV. Very well, we'll say it was all.

MIKHALKA. It's known that the water is poisoned... And... and our brigade decided not to give up any of our men...

BOLDYREV. Is that all?

MIKHALKA. Yes... and... in the days of the Tsars there never was such blaspheming of the working class.

BOLDYREV. So! And how old are you, my countryman?

MIKHALKA. That's nothing to do with it.

BOLDYREV. But that has something to do with it. You tell me your age.

MIKHALKA. Well, twenty... next autumn.

ARTAMON. Didn't I say youngsters should not put spoons into their mouths...

BOLDYREV (*amused*). Comrades, he's not much of a ringleader. Is he the spokesman for the forty-first barrack?

ZOTOV (*indignantly*). Who said he's our spokesman? He's just a pumpkin.

BOLDYREV. Well, then, I'm just wasting my time. You, my lad, should spend some of your evenings with the old men. Talk to them about the days under the Tsar. Ask them when young workers like you ever had a chance to speak to their chief directors.

ZOTOV. Aha... that's telling him.

BOLDYREV. No director would have spoken to you in those days. The least complaint, and you would have been put under arrest. You talk it over with the old men. They will tell you.

MIKHALKA. What did we make a Revolution for?

BOLDYREV. We made a Revolution? Why, you were still wetting your cradle. (*Turning to the others.*) Now, men, let me say a few words to you. We've got to handle this matter differently. Think of it! I just got a message over the 'phone that the forty-first barrack had mutinied. The forty-first barrack, my own Kostroma countrymen... I left my work to come here, and what do I find? You — fighting with a woman... It's too funny...

ARTAMON. No, Comrade Director... the water is poisoned... the people get sick...

BOLDYREV. Come, bearded one, they will laugh at you if you talk like that. The Volga is not a brook. The whole city drinks this water. If you were to say that the water is not purified, that would be a different matter. We boil as much of it as we can, but some insist on drinking the water raw. The next thing you know they suffer from a bellyache. After all, what did you drink in the village? Soda water? So let's be sensible. Send the sick one to the hospital. Send a delegate with him. Then you will know how and where he is cared for.

(WORKERS *nod approvingly*.)

ZOTOV. Well, we've made fools enough of ourselves for one day. Hey, Mikhalka... Where is he? H'm... hiding.

VALKA. Let's go.

BOLDYREV (*to* VALKA *and the* CHAUFFEUR). You two go back to the car. They will carry him over themselves.

SUMATOKHINOV. Why carry him? He can walk himself. He's the one who started all this fuss.

BOLDYREV. Now, now, you go and bring him. There is no point in wasting time.

(*Most of the* WORKERS *leave for the barrack*.)

ZOTOV (*to the* KITCHEN MAID). What are you waiting for?

KITCHEN MAID. Maybe I should 'pologize... he might arrest me.

ZOTOV. Go on, silly, scat!

KITCHEN MAID. But...

ZOTOV. Scat!

(KITCHEN MAID *runs off.* THREE WORKERS *enter carrying* LAPTEV.)

THOSE CARRYING LAPTEV. Pretty nice for you, travelling in a coach like the English chamberlain. And not alone at that — with a deputation!

LAPTEV (*delirious*). I won't give up my drawers! I won't give them up... they are mine... Hey, Mikhalka, don't let them take me away... my drawers...

BOLDYREV. He's feverish.

ZOTOV. You can see he is out of his mind.

(*All leave, except* BOLDYREV.)

(GONCHAROV *enters*.)

GONCHAROV. What happened here, Stepan Semionich?

BOLDYREV. They almost beat my sister... That's not so serious. What's more to the point, the fourth barrack mutinied today. Some went out on strike. They all complained that the water has been poisoned. Some fool started this wild rumor, damn him, and I've been trying to pacify them. Lagutin isn't here. I ought to be at a conference, but I can't leave the place.

GONCHAROV. Yes, it is a troublesome evening.

BOLDYREV. They are grumbling. What we need is some real metal workers here, and quickly... five hundred of them and the atmosphere would change. Well, good-bye.

GONCHAROV. Good night. (BOLDYREV *leaves. Alone.*) ...Sharp turns, Comrade Boldyrev. A driver may fall off his perch... and maybe his passengers, too. Today it was your sister they wanted to kill, tomorrow it may be you... or me. (*Laughs quietly.*)

(ZOTOV *enters.*)

ZOTOV. What are you laughing at, comrade chief?

GONCHAROV (*alarmed*). Who's there? What do you want?

ZOTOV. Oh, I was just walking by. I thought I heard someone talking to himself... It's queer when someone talks to himself in the night. It's strange, somehow.

CURTAIN

ACT I

SCENE 2

BOLDYREV'S *office; a room in a rough wooden shack; crowded with improvised furniture; the walls and tables covered with blue-prints and work-charts.* BOLDYREV *and the Young Communist* MAKSIMKA *are in conversation.*

MAKSIMKA. There is no work in the world that's as good as war.

BOLDYREV. What do you mean?

MAKSIMKA. I fought in the war, Stepan Semionich, and I am convinced there is no work as pure as fighting on the front.

BOLDYREV. According to you, then, building plants is not pure work, eh?

MAKSIMKA. You don't understand me. Here I stroll like Chicherin at one of Stresemann's receptions. But in the war my position was clear. I saw my enemy, I fought him, he fought me. But here everything is diplomacy. I am working with men who ought to be exiled to Solovki; still I have to go on with them as if they were really comrades. It doesn't help to complain. If one does, he is charged with over-ambition. And one feels social pressure. Or there'll be a Party reprimand, requests for resignation and charges of deviation. Ruin! And before you know it he is chairman of a village Soviet in some Turukhansk Province...

BOLDYREV. Come, now, you're wasting time. Tell me, what's happening in your Bureau?

MAKSIMKA. You forced this Bureau of Rationalization on me. It would have been better if you'd put me to work as a stonemason.

BOLDYREV. Maksim, that's enough of that rot. Give me your report.

MAKSIMKA. I can't work there...

BOLDYREV. Maksimka!

MAKSIMKA. All right, it's no use... I'll begin with foreman number five. What a bedbug he is! For the fourth time now Goncharov has signed an order directing him to instal an elevator.

BOLDYREV. More paper orders.

MAKSIMKA. What am I to do if he just won't carry out the order?

169

BOLDYREV. Do it yourself.

MAKSIMKA. That's an idea.

BOLDYREV. It's no idea, it's a practical suggestion. You are all shouting tempos, tempos, and all you do is sign orders. Well, go on.

(*The* WOMAN INTERPRETER *enters; hesitates at the door.*)

INTERPRETER. Comrade Boldyrev, may I?

BOLDYREV. Come in, what can I do for you?

INTERPRETER. Mr. Carter is here, and he would like to see you at once.

BOLDYREV. Did you bring him here?

INTERPRETER. I certainly did not. He is not the kind who has to be brought anywhere.

BOLDYREV. Good. Tell him to come in. (*Interpreter leaves.*) Something is up with the Americanetz.

MAKSIMKA. They're sabotaging him. Wait and you'll see.

(*The* INTERPRETER *returns, followed by* CARTER. *The American engineer is calmly puffing his pipe. He shakes hands with* BOLDYREV *and remains standing.*)

BOLDYREV (*to* INTERPRETER). Tell Mr. Carter I am glad to see him. Is there anything I can do for him?

CARTER. I want to talk to Mr. Boldyrev about a matter that will probably be a complete surprise to him.

INTERPRETER. Mr. Carter wants to speak to you about something he thinks will be quite surprising to you.

BOLDYREV. Indeed. Have him tell me about it.

INTERPRETER. He wants to hear what you have to say, Mr. Carter.

CARTER. I haven't the slightest desire to mix in Soviet Russia's politics, and the different political angles on this construction job don't bother me. I'm an engineer, and not a statesman. I want to make it perfectly clear that I'm not going to take sides with any group here.

INTERPRETER. He is not interested in the quarrel of the Russian engineers about the tempos.

BOLDYREV. I understand Mr. Carter.

INTERPRETER. Mr. Carter wants this point emphasized.

(BOLDYREV *nods understandingly.*)

CARTER. I have a contract with the Soviet Government and it is this contract which will govern my actions as long as I am in your country. (BOLDYREV *again nods approvingly.*) I want to remind you that I am not a tourist, and am not on a pleasure trip. (*To* INTERPRETER.) If my reasons for making this statement are not clear to him, say that the ten days which I have spent here I consider entirely wasted.

INTERPRETER. Mr. Carter feels that the time he has spent has been wasted.

BOLDYREV. I understand.

CARTER. I don't care for the nice desk you took such trouble to get me. I am not a banker or a lawyer. I am a construction engineer. My place is in the field, right on the job, not at a desk answering telephone calls. And every day the same old reply.

BOLDYREV. Which reply, Mr. Carter?

CARTER. As you Russians say, 'Na buduchi nedele.'

BOLDYREV. Next week. So?

CARTER. Yes, invariably.

BOLDYREV. Who has been saying this to you, Mr. Carter?

CARTER. Engineer Goncharov.

MAKSIMKA. I told you so, didn't I?

CARTER. As far as I can see, there is no reason why American methods of production should not be adopted in Russia. (*Pause.*) I am sorry to say that as things stand, there is nothing for me to do but break my contract and return to the States. I don't intend to take money from the Soviet Government for wasting time. I'm sorry the situation is what it is.

BOLDYREV. The dirty son-of-a-bitch!... (*To the* INTERPRETER.) Don't translate this to Mr. Carter. It's not to him I'm referring... so... That's how it is... (*Turns to window for a moment.*) Tell Mr. Carter I will give him a definite reply very soon. (*Pause.*) Tell him I will immediately issue an order putting him in charge of construction, and that he will be responsible directly to me and to me only.

INTERPRETER. Comrade Boldyrev is going to issue an order placing you in charge of construction, and you will be directly responsible to him alone.

CARTER. Swell. That suits me.

BOLDYREV. Fine. As you Americans say, Okay. (*Extends his hand to* CARTER.) You will start to work tomorrow. Dosvidanye. Goo-od-bye.

CARTER (*laughing*). So long, so long.

(INTERPRETER *and* CARTER *depart.*)

171

BOLDYREV. Maksimka, 'phone the Secretary of the Party Committee. (*Shouts.*) Rybkin! (RYBKIN, *his secretary, comes in.*) Comrade Rybkin, draw up an order for me. From now on Carter is to be in charge of construction and responsible only to me. No, no, not like that... and is to be responsible only to the administration.

(RYBKIN *makes a note and leaves again.*)

MAKSIMKA (*at the telephone*). Operator, operator! Are you having tea, comrade operator? (*Telephone rings.*) Wait a moment. Stepan Semionich, take the receiver.

BOLDYREV. Yes... Yes... On *our* land? But where is the fire brigade? You can't put it out by pouring pots of water on it. Now, don't get excited. Go back and if anything more serious develops, call me again.

MAKSIMKA. What was that, a fire?

BOLDYREV. Just a smudge. The woodpile in back of the barracks caught fire, and the kitchen workers tried to put it out with pans of water. The fire brigade is off somewhere.

MAKSIMKA. But Stepan Semionich, this is serious.

BOLDYREV. You don't expect me to run over there with a pot of water myself, do you? Please try to get the Party Secretary. (LAGUTIN *enters. To* MAKSIMKA.) Never mind, here he is now.

LAGUTIN. Boldyrev, a fire broke out in the woodpile.

BOLDYREV. Never mind. Lock the door and sit down, I have something more important to talk about.

(MAKSIMKA *locks the door.*)

LAGUTIN. What do you mean, Semionich, there is a fire there and you...

BOLDYREV. Never mind, sit down. (*Pause.*) Carter has refused to work any more.

LAGUTIN. He refuses to work for Bolsheviks, I suppose.

BOLDYREV. No, that's not it.

LAGUTIN. I don't understand.

BOLDYREV. Let me tell you what the Americanetz just said. He told me he refuses to be involved with any factions. (*Pause.*) Right deviations are no abstractions, Lagutin. I see them at work right here before my very eyes. (*Pause.*) Now, Goncharov, for example. He's an excellent engineer, and yet there is no telling. He can't be relied upon. He put Carter in an office, gave him a few blue-prints to occupy him, and for ten days the man sat at his desk doing nothing. Today Carter comes to me ready to break his contract.

MAKSIMKA. What a mess! I knew it was coming.

BOLDYREV. Do you know what I did, Lagutin? Without consulting you, I appointed Carter chief of construction. It's a big step, but I had to do it. Now, either Goncharov will resign and bring about a split in the engineering staff or Carter will resign. Personally I am convinced that our men will not be able to make the tempo. Maybe, in a year or two, but certainly not in the first year of the Piatiletka. On the other hand, we are supposed to build the plant by American construction methods.

LAGUTIN. Oh, I understand all that.

MAKSIMKA. What a mess, what a mess!

BOLDYREV. That's my dilemma. Shall I sign the order, or wait a while? I'm worn out. What a backache! Come on, help me decide.

LAGUTIN. You're a metal worker, Boldyrev.

BOLDYREV. That's right. (*Pause.*) Well, what do you say, shall I sign the order?

LAGUTIN. Hold on... perhaps you... it's a problem...

BOLDYREV. Shall I sign the order?

LAGUTIN. Sure, sign it.

BOLDYREV (*shouts*). Comrade Rybkin! Maksim, open the door for him.

(MAKSIMKA *unlocks the door;* RYBKIN *enters, followed by the* CAPTAIN *of the fire brigade.*)

RYBKIN. I have the order ready for you to sign, Comrade Boldyrev.

CAPTAIN. Comrade Boldyrev, the fire has been put out. What women! You should have seen them throwing water out of pails, teapots, frying-pans. Active as heroes of labor. One got her dress scorched.

BOLDYREV. Where was the fire brigade?

CAPTAIN. There's a story to that. We were answering another call, a false alarm.

BOLDYREV. Maksim, I want you and this comrade to look into the matter of the false alarm.

MAKSIMKA. We will. Let's go first to the operator and find out about the call. (*To* CAPTAIN.) She's a Komsomol girl, dark eyes and dark skin...   (*Exit* MAKSIMKA *and the* CAPTAIN.)

LAGUTIN. Stepan!

BOLDYREV. Well?

LAGUTIN. This is war.

BOLDYREV. War. Since yesterday evening, the water, the mutiny, the fire, Carter — all in the space of eighteen hours.

LAGUTIN. The Piatiletka, comrade.

BOLDYREV. That's right. (*Calls to the next room.*) Comrade Rybkin, bring the budget on bedbugs. (*To* LAGUTIN.) I'm appropriating five and a half thousand rubles for a campaign against bedbugs. Bedbugs, my friend, also hinder tempos.

CURTAIN

ACT I

SCENE 3

Dawn. A deep valley, and at the left a winding river, like a bright ribbon. Scattered concrete work and excavations indicate that this is an edge of the construction. VALKA, *seated on a log, is singing.*

VALKA.

> Beautiful ocean, holy Baikal,
> Brave little schooner fighting the sea.
> Hey, Baruzine, we're off to Ural...

(MAKSIMKA *enters and joins in the song.*)

> Off to be happy and free.

MAKSIMKA (*softly singing*).

> Many a year I've been dragging the chain,
> Scaling the hills of Katuya,
> Now I am fighting determined to gain
> Freedom and...

The opera is ended, on with the comedy. At last I understand you, Valentina Semionovna. You are not studying the aurora at this hour. It's too late for that, and it's too early to be dreaming. So you must be reconnoitring the locale of your future skirmishes.

VALKA. Idle talk, my boy. I've come to have a swim before those bullies get here. (*Pause.*) Mornings are lovely on the Volga, Maksim. The water is blue and delicate as Bokhara silk, and the sea-gulls are like silver arrows dropping from Heaven, while far, far in the distance the beckoning of a dark brown sail... But you don't understand that.

MAKSIMKA. Valya, if you only knew how sentimental I really am!

VALKA. You!... why, the sun is energy to you, water is moisture, and grass is only fodder...

MAKSIMKA. Damn you, Valka, you look so belligerent. It's impossible to say anything soulful to such a face.

VALKA. That's because you have nothing to say. Maybe you are ill?

MAKSIMKA. Never mind now. I don't need an ambulance. All I want is a dip to revive me. I studied all night: Fordism, Taylorism, scientific organization of labor...

VALKA. Infatuated with Americanism, just like all the rest. Stepan is spending nights conjugating English verbs, 'Ai khaz ay book, She khaz ay book.' He is planning to take a trip to America.

MAKSIMKA. One has to understand Americanism. If we could only master Americanism and suffuse it with Communist principles, then...

VALKA. Then what?...

MAKSIMKA. But you don't understand that, no use talking to you. You're only a medical student. Good-bye, I'm off for a swim. (MAKSIMKA *starts for the river, turns back.*) Val!

VALKA. What is it?

MAKSIMKA. There is something I wanted to tell you.

VALKA. Why don't you say it?

MAKSIMKA (*sitting down*). Did you ever see a suckling stallion? Well, you, Valya, look just like one.

VALKA. Thanks for the comparison.

MAKSIMKA. I mean it seriously, Valya. And, you know, later on the baby stallions get their manes clipped. You look just like one of them.

VALKA. Did you ever see a grown-up stallion? Well, that's what *you* look like.

MAKSIMKA. You don't understand, I'm using images, symbols.

VALKA. Images? All you can see is horses.

MAKSIMKA. Valya... I've been watching you for days.

VALKA. One of the functions of your Bureau of Rationalization.

MAKSIMKA. I've been watching you, Valya. You're losing weight. When you first came, you looked like a blooming poppy, and now you're like a sunflower seed.

VALKA. Go jump in the river.

MAKSIMKA. But I really mean it, Valya.

VALKA. Fordism is having a bad effect on you. Try a swim. (*Exits.*)

MAKSIMKA. That's just like her, it's impossible to speak gently to her. (*Goes off singing dolefully.*)

> You're but sixteen,
> Tripping your way,
> Seeking your share of romance;
> While I feel so old,
> Feeble and cold,
> Hardly in tune with your dance.

(*A group of the* KOSTROMA PEASANTS, *construction hands, come on the scene, dragging* TUSHA, *a dishevelled, snivelling young peasant.*)

MIKHALKA. And who would expect it of a fellow with a quiet name like Tu-usha?

SUMATOKHINOV. It's apricots like him that stir up trouble for honest people.

MIKHALKA. Let's introduce him to the Director.

SUMATOKHINOV. We don't need the Director, we'll take care of him ourselves, the son-of-a-bitch. For four days I've been trailing him. Where could Tusha be, said I. There is no Tusha. (*With thick irony.*) The bathtub lord was bathing himself, taking sun baths, damn him. (*To* TUSHA.) You'll have to answer for this to the brigade.

TUSHA. Brothers, don't hit me... I'll make up for it, only don't hit me.

MIKHALKA. A coward, ain't you?

ARTAMON. You weren't afraid to give the brigade a bad name.

KITCHEN MAID (*running toward the group*). Look at them... the...

LAPTEV (*to* TUSHA). Here is your mistress a-coming... (*To the* KITCHEN MAID.) You've been feeding him goodies, haven't you? Such a kind heart...

KITCHEN MAID. Don't be so hard on him... he's still young and tender... he's not used to it yet.

MIKHALKA. We'll harden him, all right.

SUMATOKHINOV. Tusha, you stupid ass.

MIKHALKA. We'll trim him like an Indian cock. (*Aside.*) There's no use wasting words on him... Let's drag him to the barrack.

TUSHA (*drops to his knees*). Townsmen, don't take me to the barrack... Artamon, please...

MIKHALKA. Please! Listen to him! You can't move Moscow with tears. Get up, you lazy dog. (*To the* KITCHEN MAID.) Take yourself off to the devil's mother, or you'll be getting it too.

KITCHEN MAID (*leaving*). You're brutes, that's what you are...

(*Enter the peasant* ZOTOV.)

ZOTOV. Did you catch him?

ARTAMON. He's burned as brown as a berry.

ZOTOV. You're not going to beat him, are you?

MIKHALKA. Do you expect us to kiss him or enshrine him, after what he's done?

ZOTOV. Mikhalka, shut up and keep out of this.

MIKHALKA. And who are you, a defence attorney, or something?

ZOTOV (*to* MIKHALKA). Stop barking. (*To the others.*) Come, brothers, this won't do, I won't allow it... it's ignorant... it's uncultured...

SUMATOKHINOV. Maybe he's right; why beat the lad?

ARTAMON (*to* ZOTOV). Don't you go against the brigade, Anisim! He was placed in our care by his old man, and it's up to us to bring him up right.

MIKHALKA. What kind of preda... predagogy — (*stumbles over the word*) — is this... Drag him to the barrack.

ZOTOV. I won't let you...

ARTAMON. And I'll give you a... (*Pushes* ZOTOV.) Anisim, don't you tempt me.

ZOTOV. Watch yourself, old man, or you'll be brushing the soil out of your whiskers.

ARTAMON. Me? Brush the soil out of my whiskers? (*They tussle clumsily.*)

ZOTOV. Yes, you!

ARTAMON. Mikhalka...

(LAGUTIN, *the Party Secretary, arrives on the scene.*)

LAGUTIN. Here, old man... (*Separates* ARTAMON *and* ZOTOV.) Shame on you... just like two roosters... What's going on here?

ARTAMON. Now I'll leave it to you. This son-of-a-bitch is giving a black eye to the whole brigade. A new trick he's up to. Calls in the morning, punches the clock, wags his tail, and is off for the Volga to wash his white skin.

LAGUTIN. Loafing, eh?

ZOTOV. But they want to take the law into their own hands.

LAGUTIN. It won't go. Who's idea is that, anyway?

MIKHALKA. Comrade chief, I don't know what kind of chief you are, Party or otherwise. But I'll tell you straight, nothing will come of it. Tempos, sub-tempos, it's just lip work... tempos... tempos... And what sort of tempo is this when such heroes flee from work like cats from dogs?

ARTAMON. The thing to do is knout a few of them, good and hard, then you will have tempos.

MIKHALKA. All right, let him loaf. We thought we were doing the Government a favor.

ZOTOV. Beating isn't much of a help.

LAGUTIN. Right! What we should do is warn the youngster this time. He won't repeat this trick again.

ARTAMON. My very words... Of course, a clout or two on his ears would also help...

MIKHALKA. It's your good luck, Tusha... my anger is now cooled off.

TUSHA. Comrade chief... never... never again till my very grave.

SUMATOKHINOV. Run along now, Tusha... as fast as the wind will carry you. (TUSHA, *glad to escape a beating, rushes off.*)

ZOTOV. Mikhalka is right, Comrade Lagutin, it's bad business. It hurts one's soul.

LAGUTIN. What do you mean? Speak up.

ZOTOV. What do you mean? Here is what I mean: half-days pass by and we sit around here doing nothing. True, we get paid for it, but out of whose pocket does it come? Men sit idle, just doing nothing because we have to wait for the lime.

MIKHALKA. You, comrade chief, may think there is no class-consciousness in us. We know this is *ours*. You think it makes no difference to us, but look here...

ARTAMON. The people, brother, want to work, and we have to waste half-days waiting for lime.

MIKHALKA. We ain't pleased with this... we have been hired to work.

ZOTOV. There is dissatisfaction among the people. You won't notice it at the meetings, but listen to them at work.

(*Another peasant,* DUDYKIN, *enters.*)

DUDYKIN. Hey, there, fellow Kostromites, you gentlemen of the ontilligentzia, what's this, a picnic? You should be building a monastery instead of a factory...

MIKHALKA. See, comrade chief, what it's coming to. We're being laughed at. How can we be expected to keep our tempos?

(*The construction workers troop off, except* DUDYKIN *and another — having stretched out comfortably and unseen on the ground, they remain there. Three women workers — the Production Committee of the brick factory — enter; aggressive, garrulous, racy examples of Kostroma womanhood.*)

FIRST WOMAN. Are you an engineer? Or just so and so?

LAGUTIN. Just so and so.

SECOND WOMAN. And where are the engineers, the specialists?

LAGUTIN. Do you want someone, personally?

FIRST WOMAN. We don't want anyone personally, we are married. And don't you be getting fresh.

THIRD WOMAN. What the hell are you getting fresh about, you horse-radish? Do you think you are a delegate or something?

LAGUTIN. Where do you come from, women?

THIRD WOMAN. The same place you come from.

SECOND WOMAN (*to her companions*). If we could only catch one of them specialists. The kind that wears a velvet cap.

LAGUTIN. Why do you have to catch him?

FIRST WOMAN. We know why we have to catch him... Now look here, brother, if you...

THIRD WOMAN. Why talk to *him?* Let's go, women. No point wasting words on him. He's crazy.

SECOND WOMAN. We need the big chiefs, real big ones, do you hear?

LAGUTIN. What's happened?

THIRD WOMAN. Catch me tellin' *you*... Let's go, comrades.

FIRST WOMAN. Which way, right or left?

SECOND WOMAN. Straight ahead.

THIRD WOMAN. We'll find someone, somewhere.

> (*The three of them leave and* LAGUTIN *follows.*)

LAGUTIN. Wait a moment. Explain what's happened.

> (*As the scene proceeds, it grows lighter speedily. There are signs of activity far in the background; foremen are assigning workers to sections. The peasants* TEMIN *and* GRISCHUK *enter, they have evidently had their morning eye-openers.*)

TEMIN. Let's start it.

GRISCHUK. How does it go?... 'I wish I were back on my farm, looking at the little kittens.' Now, I remember it. Let's go.

BOTH (*singing*).

> Yo-ho-ho-ho-ho —
> Wish I were back on my farm,
> Looking at my little kittens.

GRISCHUK.

> When I left they still were blind,
> Now they're wearing shoes and mittens.

BOTH.

> Yo-ho-ho-ho-ho —
> When I left they still were blind,
> Now they're wearing shoes and mittens.

(CARTER *enters, accompanied by the* INTERPRETER.)

GRISCHUK.

> There's a tree that's tall and eerie
> And it casts a great big shade.

BOTH.

> Yo-ho-ho-ho-ho —
> There's a tree that's tall and eerie
> And it casts a great big shade.

GRISCHUK.

> If a road is nicely paved,
> That means it's an avenoo...

CARTER. What's that song they are singing?
BOTH.

> If a road is nicely paved,
> That means it's an avenoo...

INTERPRETER. Mr. Carter wants to know what the song means.
GRISCHUK. We don't know ourselves, lady.
TEMIN. No. Explain to him that them is our own compositions —
that we are saying that if a gentleman buys his hats with care that
means he has no hair. (CARTER *laughs, removes his hat.*)
GRISCHUK. Listen, learned lady, you ask him whether he would
take us to America with him to build plants there.
INTERPRETER. All right, I'll ask him. (*To* CARTER.) They want
to know if you would take them to the States with you to build for
you there.
CARTER. No. I am afraid I couldn't.
INTERPRETER. Mr. Carter doesn't think he would take you.
TEMIN. He doesn't like us?
GRISCHUK (*offended*). We ain't good enough, I suppose.
DUDYKIN (*sits up*). They have skyscrapin' buildings there.
HIS COMPANION. Skies don't mean nothin'... Here we got a plant
that covers five acres and we're managin' all right.
CARTER. I couldn't take them because we have our unemployed

who want to work. Lots of them, God knows. These are good men, though. (*Pause.*) Why do they scratch themselves so much?

INTERPRETER. Mr. Carter says you are wasting too much time scratching.

CARTER. Tell them it is seven o'clock and time to start work.

GRISCHUK. These Americans, by God! Ask him what *he* does when he's got a bite.

DUDYKIN. In his country... every time you scratch you pay a ruble fine.

HIS COMPANION. How do you know it's a ruble? Maybe it's only a quarter.

DUDYKIN. You can go there and bargain with them. I'm telling you it's a ruble. Come on, Fedya, the Americanetz wants us to start work.

HIS COMPANION. The Devil, he won't let us rest a minute.

DUDYKIN. In his country, brother, if you waste a minute, you pay a ruble fine.

HIS COMPANION. Go to the Devil with your fines.

(*The three women workers return, still hunting for a real chief.*)

FIRST WOMAN (*sizing up* CARTER). One can tell by his specs that he is the chief here.

SECOND WOMAN. Who could mistake it?

THIRD WOMAN (*addresses* CARTER). Citizen, hey, citizen engineer, we have been lookin' for you all morning. We've got something important to tell you about... (*Whispers importantly.*) It's about spoilage, sabotage... (*Pause.*) Now, look here, comrade, don't you be puttin' on airs. We ain't been runnin' around all mornin' lookin' for you for nothin'.

SECOND WOMAN (*with dignity*). We, brother, are a deputation.

(CARTER *observes them uncomprehendingly.*)

FIRST WOMAN. The damn boorocrat... (*Excited.*) Pays no attention to us. We won't stop till we get to Boldyrev himself...

SECOND WOMAN (*to* CARTER). We'll make you talk at the next general meeting. We'll make you squawk all right. (*Aside.*) One can tell by his face that he's a wrecker.

FIRST WOMAN (*shouts at* CARTER). Two thousand bricks were just spoiled. Do you hear? Why don't you see to it that there is more order? What fool mixes clay with black soil? Think of it, mixing soil with clay, the fools.

THIRD WOMAN. What kind of work is this? That's no work, that's what literate people call absurd... absurd.

CARTER. Absurd... Russki?

THIRD WOMAN. Now you stop gidappin' us, we're not horses. You can't make fun of us.

SECOND WOMAN. Hold on, comrade, maybe he's deaf. Listen uncle, how are you on your ears? Kin you hear anything, uh? (*Pause.*) Of course, he's deaf. Well, what's the use! There's something wrong with every one of them here.

FIRST WOMAN. Maybe he's a German.

THIRD WOMAN. He ain't no German... he's just plain dumb. Let's go.

(*By this time work is getting under way in the distance. There are shouts: 'Send two men to section four!' 'Dig two metres,' etc. CARTER, disregarding the women, has been making calculations and sending the INTERPRETER with messages. She now returns.*)

INTERPRETER. Calling foreman four!

(*The FOREMAN comes in.*)

INTERPRETER. Mr. Carter wants the left section of the basin cleared by noon today.

FOREMAN. Impossible! Is he cra... excuse me, but that's two days' work.

INTERPRETER. But he says it must be done...

FOREMAN. It's easy enough for him to say so, lady, but I know it can't be done. This is not my first year here...

(*Enter BOLDYREV and GONCHAROV. As the scene proceeds others — workers, technicians — come and go.*)

BOLDYREV (*to FOREMAN*). What are you saying?

CARTER (*greeting arrivals*). How do you do, zdravstvuyte!

INTERPRETER. Comrade Boldyrev, the foreman says he can't clear the left section by noon.

BOLDYREV (*to the FOREMAN*). Look here, townsman, it's five minutes past seven now. By twelve o'clock that section must be cleared.

FOREMAN. I can't do it, Stepan Semionich.

BOLDYREV. You can't do it?

FOREMAN. I tell you, it's impossible, Stepan Semionich.

BOLDYREV. All right, then, I'll do it myself.

FOREMAN. You can't spare the time. You have more important work.

BOLDYREV. Will you do it, or shall I do it?

FOREMAN. I'll try, Stepan Semionich.

BOLDYREV. Report to me at noon. (*To* INTERPRETER.) Tell Carter the section will be cleared. (*Joins the technicians.*) Well, boys, how's the new tempo?

FIRST TECHNICIAN. We don't even get time to smoke.

BOLDYREV. No time to smoke, well, well...

FIRST TECHNICIAN. The minute you finish a job, and before you get a chance to sit down and smoke, you're interrupted by the interpreter, 'Mr. Carter wants you to...'

SECOND TECHNICIAN. This Americanetz works like an automat. He's just a machine.

BOLDYREV. That's good practice for you fellows, you need this sort of experience. (*To a worker.*) Look here, handsome, that's no way to hold a spade. Let me show you.

> (*Having given up* CARTER, *the three women hopefully approach the Director.*)

FIRST WOMAN. Oh, Comrade Boldyrev...

SECOND WOMAN. We've worn our feet off...   (*All talk at once.*)

THIRD WOMAN. Absurd, just absurd...

FIRST WOMAN. Mixing black soil to make bricks... two thousand spoiled already.

THIRD WOMAN. And no one to report to.

SECOND WOMAN. They all seem to be deaf or dumb.

FIRST WOMAN. They're still mixing soil.

THIRD WOMAN. Is this a game they're playing? Sabotagers...

SECOND WOMAN. Wreckers, that's what they are.

THIRD WOMAN. Absurd, that's the word.

BOLDYREV. Whew, calm down, you are getting me dizzy.

FIRST WOMAN. They ought to be put on trial.

SECOND WOMAN. We are no bats, we can see.

BOLDYREV. Now wait a minute. Let me get this. Speak one at a time. (*To* THIRD WOMAN.) Supposing you tell me, Praskovya.

SECOND WOMAN. That isn't Praskovya, it's Leda.

BOLDYREV. All right, Leda, but no speech-making.

THIRD WOMAN. I've nothing to speech-make about.

FIRST WOMAN. Two thousand bricks were spoiled today.

BOLDYREV. How?

FIRST WOMAN. They're using black soil. They are still mixing it.

BOLDYREV. Now we're getting somewhere. Are you delegates?

SECOND WOMAN. We're the Production Commission of the brick factory.

BOLDYREV. Fine, I'll get my car and go back with you.

THIRD WOMAN (*scared*). You go by car. We'll walk.

BOLDYREV. We'll all go in the car, but you'll have to quiet down, my chauffeur is a timid man.

SECOND WOMAN. No, not us, we'll walk.

(BOLDYREV *and the women leave.*)

INTERPRETER (*to* DANILO DANILOVICH). Will you please calculate the amount of cement required for the left section.

DANILO DANILOVICH. I'll have those figures ready for him to-morrow. (*Walks over to* GONCHAROV.)

INTERPRETER. Just one moment, Danilo Danilovich, Mr. Carter says it must be done today, not tomorrow.

DANILO DANILOVICH. Huh! not tomorrow, today. So that's the kind he is... strict. All right, tell him it will be ready today.

CURTAIN

ACT II
Scene 4

The study in Goncharov's *home, with a sector of the porch outside the study window. It is evening — shaded lights on the porch and over the desk in the study.* Goncharov *is at the telephone.*

Goncharov. Yes, speaking. Listen, Danilo Danilovich... pick up Carter and come down to see me. I have to talk to him about some technical matters. Don't bother about the interpreter, I'll manage myself. That's all. I'm waiting for you. (*Hangs up receiver.*) The softy... (*Picks up a newspaper. Knock at door.*) Come in.

(*Engineer* Gruzdev *enters.*)

Gruzdev. Good evening, Uri Nikolayevich... Hasn't Carter been here yet?

Goncharov. Do you expect Carter here?

Gruzdev. Don't you? The interpreter told me that you asked him to attend a conference here, and Carter asked me to come along.

Goncharov. I haven't any idea, my dear man, who invited him.

Gruzdev. Are you really having a conference?

Goncharov. Nothing of the sort. We've entered into a period where we are working without conferences, or, as Carter would put it — work first and talk later. Will you have a cigar? A real foreign brand a friend sent me. A fool in the *Pravda* has been writing about our tempos and the progress we've made. Of course, Gruzdev and Carter are praised to the skies.

Gruzdev. What difference does it make what they write?

Goncharov (*surreptitiously looking at his watch*). Stay a while. Any news about the typhoid cases?

Gruzdev. You are better informed than I am.

Goncharov. No, I am not. All the reports are given to Boldyrev. By the way, is it true that Boldyrev's sister is ill?

Gruzdev. Yes, she's been ill for a long time.

Goncharov. A long time? You don't say. Now, don't you drink any raw water. You're not, are you?

Gruzdev. No, why do you ask?

GONCHAROV. Because I naturally believe in prophylactics. In all aspects of life. You know, not only people may be afflicted with typhoid, but also the plants which they build, and at times even governments.

GRUZDEV. Why are you telling this to me, Uri Nikolayevich? Is there anything you want of me?

GONCHAROV. You are an enthusiast, my friend. You're praised in the press. It is said that you have entré to the Party Committee. You are not joining the Party, are you?

GRUZDEV. I'm not joining anything. On the other hand, neither do I understand you. What is it you expect from me, or for that matter from the engineering staff? It would be easier for all of us if you came out frankly and told us what's on your mind.

GONCHAROV. Well, if you must have it, I believe this tempo talk is just a stunt. I am an engineer and not a juggler. That should be clear. I can't make it any plainer. Furthermore, my friend, it is my opinion that we must go step by step through the stages of the older industrial countries.

GRUZDEV. Do you propose to postpone this construction for another two hundred years?

GONCHAROV. Yes, even two hundred years. These muzhiks building this plant are as far from Americanism as you and I are from the psychology of Martians. (*Glances at his watch.*) That is why, my friend, your enthusiasm seems so naïve to me.

GRUZDEV. Really, I should go.

(*Enter* KASTORKIN, *somewhat intoxicated and strumming a guitar; and at his heels, Engineer* KALUGIN *and his gay young wife,* TATIANA LVOVNA.)

KASTORKIN (*singing an American jazz tune*). 'Hallelujah, hallelujah...' (*To* GRUZDEV.) Nothing of the kind, my friend. Why should you go? Stay and be merry.

TATIANA LVOVNA (*to* GONCHAROV). We've come to see you. Kastorkin is celebrating. This is his birthday, or isn't it?

KASTORKIN (*in high spirits*). It isn't, but, Gruzdev, I won't let you go anyway. To hell with business. How about having a bottle of champagne with us, Uri Nikolayevich? (*Strums and sings.*) 'When railway men are having fun'... We are taking over your veranda. Think of it, four million stars in the heavens. Come, Kalugin, our spirits must rise to embrace those starry heights. Why are you quiet, chief engineer? A-ah, I can tell by your face, it's political economy stirring your insides again. Some believe, others doubt, and still others rejoice. Comrades, stop worrying, we don't understand a damn anyway, and you too, Nikolayevich, don't understand a damn. (KALUGIN *has wandered out to the porch.*)

TATIANA LVOVNA. Now, don't be a rowdy, Kastorkin.

KASTORKIN. Why not? It's somebody's birthday...

TATIANA LVOVNA. Uri Nikolayevich, you must pay court to me tonight.

KALUGIN (*from the porch through the window*). Hand me the glasses.

KASTORKIN. Don't sulk, my lord... you must obey the lady's wish.

TATIANA LVOVNA (*coyly*). You must.

GONCHAROV. I shall be most happy.

TATIANA LVOVNA. How chivalrous!

KASTORKIN. Gruzdev, you can't run away. Close the semaphore, Simon Semionovich. You are now a prisoner. How about a couple of glasses? Haven't we a right to it, once a month?

GRUZDEV. It's not a matter of right, it's...

KASTORKIN. Hush, hush, come along. (*Drags him to the porch, singing.*)

> Come visit me alone tomorrow,
> Let me repose upon your breast;
> Your eyes are happiness and sorrow,
> Your lips a-thrill at love's behest.

The ladies will be here presently.

TATIANA LVOVNA. Why are you so depressed, Uri Nikolayevich? Did we disturb you? Are you expecting anyone?

GONCHAROV (*preoccupied*). No one, my dear, no one. Excuse me a moment... I'll arrange everything shortly. There is something I must tell Boldyrev... It's confidential. I received a telegram just this minute. I'll say just a few words to him over the telephone and after that I'll be free.

TATIANA LVOVNA. Now, remember, no more than two minutes. (*Exits.*)

GONCHAROV. Kastorkin, the idiot. (*At the telephone.*) Operator... Extension thirteen. Danilo Danilovich...

(DANILO DANILOVICH *and* CARTER *appear at the door.*)

DANILO DANILOVICH. I'm here.

GONCHAROV (*hangs up receiver*). Oh, that's fine. (*To* CARTER.) Have a chair. (*To* DANILO DANILOVICH.) Untimely visitors out there. But after all... (*To the porch.*) Gentlemen, I'll be with you presently. (*To* DANILO DANILOVICH.) It didn't turn out quite right...

DANILO DANILOVICH. What is it, Goncharov? Perhaps you could put it briefly.

GONCHAROV. In the final reckoning... we'll decide everything briefly. You know what I want to talk to you about. You have my letter.

(KASTORKIN *rushes in, glass in hand.*)

KASTORKIN (*singing*). 'Hallelujah, hallelujah,' a-ah, Mr. Carter! (*In broken English.*) Russky vodka verry goot, Mr. Carter. I beg you. (*Offers him a drink.*)

GONCHAROV. Kastorkin, I ask you not to disturb us... this is a very important matter, it will take only a few minutes.

KASTORKIN. To hell with important matters! Hasn't an honest specialist a right to rest once in a while?

GONCHAROV. Kastorkin, we must discuss the steel work, you understand. Ask Tatiana Lvovna to play hostess for me. I'll be with you right away.

KASTORKIN. Well, if it's about the steel construction, we'll wait. (*Leaves.*)

(CARTER *observes curiously the doings of these Russians on the porch, while the other two talk earnestly.*)

GONCHAROV. And now, Danilo Danilovich, I must have your decision. Are you going to tender your resignation or not?

DANILO DANILOVICH. I'm an old man, Uri Nikolayevich. I've gone through a lot. It's not that I'm cowardly, but what you suggest is not new and for me personally it is...

GONCHAROV. Make yourself more clear. Are you declining my proposal?

DANILO DANILOVICH. Don't put it that way.

GONCHAROV. How am I to take it?

DANILO DANILOVICH. I do not agree with your plan in principle.

GONCHAROV. I didn't expect that.

DANILO DANILOVICH. Don't get yourself involved, Uri Nikolayevich. Why inject politics? You are a young engineer, and you have great opportunities...

GONCHAROV. You're aping Boldyrev.

DANILO DANILOVICH. What do you want to do?

GONCHAROV. It is hardly necessary to discuss that now. Have you spoken to Kalugin?

DANILO DANILOVICH. Yes.

GONCHAROV. How about him?

DANILO DANILOVICH. He too...

GONCHAROV. Because of principle?

DANILO DANILOVICH. No. He believes that...

GONCHAROV. I understand. He's got a young wife... Tatiana... love... That's the way it is, Danilo Danilovich. They squeal, they cry, then they get used to it.

DANILO DANILOVICH. Let's forget about this, Uri Nikolayevich. I have destroyed your letter and I give you my word of honor...

GONCHAROV. You talk as if I were a wrecker.

DANILO DANILOVICH. No. Uri Nikolayevich... but let's not speak about this any more.

GONCHAROV. You refuse.

DANILO DANILOVICH. Yes. (*Silence.*)

GONCHAROV. Allow me to say a few words to Mr. Carter.

DANILO DANILOVICH. I wouldn't advise it, Uri Nikolayevich.

GONCHAROV. You're queer. There is another matter I have to discuss with him... a brief technical interview...

DANILO DANILOVICH. I don't think you should, Uri Nikolayevich. (*Exits.*)

GONCHAROV. The old shoe! (*To* CARTER.) I would like to talk to you about your work.

CARTER. Please do.

GONCHAROV (*speaks haltingly in English*). I feel that the fraternity of technicians, Mr. Carter, transcends national boundaries. Our country is a lunatic asylum. We are ruled by madmen. You can see for yourself, a crazy experiment. This plant we are building is a phantasy. And you are helping these maniacs. I'm a Russian engineer, I speak to you as a colleague.

CARTER. I wouldn't say the Bolsheviks are crazy; lunatics don't build plants. Your politics sicken me. There is altogether too much talk and not enough work.

(*Enter* KASTORKIN.)

KASTORKIN. More political economy! (*Sings.*)

No use pining,
No use crying,
  Let's drink and drown it all.
Life is empty,
Life is weary,
  Come, heed the gypsy's call.

(CARTER *and* KASTORKIN *leave*.)

GONCHAROV (*answering telephone*). Yes, this is Goncharov's apartment, Engineer Goncharov speaking. You say the steel girders arrived. To Kastorkin? I'll call him this minute. (*Goes to the door, stops suddenly and returns to the telephone*.) Engineer Kastorkin speaking...

CURTAIN

ACT II

SCENE 5

VALKA'S *room in* BOLDYREV'S *apartment, at night. A shaded lamp throws a dim light on the bed, where* VALKA *is stretched out. Medicine bottles, a thermometer, and hot-water bottle are on a stool near the bed. For a minute after the curtain rises, the scene is deserted and quiet. Then* BOLDYREV *enters.*

BOLDYREV. Tonight I am free, Valya. No work.... (*Walks in stocking feet to the bed and looks intently at* VALKA *for several moments.*) No! I must be imagining! (*Drops panic-stricken to his knees and puts his ear to* VALKA'S *bosom. Rises frightenedly.*) Valka, are you sleeping? Valichka, Valushka... (*In a whisper.*) My little sister, my Valushka. (*Kisses her. Rises and slowly walks away from the bed.*) ... Dead. (*Stands in dark silhouette in centre of room.*) I am tired. Wait, Stepan Boldyrev... cry, old man, it helps. Someone give me a cigarette. Valka, Valka, you won't be with me any more. (*Walks over to the bed, looks into* VALKA'S *face, covers her up.*) What shall I do? What shall I do? (*Telephone rings in adjoining room.*) That 'phone has been ringing all night. Of all people, I alone must never sleep. I am going, I'll answer no calls tonight. (*Telephone rings, ceases, then resumes. Mechanically* BOLDYREV *lifts the receiver. As he talks,* VALKA *stirs on the bed — her brother has given her up too soon.*) What is it? Boldyrev speaking. Come to see me tomorrow, Maksim ... What are you shouting about? I can't understand. Not so loud. Yes... I understand... what did you say, say it again. How dare they! I'll shoot them on the spot. Stop them. Call out the G.P.U. Wait a minute, I think you're right. I can get there in fifteen minutes in the car... What? Regards? Wait a minute, Maksim, don't talk so much. She isn't here... I found her dead when I came home ... (*Pause.*) That's the way it goes. (*Hangs up receiver; dejectedly, looking at the bed.*) Regards for you, Valka. He says he is coming to see you. (*Exits.*)

(VALKA *is motionless for a few moments, then she stirs again and sighs deeply.*)

(MAKSIMKA *enters, thoroughly frightened, heart-broken.*)

VALKA (*weakly*). Maksim, give me a drink.

192

MAKSIMKA (*startled*). Is it you, Valya?

VALKA. Stop playing, Maksim, bring me a drink.

MAKSIMKA. I'm damned if it isn't Valya herself speaking! (*So overjoyed that he seems to lose control of his senses.*) What a colossal mistake — Valya, my darling, I love you! I was just crying like a fool because Stepan told me you had died. My little Komsomolka, my comrade, my little girl. Oh, Valya...

VALKA. Maksim, a drink.

MAKSIMKA. Oh, yes, a drink. I'll bring you oceans of water, I'll bring you mineral water. (*Runs helplessly around the room.*) I'll get you champagne. Oh, Valya, I am so happy. I could sing lyrics, operas, preludes, symphonies. Valya, you are with me! I shall never leave you. I shall take care of you myself. I will sit right here on this chair and never leave you.

VALKA. Maksim, let me have a drink.

MAKSIMKA. A drink... instantly. (*Rushes to the kitchen singing, 'Bravely, comrades, onward.'*) A drink, a drink. (*Rushes back with glass.*) Drink, drink it all, you have my permission.

VALKA. Maksim, you brought me raw water.

MAKSIMKA. I'll boil it instantly...

VALKA. Maksim, you've gone mad.

MAKSIMKA. Yes, I've gone mad, it's a fact.

VALKA. Give me the boiled water. It's in the pitcher on the window-sill.

MAKSIMKA. Instantly. (*Drinks the water from the glass and refills it from the pitcher.*) Drink. Let me run down to the city and get you some mineral water. Why are you smiling, Valya? I'm serious. If you only knew how I love you! I'm madly in love with you. Who says there is no such thing as love? I'll kill him instantly. (*Pause.*) Is there anything else you want me to do?

VALKA (*playfully*). Yes, dance.

MAKSIMKA. You're always the same, even when you're sick.

VALKA. Sit down... you may sit here on the bed, but sit quietly, Maksim. I am very weak. Let's talk seriously. Give me your hand. You are nice, Maksim. I love you.

MAKSIMKA. Valya... Valka... Valichka.

VALKA. Be quiet, Maksim, please.

MAKSIMKA (*jumps up*). I can't. I must have music, a rhapsody by Liszt, Beethoven, Glazunov! (*Sings unintelligibly and does an impromptu jig.*)

(*Enter* Nurse *and* Physician.)

Doctor. What *corps de ballet* is this?

Maksimka. Excuse me, please.

Doctor. Who are you, where did you come from, young man?

Maksimka. I swear to God, comrade doctor, I don't know. Now don't be offended. Don't you know what happened?

Nurse. Why, that's only Maksim, he's always here. But look at her, she's laughing. Valya, my dear, and I thought that you... Valusha, my joy.

Maksimka. Comrades, none of you know anything... anything.

CURTAIN

ACT II

SCENE 6

Night. A sector of railroad track. KOMYAGIN, *a switchman, is quietly speaking to* BOLDYREV. LAGUTIN *paces to and fro, worried.*

BOLDYREV. ... Kastorkin's orders. So, it was Kastorkin's orders.

LAGUTIN. Stepan, you're getting excited.

BOLDYREV. Quite the contrary, Lagutin. I am being extremely patient. I've been pampering Goncharov as though I were his nurse. Goncharov has been plaguing me with his principles and doubts. I've had enough. It's time to strike back, even if it's at Kastorkin. We must show strength here and now. We must be decisive. No more pampering.

LAGUTIN. I think it is only petty vengeance on Carter.

BOLDYREV. It's all part of the same thing, Lagutin. These bickerings have gone too far.

(GRUZDEV *enters.*)

GRUZDEV. What's the matter?

BOLDYREV. The gentlemen technicians are up to their pranks.

GRUZDEV. Technicians will have their fun.

BOLDYREV. Were you at Goncharov's today?

GRUZDEV. Yes.

BOLDYREV. Was Kastorkin there?

GRUZDEV. Yes.

BOLDYREV. What instructions did he give over the telephone about the unloading of the steel girders?

GRUZDEV. I have no idea.

BOLDYREV. What conversation took place there?

GRUZDEV. Comrade Boldyrev, don't talk that way to me.

BOLDYREV. Look here. This is damned serious. During that party in Goncharov's apartment, Kastorkin gave orders to unload the girders on the eighth track.

GRUZDEV. Hell, I didn't hear a thing.

(MAKSIMKA *arrives, and close behind him,* KASTORKIN.)

MAKSIMKA. What a mess... what a mess... He's as drunk as King David.

KASTORKIN. Stepan Semionich, forgive me, I've had a couple of drinks... but not during working hours.

BOLDYREV. Comrade Kastorkin, do you remember what you did tonight at Goncharov's apartment?

KASTORKIN. I don't remember a thing.

BOLDYREV. Maybe I can remind you. You, as chief of the Transport Division, instructed Switchman Komyagin over the telephone to run the cars of girders to the eighth track.

KASTORKIN. What do you mean, Stepan Semionich? That's ridiculous. I may have had a few drinks, but I'm not crazy.

BOLDYREV. You gave those orders and you said that you would be at the place of unloading at midnight.

KASTORKIN. Stepan Semionich, you're not serious.

BOLDYREV. You don't suppose I got you out here at three in the morning to tell you a joke, do you?

KASTORKIN. Stepan Semionich, it's impossible! Why, I was the one who made out the plan... I know the eighth track is supposed to be torn up tomorrow. It can't be...

BOLDYREV. That's just it, it can't be.

KASTORKIN (*frightened and confused*). I don't understand a thing you are saying, comrade.

BOLDYREV. No? Citizen Kastorkin. I suggest one of two things, either you tell me everything, fully and frankly, or I'll hand you over to the G.P.U.

KASTORKIN. Stepan Semionich, how can you talk like that — to the G.P.U.? Why should you hand me over to the G.P.U.? No, I'm not drunk any more, Stepan Semionich. I remember everything clearly... I did not 'phone anyone from Goncharov's apartment. It wasn't I, Stepan Semionich... Comrade Lagutin, you know I didn't.

BOLDYREV. The switchman says you told him it was with my approval.

KASTORKIN. I said... hell, I didn't say...

BOLDYREV. You didn't say what?

KASTORKIN. I didn't say anything to anyone, I didn't speak over the telephone at all. It's a lie.

BOLDYREV. Komyagin told you twice that the track is to be torn up in the morning, and you replied each time that the track was not going to be torn up. (*To* KOMYAGIN.) Isn't that true?

KOMYAGIN. It's true.

KASTORKIN (*bewildered*). I told you twice?

196

KOMYAGIN. You did.

BOLDYREV. Then Komyagin switched the cars onto eight.

KASTORKIN. Onto eight?

BOLDYREV. Yes, track eight. Fortunately he 'phoned first to Maksim. He told him that he was carrying out the orders because they were given to him by his chief. Had Komyagin not done this, what would have happened to our program? Kastorkin, we understand each other. Now you may go home and make your own deductions.

KASTORKIN. Don't chase me away, Stepan Semionich. Why are you sending me to the G.P.U.? I implore you, don't give me up. Take pity on me, I have a mother, an old woman. She'll die, she won't believe anyone. Gruzdev, speak up for me. Why are you silent? How can you turn against one who is being slandered? It's all lies, lies.

MAKSIMKA. Go along, Comrade Kastorkin. Why fuss? They will look into everything.

KASTORKIN. You want to send me to the G.P.U. I won't go. I'm a free Soviet citizen. I have two commendations for my work. My God, my God! I worked day and night to organize the transport, introduced iron discipline... yes. I was envied, I was considered a fool for working so hard. Stepan Semionich, is it possible that you don't appreciate me? This is a judicial mistake! Please, Stepan Semionich, have pity on me, try to understand...

BOLDYREV. Comrade Kastorkin, leave immediately.

KASTORKIN. All right... where is my cap? Very well, I'll go. Good night. (*Goes.*)

MAKSIMKA. A pitiful creature.

BOLDYREV. What do you think of this, Gruzdev?

GRUZDEV. I'm a technician, not a prosecutor.

BOLDYREV. Are you alive to the responsibility of the work entrusted to you?

GRUZDEV. I have been for eleven years.

BOLDYREV. Then, what would you have done in a case like this?

GRUZDEV. Precisely as you did.

BOLDYREV. Then, I'm right.

GRUZDEV. Not at all.

BOLDYREV. That's sophistry.

GRUZDEV. Even though I would have acted as you did, I would not have considered myself right until...

BOLDYREV. I understand.

GRUZDEV. Secondly, I would not have been so sharp with the lad.

BOLDYREV. You're right. Lagutin believes one should not be too hasty. All right, let's go home. Excuse me for dragging you out at this hour.

LAGUTIN (*to* BOLDYREV). Don't forget the Bureau meeting at eight.

BOLDYREV. All right.

GRUZDEV. Stepan Semionich, drink a large glass of vodka, you will sleep better. And in the morning have some tea. That will give you the wisdom of Solomon and the courage of Alexander of Macedonia. Your eyes are like projectors.

BOLDYREV. My eyes hurt. Good-bye.

(LAGUTIN *and* GRUZDEV *depart*.)

MAKSIMKA (*singing*).

> You're but sixteen,
> Tripping your way,
> Seeking your share of romance;
> While I feel so old,
> Feeble and cold,
> Hardly in tune with your dance.

BOLDYREV. How can you be so gay, Maksim?

MAKSIMKA. There's nothing to be tragic about, Comrade Director.

BOLDYREV. Maksim, my nerves are giving out. They're shattered... I feel unpleasant about this case. There's something strange about it... Maybe it's just hooliganism... maybe Kastorkin is not guilty.

MAKSIMKA. I don't see why you have to go into all this psychology.

BOLDYREV. All right, do as you think best. By the way... you come along to our place... I mean to my place...

MAKSIMKA (*stares at* BOLDYREV; *suddenly breaks into laughter*). Stepan Semionich... I forgot completely. You made a terrible mistake. Throughout the universe this night not a single soul has died. (*Happily, dancing around* BOLDYREV.) Valka is alive! Valka is alive, and she and I... but this is no concern of yours...

CURTAIN

ACT III

SCENE 7

The same construction site as in the opening scene, but with new wall sectors showing and other evidences of progress on the job. All the workers, engineers, and officials are gathering for a production meeting. The Chairman and Secretary of the Production Commission are already on an improvised platform to the left and other officials — BOLDYREV, LAGUTIN, foremen—are disposing themselves at a table on the platform.

The curtain rises on sounds of laughter and loud talk. The workers are in excellent spirits. A group of construction workers enters in the foreground, one of them, GRISCHUK, reading a newspaper.

GRISCHUK (*reads haltingly*). Dis... sen... sion... is drowned...

TEMIN. How they write, those devils! Why should they write about dysentery?

GRISCHUK. Dysentery? No, it isn't dysentery. Just dis... sension... that's something entirely different...

DUDYKIN. All right, read on.

WORKER IN PINK SHIRT. But leave out them big words that don't mean nothing.

GRISCHUK (*reads*). Dis... sen... sion is drowned in the... tide of ... Socialism.

TEMIN (*insistent*). Sure, they're writing about dysentery. See, they say tide... the river... you should always go to the river when you...

GRISCHUK. You shouldn't be listening to newspapers, you should be cleaning boots. It says disten... I mean dissension here, do you understand?

DUDYKIN (*admiringly*). Anyone can tell that was written by some educated bastard — you can't understand what it says.

TEMIN. There's nothing to understand.

GRISCHUK. What an idiot you are! It says dissension, dissension. Is that a head on your shoulders or a cabbage?

DUDYKIN. If a man says dissension, it's dissension, and don't you be conerdictin'. Read on, Grischuk, read on.

GRISCHUK (*reads*). Dis... sension is drowned in the tide of Socialism...

TEMIN. Some new ideas they have these days. Dysentery and Socialism!

DUDYKIN. Shut up, you devil!

TEMIN. Imagine, mixing that with Socialist competition... Dysentery!

GRISCHUK. Will someone tell this fool what I mean... Dissension, do you hear?

WORKER IN PINK SHIRT. Say, brothers, what is this dis... sension?

DUDYKIN. Just some big word. Doesn't matter.

WORKER IN PINK SHIRT. What does it mean?

DUDYKIN. How should I know? Am I a bookkeeper or professor or something?

TEMIN. There is no such word in our language.

GRISCHUK. How do you know? Do you read words, perhaps?

(KRALICHKIN *and other metal workers enter. They are city-bred, a little farther from the village than the ordinary construction hands.*)

WORKER IN PINK SHIRT. Comrade Kralichkin, you're a Communist, you understand all kinds of words.

GRISCHUK. That's right. You tell us. (*Points to the passage in the paper.*) Are they writing here about dysentery or not?

KRALICHKIN. Where?

TEMIN. Dysentery and dissension is the same word, but Grischuk is putting on airs.

DUDYKIN. Will you shut up! What a leech!

KRALICHKIN (*reading*). Dissension is drowned in the tide of Socialism. Well, what's wrong? Dissension, of course... that's clear.

WORKER IN PINK SHIRT. What sense is there to the word? What is it used for?

KRALICHKIN. Wait a minute. (*Laughs.*) How funny, these fellows don't understand the meaning of the word dissension. Dissension is ... I'll explain it to you right away. How shall I put it? It shakes you...

TEMIN (*triumphantly*). There you are, I told you.

DUDYKIN. Something like a bucking donkey?

KRALICHKIN. No, what do you mean, donkey? It's rather more like when you... (*Greatly relieved as he notices* GRUZDEV *approaching.*)

200

Comrade Gruzdev, you come here and explain the word dissension. We are rotten professors.

DUDYKIN. Let's hear you, comrade engineer.

GRUZDEV. Dissension is an enemy of the workers. Here you are, happy, working, building your own plant. Should anyone come here and sow seeds of dissension, all this wonderful work of yours would be endangered.

DUDYKIN. I see. When one scratches himself instead of working, that's dissension...

KRALICHKIN. Dissension is fighting among ourselves instead of building.

GRISCHUK. Dissension, is that the word I was reading?

TEMIN (*sneeringly*). What a reader, mumbles and mumbles until it sounds like dysentery.

WORKER IN PINK SHIRT. Makes no sense, anyway, just a big word.

DUDYKIN. And you, you poor flounder, how many times has the brigade told you not to scratch so much? You can't even be moved by dissension.

GRISCHUK (*reading*). Dissen... sion is drowned... in the tide of Socialism.

TEMIN. Now everything is clear.   (*Chairman rings for order.*)

VOICES. It's about time. Why all this delay?

MIKHALKA. Don't keep the working class waiting.

ZOTOV. Eh, Mikhalka, shut up!

CHAIRMAN (*sounds bell again*). Order, please. We shall now continue with our meeting. (DUDYKIN *clambers to the platform.*) The next speaker is... (*Laughter.*) The next speaker is... (*Looks around.*)

VOICES. There's an orationer of the first water. Let 'er go, uncle.

CHAIRMAN (*to* DUDYKIN). Speak, comrade.

VOICES. On with the speech! Don't forget to clear your throat!

DUDYKIN. You stop laughing. Go ask the Americanetz, he'll tell you that if one scratches in his country, he's fined a ruble, but here with us...

WORKER IN PINK SHIRT. You must have just returned from America, your face looks salty. (*Laughter.*)

DUDYKIN. You, Fetiska, shut your mouth, or I'll tell about you in front of the comrades. He laughs at me, but he's always losing his pants. And he calls himself a proletariat.

WOMAN WORKER. That's telling him, uncle, that's telling him.

DUDYKIN. You old hayseed, if you can't take care of your pants, what kind of a citizen are you for the Soviet State? And why am I saying this? I see that times are different now. One has to be on the lookout or he'll break his neck. And you go losing your pants, you fool. That's what I mean when I say that you are uncultured.

WORKER IN PINK SHIRT. You're a crocodile yourself.

DUDYKIN. Comrade Secretary, put down in the 'greement that we masons will beat all the other brigades. We can beat them. (*General commotion.*) That's my opinion. I'll be the first in the brigade to see to it. Socialist competition! We were told that if we want to we can finish the stonework before the cold weather sets in, if not we can let the beams rust in the winter-time. What sort of a proprietor would permit such shame? We need brigades of fighting fellows. I'll put my name down. Kondrat will go too.

VOICE. I'll go.

DUDYKIN. Likhomanov, Ignashka, will you sign up?

VOICE. I'll sign up.

DUDYKIN. The brothers Grazev will go, my kin will go. And even that Fetiska, who loses his pants — he'll go.

WORKER IN PINK SHIRT. Sure I'll go. Do you think that you're the only Jack of Clubs here?

THIRD WOMAN (*jumps up*). The production meeting of the brick factory...

FIRST WOMAN. You wait a minute.

THIRD WOMAN. The production meeting...

FIRST WOMAN. What a hothead you are... (*Forces her to sit down.*)

DUDYKIN. You, comrade, with the pen there, put down the entire brigade of masons. Don't scratch, write. Since we are all here, I'm going to say in this respect, long live the Piatiletka! (*Retires in confusion, but satisfied with himself.*)

CHAIRMAN. The next speaker is a representative of the Komsomol, Comrade Valentina Boldyreva.

(VALKA *appears on platform.*)

LAPTEV (*to* MIKHALKA). There she is.

MIKHALKA. It's her.

LAPTEV. Her, as I live! That one!

MIKHALKA. Are you in love with her, or something?

LAPTEV. Comrade Chairman, let me speak.

CHAIRMAN. When your turn comes, I'll let you speak.

LAPTEV. But I'll forget by then. Have mercy, I swear to God I'll forget.

KITCHEN MAID. I want to speak too.

MIKHALKA (*to the* KITCHEN MAID). What are you jumping around for?

KITCHEN MAID (*shouting*). Let me speak.

CHAIRMAN. Comrades, we can't upset the program.

LAPTEV. What's there to upset? I want to say a few words from my soul. Don't stop me.

BOLDYREV. Let him have the floor.

CHAIRMAN. You will have to come up here.

ARTAMON. The world has come to an end. Yermolay is doing speech-making.

LAPTEV. The lady that was here... it's about her I want to say a word. Yes, we shamed her, there is no denying it. I'm the first to blame. She comes to me and, without much ado, orders me: 'Take off your drawers...' (*Laughter.*)

CHAIRMAN. Comrade, we are discussing the Socialist competition agreement.

LAPTEV. That's what I'm talking about, and don't you be shoving me off the track, it's hard enough to remember. So she says to me, 'Take off your drawers...' I started running from her like she was a plague.

MIKHALKA. There you go chattering like a Turk.

LAPTEV. You better keep still, you're the one who wanted to beat her up. I'm speaking from my soul. I just waited for a time like this... She's a girl of the first sort... She came to us simple folks and saved us, and we were ready to smash her head... We are ashamed of ourselves. She is good, she worked night and day in our barracks until she caught it herself. We ought to carry her on our hands. I will always remember. And you sheep's head mewing there... Now you've got me all mixed up... What is it I wanted to say... how shall I put it? We must love the comrades who are among us. They are good people, yes... yes. (*To the* CHAIRMAN.) You've got me all mixed up... I'll go for those tempos. I'll sign the 'greement, even though I'm illiterate. I'll put a cross there, and the very first cross there will be me, Yermolay Laptev.

CHAIRMAN. The next speaker will be Kralichkin, a riveter.

THIRD WOMAN. Be fair! Why don't you let the women talk?

WORKER IN PINK SHIRT. It's no use opposing the like of you.

THIRD WOMAN. Go chase the flies off your nose.

SECOND WOMAN. Hold your tongue, Leda.

WORKER IN PINK SHIRT. Leda? That's not Leda, that's a devil.

KITCHEN MAID. I, too, want to speak.

MIKHALKA. Sit down.

KITCHEN MAID. I protest.

ARTAMON. Who let her in here?

KRALICHKIN. We riveters challenged the masons and carpenters to Socialist competition because we feel that our tempos must be increased further. They must be doubled. I know you have worked hard as the Devil, you have reached an unusual pace. But how about us? When I came, I saw there was work for six months for us, but the Americanetz said it must be done in ninety-five days. How was it possible? But Boldyrev told us: 'Boys, the construction of the plant is in your hands.' We each understand that the responsibility rested on us. After all, we are the bosses of our own country, and this is our plant. We accepted the Five-Year Plan, and we are building it with our own hands. Socialism won't drop on us from Heaven. No one is going to help us. These ninety-five days are a political matter, it is our challenge, and our blow at all our enemies. We are considered backward, they sneer at us and try to convince us that we cannot surpass the leading capitalist countries. You lie, you snakes! We were given ninety-five days, but we did it in eighty! The framework is up. There it is. Such tempos are unknown even in America. We worked hard, that's true, but we are strong and determined. We made a decision yesterday that in the event that we failed to maintain the control dates on our work, we will work not eight hours, but ten or twelve. If a capitalist compelled us to work a half-hour overtime, we would strike, but here we will work twelve hours. It isn't easy to work twelve hours. I, as a riveter, know what it means. After ten hours my feet give in, I can hardly get to my bunk, can't even look at the grub. It seems as if I haven't slept for a year. We worked like that for eighty-two days, and the Devil didn't take us. Our plant, our proletarian pride, our fort will be erected in a year and a half. Then let them tell us we cannot catch up with the capitalist countries. That's why we riveters and steel workers challenge you, comrades carpenters and stoneworkers, to a Socialist competition. Do you want to come with us or not? We put the question directly: Will you sign the agreement or do you refuse? Answer our question in simple language as workers to workers. No use beating around the bush. I'm finished. (*Applause.*)

THIRD WOMAN. Comrades, we women brickmakers... the Production Committee. How do we mix clay? We wet the clay...

MIKHALKA. There she goes wetting again.

WORKER IN PINK SHIRT. Move her away from here or she'll be wetting us all.

FIRST WOMAN. Hooligan, don't talk like that!

THIRD WOMAN. We did wet the clay and we...

SUMATOKHINOV. Talk up like a man.

ARTAMON. So help me God, these women should be chased out; who let them in here?

BOLDYREV. Your name is Leda, isn't it? Now you wait, Leda. (*Turning to the assembly.*) There is nothing to laugh about. We understand you, Leda. I express my deep admiration for the women workers of our brick factory who are present, for their class-consciousness and commendable attitude towards production. They are doing good work. You workers here should all thank them for it. Hurrah for the women brickworkers!

(*The workers slowly follow* BOLDYREV *and the præsidium, and break into applause.*)

BOLDYREV. Speak, Leda.

THIRD WOMAN (*to* FIRST WOMAN). You speak.

FIRST WOMAN (*to* SECOND WOMAN). You ought to speak.

SECOND WOMAN (*to* THIRD WOMAN). You started, why don't you finish?

LAPTEV. Look at them, they will all be crying yet.

DUDYKIN. Hey, you beauties.

CHAIRMAN (*to* LEDA). Comrade, go on with your speech.

THIRD WOMAN. Well... we, of course... (*Suddenly very firmly.*) A tempo is a tempo! But such... (*A gesture of energy.*) Such tempo... (*Sheepishly.*) But what can I teach you? You devils know it already. (*Embarrassed by laughter.*) That's all, if I go on, I'll only get mixed up. (*Sits down.*)

CHAIRMAN. Engineer Gruzdev has the floor.

GONCHAROV (*to* INTERPRETER). Evgenia Eduardovna, what is Mr. Carter's impression? Has he ever seen anything like this before?

CARTER (*to* GONCHAROV). The meeting is unusual, characteristic, I should say, of the present spirit in Russia. It is fascinating. (*To* INTERPRETER.) Don't let me miss anything.

GRUZDEV. I just want to say a few words. It seems to me that you fellows forgot to say the most important thing. You talk about tempo, but what tempo is, many of you don't know. Listen to me. (*Pulls out a sheet of paper.*) Our normal average Russian tempo in stonework may be fixed at sixty. That's how we always worked. The chief engineer's office considers it possible to increase the tempo to eighty. Do you understand?

VOICES. That's clear.

GRUZDEV. German specialists, having studied our conditions, set the figure at one hundred.

VOICES. A hundred...

GRUZDEV. And finally, Mr. Carter calls for the American tempo, which means a hundred and twenty. This, fellows, is the official statement, but... I must inform you that only if we work according to American tempos, that is, if we raise it to a hundred and twenty, only that way can we finish the work before the cold weather sets in. If we don't, we are lost. Do you understand? Now a word unofficially. If you ask me whether I personally agree with Carter, I'll tell you: yes, I agree. I know all of you. I have lived with your kind, thank God, for some twenty-odd years. It's up to you. Decide. Eighty, a hundred, or a hundred and twenty.

(*Silence.* GRUZDEV *slowly descends from the platform.*)

CHAIRMAN. Comrade Zotov, a stoneworker, has the floor.

ZOTOV. In my opinion, it shouldn't be sixty, it shouldn't be eighty, it shouldn't be a hundred and twenty, but a hundred and fifty. Is that plain? (*Pause.*) A hundred and fifty! We challenge Mr. Carter to a Socialist competition. I don't know about the rest of you, but as far as section two is concerned it's decided. It's a hundred and fifty and we stand by it. We'll show them how Soviet masons work.

(MIKHALKA *hurriedly ascends the platform.*)

MIKHALKA. Comrades...

ARTAMON. There's the yearling again...

MIKHALKA. Comrades, I'm not joking. What differences can there be among us when we are all one family?... Why meetings, a hundred and fifty? I take it upon me. No use talking too much.

ZOTOV. H'm... he didn't let me speak and he is all mixed up himself.

CHAIRMAN (*to* MIKHALKA). Are you through, comrade?

MIKHALKA. I? Yes, I guess so.

ARTAMON. He's all heated up and snorting, doesn't know if he is through or not.

CHAIRMAN. Our next speaker is a representative of the engineering-technical personnel.

ARTAMON. Who wants him? There is nothing in the agreement about the engineers. They didn't challenge us, and they can't teach us.

CHAIRMAN. Comrades, no one is trying to teach us, but we must enlist...

ARTAMON. Stop starting things. We don't want to hear no engineers. It's their business to give us work and see to it that the people have enough work... We've had men waiting half-days for work.

SUMATOKHINOV. Comrade Chairman, now don't mix us up. Wait ... let me say a word. This is our own affair, among us workers. Why drag the chiefs in?

ARTAMON. Let the comrades engineers and technicians sign agreements among themselves.

KRALICHKIN. Comrade Chairman, one word. Comrades, it's unimportant whether the floor is given to a representative of the engineering-technical personnel or not. What matters is that the engineers should join the workers on the Socialist competition. They can do that without any speeches. We don't drive anyone away, but neither are we going to beg anyone. I am saying this frankly and sincerely. Who is with us will receive our hearty co-operation, but whoever opposes us will learn to respect proletarian enthusiasm. That is all.

VOICES. True and to the point.

LAPTEV. Comrade, you put it well... those who are against us... (*Threatens with a clenched fist.*) Those who are with us, welcome.

KITCHEN MAID. We kitchen maids... we too... we'll feed them...

ARTAMON. Shut up, you maw. Can't you see it's an affair of state we're deciding here? Sit down. (*Forces her down.*)

CHAIRMAN. I'll put it to a vote. Who is in favor that the discussion be closed? (*Counts.*) The majority. Fine. Now, who is in favor of the immediate signing of the agreement? And, first of all, who is for accepting the tempo as proposed by the stoneworker, Zotov, of the second section? Who is for the tempo of a hundred and fifty?

GONCHAROV (*ironically*). Danilo Danilovich, are we for an index of a hundred and fifty?

Danilo Danilovich. Absolutely.

Goncharov. They have put it through without any discussion.

Danilo Danilovich. What is there for us to discuss?

Goncharov. Nothing. We should just keep still and raise our hands, I suppose.

Chairman. Who is against it?

Danilo Danilovich. You ought to get a vacation, Goncharov, and go to the seashore.

Goncharov. I'm no longer needed, I'm beginning to see it.

Chairman. Anyone abstaining? (*Pause.*) Adopted unanimously. (*To the* Secretary.) Sasha, read the list.

Secretary. Will the representatives of the building-trades workers please come here to sign the contract: Comrades Zotov, Dudykin, Grischuk, Govorov, and Sumatokhinov. And the following workers representing the riveters, and the other metal trades: Comrades Kralichkin, Zutov, Tulsky. Will you all come up here and sign the agreement?

Kalugin (*to* Gruzdev). So far everything is very business-like. We'll see how they make out later on. The figure they set is terrific.

(*The workers named crowd on the platform, ready to sign the agreement.*)

Gruzdev. How did you like the metal workers? What lads... there's drive in them.

Kalugin. You and your metal workers... I know them... they're daring bastards. Real progeny of Communists.

(Carter *pulls out notebook and writes busily.*)

Danilo Danilovich (*to the* Interpreter). We suggest that Mr. Carter apply this experience in America. It isn't always that Americans will teach us. Our turn will come to teach them.

Carter. This is a new experience to me. If it were not for politics, I would join in the business end of this meeting myself.

Mikhalka. Sumatokhinov is here. Hey, Sumatokhinov, put your name down first.

Voices. Take your hat off, Govorov, you're on the tribunal... oh, brother, what have we started? We're challenging America... a hundred and fifty.

Chairman. The metal workers are to sign the agreement first.

Artamon. By what authority do they sign first?

Chairman. The metal workers were the first to throw the challenge.

KRALICHKIN. That's not important. Sign it up, fellows.

SUMATOKHINOV. Zotov, let's see you begin.

ZOTOV. Oh, well, what the hell. (*Signs.*) There, Zotov, Anisim, son of Petrov.

MIKHALKA. Who cares whose son you are? Write down your name, and don't forget your nickname.

ZOTOV (*to* SUMATOKHINOV). Now put yourself down.

(SUMATOKHINOV *drops to his knees and edges over to the table.*)

ARTAMON. Hey, you're not breaking into prayer, are you?

SUMATOKHINOV. And what if I can't write on my feet?

MIKHALKA. You don't have to write with your feet, write with your hands.

SUMATOKHINOV. All right, here I go... what a terrible pen! (*Scrawls.*) Su-ma-tokhi-nov, La-vren-ty.

MIKHALKA. Otherwise known as 'Red-Nose.'

GRISCHUK. The brazen fool, to poke fun on such an occasion... (*Removes hat, solemnly, and signs.*)

SECRETARY. Next.

DUDYKIN. Let me do it. (*Signs.*) Dudykin. Anything else?

SECRETARY. That's all. Next: Govorov.

GOVOROV. The fifth section is signing up for a hundred and fifty. Don't let me down, comrades.

VOICES. It's all right, we won't let you down.

(*Metal workers sign up quietly. All delegates remain on the platform.*)

(*Enter* MAKSIMKA.)

MAKSIMKA. Order, comrades. A red light is going to be raised to the tower on the left side of the Volga. Do you know what that means? As soon as the red light appears there, it will be a signal to us that we have surpassed the American tempo. Watch the left tower, comrades. A red signal from the tower means our victory.

LAGUTIN (*jumping to his feet*). In the name of the Communist Party Committee of the plant, I congratulate you, comrades, with the beginning of an important revolutionary deed. The proletarian agreement is signed. Here on this sector of socialist construction burns the flame of Leninist ideas. Leninism lives and guides us in our work! Long live Leninism!

CURTAIN

ACT IV

SCENE 8

The porch of GONCHAROV'S *house, as in Scene 4, with a corner of the study visible through the window. It is early evening.* GRUZDEV *is on the porch when the curtain rises.*

GRUZDEV (*looking offstage intently*). Who is that?... impossible... as I live, Kastorkin!

(KASTORKIN *enters, unshaven, shabby.*)

KASTORKIN. I suppose you thought Kastorkin was through.

GRUZDEV. Why do you suppose that?

KASTORKIN. Well, you didn't make any attempt to help Kastorkin that evening in Boldyrev's office, if I recall correctly. You were quite ready to accept as a fact that Kastorkin was a scoundrel. Really, Gruzdev, is it possible that you thought I gave those orders over the telephone? You see there was no trial. I have just been released and now I am back working on the construction. Boldyrev and the authorities are sparing Goncharov. Everything is known, now. It was Goncharov who disguised his voice and issued instructions to Komyagin. Our Mister Goncharov underestimated the efficiency of the G.P.U. He slandered me. You should have heard him testify at the investigation: 'I believe it was Kastorkin who spoke over the telephone'... The dirty dog!

GRUZDEV. That's the way it is, Kastorkin...

KASTORKIN. This is the kind of people we have among our engineers these days.

GRUZDEV. Scoundrels.

KASTORKIN. Goncharov is of aristocratic origin. He received his education abroad. He looked down upon us. He thought he could lay down the law to the entire engineering staff.

GRUZDEV. See here, Kastorkin, you go home and rest a while.

KASTORKIN. I've rested enough.

GRUZDEV. Come, my friend... don't be offended... you go home ... we'll go to him.

KASTORKIN. I'll go... the old woman is waiting... poor mother ... but I want to speak to him myself.

GRUZDEV. You'll still have a chance to talk to him, that's your own affair.

KASTORKIN. I'll present my note to him... Good-bye, Comrade Gruzdev.

GRUZDEV. Good day, Kastorkin. (KASTORKIN *leaves*.) (*His tone changes*.) He's bitter.

(*Enter* TATIANA LVOVNA, *arm in arm with* GONCHAROV, *followed by* DANILO DANILOVICH *and* KALUGIN.)

TATIANA LVOVNA. Do you recall, Uri Nikolayevich, the song of our unfortunate friend, Kastorkin? (*Sings*.)

> Come visit me alone tomorrow,
> Let me repose upon your breast,
> Your eyes are happiness and sorrow
> Your lips a-thrill at love's behest.

(*Laughs*.) Gruzdev, why is your face so Napoleonic? Let me cheer you up. We've just been discussing ghosts. (*Laughs*.) Do ghosts exist? On our way here Simion Simionovich happened to see a real ghost. He saw an eery, black ghost. (*Laughs*.) A most dismal black ghost, and do you know what Simochka said? He says that he has military eyes and that with his military eyes he recognized in the black ghost, Kastorkin. (*Laughs*.) He doesn't know that poor Kastorkin is up North or in Siberia. That's true, Uri Nikolayevich, isn't it? Oh, Simochka, admit that you are getting old and your eyes are failing you.

GRUZDEV. There is no doubt that your Simochka is getting old, but his eyes are truly military. There are no ghosts. That was Kastorkin in the flesh.

DANILO DANILOVICH. We are joking... it was just a play of the imagination.

GRUZDEV. You'll soon find out whether it was a play of your imagination... Take care, Danilo Danilovich, or you may be imagining yourself in the North or Siberia.

DANILO DANILOVICH. What do you mean?

GRUZDEV. I am merely explaining that when our mutual friend plans a little fight, he is wont to send his recruits out ahead. I am referring to you, Comrade Goncharov.

TATIANA LVOVNA. There you go arguing political economy again.

GONCHAROV. Recruits? What sort of allegory is this?

GRUZDEV (*suddenly angry*). It was foul play, Goncharov. Simion

Simionovich served in the Guards. He can tell us how, in accordance with the traditions of the nobility, an army man was treated who made his colleagues answer for his own misdeeds. It was not Kastorkin who telephoned that day from your office. It was you, Goncharov.

GONCHAROV. That's a lie... a contemptible lie!

GRUZDEV. You better explain that to Kastorkin himself; he was just here...

TATIANA LVOVNA (*pulling her hand away from* GONCHAROV's). Well, what do you say to that?

GRUZDEV. Instead of Kastorkin, you might have slandered me... (*indicating* DANILO DANILOVICH) or him.

DANILO DANILOVICH. Come, now, let's stop this talk, there's nothing in it. It will be straightened out... trifles, trifles.

GRUZDEV. No, Danilo Danilovich, it's not a trifle. An engineer slandered his colleague. When petty, cowardly people drag honest, innocent workers into crimes, it's not a trifle. I'm glad I found you out. (*Departs.*)

TATIANA LVOVNA. Simochka, where are you going?

KALUGIN. For some cigarettes, my dear. (*Also departs.*)

DANILO DANILOVICH. Oh, I'd forgotten, the boat is waiting, won't you all come with me? (*Pause.*) You can't... well... (*Leaves.*)

TATIANA LVOVNA (*in tears*). You, you might have named my husband, you —— (*Leaves.*)

GONCHAROV. Terrible, terrible.

(*A* DRUNKARD *enters, singing lustily.*)

DRUNKARD.

> A pretty maiden on the shore
> Embroidering her silken shawl.
> Her work is delicate in stitch,
> But, ah, the piece is much too small.
>
> A huge white sail looms from afar,
> A boat is making for the shore,
> The pretty maiden sits and sews,
> But, ah, the piece is much too small.

(*To* GONCHAROV.) Here I am looking at you. You seem so pensive. Can't make out whether you are dark or fair. Listen, citizen, now don't get offended, please, I have a big heart. Imagine, I come home for a vacation, after a long absence, and can't recognize my native city. It used to be a wide, steppe-like stretch, a grey, unimaginative landscape. By nature, I am a non-partisan, but under the influence of this grandiose change I am becoming a Marxian. Why, look, this isn't a plant, it is a gigantic transformation. Sure, I know I'm drunk, and you loathe me, but I am moved with all the fibres of my noble soul, I am deeply affected. (*Pause.*) If you want me to, I'll be as quiet as a clam. I suppose it's all the same to you, but to Sergei Tishkin who was raised here as a child, it's not the same. And if he were a Balmont, or a Vladimir Mayakovsky, he would create a poem out of life... Literature, you know, is the inspiration of the heart. For all you know, I might have just been kissing the soil here, like a pilgrim, and there you stand laughing at me. People always laugh at drunkards, but drunkards penetrate into the abyss of the emotions. What a sober man has in his mind, a drunkard has on his tongue... I'm beginning to think that you are a hard person. You have a self-complacency in your face... I'm not going to talk to you any more. Ha, ha, ha... Sergei Tishkin, a fakir? Sergei Tishkin is a psychologist. (*Sings.*)

> I'm lonesome, I'm weary,
> All my hopes are gone...

(*Exits.*)

GONCHAROV. What is it I wanted to do? There was something I intended to do. (*Rises. Reaches for the telephone through the window and removes the receiver.*) That's better.

(*Enter* BOLDYREV.)

BOLDYREV. Are you alone?

GONCHAROV. Sit down, Stepan Semionich. I just came in, and I'm rather lonesome. (*Removes his hat and coat.*)

BOLDYREV. There is no one here with you?

GONCHAROV. No. Who could there be?

BOLDYREV. Very well. There is something I want to say to you.

GONCHAROV. Yes, I understand... you want to talk to me.

BOLDYREV. First of all, Comrade Goncharov, I believe that you ought to resign at once.

GONCHAROV. I will submit my resignation immediately.

BOLDYREV. Well, this is essentially all I want to say to you now. (*Looks at him for a long moment and leaves abruptly.*)

GONCHAROV. He didn't shake hands. They are all spitting into my face. What a change! Can one speak of the zenith of the abyss?

... Nonsense, I must be getting... where are my cigars?... I had some good strong ones.

(*Walks into the house. At the same time* KASTORKIN *enters dressed as before his arrest. He is again in high spirits, slightly intoxicated and strumming the guitar.*)

KASTORKIN (*sings*).

> Tonight I want to sing and dance —
> Play, little gypsy, play —
> Tonight's the night for real romance —
> Play, little gypsy, play...

Merely calling to visit an old friend. (*Sings.*)

> The moon is high,
> Your lips are ruby...

It's three months since I saw my friend... It's so nice to see a friend after such a long, sad separation. (*Sings.*) 'Hallelujah, hallelujah, oh, hallelujah.' Damn it, that is certainly a gay foxtrot... 'Hallelujah, hallelujah'... Uri Nikolayevich, are you home?

GONCHAROV (*speaking from his study*). Sit down, Kastorkin, I'm home.

KASTORKIN. Thanks for the hospitality... 'Hallelujah, oh, hallelujah.' Why is the receiver down?... I can't hear you. 'Hallelujah, oh, hallelujah.' I suppose telephone calls annoy you?

GONCHAROV. Yes.

KASTORKIN. 'Hallelujah, oh, hallelujah'... Excuse me, Uri Nikolayevich, for singing in your house, but I feel very gay. It's three months since I have spoken over a telephone... since the time when right here at this table you spoke over the telephone impersonating Engineer Kastorkin... Do you recall, Uri Nikolayevich?

GONCHAROV. I remember, Kastorkin.

KASTORKIN. You're not denying it, Uri Nikolayevich?

GONCHAROV. I'm not denying it, Kastorkin.

KASTORKIN. 'Hallelujah, oh, hallelujah'... Don't you think my voice is changed somewhat? Still, one can recognize my voice, don't you think? You, too, can be recognized by your voice... Goncharov... yet you forgot all about the telephone operator! The dark-skinned, dark-eyed Komsomol girl at the switchboard... dark-skinned, dark-eyed... (*Sings.*) 'Ochi, chornye'... But we, Goncharov, thought of her. I feel very gay... why are you hiding like a rat? Come, let's sing together. I want to go on with the party that was interrupted three months ago. Goncharov, after all, it's impolite. An honest, simple fellow invites you to join in his festivity. (*Plays the guitar, dances.*) And you are hiding, aren't you ashamed? Is it possible you are afraid, Goncharov? Afraid? Come, my philosopher, I would like to talk to you, talk to you about our tempos, or about my locomotives... that is, if you will condescend to talk to me. Come, Engineer Goncharov, show yourself. (*Walks toward door of* GONCHAROV's *room.*) 'Hallelujah, hallelujah'...

(*Stops short at the door, suddenly sobered by what he sees —* GONCHAROV *has killed himself; nervously plucks the strings of his guitar, raises it, thrusts it in front of him as if to shield himself, then rushes out covering his eyes.*)

CURTAIN

ACT IV
SCENE 9

The construction site. By now a huge structure rises to the sky; several men are working on the upper stories. Through the morning mist, in the distance and to the left, a tower can be seen.

BOLDYREV enters, looks around, then sits down on a barrel, absorbed in thought. WORKERS are pushing wheelbarrows. One walks over to the water tank, removes his shirt and splashes water over himself.

THE WORKER. Ekh, it was a clever fellow who invented water. (*Puts on his shirt and walks off.*)

(*The* THREE WOMEN WORKERS *enter, in holiday attire.*)

FIRST WOMAN. It's him... so help me God, it's him sitting there thinking.

THIRD WOMAN. Women, women...

SECOND WOMAN. Let's tell him now...

THIRD WOMAN. But he's thinking... maybe we better not bother him...

SECOND WOMAN. It's all right.

FIRST WOMAN. You, Leda, know how to hypo... tamize men. You have a female face and dark eyes. You go up to him.

THIRD WOMAN. What do you expect me to do, lure him? I'm a quiet woman.

FIRST WOMAN. You tell him in a sweet voice: 'Comrade Boldyrev, you see, it's like this, and then say to him, '*We are still on guard.*' (*Pleased with herself.*) There!

THIRD WOMAN (*to* BOLDYREV, *very softly*). Comrade... Comrade Director... it's us... I, Leda... (*Embarrassed.*) Please excuse us. We delivered the brick on time, and the fire-brick, too. Greetings, Comrade Boldyrev.

BOLDYREV. The brick... yes... where? Oh, it is you, the Production Committee; hello, Leda.

FIRST WOMAN (*to* THIRD WOMAN). Go on. Don't stop.

THIRD WOMAN. We are still on guard, Comrade Director... we — (*almost in tears*) — how we worked!... It still hurts me, here, in my side... and our eyes, blue circles, just as if we were drunk...

FIRST WOMAN. The food... you know yourself — mostly sympathy and not much else.

THIRD WOMAN. It was hard, Comrade Director. Take her or me, you know... The bricks, they were like our children, we felt like patting them with our hands. Poor Leedka, she couldn't sleep nights worrying about them. How she would swear at the engineer... There is class-consciousness in us, but we can't put it in words.

FIRST WOMAN. We've come to say good-bye, Comrade Boldyrev.

BOLDYREV. Where are you all going?

SECOND WOMAN. The program we have over-liquidated — to the very top shelf, Comrade Director, a full hundred per cent.

FIRST WOMAN. And now we are leaving.

BOLDYREV. Where to?

SECOND WOMAN. I'm getting my social insurance and I'll take myself off to the Crimea... it's for my organism.

BOLDYREV. I envy you.

SECOND WOMAN. You too should go... for your organism.

FIRST WOMAN. Yes, you have got seedy, Comrade Boldyrev... no man should get seedy. I'm going to my husband for the winter... my man is in the Red Army. He's returning from there and I am returning from here. I've got that way too... He writes to me in his letters... 'Don't touch me with your bare hand!' (*Giggles.*) That's how I feel too.

BOLDYREV. Well, good-bye, my dears... and you, Leda, are you also going to your husband for the winter?

THIRD WOMAN. Me? (*Laughs.*) I'm not married. I'm going to do some learning. You know the kind of sciences we understand. Well, Director Comrade, there was something we wanted to say to you in parting... we can't find the words for it. Good-bye.

FIRST AND SECOND WOMEN. Good-bye.

BOLDYREV. Good luck.

(*The* WOMEN *leave. A group of* WORKERS, *among them the* KOSTROMA PEASANTS, *approach the Director.*)

MIKHALKA. Stepan Semionich... how did you like that? Three hours' work in one.

SUMATOKHINOV. Tempo, that's what it is, tempo.

(*At the left, rear, near the new wall, a large improvised wooden elevator car is lowered on a cable. In the car are* LAPTEV *and* CARTER.)

MIKHALKA. Brothers, look! Our Yermolay has hired himself as

217

secretary to Carter. (*The elevator suddenly stops and the car remains suspended in the air.*) Little brothers of mine, look at Yermolay floating in the air like a holy spirit.

(*Enter* DANILO DANILOVICH.)

DANILO DANILOVICH. Why do they stop?

MIKHALKA (*to* ZOTOV). We must have gone over two hundred by now.

ZOTOV. Why not five hundred, you fool?... We're still far from it; before we get to a hundred your belly will bust. America is no easy country to beat, brother.

SUMATOKHINOV. The sons-of-bitches must have smashed something... it ought to be stopped.

BOLDYREV. What's the matter? Why did the car stop?

MIKHALKA. Hey, you cherubs, why don't you fly down here?

ZOTOV. You fool, he's a foreigner, and you...

MIKHALKA. What the hell! he can't understand us, anyhow.

ARTAMON. Of course, for all he understands he may take our swearing for compliments.

MIKHALKA. And how thick the two of them got... we ought to take a picture of them... One without a tongue, and the other just stupid.

ZOTOV. The Devil take you, Mikhalka, you're so brazen.

DANILO DANILOVICH (*shouts*). Hello, Mr. Carter, hello.

SUMATOKHINOV (*waving his hand*). Hey, there.

CARTER. Hello!

DANILO DANILOVICH. Hello!

CARTER. Hello!

DANILO DANILOVICH. Mr. Carter... how shall I say it to him? Very well?

BOLDYREV. What are you saying 'very well' to him for? You can see there is something wrong with the cable. Do something about it.

MIKHALKA (*shouting up to* LAPTEV). Hey, Yermolay, say something.

LAPTEV. Stop barking.

MIKHALKA. Hey, you aviator, don't break your head flying from the heavens.

(CARTER *takes out his pipe and fills it calmly.*)

LAPTEV (*to* CARTER). Ahem... give me some tobachko, maybe?

CARTER. How long are you going to keep us up here in the air?

LAPTEV. Nice to smoke up here.

CARTER. Tell those damned fools to get me out of here. What in hell is the trouble?

LAPTEV (*offended*). Not my fault. (*Very politely.*) Meester, some tobachko? Leave me your smoke to finish?

> (CARTER *does not understand him and smiles blankly.*)

MIKHALKA (*to* LAPTEV). No use, old man, he won't give you any.

BOLDYREV. Why are they standing there, Danilo Danilovich? They will hang there all night. What kind of technology is this, anyway?

> (*Enter* KASTORKIN.)

KASTORKIN. Stepan Semionich, the transport is moving on seventeen tracks, just like in the moving pictures. American rationalization, I call it.

BOLDYREV. Just like in America, huh? Well, look up there.

KASTORKIN. Well, well...

BOLDYREV. Disgraceful. I want that car brought down immediately. (*Sits down on a barrel of cement.*)

LAPTEV (*explains in gestures that he wants tobacco and* CARTER *finally understands*). Most grateful to you, esteemed one. Now we are acquainted.

> (DANILO DANILOVICH *and* KASTORKIN *rush to left wing of structure. The* INTERPRETER *arrives.*)

CARTER. Tell them I have no time to spend joy-riding in the air.

INTERPRETER (*to* BOLDYREV). You see the minute I go away, he gets into some trouble... he wants me to tell you he can't waste time up in the air.

BOLDYREV. They will let him down right away.

INTERPRETER. They will pull you down soon.

LAPTEV. Comrade Director, I too ain't got much time to waste... flying like the archangel Michael. I'm getting a pain in my stomach. (*The car is lowered.* BOLDYREV *walks away.*) Say, what did I come down for?... Oh, I remember... Mikhalka, hey, Mikhalka, to what section do the bricks go?

MIKHALKA (*to* DANILO DANILOVICH). To what section shall we cart the bricks?

DANILO DANILOVICH. Section seventeen.

ZOTOV. All right, Yermolay, you look after it, and see that there is no delay... Let's go.

MIKHALKA. That's queer, where is she hanging?

ARTAMON. Who?

MIKHALKA. The electric lamp.

ZOTOV. There, yonder, to the left, see it?

MIKHALKA. The agreement says that as soon as it starts burning, Carter will have to pay for our drinks. (*Exit.*)

(LAPTEV *and* WORKERS *load bricks into elevator until the car is loaded.*)

LAPTEV (*to worker operating elevator*). Now, townsman, let her go, up there. (*The operator presses a button, but the car remains motionless. He shrugs his shoulders helplessly.*) What's the matter with her, is she pregnant? Maybe you ought to grease her, eh? Will she go, or won't she go? (*The operator nods negatively.*) She won't go, she's got tired... (*Stirs suddenly.*) What the hell am I airing myself here for... Mikhalka!... Mikhalka!

MIKHALKA (*from above*). What's wrong?

LAPTEV. Tell them she won't go.

MIKHALKA. Who won't go?

LAPTEV. The damned machine, curses on her! She is sick.

MIKHALKA. Why?

LAPTEV. I don't know why... come down. (*Examines elevator.*) What do you know... a machine won't work.

(BOLDYREV *returns with* LAGUTIN.)

BOLDYREV (*to a foreman*). Have you a report about the concrete work?

FOREMAN. I'll send it to the office right away.

(BOLDYREV, *about to leave, is detained by* DANILO DANILOVICH.)

DANILO DANILOVICH. Stepan Semionich, I'm taking all the men away from here until tomorrow.

BOLDYREV. Where are you taking them to?

DANILO DANILOVICH. The floor work has to be done in the forge shop.

BOLDYREV. All right. (*To* LAPTEV.) Hey, you, little father, are you on sentry duty here?

LAPTEV. She don't go.

BOLDYREV. Who doesn't go?

GRUZDEV. Stepan Semionich, I have something important...

BOLDYREV. Who doesn't go? (*To* GRUZDEV.) What did you say? ... I've got to get over to the stone quarry.

(*Enter* RYBKIN.)

RYBKIN. Comrade Boldyrev, are you here?

BOLDYREV. Here.

RYBKIN. Two Germans and an American have arrived.

BOLDYREV. Rybkin, apologize to the Germans for me and tell them I will see them tomorrow. Ask the American to wait... I must get away from here. Is there anything else?

RYBKIN. Some telegrams.

BOLDYREV. Let me have them... What is it you wanted, Gruzdev? (*Opens telegrams, reads them while listening to* GRUZDEV.)

GRUZDEV. No glass work has been done in unit four... it's a jam ... can't get any glaziers from the Labor Division... it's holding up the installation of the lathes. Imported equipment, being held up for want of glaziers.

BOLDYREV (*reading telegrams*). Let's see... you say no glaziers?

GRUZDEV. The entire unit is completed as far as the equipment is concerned, but the windows are not in.

BOLDYREV. There are no windows? (*To* RYBKIN.) Rybkin, take this telegram: 'TOLOKONTSEV, GLAVMASHINSTROY, MOSCOW: URAL FAILED DELIVER RAILS STOP TAKE MEASURES BOLDYREV.' (*To* GRUZDEV.) Take my car and go to town; pick up the first two glaziers you see in the street. Get them into the car and bring them back. Do you understand?

GRUZDEV. Say, that's an idea...

BOLDYREV. Rybkin, wait a moment... have you got a notebook?

GRUZDEV. Stepan Semionich, one more thing...

BOLDYREV. Wait... (*To* RYBKIN.) 'Kuybishev, V.S.N.Kh., Moscow. Kuybishev...' (*To himself.*) Say, why not Stalin? (*To* RYBKIN.) Let me have your notebook. (*Writes a message.*)

RYBKIN (*takes the paper*). Anything else?

BOLDYREV. Nothing more. (RYBKIN *leaves. Suddenly aware of* LAPTEV *again.*) What sentry work are you doing here, townsman?

LAPTEV. She won't move... has no tempo... this damned air machine... it's balking.

BOLDYREV. It won't go? (*To* GRUZDEV.) Say, Gruzdev, could you take over the Bureau of Rationalization for a while?

GRUZDEV. I don't know.

BOLDYREV. Well, you won't have to ask a fortune-teller, I'm ordering you to. You'll be responsible for it from now on, and what's more, you're also responsible for this... (*Pointing to the elevator.*)... Do you understand? I have no one else.

GRUZDEV. I understand. But I have one more question.

BOLDYREV. When will I get to that stone quarry? Come along and tell me about it.

GRUZDEV (*following him*). The Smith machines... (*They leave.*)

(MIKHALKA, ARTAMON, ZOTOV, *and others enter.*)

MIKHALKA (*to* LAPTEV). Yermolay, are you waiting here to get married?

LAPTEV. She won't budge.

MIKHALKA. Is the car stuck? H'm... There goes our tempo. I suppose we'll have to stay around here and wait.

ZOTOV. You ought to report to the engineer that the bricks are not being moved.

ARTAMON. We have nothing to do with that. That's not our affair.

MIKHALKA. Let's smoke, brothers. (*They sit down.*)

LAPTEV (*to* ZOTOV). Anisim, Anisim, useful you are, honest... signed the agreement, didn't you? Anisim, son of Peter... pledged yourself. Why am I saying this? You signed, you sons-of-bitches... the machine stopped and we... Anisim, do you understand?

ZOTOV (*rises and shows by gestures that the bricks should be carried on their shoulders*). Understand? (*Points to his shoulder.*) Clear? (*Bends down.*) See? (*Gesticulates as if swearing at them.*) Come on! (*Quietly, without a word, the* WORKERS *bring hods and* YERMOLAY *begins to load them with bricks.*) Understand?

(*The* WORKERS *carry off the bricks in feverish haste.*)

DANILO DANILOVICH (*hoarsely, to* DUDYKIN). Are you coming from the chief?

DUDYKIN. Yes.

DANILO DANILOVICH. In reference to the concrete work?

DUDYKIN. Yes.

DANILO DANILOVICH. Is Sumatokhinov there?

DUDYKIN. He was.

DANILO DANILOVICH. Call him.

DUDYKIN. Sumatokhinov.

VOICE FROM ABOVE. Here.

DANILO DANILOVICH. Let's see... (*Studies his notebook.*) Have him wait.

DUDYKIN. Sumatokhinov, wait there.

DANILO DANILOVICH. Ask him whether the third square on the diagonal was cemented yet.

DUDYKIN (*shouting through his hands*). Sumatokhinov, has the third square been cemented yet?

VOICE FROM ABOVE. No.

DUDYKIN. No.

DANILO DANILOVICH. Ask him if the fourth square has been cemented yet?

DUDYKIN. Sumatokhinov, how about the fourth square?

VOICE FROM ABOVE. No.

DUDYKIN. No.

DANILO DANILOVICH. Disgraceful... these fellows must be drunk ... find out about the cementing along the straight horizontal.

DUDYKIN. Sumatokhinov, and the straight horizontal?

VOICE FROM ABOVE. No.

DUDYKIN. No.

DANILO DANILOVICH. Something has got to be done...

DUDYKIN. Comrade engineer, let me ask him. (*Shouts.*) Sumatokhinov, I'm asking you in plain language. Listen with your ears, not with your navel. How much, you lousy son-of-a-bitch, how much cementing has been done?

VOICE FROM ABOVE. The whole damn thing, less half a metre.

DUDYKIN. There, see... They cemented the entire job less half a metre.

DANILO DANILOVICH. What was that?

DUDYKIN. A man is telling you in simple Russian: all the cementing is done except half a metre. (*Goes.*)

DANILO DANILOVICH. Can't understand a thing. (*Goes.*)

(*Enter* BOLDYREV, *flanked by* CARTER *and the* INTERPRETER.)

BOLDYREV. I don't know when I'll ever get to the quarry.

(GRUZDEV *enters and hands several sheets of paper to* CARTER. *The* INTERPRETER *busies herself writing out the translation.* BOLDYREV *makes several attempts to leave, but is detained by others.*)

INTERPRETER. Comrade Director, I believe you should... (*Points to* CARTER.) He must see you... you ought to wait...

BOLDYREV. What is it?

INTERPRETER (*nervously*). He must... (*Writes quickly.*) There, it's finished... (*Hands* CARTER *the papers, the original and the translation.*)

223

BOLDYREV. Well?

CARTER. Ask him to wait for a moment.

(CARTER *reads the paper, compares the figures with those on the original, pulls out his own notes from the back pocket of his trousers... The calm, methodical American loses his austerity. He breaks into laughter, shaking violently. He laughs for a long time, then utters the Russian word 'Svoloch' — scoundrel.*)

BOLDYREV. What does he mean 'svoloch'?

CARTER. Mr. Boldyrev, 'svoloch.' (*Laughs.*)

GRUZDEV. Say, what's the matter with him?

INTERPRETER (*embarrassed*). ... He's heard the men use it so much around here, he thinks it must be a compliment.

CARTER (*signs original, hands it to* BOLDYREV). My heartiest congratulations to everybody. I am far from politics, but I am sure that such a record is outside the reach of any country with a different political organization from yours here. I am happy to inform you that the figures for the last ten days show not one hundred, or a hundred and twenty, or a hundred and fifty, but a hundred and sixty-eight per cent of the program.

BOLDYREV. A hundred and sixty-eight! Fine! Thank you, Mr. Carter.

CARTER. Ochin horosho... (*Pats* BOLDYREV *on the shoulder.*)... Svoloch. (*Departs.*)

(BOLDYREV *is alone in the centre of the stage. The rhythmic sounds of machines rise, scatter, then rise again with increased volume. In the haze of the evening the red signal flashes on top of the tower. There is sudden quiet.* WORKERS *appear from the bays of the structures.*)

BOLDYREV. On one sixth of the globe, in pain and joy, a Socialist world is being born.

CURTAIN

BREAD

A Play in Five Acts and Nine Scenes

By VLADIMIR KIRSHON

Translated from the Russian
By SONIA VOLOCHOVA

INTRODUCTION

THE autumn and winter of 1929–30 remain memorable in Soviet history. It was then that the Kremlin was pushing through its headlong and costly collectivization of agriculture, with the accompaniment of the 'liquidation of the kulaks as a class,' intense class warfare in the villages and the emergence of a new Opposition in the Communist ranks.

Vladimir Kirshon took a personal share in the drive, as a Communist volunteer in the villages. Fresh from the scenes of struggle, he wrote *Bread* in the spring of 1930. The play was consequently as topical as a news report. It was an argument in dramatic form for the Communist Party 'line' on the 'agrarian front,' and an attack on Communists who 'deviated' from that line.

Bread is an almost perfect example of the agitational or propaganda type of Soviet drama. It is a sort of Soviet morality play. Mikhailov is the incarnation of the Party line; Rayevsky is equally the embodiment of political heresy in the ranks; Kvassov is the archtype of villainous kulak or well-to-do peasant. Kirshon's great technical skill as a playwright, however, has turned what is essentially a political editorial into a living human drama.

Born in Leningrad in 1902, Kirshon was only fifteen when the Revolution came. He joined the Communist Youth League and fought on the Caucasian front in the civil wars. By 1920 he was a member of the Communist Party and active in its work, and in the following years he completed a course at the Sverdlov Communist University. From the beginning of his literary career he was therefore among the leading exponents of orthodox Communist tenets in the domain of art. In 1925 he organized first the Rostov and then the North Caucasus Association of Proletarian Writers and later he became one of the guiding spirits of the national organization, the Russian Association of Proletarian Writers (RAPP). At present, RAPP having been dissolved by the Government, he is a member of the Presidium of its successor, the Union of Soviet Writers.

Kirshon's first play, produced in 1926, was written in collaboration with A. Uspensky. It was called *Constantine Terekhin* and won production (under the title *Red Rust*) in the United States, England,

and other countries. His play *The Rails Hum*, in 1928, and *City of Winds*, in 1929, were both staged by the Moscow Theatre of Trade-Unions. The latter play Kirshon subsequently turned into a libretto for the opera *Northwind*, now on the repertory of Nemirovich-Danchenko's Moscow Musical Studio.

Bread was first produced by the Academic Theatre of Drama in Leningrad, in the autumn of 1930, and in the following January was staged by the Moscow Art Theatre. It is still extensively played all over the Soviet Union.

Recently Kirshon won the highest award in a nation-wide contest for the best new play, with a comedy called *Miraculous Alloy*. He has also written a number of motion-picture scenarios and several volumes of literary criticism.

CHARACTERS

MIKHAILOV, DMITRI PETROVICH: Secretary of the Regional Committee of the Communist Party, in his late thirties; a stalwart, level-headed Communist.

OLGA: his wife, a pretty blonde of about twenty-five, chafing under the harsh, small-town existence.

RAYEVSKY, PAVEL: a newly arrived delegate to the Regional Committee, in his early thirties; a true and tried Communist, but with a romantic flare and a hankering for the flesh-pots.

ZHUKOV: Director of the Organizational Section of the Regional Committee.

KONONOV: a worker in the local Communist Party branch.

PEREVOZHNIKOV: editor of the regional newspaper.

LARYONOV: assistant superintendent of roads.

KOSYAKOV: Director of the 'Communkhoz' (Communal Property Department) of the region.

GROMOV: Manager of Public Accounts, a Communist.

LOKTEV: Secretary of the local Communist Party 'cell'; about thirty years old.

ZOTOVA: Secretary of the local Communist Youth League, about eighteen; a vigorous peasant girl whose chief failing is excessive zeal.

DYEDOV, MIKHAIL PAVLOVICH: Chairman of the village Soviet; an old peasant, respected in the village.

ROMANOV, NIKOLAI: a peasant, formerly a member of the Communist Party; between thirty-five and forty; has lost an arm in guerilla fighting during the civil war; hot-tempered and vengeful towards the 'class enemies.'

SOTIN: a landless peasant and an active Communist.

KVASSOV, IVAN GERASIMOVICH: a typical 'kulak' or well-to-do peasant, nearly sixty years old; bitterly anti-Soviet; shrewd and conniving.

PASHA: his daughter, about twenty-two, an attractive, buxom girl.

MIKHAIL: his son, about twenty-four, a chip of the old block.

KOTIKHIN, VASILY AFANASYEVICH:
ZUBOV, PAVEL IVANOVICH: } 'kulaks' or well-to-do peasants.
PROSHKIN, SOFRON KUZMICH:

CHARACTERS

OLKHA, VASILY PAVLOVICH:
KORITKO, IGNAT VASILYEVICH: } less prosperous or 'middle' peasants.
SHILOV, VASILY:

GRUNKIN, NIKANOR SEMIONICH: a poor peasant.

MISHKA AFANASYEV: a member of the Communist Youth League.

MOKRINA: a nun, with a mystical turn of mind and a flaming hatred of the Soviets.

KATERINA: a peasant woman.

DASHA: a girl typist.

Peasants, Men and Women: Communist Youth Boys and Girls

Time: The autumn of 1929.
Place: A grain-growing district of the U.S.S.R.

ACT I

SCENE I

The study at the MIKHAILOVS' *home, a crowded, busy room, its tables strewn with papers and documents and part of the rear wall covered with crude bookshelves. A telephone stands on a small desk in a litter of reports and office paraphernalia. The room conveys a sense of intense activity, in which appearances are sacrificed to speed and accomplishment. In front of the bookshelves is a denim-covered sofa. One door leads to a vestibule and another to the rest of the apartment.*

MIKHAILOV *is engrossed in work at the table. He is a tall, slender man in his late thirties, rough-hewn in feature and negligent in dress. At the moment he is unshaven, tired-looking, and clearly overworked. One of his legs is swathed in bandages. His speech, like his personality, is blunt, without frills. His wife,* OLGA, *is a pretty, buxom blonde of about twenty-five, who obviously takes some pains with her toilette. She is now wearing a deep-red woollen dress, with some effort at style. She is at the shelves, sorting the books and flinging some of them on the sofa.*

MIKHAILOV. Why do you throw the books? Can't you pick them out calmly?

OLGA. I'm sick of being calm.

MIKHAILOV. You're moody again, Olka.

OLGA. Oh, I'm fed up with this petty little town, with its age-old ignorance and its paltry three hundred and eleven street-lamps.

MIKHAILOV. How do you happen to know there are only three hundred and eleven street-lamps here?

OLGA. I read it in your reports.

MIKHAILOV. If you had read to the end, you would have learned that we are adding five hundred and nineteen more within the year.

OLGA (*sighs*). I want to live in a big city.

MIKHAILOV. In five more years we'll have a population of five hundred thousand.

OLGA. I'm just miserably bored, Mikhailov.

MIKHAILOV. That's beyond my comprehension.

OLGA (*sighs again*). Yes, that's beyond your comprehension.

(*The doorbell rings sharply; there is a second's pause.*)

MIKHAILOV (*takes his cane and rises*). I'll open, Olka. It's the engineers.

OLGA. Sit still, please. (*Goes out through the vestibule door.*)

(*Voices behind the scenes.* RAYEVSKY *runs into the room. He is wearing a fashionable European topcoat and a new felt hat and is carrying a calfskin suitcase, which he flings to the side. He grabs* MIKHAILOV, *kisses him, hugs him and slaps him vigorously on the back — all simultaneously.* RAYEVSKY, *a few years younger than* MIKHAILOV, *is more polished and worldly, well-dressed and rather handsome.* OLGA *comes in from the vestibule, a barely perceptible smile on her lips.*)

RAYEVSKY (*joyously*). Mitka!

MIKHAILOV (*equally pleased*). The Devil! Always unexpected. Let me look at you.

(*They inspect each other with genuine pleasure.*)

RAYEVSKY. What's the matter with your leg, Mitka?

MIKHAILOV. It's nothing. I fell out of a droshky. Our Russian roads, you know... Well, so I tumbled out of the droshky. But where did you come from?

RAYEVSKY. I'm to work in your region. Here. (*Takes out and exhibits his documents.*) I spent three years in Germany, Mitka.

MIKHAILOV. So that's it! You're going to work with us? Well, take off your things. But how stupid of me. This, my friend, is Olka. (RAYEVSKY *and* OLGA *shake hands.*) And this, Olka, is Rayevsky, Pavlushka, my commissar in the army.

OLGA. So I gathered.

RAYEVSKY (*to* OLGA). How did you know?

OLGA. Dmitri had told me you were a lunatic.

RAYEVSKY (*playfully grabs his hat and makes a sweeping bow to* MIKHAILOV). Many thanks, Mitya.

(*The telephone rings;* MIKHAILOV *picks up the receiver and listens.*)

OLGA (*to* RAYEVSKY). How long are you from Germany?

MIKHAILOV (*into the receiver*). Yes...

RAYEVSKY. Some three weeks... Mitka has grown very thin, and ne stoops. What a dashing commander he was... the best dancer in the brigade.

MIKHAILOV (*as before*). Yes...

OLGA. He danced!? Were you attached to the embassy?

MIKHAILOV. Yes...

232

RAYEVSKY. No, I was with a research group.

OLGA. Then you're a professor? (*Smiles.*)

MIKHAILOV. Yes...

RAYEVSKY. That amuses you?

MIKHAILOV. I agree. (*Hangs up the receiver.*) What's amusing?

RAYEVSKY. Olga — I shall call you Olga, may I? (OLGA *nods.*) Olga is laughing because I'm a professor. I find it amusing myself.

MIKHAILOV. And I, on the contrary, was always sure that some day you would be a professor. But do take your things off. (RA-YEVSKY *takes off his coat. He is wearing the Order of the Red Banner.*) You'd like to wash up, I suppose?

RAYEVSKY. No. I attended to that at the station... You've grown thin, Mitka.

MIKHAILOV. Nonsense. What's going on in the European countries?

RAYEVSKY. The European countries? There's no more Europe. Only the steeple of the Eiffel Tower is still scraping the sky. And a peak of the Alps. The rest is shut out from view by our Russian hats.

MIKHAILOV. So you're offended because I've insulted the old lady?

RAYEVSKY. I'm irritated by our immemorially stupid and sneering attitude towards all those things about which we know nothing.

MIKHAILOV. You've become neurotic!

RAYEVSKY. I'm incensed because you are not the first who has spoken to me in this vein. They can still teach us a thing or two, these Europeans. Mitka, I could shoot all those vulgarians who see and hear nothing but the music of the foxtrot in Europe...

MIKHAILOV. Were you in Germany?

RAYEVSKY. In Berlin, Hamburg, Dresden... The whole country is working like a well-oiled, glistening machine. You take a plane at Königsberg, and all Germany is spread before your eyes like the mechanism of a watch. (*With mounting enthusiasm.*) The machines roar incessantly, the thunder of the many underground railways shakes the earth. That's something worth listening to!

OLGA. Are the lights very bright at night?

RAYEVSKY. It's impossible to read on some of the streets, so glaring are the electric lights there. And there are buildings which are completely flooded with light. An electric champagne glass flares up every night over one of the buildings in the Tauenzenstrasse. A champagne bottle appears, and, outlined against the dark background of the sky, champagne begins to foam.

(*The telephone rings.* MIKHAILOV *picks up the receiver.*)

MIKHAILOV. Speaking... Yes, I asked about it... Why aren't you supplying the Ruchievsky District with kerosene? The secretary telephoned me. They had to burn candles in the Party cell last night. Soon you'll be giving the peasants nothing but matchwood... That's a lie! You received five tanks three days ago... Take care, you may find yourself in serious trouble... Very well... (*Hangs up the receiver. To* RAYEVSKY.) Champagne?

OLGA. And is it true that one can't see the people for the automobiles which fill the streets?

RAYEVSKY. Yes, it's true. When seen from an aeroplane, they seem so tightly squeezed together one couldn't find room to drop a pin among them. They take up the whole street. And they stop only at crossings, and not even there, unless an automatic signal indicates that they should do so. Only then are the pedestrians allowed to cross the street.

MIKHAILOV. Very pretty.

RAYEVSKY. What is?

MIKHAILOV. You tell a story very prettily. And what about the revolutionary movement over there? (*The telephone rings again.*) Excuse me. (*Picks up the receiver.*) Yes... Yes, yes. I've read it... It's very good... The writing is lucid... Add a few words about the manure at the end... Say that it must be collected right away and transported to the fields... Let them heap it up in piles afterwards and then manure it. How many are you printing? Fifty thousand? Agreed. Have you already delivered them? When will they be ready? All right. (*Hangs up the receiver. To* RAYEVSKY.) Well, what is your opinion — are there any prospects of a revolution in the West?

RAYEVSKY. Is this an idle question? Or do you really want to know?

MIKHAILOV. I... (*The doorbell rings.*) Olga... It's the engineers ... You wait here, Pavel, it won't take long. Olga, you sit in on the conference, too. You'll find the information useful for your paper.

(OLGA *leaves to open the door.* MIKHAILOV *searches for a report among the papers on the table.* RAYEVSKY *examines the books scattered on the sofa.* OLGA *returns, followed by the assistant road superintendent, Engineer* LARYONOV, *and* KOSYAKOV, *Director of the 'Communkhoz' or Communal Property Department.*)

KOSYAKOV. Well, here we are. But what's wrong with your leg?

MIKHAILOV. Nothing much. A slight dislocation. You're late, comrades. Fifteen minutes late.

KOSYAKOV. It isn't my fault, I swear it isn't... My comrade here...

LARYONOV. I'm Laryonov, assistant to the road superintendent.

MIKHAILOV. So you've arrived? Please. (*Points to a chair.* LARYONOV *sits down. To* LARYONOV.) Well, now. So you refuse to contribute?

LARYONOV. We can't contribute.

MIKHAILOV. But you can use the water?

LARYONOV. The water is national property.

MIKHAILOV. Everything is national property. Who is building the canal? We or someone else?

KOSYAKOV. We are.

MIKHAILOV. Then let's have some money, comrades. The road needs water. Contribute the money.

LARYONOV. We can't. It's your canal, not ours.

MIKHAILOV. So you won't contribute?

LARYONOV. We can't.

MIKHAILOV. Very well, then. We'll collect it kopeck by kopeck.

LARYONOV. What do you mean, kopeck by kopeck?

MIKHAILOV. We'll charge you a kopeck for every hundred pails of water you use. Here are the figures. (*Picks up a paper.*) In two years you will have paid the first instalment, in five the whole cost, in ten...

LARYONOV. One moment... What does this mean? Who gave you the right?

MIKHAILOV. You said yourself the canal is ours.

LARYONOV. No, but wait a moment... And when the second branch is built there will be a kopeck assessment for that, too?

MIKHAILOV. Yes, for that, too, we will charge a kopeck for every hundred pails of water.

LARYONOV. Will you wait until tomorrow for an answer? I'll wire the Board of Directors right away.

MIKHAILOV. All right. But tell them to hurry with the money. We need it.

(LARYONOV *gets up, makes his farewells, and goes.*)

KOSYAKOV. You think they'll pay up?

MIKHAILOV. What else can they do? You can't get the best of a little kopeck assessment. Have you examined all the clay yet?

KOSYAKOV. We have fourteen hundred sazhens more to do.

MIKHAILOV. Have you done anything about the bricks?

KOSYAKOV. They are still figuring.

MIKHAILOV. Your estimate was due yesterday. One moment. (*Reads from a notebook.*) 'Kosyakov, the 12th, brick factory estimate.'

KOSYAKOV. I swear I didn't have the time. May God be my witness, I didn't have the time.

MIKHAILOV. So they are still figuring?

KOSYAKOV. I'll bring the estimate tomorrow. I swear I will. Let me off this time.

MIKHAILOV. Tomorrow at eleven. (KOSYAKOV *shakes hands with* MIKHAILOV *and leaves.*) They simply cannot learn to be on time. (*Writes in his little notebook.*) We'll stick them with the little kopeck as one sticks a grasshopper on a pin. What were you on the point of saying about the West, Pavel?

RAYEVSKY (*irritably*). Things are different in the West. There blood is spilled when the proletariat takes the street.

MIKHAILOV. Are you referring to the large demonstrations?

RAYEVSKY. All demonstrations are dispersed, large or small. I went to the Reichstag with a crowd of unemployed. The police beat us with rubber clubs and with the butts of their revolvers. One of my arms was broken, and I barely managed to elude the Schutz-polizei.

MIKHAILOV. What a wasted gesture! You shouldn't have gone.

RAYEVSKY. You think I should have stepped aside and watched from the sidelines how the workers were being clubbed?

MIKHAILOV. If you had been caught by the Schutz-polizei, the German police could have framed some fable about Russian spies who organize workers' demonstrations. Believe me, that would have been more harmful than your standing aside.

RAYEVSKY. You have a very level head. But there are times, if you know what I mean, when reasoned behavior borders on the criminal.

OLGA. Dmitri, I am sure, would not have gone to the Reichstag.

MIKHAILOV. You're right. Unreasoned behavior, it seems to me, is always criminal.

RAYEVSKY. Then I'm a criminal. But if the same situation were to be repeated tomorrow, I should again throw myself in front of the Schutz-polizei's clubs together with the German workers. I'd let you do the watching while we were being beaten.

236

MIKHAILOV. Spoken like a hero. From my point of view, however, purposeless heroism is but the reverse side of cowardice.

RAYEVSKY. You would not have spoken like this five years ago... Ah, but... (*Jumps up, paces about the room, sits down on the couch, examines the books.*)

MIKHAILOV. But you must be hungry, Pavel. You're jumping on people because you haven't had anything to eat. Olka...

OLGA (*to* RAYEVSKY, *ironically*). Dmitri always has a very delicate appreciation of the psychological moods of others...

MIKHAILOV. Give him something to eat, Olka...

RAYEVSKY. I don't want anything to eat.

MIKHAILOV. You haven't stopped raving, Pavel. (*Remembering something, he begins to dig among the papers on the table.*)

RAYEVSKY. And you, Mitka? Have you really stopped raving so soon? Have you really become leaden?

OLGA. Leaden, did you say?

MIKHAILOV. No... (*Going through his papers.*) So you aren't hungry? Perhaps you'd like some vodka? We have some.

RAYEVSKY. No.

(*The telephone rings;* MIKHAILOV *answers.*)

MIKHAILOV. Yes, yes, Mikhailov. Very well. I'm waiting. (*Sits down at the table.*) The District Committee is calling.

OLGA (*in a low voice to* RAYEVSKY). Why are you so nervous?

RAYEVSKY. So much has changed in Russia during the last few years. On the faces of my friends I see dull and fatal reflections of the last rays of the sunset. Our people had been on fire, now they are smouldering... I look at Mitka... and I want to weep. He was once astride a winged horse... He wanted to ride to Berlin on this horse... And now...

MIKHAILOV (*at the telephone*). Yes, yes, Mikhailov speaking, Comrade Antonov. We delivered everything during the last five days. Yes, sixty men have departed. We left a hundred thousand for ourselves. H'm, I understand. I'll begin to load·tomorrow. Very well, we'll gather what's left. It will be done. Good-bye. (*Hangs up the receiver.*) Russia needs bread!

CURTAIN

ACT I

SCENE 2

The same room. MIKHAILOV *is at the table, examining a list of names, and near him is* ZHUKOV, *Secretary of the Organizational Sector of the Regional Committee. A youthful girl typist,* DASHA, *is at work near-by. The editor of the local paper,* PEREVOZHNIKOV, *is laboring over an article at a table in another part of the room; he is an elderly man, with a wisp of greying beard and moth-eaten clothes.*

MIKHAILOV (*crossing out a name*). Chistyakov can go to the Devil. These, on the other hand, are fine chaps. Why is there a question-mark after Kononov's name?

ZHUKOV. He refuses to go — categorically. He's raising hell. Wants to write to the Central Committee.

MIKHAILOV. Did you send for him?

ZHUKOV. He's coming here.

MIKHAILOV. Which Lobsikov is this? From the Okrzu?

ZHUKOV. The same.

MIKHAILOV. But he stutters.

ZHUKOV. Well, he's not going to read a lecture.

MIKHAILOV. His name goes out. Before he gets one word out, the peasant will have twenty ready for him... Does Gromov also refuse to go?

ZHUKOV. I sent for all of them.   (*The telephone rings.*)

MIKHAILOV. Speaking. The chairman? You drop in here. I guess we'll have to make the rounds of all the districts tomorrow. Yes. Yes. All right. (*Hangs up the receiver. To the editor.*) Have you finished the article?

PEREVOZHNIKOV. Just fancy! I don't seem to be able to get any-where with it.

MIKHAILOV. What's wrong?

PEREVOZHNIKOV. Just fancy, it sounds bombastic, somehow.

MIKHAILOV. Out with the bombastic phrases!

PEREVOZHNIKOV. Just fancy, it will be too dry, then.

MIKHAILOV. Well, go on, go on, write... Dasha, are the proofs here?

238

DASHA. No, the proofs haven't come yet.

MIKHAILOV. The usual story. (*The doorbell rings.*)

ZHUKOV (*goes to the door and shouts*). The door is open!

MIKHAILOV (*telephoning*). Give me 1–16. Yes, yes, 1–16... Particularly where Popov is concerned. Popov? Hello. Listen, Popov, where are the proofs? It's ten minutes to one. I'll put you under arrest, Popov. I warned you yesterday. Your messenger is not my affair. Possibly he is a congenital alcoholic. The proofs were supposed to be here at twelve sharp. It's twelve minutes to one right now... and no proofs. Better put away a little bag of biscuits for future use... The food in our House of Correction is only fair to middling...

(KONONOV *enters and listens with interest to* MIKHAILOV's *threat.* MIKHAILOV *hangs up the receiver.*)

MIKHAILOV. Ah, Kononov, greetings! What's this I hear about your refusing to go to the country?

KONONOV. I? Who said so? Nothing of the kind. I'm only too happy to go.

ZHUKOV (*astonished*). Happy? Then what were you raising such a row about?

KONONOV. I was joking. Just joking. That's all there is to it. And you, you've already told Mikhailov?

MIKHAILOV. Then what did you come here for?

KONONOV. I... I... Why, I came to say good-bye.

MIKHAILOV. In that case, a pleasant journey, Kononov. You'll find your travelling pass in the office of the Regional Committee.

KONONOV. Good-bye, Mikhailov, good-bye. (*Leaves.*)

MIKHAILOV (*to* PEREVOZHNIKOV). How's the article coming along?

PEREVOZHNIKOV. Just fancy, it sounds kind of pathetic.

MIKHAILOV. Out with the pathos!

PEREVOZHNIKOV. Well, just fancy, in that case it sounds like a decree.

MIKHAILOV. Well, try harder, try harder.

(GROMOV *enters, goes to the table.*)

GROMOV. I can't go to the country.

MIKHAILOV. And why not?

GROMOV. The Inspection Committee from Moscow is due here shortly, isn't it?

MIKHAILOV. It is.

239

GROMOV. I must finish the construction job on time, mustn't I?

MIKHAILOV. You must.

GROMOV. Raw materials for next year have to be stocked, don't they?

MIKHAILOV. They do.

GROMOV. We are thirteen per cent short of our quota. We must catch up, mustn't we?

MIKHAILOV. Without fail.

GROMOV. I have to remain here to direct operations, don't I?

MIKHAILOV. No, you do not. You, Gromov, must go to the country. Stop at the office of the Regional Committee and get your travelling pass.

GROMOV. And who will be responsible for the work here?

MIKHAILOV. You, Gromov, will be responsible. If you haven't selected capable assistants, you will suffer the consequences. If your quota isn't fulfilled, you will suffer the consequences. If the construction work isn't finished on time, you will suffer the consequences.

GROMOV. And in addition I must go to the country?

MIKHAILOV. And you must also go to the country. These are difficult times, Gromov... Have you any more questions?

GROMOV. I have many more questions. But I shall ask them at the Party Conference.

MIKHAILOV. If you are chosen delegate to the Conference. *If* you are chosen. You haven't been a frequent visitor to the Party cell of late, have you?

GROMOV. So you have informers?

MIKHAILOV. There are no informers in the Party. Don't waste so much time talking.

GROMOV (*insolently*). In the Communist Party...

(*The door opens with a bang, and, pushing* GROMOV *aside, the printer's messenger — an old man — rushes in, headlong.* GROMOV *departs angrily.*)

MIKHAILOV (*rising, shouts after him*). What about our Party? What about it?

MESSENGER (*panting and trying to catch his breath*). The proofs ... by twelve.

MIKHAILOV. Give them to me. (*Takes the papers and examines the proofs.*) He's disintegrating, the scoundrel...

MESSENGER (*very loudly*). It's not true!

MIKHAILOV. What are you talking about — not true?

MESSENGER. Not disintegrating a bit. As for my shortness of breath, that's from running.

MIKHAILOV. I wasn't talking about you. (*Examines the proofs.*) And don't run. Tell them to give you the proof ten minutes earlier, hereafter. Otherwise you'll never catch up with the times.

MESSENGER (*pacified*). Exactly so.

MIKHAILOV (*to the messenger*). You may go. (*To* ZHUKOV.) You go, too. Everybody must get going tomorrow. Telephone all the secretaries.

ZHUKOV. Have they 'phoned you from the factory yet?

MIKHAILOV. No. Why?

ZHUKOV. They have some business they want to discuss with you. (*Leaves with the messenger.*)

(MIKHAILOV *busies himself with his work.* PEREVOZHNIKOV *is undergoing the tortures of creative effort. He reads his article to himself, gesticulates, crosses out lines, writes, ponders. All around him are crumpled papers.* OLGA'S *laughter is heard in the vestibule. She enters, followed by* RAYEVSKY. *They are both gay and animated.*)

OLGA. He really is a lunatic, this Rayevsky of yours. First, he stops to play jacks with the children on the street. Then he carries an old woman across a puddle, and finally he is almost run over by an automobile, right in front of the house.

PEREVOZHNIKOV. How did that happen?

OLGA. Good morning, comrade editor. We were walking along the street when a car flew out from behind a corner and raced along. Then, suddenly, before I knew what was happening, he left me and made a broad jump across the street under the very nose of the car. I screamed so loud, the whole town must have heard me.

MIKHAILOV. What a fool stunt!

RAYEVSKY. Don't worry, I have sturdy legs.

MIKHAILOV. I know. It's a fool stunt because the chauffeur feels rotten at such moments. He hasn't time to stop the machine — and it is no great joy to him to run you over if you should stumble. For you the whole thing was just a prank.

OLGA. Heavens! How dull everything has become!

RAYEVSKY. Perhaps you're right. But you can't always stop to reason out every move you make, Dmitri.

MIKHAILOV. It seems to me that one can't afford not to stop, that

241

it is impossible not to weigh beforehand every move one makes. (*Pause.*) You're to go to the country to collect bread from the peasants. That will be your first job.

OLGA. When?

MIKHAILOV. Tomorrow.

RAYEVSKY. Tomorrow? Are you, Dmitri Mikhailov, merely advising me to go tomorrow, or is this an official order from the Secretary of the Regional Committee?

MIKHAILOV. What's the difference?

RAYEVSKY. If this is an official order, I shall leave tomorrow.

MIKHAILOV. Such is the decision of the Regional Committee. (*To the editor.*) How are you getting on with the article?

PEREVOZHNIKOV. Just fancy...

MIKHAILOV (*shouts*). Go to the Devil with your 'just fancies.' I'll write the article myself. (*More calmly.*) Dasha, take the typewriter. Come, I'm going to dictate.

(DASHA *takes the typewriter and* MIKHAILOV *follows her, leaning heavily on his cane. The frightened* PEREVOZHNIKOV *also leaves.*)

OLGA (*in agitation*). So you're going tomorrow?

RAYEVSKY. I have never yet refused to carry out an order of the Party, Olga.

OLGA. But this is absurd. The Party should take advantage of your abilities as a leader.

RAYEVSKY. The Party will take advantage of whatever it happens to need at the moment.

OLGA. But men may be motivated by personal considerations. They can't hide behind the word 'Party.' What is the Party? People — men and women.

RAYEVSKY. No.

OLGA. What then?

RAYEVSKY. The Party is a ring. It's an iron thong which holds people together.

OLGA. That may be so. But there are times when this thong cuts into the flesh. Human beings are not, after all, as like as peas. They are not bushes which can be levelled and trimmed to a standard size. You, for instance, are not like...

RAYEVSKY. I've thought of that. Yes, the thong often cuts into my flesh, but I can't live without it...

OLGA. Your words are incomprehensible to me.

RAYEVSKY. It's all very complex, Olga. I haven't had to explain before. Picture a crowd. A crowd composed of identical people, a crowd composed of standardized people. They are all wearing neckties of the same color. They are all walking in the same direction. They all speak the same measured words. I don't want to be one of this crowd. There are times when I'm horrified at the thought that each day I put on the same kind of necktie everyone else is wearing. But I know a feeling which is even more terrifying. Picture, Olga, this crowd going by without you. And that you are left alone, all alone with your thoughts, with your doubts, while the columns keep passing by. They pass by forever without you. They reiterate their words. They sing their songs. Not a single one of them turns his gaze in your direction. Their measured steps are merciless. And precisely because I myself am filled with thoughts which are not attuned to those of the others, with emotions which do not correspond to those of my companions, I cannot step out of the ranks. I dare not leave. I must feel another shoulder next to mine. I need someone to give me orders, someone to discipline me. I can't get along without those iron fetters which weld together the diverse sides of my 'I.'

OLGA. And if you should not be led in the right direction?

RAYEVSKY. I'll follow and die with the rest. I fought for the Party. I'm its soldier.

OLGA. A soldier who has no confidence in the ultimate victory? Can such soldiers conquer?

RAYEVSKY. Who told you that I have no confidence in the ultimate victory? It's impossible for the proletariat not to conquer. Victory is inevitable, as inevitable as death. I'm not sure that we — that Russia — will be the final victors. Perhaps we are but another Paris Commune which has managed to hold out for twelve years. If so, I shall know how to stand up against the wall.

OLGA. You don't want to go to the country, do you?

RAYEVSKY. I don't like the country. I don't like snowstorms, rain, frost. I don't like all those stupid elements which man cannot harness to do his bidding. The country — the village — is such an element. No... I don't like the country. But I leave tomorrow.

OLGA. Do you know...

RAYEVSKY. What?

OLGA. No... I haven't come to a decision yet.

RAYEVSKY. I'm going to my room. I have some writing to do. (*Leaves.*)

OLGA (*paces the room excitedly. Her head is lowered, her hands clasped. She bends, looks at the sheets* PEREVOZHNIKOV *had thrown down, and reads*). 'Peasants! The Party is sounding the trumpet and unfurling its crimson banners. Twelve years...'

(DASHA *and* MIKHAILOV *come in.* DASHA *puts away some papers and leaves silently.* MIKHAILOV, *leaning heavily on his cane, goes to the table.* OLGA *takes a step toward him. They both stop when they come face to face.*)

OLGA. Are you sending Pavel to the country because you're jealous of him?

MIKHAILOV (*is silent for a moment, then looks at her in consternation*). I can't believe you're asking this seriously.

OLGA. Oh, yes, certainly! There is the resolution issued by the Regional Committee. He's not the only one who's going. It is the will of the Party. The people need bread. Well, speak, speak! You're never at a loss for words, clever, ingenious words, like the headlines of your articles... 'Peasants! The Party is sounding its trumpet...'

MIKHAILOV. Are you ill?

OLGA. Certainly I'm ill. Isn't that self-evident? Just feel my brow, see if I haven't a fever. How simple life is, Mikhailov. Olga is sick. Pavel is hungry. The Party is sounding its trumpet.

MIKHAILOV. What trumpet are you talking about? Get hold of yourself, Olka.

OLGA. Just once, Mikhailov, just once. Stop being the Secretary of the Regional Committee for one second. Tell me honestly, looking me straight in the eyes. Are you sending Pavel away because you're jealous? Well, go on, answer me!

MIKHAILOV. Your question is insane.

OLGA. Why insane? Why are you hiding, Dmitri? Don't you think I can sense this? I know your hidden thoughts. You want to get him out of the way! Honorable people seize each other by the throat in open battle. They fight with the same weapons. But you — you are the Secretary of the Regional Committee. You can get your friend out of the way because such is the 'will' of the Party. (*Practically screaming.*) A travelling pass for Pavel Rayevsky! (*Without saying a word, leaning on his cane,* MIKHAILOV *crosses over to the table and sits down.* OLGA *paces the room, stops, and looks at* MIKHAILOV.) Forgive me. I suspected you of feelings which are not natural to you. (MIKHAILOV *quickly raises his head.*) No, not natural, because you are completely devoid of feelings of any kind. I had forgotten that your affection is lavished only on resolutions, decrees, regulations. I imagined, for some reason, that you had suddenly turned into a human being; that you had deviated, for a moment, from the set of Party principles you have transformed yourself into. You're not a man — just a set of Party principles. (*Shouts.*) Do you hear? You're a set of Party principles!

MIKHAILOV (*quietly*). Party principles have their deviations.

OLGA. Then you're not even a set of Party principles. You never deviate. Your insides are stuffed with prudence, common-sense, logic. You're a walking rule of order. Your exactitude makes me want to vomit. You would like to make methodical entries of all the problems of life with the appropriate answers on the following page, like the interpretations of dreams in a dream-book. You have drawn up an emotional time-table for yourself, and, like trains, your desires and longings can follow only one set of railway tracks, and even those not before the second bell has rung. Keep quiet!

MIKHAILOV. I'm not interrupting you.

OLGA. I have more than once tried to arouse your anger. You never lose control of yourself. I have done everything I could to insult you, but it is beyond the power of any human being to hurt you. Nothing that is outside your world of reports and telephone orders can touch you. You're a Party automaton. I can't stand it any longer. (*Falls into a chair and weeps.*) You can't even be jealous, Dmitri!

MIKHAILOV. Olka! Olka! You really are ill. I'll bring you some water right away... (*Gets up.*)

OLGA (*jumps up*). I don't need any water. Journalists are needed in the country. I'll write sketches. I'm going with Rayevsky tomorrow! (*Turns around and starts to leave.*)

MIKHAILOV (*takes a step after her; cries out as if hurt*). Oh!

OLGA (*turns around sharply*). What is it, Mitya?

MIKHAILOV. I stepped on my bad foot.

OLGA (*disappointed*). I see... (*Leaves.*)

MIKHAILOV (*gazes after her for a second, then throws away his cane, leaves the table, and limping, follows her. The telephone rings sharply. MIKHAILOV stops. Pause. It rings again. MIKHAILOV goes to the telephone*). Speaking... Yes. Hello, old man... You want a report at the general meeting? But why didn't you let me know earlier?

ACT II

SCENE 3

A large, comfortable room in the home of the 'kulak' or well-to-do peasant, IVAN GERASIMOVICH KVASSOV. *The furniture is solid, well-made. One wall is covered with ikons and a lamp burns under an ikon in one corner.* KVASSOV *is a robust, bearded man nearing sixty, wearing the belted shirt, its tails flaring under an embroidered waistcoat, characteristic of the more prosperous peasants. His daughter* PASHA *is laying out cards in a bored manner; she is about twenty-two, attractive, with thick yellow plaits down her back.*

There is a knock at the window; KVASSOV, *who is reading a newspaper, raises his head;* PASHA *goes to the window and draws aside the curtain.*

PASHA. It's the chairman of the Soviet. There are others with him.

DYEDOV (*behind the scenes*). Open, Ivan Gerasimovich. You have guests.

(KVASSOV *rises quickly and goes to the door. He can be heard raising the bolt in the hall and unlocking the door.* RAYEVSKY, OLGA, *and* DYEDOV *come in.* RAYEVSKY *is wearing his neat European topcoat, but a cap has replaced the felt hat.* DYEDOV, *an old, kindly peasant, is carrying* RAYEVSKY'S *suitcase.*)

DYEDOV. You'll be comfortable here. Ivan Gerasimovich will set a room aside for you. As for vermin... (*To* KVASSOV.) Comrade Rayevsky, District Delegate. We're going to collect bread, Ivan Gerasimovich.

KVASSOV. Welcome, welcome. What did you say, Mikhail Pavlovich? But we've already delivered our quota of bread.

DYEDOV. The State needs more.

KVASSOV. It knows best, of course. Pashka, show the masters to the bedchamber.

RAYEVSKY. What masters are you talking about? I've ducked more than one master in the Black Sea in my time.

KVASSOV. I beg your forgiveness, it's our ignorance.

OLGA (*to* PASHA). Don't bother. I'll stay here.

RAYEVSKY. You won't be comfortable here. I'll stay in this room.

OLGA. Don't argue, please. I prefer this room. (*To* KVASSOV.) But have you another room? Where will you stay?

KVASSOV. Many thanks. There is room enough.

RAYEVSKY. Excellent. Then I'll go to the other room. (*Picks up the suitcase.* OLGA *walks out after him.*)

KVASSOV (*satirically*). A hero!

DYEDOV. Presented with the Order of the Red Banner for military exploits.

KVASSOV. How now? Do they want much from us?

DYEDOV. We'll receive the decree shortly.

KVASSOV. Where are we to get it, Mikhail Pavlovich?

DYEDOV. If the State needs it, we'll find it.

KVASSOV. Bitter is our bread, Mikhail Pavlovich. Haven't we already sent a whole trainload?

DYEDOV. We'll give more.

KVASSOV. Oh, peasant tears, peasant tears...!

(PASHA *is in the doorway, watching* RAYEVSKY *as he returns.*)

RAYEVSKY. Let's not waste any time, Comrade Dyedov. Have you informed the Secretary?

DYEDOV. I haven't had time. I'll do it in a moment. I'll bring both Secretaries, the Party Secretary and the Secretary of the Communist Youth.

RAYEVSKY. Right. I'll wait.

DYEDOV. Give Comrade Rayevsky something to eat.

KVASSOV. Whatever God has sent us. Pashka!

RAYEVSKY. I'll pay for everything.

KVASSOV. I dare say we won't have to quarrel about that, we'll manage to settle accounts. Our food is plain, a peasant's food.

(PASHA *brings in sour cream, bread, butter, cheese curds, and jelly puffs.*)

RAYEVSKY (*looks at the food*). It's magnificent food. But what are these? Fritters?

PASHA. Jelly puffs.

RAYEVSKY (*takes one, eats it*). Marvellous jelly puffs! They're as ruddy as your cheeks.

PASHA. My cheeks *were* ruddy. They are fading now.

RAYEVSKY. How so?

PASHA. Shall I call your wife?

248

RAYEVSKY. My wife? (*Laughs.*) Yes, call her, call her. (*Shouts.*) Wife! Olga! Missus!

OLGA (*comes in, she has changed her clothes*). What is it?

RAYEVSKY. Breakfast is served, dear little Missus. The milk is steaming. The cheese curds are crumbling, and the jelly puffs are like a red flame.

OLGA. So you're also a poet, Rayevsky.

RAYEVSKY. The morning has raised my spirits, Olga. The beautiful ride put new life in my veins. The forest inspires me. Didn't you notice? It couldn't restrain itself; it smiled when it saw us passing through.

OLGA (*laughing in a low voice*). I notice that our landlord is staring at you as one stares at a lunatic.

RAYEVSKY (*in the same voice*). He's a nice old man. And the young maiden... How lovely she is! Just look at her.

OLGA. Yes, she is. Well, let's have breakfast, Pavel. (*They sit down.*)

RAYEVSKY (*to* KVASSOV). Why don't you sit down? And Pasha, too?

KVASSOV. Oh, we get up with the roosters. We've breakfasted. Many thanks.

RAYEVSKY (*eating*). But sit down, sit down. There is no mistress in the house?

KVASSOV. She left us, my dear little mistress left us. She's been gone almost a year now.

RAYEVSKY (*in astonishment*). Where did she go to? With whom?

KVASSOV. Where she went to no man knows.

OLGA. She's dead. Why are you asking such nonsensical questions?

RAYEVSKY. Dead? I didn't understand. I thought... (*He eats. Pause.*) Are you going to organize a Kolhoz, a collective farm, soon?

KVASSOV. We haven't heard anything about it.

RAYEVSKY. What is there to hear? You must organize one yourselves.

KVASSOV. We ourselves? H'm, yes... Our people are an irresolute lot, timid. They're afraid.

RAYEVSKY. What is there to be afraid of? Would you rather live according to the old ways?

KVASSOV. Yes, that's true, too. The days of yore were not sugarplums either. They, too, were unsweetened. But there is a saying among our people: the old ways are already familiar to us — our grandfathers lived according to these ways, our fathers had inherited them from their fathers, and they, in turn, left them to us. While the new life... Well, it's like the Heavenly Kingdom: we have faith in it, still we find it more agreeable to live in the kingdom on earth.

RAYEVSKY. But one should at least try the new ways, shouldn't one?

KVASSOV. Right. Only our people live in such darkness. They reason thusly: said the woodchuck to the horse, 'Come on, let's cross the mud; let's,' he said, 'try it. You try to drown and I'll try to remain alive.'

RAYEVSKY. Does everybody reason this way?

KVASSOV. The whole world does.

OLGA. And what do you think?

KVASSOV. What are we? Whatever direction we're turned to, there we will go. In the meantime we're holding our own.

RAYEVSKY. You wait. Chicks aren't counted until they're hatched.

KVASSOV. That's a true proverb. Only we haven't many chicks left.

RAYEVSKY. What kind of chicks?

KVASSOV. The usual kind — the offsprings of chickens.

(PASHA *laughs.*)

OLGA. Why are there so few left?

KVASSOV. The city people have eaten them. When the peasant hasn't enough bread to eat, he sells his fowl and buys bread with the money.

RAYEVSKY. As if there really were so little bread...

KVASSOV. Where, in Heaven's name, is it to come from? We've paid our bread tax, the surplus assessment we've also paid, and the voluntary contribution, too. How, then, are we to have enough bread left?

RAYEVSKY. Aren't the kulaks hoarding some?

KVASSOV. Everything is possible. (*There is a knock at the window.*)

RAYEVSKY (*jumps up*). They're here.

KVASSOV (*to* PASHA). Open the door.

(PASHA *opens the door.* DYEDOV *comes in, followed by* LOKTEV, *Secretary of the local Communist Party cell, and* ZOTOVA, *the eighteen-year-old Secretary of the local Communist Youth League. Both of them are peasants who have been transformed by the Revolution;* LOKTEV *is clean-shaven, about thirty, neatly dressed, ener-*

getic-looking; young ZOTOVA *is a sturdy girl, her eyes aflame with zeal.* PASHA *returns to the room behind the others.*)

DYEDOV (*jokingly*). Here is the whole Council of People's Commissars.

LOKTEV. The complete assortment. (*Presses* RAYEVSKY'S *hand.*)

ZOTOVA (*to* RAYEVSKY). Secretary of the Communist Youth, at your service. (*Shakes hands with* RAYEVSKY.)

RAYEVSKY. Let us begin, comrades. (*Catching* LOKTEV'S *questioning gaze on* OLGA.) This is Comrade Belotzerova. From the Regional paper. Olga, be so good. (*They all sit around the table.* DYEDOV *makes a sign to* KVASSOV, *who leaves together with* PASHA.) And so comrades, to business. You collected twenty-one thousand poods for the bread quota?

DYEDOV. Twenty-one thousand one hundred.

RAYEVSKY. Excellent. Our task now is to collect another seven thousand out of what remains.

DYEDOV. Seven thousand!

ZOTOVA. We can get seven thousand. The kulaks alone have bought up thirty thousand.

LOKTEV (*warningly*). Zotova!

ZOTOVA. Well, twenty.

LOKTEV. Twenty?

ZOTOVA. All right — fifteen thousand. At any rate, they have bought up.

(LOKTEV *shakes his head and looks at her reproachfully.*)

DYEDOV. We haven't got seven thousand poods. But we'll squeeze them out!

LOKTEV. There *is* bread, Dyedov. Your remark was unnecessary.

DYEDOV. Whether there is bread or not, one thing I do know. In short, we'll get the seven thousand poods.

RAYEVSKY. But we can't just take it, comrades. Right now it would be well for us to discuss the various methods to be used to get the bread.

DYEDOV. There is nothing to discuss. We'll announce an assessment. Period.

LOKTEV. No, that won't do.

ZOTOVA. Let's take all of it from the kulaks. Half of the peasants in this village are kulaks, and the rest follow them like sheep.

LOKTEV (*reproachfully*). Half?

ZOTOVA. You haven't been here very long. You don't know.

The whole village is kulak. You just go out, spy upon them a little, listen to what they're saying. We have kulaks of all sorts and colors here. We have to keep twenty orderlies.

DYEDOV. Seven.

ZOTOVA. Seven, then. What's the difference? We must take the bread away by force. We must use arms.

LOKTEV. You're jabbering like a magpie and riding a high horse. But it's all empty chatter.

RAYEVSKY (*to* LOKTEV). What is your opinion?

LOKTEV. The greater part of the assessment we will have to get from the kulaks. And the kulaks will put up a big fight. It would be well, therefore, to carry on a little propaganda campaign for several days.

RAYEVSKY. What do you mean by several days? Several days before we even begin our collection?

LOKTEV. Before we do anything.

RAYEVSKY. And then spend several more days in collecting the bread?

LOKTEV. Let us first prepare the ground — we'll then spend less time collecting. It's dangerous for us to open the battle without some preliminary rigging. Down with all unnecessary sails! Make sure that the rigging is all right! A strong wind is on the way!

RAYEVSKY. And the workers, in the meantime, will have to wait? You expect them to sit without bread while you're rolling up your sails?

DYEDOV. What is there to talk about? If the State orders us to get bread, we'll get it. We'll call a meeting for tomorrow. Period.

LOKTEV. As you please. But we'll merely be knocking our heads against the wall, comrades.

RAYEVSKY. You're following the old ways, Comrade Loktev. It does not become us to run away from a fight.

LOKTEV. But it does no harm to strengthen one's forces before beginning the fight.

RAYEVSKY. We're leading an attack. The Party is beating a march.

LOKTEV. All the same, I would at least get the poor peasants together once or twice. And I would discuss the situation a little with the middle peasant, too. The kulak will move all his forces.

RAYEVSKY. Your military tactics are bad, Comrade Loktev. It is evident that you've never been at the front.

LOKTEV. On the contrary. I fought for five years.

RAYEVSKY. Then you haven't learned the lesson well. The enemy should always be taken by surprise. While he is still sitting in an easy-chair, while he is still scratching his head, we are already marching on the road, we are already putting out to sea. We appear suddenly, and the attack is on. Don't give the enemy a chance to collect himself. Your kulak will be asleep, he will be reposing in his feather-bed, while we beat the alarm. One, two! First the meeting, then the collection. And if the kulak as much as squeaks, he'll find that he's too late. We will have already prepared the ground, we will already have carried out our plans, so it's all settled. Tomorrow at eight, then. (*Gets up.*)

ZOTOVA (*to* LOKTEV). There's a man for you!

DYEDOV. Your orders will be carried out to the letter.

LOKTEV. Until tomorrow. (*Worried.*) Only...

RAYEVSKY. Good-bye. Don't be offended because I lectured you a little. You'll work all the better.

LOKTEV. Who's offended? Thank you!

ZOTOVA. We're giving a play at the Club tonight. Will you come?

RAYEVSKY. I'll... we'll both come. Olga and I. Who's playing at your Club?

ZOTOVA. Our own local talent. But they play like regular troopers. They can make the whole auditorium burst into tears.

LOKTEV. That's right. They can make the audience burst into tears when it should be laughing and guffaw when it should be weeping.

ZOTOVA. You're always jeering. We get no help from you, no guidance. Only sneers and more sneers. (*Leaves.*)

LOKTEV (*shaking hands with* RAYEVSKY). What about arms, Comrade Rayevsky? We ought to have some in reserve. It's safer.

RAYEVSKY. I wasn't born yesterday. (LOKTEV *and* DYEDOV *leave. To* OLGA.) The Secretary is a coward. Spend several days in conferences, in preparing the ground! I'll be all through in three days. Four villages have been assigned to me. I'll go through ten within the time allotted to me. I'll collect my whole quota long before my time is up. I'll show these provincial moles what military tempo is.

OLGA. How well you spoke! With such force, such ardor!

RAYEVSKY. I am simply a resolute man, Olga.

OLGA. Yes, you're a man, a real man. Do you know, I had practically given up hope of ever meeting you.

RAYEVSKY. Of meeting me?

OLGA. Yes, you. Someone like you.

RAYEVSKY. What sort of a person am I?

OLGA. You're... you're... I find it difficult to explain.

RAYEVSKY. But we shall stay together, Olga... Won't we?

OLGA. In what sense?

RAYEVSKY. In this sense... (*Seizes* OLGA *suddenly and kisses her.*) Olga! Olga, dear one. Blood, not water which can be appraised in kopecks, flows in our veins. (*Kisses her again.* OLGA *breaks away. He pursues her around the table. Unable to catch her, he finally jumps on the table. At that moment the door leading into the hall is opened and a nun,* MOKRINA, *enters. She remains rooted on the threshold as if turned to stone, her arms raised over her head so that her face is hidden from* RAYEVSKY.) What do you want, Matushka?

MOKRINA (*crosses herself*). Amen! Amen! Begone, Satan!

RAYEVSKY (*laughs*). Amen! (*Jumps off the table.*)

MOKRINA. Don't dare come near me, enemy! (*Makes the sign of a large cross over him.*)

RAYEVSKY. But what do you want?

MOKRINA. What do you want here, accursèd one? What do you, who are branded with the seal of Hell, want here? Why were you flying all over the house? Begone!

KVASSOV (*comes in with* PASHA. PASHA *again remains standing at the door*). Go to your chamber, Mother. (*To* RAYEVSKY.) She's a nun. Paying me a visit. Jabbers the word of God day and night.

OLGA. Did you see the glitter in her eyes? How old is she? She must be quite young.

KVASSOV. I never had the curiosity to find out.

RAYEVSKY. Oh, to the Devil with her! Olyenka, let's go walking. There are woods on the outskirts of the village. And the snow is deep and crisp. Come on.

OLGA. Come with us, Pashenka.

PASHA. No, many thanks.

RAYEVSKY. Yes, do come, Pasha. Show us the forest.

PASHA. There it is, the forest. You'll find it without me. It's no treat to me to stroll in the middle of the afternoon.

RAYEVSKY. Why are you so melancholy, Pashenka? You should be merry, have friends.

PASHA. Merriment won't fill your stomach.

RAYEVSKY. What would you like to have?

PASHA. What wouldn't I like to have? The ceilings, for instance, are low here, and I should like to live under high ones.

RAYEVSKY. Tell your father. Ask him to make them higher.

PASHA. Tell father? He will never do it.

KVASSOV. Get to work, Pashka.

OLGA (*to* PASHA). Have you some special activity?

KVASSOV. Our tasks are peasant tasks. Did you bring any arms with you? I beg you to forgive me for my familiarity. I don't know your patronymic.

RAYEVSKY. I'm called Comrade Rayevsky.

KVASSOV. Comrade Rayevsky, take at least a little pistol along with you.

RAYEVSKY. Why do you keep harping on the subject? Is there any trouble here?

KVASSOV. No. God has saved us from disturbances. But your business here is such that anything may happen.

RAYEVSKY. Don't worry. Let's go, Olyenka. Don't be moody, Pasha. (*Waves to her.*)

> (*He and* OLGA *leave.* PASHA *remains standing in the same place.* KVASSOV *goes to the window and follows them with his eyes.*)

PASHA. Why did you want to know whether he had a revolver?

KVASSOV (*turning around slowly*). Did you say something?

PASHA. Don't pretend to be deaf. What have you got up your sleeve?

KVASSOV (*gently*). From whom are you demanding an explanation, Pashenka?

PASHA. I'm demanding an explanation from you. From Kvassov, Ivan Gerasimovich. From my father.

KVASSOV. Pashka! Our Lord is not overjoyed by anger. Don't incite me to sin, Pashka!

PASHA (*angrily*). If you throw but one stone under his feet, if you harm one hair on his head, look out for your head, Ivan Gerasimovich. I won't have it! (*Leaves.*)

KVASSOV. You won't have it? So that's how the wind blows! Just you ask him prettily, dear little daughter of mine, and he'll make you a present of a tall building in the city, so that you can parade the streets in front of it. He'll make a city street-walker out of you!

PASHA (*flies into the room, screaming into* KVASSOV'S *face*). What did you say? What?

KVASSOV. Why, little daughter! Why, dear little daughter! Now, now! (PASHA *walks away.*) You should never have even asked such a question. What are we? Murderers? Hasn't the Lord given us souls? What we haven't given is not for us to take away. Lord! (PASHA *throws a short fur jacket over her shoulders and a kerchief over her head.*) Where are you going?

PASHA. I'm going to Anka's.

KVASSOV. Go, Pashenka. Go to Anka's. Only send Mikhail to me. And knock on Grunkin's window. Tell him I want to see him. Will you send him?

PASHA. I'll send him. (*Leaves.*)

KVASSOV (*goes into the hall and bolts the door behind her. He can be heard from there*). So that's the kind of daughter I raised! Seed of the Devil! (*Comes in.*) But my flesh and blood. (*Loudly.*) Mother, Matushka!

MOKRINA (*comes in.*) Here I am, Ivan Gerasimovich.

KVASSOV. We must defend ourselves, Matushka. The city has sent us a precious gift. A red broom that's going to sweep our barns clean. They've come to pillage our bread.

MOKRINA. Is it that madman? The one branded with the seal of Satan?

KVASSOV. Stamped with a red seal, Mother. Enormous powers have been conferred upon him. He won't leave a single house unsearched.

MOKRINA. That shall not be.

KVASSOV. We must defend ourselves. Go call on all the women. Open their eyes. So that tomorrow, when the meeting is called, they'll know who's calling it and why. Make haste, Matushka, make haste.

MOKRINA. Good-bye, Ivan Gerasimovich. A day and a night are ahead of us. The Saviour will watch over us.

KVASSOV. Glory to Him! (*Follows her and is heard bolting the door; returns and gazes out of the window.*) Stroll, comrade, stroll! We have nice snow, we have nice woods. Stroll, while we are turning over on our feather-beds. While we are scratching our heads. While we are... (*A knock at the door; he lets in* PASHA, *her brother* MIKHAIL *and* GRUNKIN. MIKHAIL *is a few years older than* PASHA, *well-fed, dressed in the height of village fashion — his boots glitter.* GRUNKIN *is*

a poor peasant, obtuse and under the influence of the shrewd kulaks.)
Come in, dear guest. (*Greets* GRUNKIN *with oily, flattering cordiality.
Shows him to the best chair.*) Sit down, sit down right here. (PASHA
leaves as the others are seated.) What a life we lead these days...
(*Sighs.*)

GRUNKIN. Don't I know?

KVASSOV. So you know — that's good, that's good. And what
do you think will be the end, Nikanor Semionich?

GRUNKIN. I don't know.

KVASSOV. But I know. We'll all be carrying a beggar's knapsack.
They'll squeeze the last drop of blood out of us peasants. How much
does the State pay you for bread?

GRUNKIN. Eight rubles a pood.

KVASSOV. And I? How much did I pay you?

GRUNKIN. Sixty rubles.

KVASSOV. And why did I pay you so much, Nikanor Semionich?
Because I know how hard we peasants labor. Because I myself get
out into the field before dawn. I've fed Mother Earth with the sweat
of my brow. And so have you. She is salty, our Mother Earth —
salty with our tears and our sweat. But in Moscow the cab-drivers
feed their horses with baked bread. How should they know how
much our bread costs us!

GRUNKIN. But what can we do? They'll take the bread if we
don't give it to them.

KVASSOV. Why should they take it? If there is no bread, they
can't take any. We must all stand by each other, Nikanor Semionich.
One for all, and all for one. Most important of all — we mustn't let
them divide us. We mustn't let them destroy our family. If but one
of us is betrayed, we all perish.

GRUNKIN. But what shall I do with your bread?

KVASSOV. Let it lie in your barn, Nikanor Semionich, let it lie in
your barn. It isn't crowding you. If they search your house, tell
them it's yours. They have no right to take it away from *you.*

GRUNKIN. I'll hold it.

KVASSOV. Attend the meeting tomorrow. And tell everybody
else to go, too. They think the Devil has eaten the peasant's wits.
They'll soon find out how mistaken they are.

GRUNKIN. Well, good-bye, Ivan Gerasimovich.

KVASSOV. God be with you, dear guest. Don't pass our house by.
(*Sees him out, comes back.*) Mishka, we must play our last card. We

will be denounced. They'll pick out some sixty of us and make us pay for the whole village.

MIKHAIL. Do they want much?

KVASSOV. Seven thousand.

MIKHAIL. Whew!...

KVASSOV. We must call on every person in the village instantly. No sleep for us tonight. We have a difficult riddle to unriddle.

MIKHAIL. What sort of a man is the new delegate?

KVASSOV. All flame. But it can be put out.

MIKHAIL. He can be bribed?

KVASSOV. If we play mice, the cat will follow.

MIKHAIL. What scheme have you up your sleeve, Papasha?

KVASSOV. I have a little plan. Oh, bitter is the fate of the peasant! (*Gets up and walks towards the room* PASHA *went into; in a low voice.*) I'll whisper it to you. Our kitten...

MIKHAIL (*astonished, in an undertone*). What are you saying, Papasha?

KVASSOV. Nothing, perhaps... Pasha's springs are rushing by... The meeting is tomorrow... (*Bends towards* MIKHAIL *and whispers.*) Mishka, listen carefully...

> (*A broad grin gradually spreads over* MIKHAIL'S *face as the older man whispers into his ear. He nods understandingly and departs.*)

CURTAIN

ACT III
SCENE 4

The village square, with a general meeting in progress. The church with its onion-shaped dome, the village Soviet Headquarters hung with inscriptions on red bunting and the co-operative store are in the background. Dozens of peasants, men and women, are standing about an improvised platform. A few of the older men and women sit on rough benches. KVASSOV and ZUBOV sit on a log, somewhat apart from the others — as known kulaks they are not entitled to take part in the proceedings. Several of the younger peasants are flirting. DYEDOV and RAYEVSKY are standing on the platform. On a bench at the foot of the platform, facing the milling crowd, sit OLGA, LOKTEV, ZOTOVA, and several Communist Youths. The crowd is noisy.

DYEDOV. Citizens! Citizens! You have heard the report of Comrade Rayevsky, who was sent here, specially empowered by the State to collect bread. The exact amount of wheat and rye each one of you must sell to the State has already been decided upon. I'll read the list. Period!

KOTIKHIN. And what about questions? Aren't we to be allowed to ask questions?

SHILOV. That's right! –

KATERINA. Answer our questions.

GRUNKIN. There must be questions.

OLKHA. It's not clear...

DYEDOV (*after consulting with* RAYEVSKY *in a low voice*). You may ask questions. Only let's have order, citizens. This is a meeting, not a market-place.

KOTIKHIN (*rising*). Will you give me permission?

DYEDOV. Go ahead.

                    (*Protests are heard from several directions.*)

ROMANOV. He has no right to ask questions. He's been deprived of his vote. He's disfranchised.

ZOTOVA. Don't recognize him. He has no right to speak.

MISHKA AFANASYEV. He can't speak.

KOTIKHIN. Whatever your will is. I only wanted to clear up a point for the citizens.

KATERINA. Why shut him up? His vote has been taken away from him — but his tongue is still in his mouth. Let him ask.

GRUNKIN. Questions are for the common good, to make things clear.

SHILOV. We want free speech, Citizen Chairman.

VOICES. Give him permission to speak! Let him ask his question.

(RAYEVSKY *and* DYEDOV *again consult in an undertone.*)

DYEDOV. Let's have your question.

KOTIKHIN (*takes off his hat and reads from a note*). Our comrade delegate spoke about sacrifices. How are we to understand this? Are we asked to sell our bread or to give it away — to make a contribution, that is, like a contribution for the building of a church?

(*Laughter.*)

RAYEVSKY. I spoke about the sale of bread to State and co-operative organizations.

KOTIKHIN. But you did say something about sacrifices. We must conclude, then, that when we sell our bread at government prices, it's like sacrificing it. It comes out, then, that we're giving our bread away for nothing.

SHILOV. And where are we to get the bread?

GRUNKIN (*angrily*). Eight rubles for wheat!

KATERINA. If we had, at least, something to sacrifice. But we'll all soon go begging. We'll beg crumbs from each other.

RAYEVSKY. I spoke about the sacrifices which we must all make for the industrialization of the country. But we know that industrialization is for the good of everybody, for the good of all of us here.

GRUNKIN. And how are we to help build industrialization? On a full belly or on an empty one?

KATERINA (*in facile tears*). Dear friends, I'm hungry. I haven't eaten anything for three days.

KOTIKHIN. It seems, then, that large sums of money are needed for industrialization. And that is why we peasants are ordered to contribute more bread? Is that correct?

RAYEVSKY. Correct.

KOTIKHIN. But why the peasants, if I may be allowed to ask? Why not reduce the salaries of the workers and the government employees? Why should the factory worker get new houses, clubs, theatres, and the peasant keep only his bitter fate?

(*There is a commotion — feelings are gradually inflamed.*)

OLKHA. You forgot about the tax. The peasant is taxed. And if the tax isn't paid on time, he is hung by the neck.

KATERINA. They don't bother their heads about that. Just give them bread.

RAYEVSKY. Comrades!...

GRUNKIN. We used to receive manufactured goods. Where are they now? What's the matter? Have the factories closed down out there? Or have all the workers died? I beg you to give me an answer. (*Laughter.*)

RAYEVSKY. The reason...

OLKHA (*interrupts*). Why have you used up all the leather for your portfolios? We have no boots.

DYEDOV (*shouts*). Order, citizens! Ask your questions in turn. You don't give us a chance to answer.

KOTIKHIN. We've had enough of words.

DYEDOV. I won't allow any more questions. Period. Whoever wants to can ask his questions from here. (*Pointing to the platform.*)

GRUNKIN. I'll speak from here. My voice carries. Citizens, we've already given a trainload of bread. We've paid our taxes. We're glad to give our last kopeck to the State, but we haven't any bread. Am I right, citizens?

VOICES. Right!... We've no more bread!... Enough!... We've fulfilled our quota!

KATERINA. I'm hungry, friends, I'm hungry...

GRUNKIN. If they refuse to take our words into consideration, let them take our bread by force. Am I right, citizens? (*Noise, shouts of approval.*)

ROMANOV. What *is* this? Why are we silent? (*He runs up to the platform and jumps on with ease, despite the fact that his left sleeve is empty and pinned up. He is excited, almost foaming with indignation.*) Why don't we Party men say something? Kotikhin, you damned kulak, why have you poured wax in our ears and smeared our mouths with honey? Who's supposed to sell the bread the State is asking for? We who have about three grains of barley, or those of you who have to repair your barns because they're bursting with too much grain and those who have bagfuls buried deep in the ground?

KATERINA. What a liar!

ROMANOV. Why is the whole meeting following one shepherd, like a blind flock of sheep? You don't say anything, Ivan Gerasimovich? You're sitting quietly on your log, but I know your bite...

DYEDOV (*stares into the distance offstage*). One moment! Stop! Who is that, driving a wagonful of grain in the middle of the day? (*The whole crowd turns around and looks.*) Young Communists, find out! Period.

> (*Several* YOUNG COMMUNISTS *dash off. The crowd is watching intently.*)

SHILOV. They've caught up to him.

OLKHA. They're bringing him here. Why, that's no one else but Kvassov's Mikhail.

> (*General excitement. Shouts of 'Kvassov!' 'Mishka!' 'Mikhailo!' Some of the peasants run towards the wagon.*)

ROMANOV. Did you see? He was driving it to the market. A whole carload — four wagons. Reptile!

VOICES. A fine time he found... The idiot... what a trick to play ... What a lot of bread... Mishka has lost his mind... Wheat, it seems...

> (*Several* YOUNG COMMUNISTS *drag in* MIKHAIL, *the peasants who ran to the wagon follow them.* MIKHAIL *is propelled to the platform and the crowd mills around in increasing agitation.*)

DYEDOV. Kvassov, Mikhail! Where are you taking almost a hundred poods of wheat at a moment when the State is in need of bread?

MIKHAIL. Not guilty before the State.

ROMANOV. Perhaps he's taking it to the market.

MIKHAIL. I was bringing the bread here.

> (*Excitement in the crowd. Cries of 'What do you mean, "here"?' 'Why bring bread here?' 'Why here?'*)

ROMANOV. Don't talk to us in riddles. We might guess one of them.

KOTIKHIN (*to* ROMANOV, *angrily*). And what exactly is your official position? What's your address?

ROMANOV. I'll send you my address by letter. You'll read it on the envelope.

DYEDOV. Where were you taking the bread to? Answer and period!

MIKHAIL. I brought the bread here, to be distributed among the people, in compliance with the slogan of the Soviets — 'Help the poor.' Citizen villagers, knowing the bitter need of the peasants, through my own hard work as a tiller of the soil, I make you a present of this bread. Accept my offering, for Jesus Christ's sake. (*Bows low*

262

in three directions. There is a second's pause, during which everybody, as if impelled by some invisible force, turns to stare at the wagons of bread.)

KATERINA. Free bread! Free! Free! (*Dashes towards the wagon.*) (*The crowd, caught up by a whirlwind of greed, rushes to the free wheat. Only the few Party members and Communist Youths remain near the platform — chagrined and dejected.* MIKHAIL, *smiling unctuously, watches the peasants. His father, old* KVAS-SOV, *continues to sit immobile on the log, as if all of this does not concern him.*)

CURTAIN

ACT III

Scene 5

Kvassov's *house.* Rayevsky *is alone, writing. There is a knock on the door.* Pasha *comes from the adjoining part of the house, crosses the room and opens the door.* Kvassov *enters.*

Rayevsky. Oh, it's you?

Kvassov. Yes, I. Good morning.

Rayevsky. Thank you.

Kvassov. How did you sleep? Our feather-beds are soft.

Rayevsky. Oh, the Devil take your feather-beds! I tossed the whole night.

Kvassov. Habit. As for us, we manage to sleep on them.

Rayevsky. They're stuffy.

Kvassov. That's healthful.

Rayevsky. Did you see Olga this morning?

Kvassov. I didn't happen to. (*Pause.*) Whom are you planning to see?

Rayevsky. People are coming here, to see me. The Chairman of the Soviet and others.

Kvassov. So, so... It was very offensive, to see our citizens' lack of discernment yesterday.

Rayevsky. Come, now, quit this pretence. You were happy enough about it. I can see right through you.

Kvassov. I? What did I do?

Rayevsky. And who was responsible for the hocus-pocus affair with the wheat? Wasn't it your son?

Kvassov. That's not just. I swear before God, that's not just. This very minute I've come from him. I heaped abuse on his head as only a father can. Why bring the bread during the meeting, why create confusion? But he won't even listen. You know how children are these days. He's only waiting to get his share, and then... to the Devil with his father.

Rayevsky. I'm going to arrest him today for breaking up the meeting.

Kvassov. That also is not just. He had good intentions. Still, whatever your will is. The law, I believe, hasn't foreseen such incidents. But you know better, you're closer to the law. (*Pause.*) Pasha, go to your room.

PASHA. I haven't spoiled anything so far, but look out, I'll spoil things yet.

KVASSOV. Go, I told you. I told you gently.

(PASHA *gets up abruptly.*)

RAYEVSKY. Why are you always sending her out? You've shut her up in the house and order her about. She's a grown-up girl.

KVASSOV. I'm her father.

RAYEVSKY. And you think that gives you the right to torture her. You must stop it. Olga and I are going to take her to the city with us when we leave.

KVASSOV. If she wants to go, she'll go.

RAYEVSKY. Will you come, Pasha?

PASHA. Why talk nonsense? (*Leaves.*)

RAYEVSKY (*calls after her*). I'm serious, Pasha. I mean it, really. (*Sits down at the table. Pause.*)

KVASSOV. What are you going to do now, dear comrade?

RAYEVSKY. I'm going to get the bread. I myself will go from house to house. I'll take assistants with me. I'll dig up all the vegetable gardens. I'm not accustomed to retreat, damn it all!

KVASSOV. That's just what I was afraid of. Comrade, dear, take the word of an old man. I know everybody here. I know how much everyone has — not only what each one has in his barn, but which one of them has a thing or two hidden in a stocking, which one keeps his savings in a pitcher, and which one under a plank in the floor. We haven't got seven thousand poods. I talked to the peasants today. We'll give what we can to the authorities — but on the quiet, without a meeting. We'll collect two thousand poods. More we cannot.

RAYEVSKY. What do you mean, two thousand? I'll turn the whole village inside out.

KVASSOV (*crossing himself in front of the ikons, sanctimoniously*). Lord, save the soul of your slave, Pavel, and take pity on it!

RAYEVSKY. Stop playing the fool! What's all this about?

KVASSOV. I can't even get the words out of my mouth.

RAYEVSKY. Listen, stop playing the clown. This is no time for jests.

KVASSOV. Comrade delegate, they'll kill you, the devils. When you begin to go from house to house, they'll kill you. I know they will.

RAYEVSKY. Well, they can't scare me with threats.

KVASSOV. But they won't stop to threaten. They'll smack a bullet into you from behind some corner. At night, or in broad daylight even. Ours is a desperate village. Such turbulent people, so hot-headed! You saw it yourself.

(*There is a sharp knock at the window.*)

RAYEVSKY (*starts*). What's this?

KVASSOV (*goes to the window*). He's come. Romanov has come. A mischief-maker. He's the chief trouble-maker of the whole district. He's already lost one arm. You'd think the man would quiet down, live peacefully, but no, he fairly breathes malice, like a dragon breathing fire. Shall I let him in?

RAYEVSKY. Let him in, let him in. As it happens, he was on the point of saying something about *you* yesterday.

KVASSOV. It doesn't cost anything to talk.

(KVASSOV *opens the door and comes in with* ROMANOV.)

ROMANOV. Greetings, Comrade Rayevsky. Only I won't talk to you in front of this abomination. Order him to get out.

RAYEVSKY. Come, now, don't be so abusive. This is his house.

ROMANOV. His house was built with our hands. Let him be crowded for a change. Soon we'll crowd him out altogether.

KVASSOV. I'll leave, Comrade Rayevsky, for the sake of your comfort. You've always been hot-headed, Kolya. Akh, be careful, there may not be room enough left for *you* soon.

ROMANOV. What will you do? Throw me into the well? I haven't forgotten.

KVASSOV. The law metes out punishment for such falsehoods.

ROMANOV. And will you be the one to turn the Soviet law against me?

KVASSOV. Even you will get your deserts some day. Go ahead, talk... (*Leaves.*)

RAYEVSKY. What well are you talking about?

ROMANOV. When the Whites were here, he betrayed twelve men. He himself helped hack them to pieces. And then he threw the pieces into a well. I know this positively to be the truth. But there are no witnesses. No one will tell. Everybody's afraid. There was an inquest, but since no one testified against him, he slipped out of the whole mess like an eel. I'll give my second arm this very minute if he didn't do it.

RAYEVSKY (*incredulous*). That old man?

ROMANOV. That old man! He's the main head of the whole hydra-headed serpent. May I drop dead this minute, if I'm not telling you the absolute truth.

RAYEVSKY. Not really? And where do you live?

ROMANOV (*bitterly*). Didn't you see the Tsar's palace as you were coming into the village? It's dug in the ground — you can't see it with the naked eye.

RAYEVSKY. So that mud hut is yours.

ROMANOV. Mine. I have royal blood in my veins. Kolka Romanov. Didn't you guess?

RAYEVSKY. What are you? A member of the Party?

ROMANOV. I'm a one-armed man.

RAYEVSKY. I'm not joking.

ROMANOV. If you're not joking, I'll tell you. I was thrown out.

RAYEVSKY. For what?

ROMANOV. Because wild blood runs in my veins, because I'm young. It doesn't matter, they'll take me back.

RAYEVSKY. Yes, you really should rejoin the Party.

ROMANOV. I shall rejoin, and I will bring the whole Romanov regiment into the Party with me. I have organized a regiment. We have uniforms, and shoulder-knots too. But we have no boots. So we stand at attention in our bare feet.

RAYEVSKY. How soon will this event take place?

ROMANOV. Only get our membership cards ready.

RAYEVSKY. Aren't you a little drunk?

ROMANOV. I'm always drunk. You just go ahead, crawl into my hole, take a look at the walls. They're weeping, weeping salt tears. So you, too, begin to whimper like a dog. Gloom envelops you. But you come to the regiment — and everything turns so gay. The walls are higher. The earth is warmer.

RAYEVSKY. Why don't they give you other quarters? You're an invalid.

ROMANOV. Where should they put me? But when we build our Community House — I'll have an apartment then, three rooms and a toilet.

RAYEVSKY. Are you people going to organize a collective farm?

ROMANOV. Of course. Do you think it will organize by itself?

RAYEVSKY. But when?

ROMANOV. We're preparing the ground. Soon we'll storm the fort. Ah, comrade! If you only knew how gay my life is now! I am being borne along by a wind, a strong wind. Such a gay, joyous wind. And my mud hut even is no longer a mud hut. It's a sailing ship. And I am the skipper. The sails rustle, the mast bends, and I myself am thrown up and down, up and down. But I guide it ever — forward! The waters rise, they overflow the banks, all the huts are floating away. On the roofs of these huts are peasants. 'Kolka,' they are crying, 'catch us with your hook... Kolka, take us with you.' And I keep on hooking them. I keep on and on. I am carrying the whole village with me — and I laugh, and I cry... (*Tears stream from his eyes.*)

RAYEVSKY. But you are crying. What's the matter with you?

ROMANOV. I'm crying because I'm so happy, or maybe I'm crying because I'm such a fool... But you, are you going to collect the bread?

RAYEVSKY. We must collect it, of course. I'm not sure, however, that we'll be lucky enough to get the whole seven thousand poods.

ROMANOV. What do you mean you're not sure. Even twelve thousand could be collected here if we needed them. We must go from house to house and search.

RAYEVSKY. I don't know. I don't believe that... (*A knock at the door.*) Just a moment, I'll open... (*Opens the door and lets* OLGA *in.*) Where were you, Olyenka? I was so worried.

OLGA. You sleep till God knows what hour! I walked around the village, and farther on, into the fields.

RAYEVSKY. Why didn't you wake me? I would have gone with you.

OLGA. I didn't feel like it — I don't know why.

RAYEVSKY. Are you upset?

OLGA. It hurt me to watch our terrible defeat yesterday.

RAYEVSKY. *My* defeat, you mean.

OLGA. I said *our* defeat.

RAYEVSKY. We are far from being completely beaten yet. I told you — the country is an elemental force.

OLGA. But I thought that you would conquer it in an instant.

RAYEVSKY. It stood on its haunches yesterday — it bellowed. I felt, as I sat on the platform yesterday, that I was on a ship, on the captain's bridge, while all around me a storm was raging. The waves rose, they flung themselves against the sides of the ship, and then they broke against the planks.

OLGA. What are you planning to do now?

(*A knock at the window.* DYEDOV, LOKTEV, *and* ZOTOVA *come in, General greetings.*)

LOKTEV. We must confer.

RAYEVSKY. I don't know the situation as well as you do. What do you advise?

OLGA. Let's be seated.

(*They all sit down.*)

DYEDOV (*to* ROMANOV). You may go. You can come again later.

LOKTEV. Why should his presence bother you? Let him stay.

ROMANOV. I'll go. I have only one arm...

ZOTOVA. Stay here, Kolka. (*To* DYEDOV.) Don't you dare send friends of the Party out. Comrade Rayevsky, you tell him.

RAYEVSKY. Stay here. I'm waiting, comrades.

DYEDOV. The situation is just as I reported. The whole population has risen. They have no bread. We must beat a retreat. Period!

LOKTEV. And not collect any bread?

DYEDOV (*mockingly*). Why not? We can make a collection. We can go from house to house and collect a grain or two here and there.

LOKTEV. So there are only a grain or two left in the whole village?

DYEDOV. Whatever our comrade delegate decides upon, whatever he orders, I'll collect.

ROMANOV. Comrade Chairman, allow me to ask a question.

DYEDOV. Go ahead.

ROMANOV. What are you wriggling for, like the Devil in a frying-pan? Shoot straight now — has the kulak bread or hasn't he?

DYEDOV. Nikolai Romanov, the time has long passed since you were allowed to insult people.

ROMANOV. I will continue to say this with my dying breath. I will continue to repeat it even after my last breath is drawn. I will poke my head out of the grave and I will shout so that the whole village can hear me. (*Shouts.*) The kulaks have bread!

RAYEVSKY (*irritably*). Stop your shouting — do you think we're deaf? You're not in your grave yet.

DYEDOV. Shouting such as yours only harms our Soviet Power. Who protested at the meeting yesterday? The kulaks? Period.

269

One must have some understanding, Comrade Romanov, of the economics of an agrarian society. You, of course, never had a farm of your own. There is a great deal you haven't yet comprehended.

ROMANOV. Your kind of farming cost me my right arm. Abuse me, Dyedov, abuse me, Comrade Chairman. All the kulaks call me a ne'er-do-well.

LOKTEV. That's enough from both of you! Comrade Rayevsky, we must arrive at some decision. There *is* bread, no question about that. But what is to be our next move?

ZOTOVA. Arrest the kulaks — and we'll collect all the bread in one day.

RAYEVSKY. What do you mean, arrest them — without cause?

ZOTOVA. Keep 'em in jail until they give up the bread.

DYEDOV. If we arrest them today, the whole village will be rioting by nightfall.

RAYEVSKY. Rioting?!

DYEDOV. It's all very simple. The whole district for miles around will be in an uproar. And who will be held responsible — the Secretary of the Communist Youth cell, Zotova? Pardon me, but she will be overlooked completely. Or the hot-headed Kolya Romanov, perhaps, will be held responsible? No! Dyedov will be held responsible. Comrade Rayevsky will be held responsible...

RAYEVSKY (*gets up and walks nervously around the room*). True...

LOKTEV. What are we going to do, then?

RAYEVSKY. The situation, comrades, is more serious than you think. Yesterday we saw before us the solid peasant mass, united and organized.

ZOTOVA. The kulak mass. I told you — the whole village is kulak.

RAYEVSKY. There are two ways open to us. We can, as has been suggested, begin to make arrests and search all the houses. My own original intention had been to put such pressure upon the peasants. But I have become convinced that Dyedov is right. Not only will the whole village rise in arms against us, not only will we not succeed in collecting any bread: we may also have to answer for the serious consequences our actions may lead to.

LOKTEV. A little preparedness would not have come amiss.

RAYEVSKY. The second method — and, in my opinion, the only correct one, the only one in agreement with Bolshevik methodology — is to remember that it is far more important for us to have the peasant as an ally than to collect two or three thousand additional

270

poods of bread. I propose, therefore, that after setting before ourselves the task of collecting the largest amount of bread possible under the circumstances, we should not be upset if we succeed in collecting no more than two or three thousand poods.

DYEDOV. Period!

ROMANOV. Ah, comrades, dear comrades! (*Quite unexpectedly he runs up to the table and puts his one arm upon it.*) Here, Dyedov, hack it off! Hack off my second arm! It's of no use to me. You won't let me raise it! I have an axe in my hand. And there are people who should be struck with that axe. But you won't let me!

(*While* ROMANOV *is talking,* MIKHAILOV *comes in. He wears an old military greatcoat and a grey karakul hat. His expression is earnest to the point of grimness.* RAYEVSKY *is visibly disturbed by his sudden arrival.*)

MIKHAILOV. What's going on here? Have you opened up a butcher shop? What are you going to hack off? Hello, Pavel! Greetings, Comrade Loktev. Hello, Olga. (*To* ROMANOV.) Oh, so it's you, Your Imperial Majesty, who are rioting? Dissatisfied with your subjects again?

ROMANOV. I have no tongue in my mouth for jests, Comrade Mikhailov. I have only two more years to live. Is it possible that all my life has been wasted?

ZOTOVA. Are you going to stay here long, Mikhailov? Will you speak at the Party meeting?

MIKHAILOV. I'm making the rounds of the districts, to speed up the bread collection. How are you getting on, Pavel?

RAYEVSKY. So-so. We've been slowed up a little at the moment, but there are certain local conditions here which must be taken into account.

MIKHAILOV. You've been delayed? What sort of delay? There shouldn't be any here. There is plenty of bread in this village.

DYEDOV. There *was* plenty of bread.

MIKHAILOV. And who are you?

DYEDOV. Chairman of the local Soviet — Dyedov, Mikhail Pavlovich.

MIKHAILOV. Then you, Mikhail Pavlovich, ought to know that there *is* plenty of bread here, not that there was.

DYEDOV (*retreating*). Just so...

LOKTEV. In the meantime we certainly have failed.

MIKHAILOV. What? What do you mean, failed?

271

LOKTEV (*hands him a sheet of paper*). Here, read the report of what happened yesterday!

MIKHAILOV (*reads, shakes his head, frowns*). So that's it... (*Returns the report to* LOKTEV. *To* DYEDOV.) Has Mishka Kvassov been arrested?

DYEDOV. I was waiting for an order.

MIKHAILOV. Waiting! To prison with him this instant! Call a meeting for tonight.

DYEDOV. At your service!

RAYEVSKY. In my opinion, a meeting for tonight, without any preparation, will do no good.

MIKHAILOV. You should have organized all preparatory measures before this, Comrade Rayevsky.

LOKTEV. That's what I said, too.

MIKHAILOV. That's what you said, too? You should have acted, not talked.

LOKTEV. But Comrade Rayevsky...

MIKHAILOV. Rayevsky! Rayevsky! You are the Secretary — when you disagree with someone, you should be able to convince your opponent that he is wrong and you are right. And if you can't convince him, telephone the District Office. Demand, insist. Otherwise you prove yourself a spineless creature. It is too late now, after the kulak has beaten us before the whole meeting, to take preparatory measures. We must turn the tables on them without any further loss of time.

RAYEVSKY. You won't be fighting merely the kulaks. You'll be fighting a united peasant mass.

MIKHAILOV. Such a thing as a united peasant mass doesn't exist. Country and city — those are but geographical and poetical labels — they have no sociological meaning.

RAYEVSKY. That's a good theory, but when it is a question of bread, all the turbid currents of the peasant's soul begin to flow against us.

MIKHAILOV. They are false currents, Pavel. Different currents — different waters — different eddies. You must know how to steer your boat.

ZOTOVA. And I say that this is a kulak village.

MIKHAILOV. It isn't you who is saying it. You only think you are the one who is saying it.

ZOTOVA. Amazing, Maria Dmitryevna! Who, then, is saying it?

MIKHAILOV. The kulak is saying it.

ZOTOVA. I would strangle a kulak with my own hands — and I repeat kulak words!

MIKHAILOV. Such things happen. Let's get going, comrades! Romanov, you will have to run a few errands. Dyedov, get the list of names. The checked list, be sure. Loktev, call all our active members together right away. But first of all, let's get out of this house!

(MIKHAILOV, DYEDOV, LOKTEV, ZOTOVA, *and* ROMANOV *leave.*)

RAYEVSKY (*after them, very loudly*). There will be rioting.

MIKHAILOV (*at the door*). We'll meet force with force.

ROMANOV. I shan't give my arm up yet, Comrade Chairman. (*Raises his arm.*) It will be needed.

CURTAIN

ACT IV

Scene 6

The village square. Towards sundown. The platform is still there, but as yet unoccupied. In the centre of the square is NIKOLAI ROMANOV, digging. The peasants — men, women, and children — are assembling in the square. They come singly and in groups. They stop when they see ROMANOV and look on in astonishment.

FIRST PEASANT WOMAN. What are you doing, Kolya?
(ROMANOV *answers neither her question nor any which follow. He continues to dig energetically. The comments of the spectators are met with laughter and exclamations.*)
SECOND PEASANT WOMAN. Kolyushka, what are you making?
FIRST YOUNG PEASANT. Brothers, Kolka is looking for treasure.
SECOND YOUNG PEASANT. Treasure! Kolya, let me help you! We'll divide the treasure.
SHILOV. No, seriously now. What are you doing, Kolya?
KATERINA. Why doesn't he answer, the accursèd one? It augurs ill, I know!
FIRST PEASANT. What did you lose, Kolya?
SECOND PEASANT WOMAN. No one knows. He just digs and digs and doesn't open his mouth.
KOTIKHIN. A clown, a regular clown.
SOTIN. You just wait, Vasily Afanasyevich, perhaps it isn't going to be so funny.
THIRD PEASANT. Brothers, look! I do believe he's digging a grave for himself.
THE WHOLE GROUP. A grave?
FIRST PEASANT GIRL. Or perhaps he's digging out a dowry for his Nyushka.
KATERINA. Oy, dear ones, it augurs ill...
FIRST PEASANT. Perhaps you're digging another mud hut for yourself? Only tell us, Kolya, and we'll take up a collection of boards for you.
A LITTLE BOY. I know. He's digging a radio.
FOURTH PEASANT (*approaching*). What's he doing?

274

SECOND YOUNG PEASANT. Building a new church.

SECOND PEASANT WOMAN. Tell us, Kolya, don't torture us.

VOICES. Tell us, Kolka! Come on, speak up! What are you doing? There's a devil for you! Not a word out of his mouth!

KOTIKHIN. We ought to chase him out. For indecent behavior while drunk.

SOTIN. Was it, perhaps, at your apiary, Vasily Afanasyevich, that he snatched a drink?

THIRD YOUNG PEASANT. What's going on here, lads?

SECOND YOUNG PEASANT. News! Someone slashed a calf's throat with a cucumber.

FIRST PEASANT WOMAN. Kolyushka, the whole assembly is begging you. Tell us now. What are you digging?

SECOND PEASANT. Don't be so proud, Kolka!

AN OLD MAN. Kolya, why are you ransacking the earth? The earth doesn't like it.

GRUNKIN. Kolya, have you, perhaps, some bread hidden underground which you'll sell to the State?

(*The peasants double over with laughter at every new sally.*)

FIRST PEASANT. Okh, this is killing me!

FIRST PEASANT WOMAN. It's bread he's got there, dear ones, bread. (*Holds her sides with laughter.*)

KOTIKHIN (*titters*). Bread!

ROMANOV (*shouts wildly*). Shut up, all of you! (*To* KOTIKHIN.) And you, reptile, you in particular shut your trap! (*Silence.*) I'm building a railroad.

VOICES. What? What did he say? What's that he's saying?

SHILOV. A railroad? You're building a railroad with this little spade? (*Suppressed laughter among the crowd.*)

SECOND PEASANT WOMAN. He's lost his mind, dear ones. Poor little Kolyushka!

OLKHA. A fine time he found to play jokes in. What a fool!

ROMANOV. I'm a fool, am I? But you aren't a fool? And what are all these people around me? They are the fools. (*Points all around him.*) I'm a fool — because I'm building a railroad without help from anyone. But here they are — fifteen hundred fools — whom Kvassov and his gang are skinning alive, but who follow him blindly, who even bow to the ground before him — 'Thank you, dear little father...' He is only one man, yet he fools the whole village, but I, I can't build a railroad single-handed? We'll see.

KOTIKHIN. So that's what you were leading up to? All he wanted was to gather a crowd to spout nonsense to!

KVASSOV. What a restless soul you are, Kolya. You shouldn't call all the peasants fools. It's not right. You're putting yourself above everyone else.

KOTIKHIN. From within, citizens, from within the worm is eating our entrails away. That's why he's digging.

SOTIN. There are worms and there are reptiles. Kolka is not the only one. What do you say, brothers?

VOICES. Right! Clever lad, Kolka! We've had our fill of bowing and scraping to Kvassov. The assassin!

KATERINA. Didn't I tell you, no good would come of this!

GRUNKIN. There they go, bawling their heads off, the scum. An idler drinks his farm away, and then yells for the one which doesn't belong to him. Just give him what another has earned with the sweat of his brow, and that, too, he'll spend on guzzling. That's what you're waiting for.

KOTIKHIN. Just as Kolya said — the whole village is filled with fools.

KORITKO. You shouldn't have made this exhibition, Kolya, you shouldn't have made it. This is a serious business.

KVASSOV. What business?

KORITKO. About you, for instance.

KVASSOV. What about me?

SOTIN. Everything. It's long past time for the whole world to see you as you really are. Come out in the open.

KOTIKHIN. And whatever's in the open, you will steal.

SOTIN (*raises his fist*). Uncle Kotikhin, I'll clout you just once — and where you are now standing a well will begin to flow.

OLKHA. Don't shove your fists! Don't shove your fists! You've come to a meeting, not to a brawl.

KORITKO. You see, Kolya, what has happened, instead of a serious discussion. You shouldn't have done this!

ROMANOV. Abuse me, go on, abuse me! I have only one arm!

KOTIKHIN. What is this, brother peasants? A tramp and a drunkard want to sit on top of us! They're making fools out of the whole village. Threatening to beat us. Are we going to let them? No, this shall not happen in *our* village.

ROMANOV. You shall not be on this earth. (*Throws himself upon* KOTIKHIN.)

276

(*As a free-for-all brawl starts,* MIKHAILOV, DYEDOV, RAYEVSKY, OLGA, LOKTEV, ZOTOVA, *several Party members, and Young Communist boys and girls arrive.*)

MIKHAILOV. Stop! Stop, I said!

(*The crowd separates.* ROMANOV *is dragged away from* KOTIKHIN.)

KOTIKHIN (*piteously*). He drew blood from me! Blood!

ROMANOV. I'll get you! I'll get you! I'll smear honey out of your own beehive all over your body and throw you into an anthill!

MIKHAILOV. Stop rioting! I'll have you removed from the meeting!

ROMANOV. Ah, I haven't a second one. I'd...

MIKHAILOV. What's happened?

OLKHA. A little quarrel. A peasant always tries to prove his point with his fist.

KORITKO. Kolya here put on some sort of theatrical performance and succeeded only in exciting everybody.

MIKHAILOV (*to* ROMANOV). You're always flying into a passion. You're in too much of a hurry.

ROMANOV. I haven't long left to live.

KVASSOV (*ironically*). That's true!

MIKHAILOV (*turning around sharply*). Ah, Kvassov! (KVASSOV *bows.*) Come on, Dyedov, let's open the meeting. How do you do, Ignat Vasilyevich. (*Greets* KORITKO.) Why didn't you speak up at the meeting yesterday? You see what the consequences are.

KORITKO. How do you do, Dmitri Petrovich. No one recognized me, or I would have spoken up.

MIKHAILOV. That's bad, very bad. You shouldn't have waited to be recognized. When you see that things are going wrong, speak up.

KORITKO. I thought it would blow over. It all happened so quickly.

MIKHAILOV. Yes. (*Goes towards the platform.*)

KVASSOV (*draws* GRUNKIN *aside*). Did you bring it?

GRUNKIN. I have it with me.

KVASSOV. Where?

GRUNKIN. Here. (*Slaps his pocket.*)

KVASSOV. See that you're not too late. Go ahead the minute he finishes. Don't give him time to collect his wits.

GRUNKIN. On the dot. I'll not give him a chance to say 'Oh!'

DYEDOV (*climbs up on the platform*). Citizens! We will now continue yesterday's meeting which was interrupted by a kulak conspirator who is now locked up. (*There is a movement among the crowd.*) The Secretary of the Regional Committee, Comrade Mikhailov, has the floor.

MIKHAILOV. I was here last in the spring of last year. You remember? We were trying Proshkin for speculating with bread. He had bought up all the bread at a ruble and twenty kopecks the bushel in the autumn, and later sold it to you at four and a half rubles. He had sold six, or perhaps seven hundred bushels. How much would that amount to? Perhaps someone here will add it up?

SECOND PEASANT. Mishka Afanasyev. Figures buzz around in his skull like flies.

MISHKA. If six hundred — (*mumbles*) — one thousand nine hundred and eighty rubles — and if seven hundred — (*mumbles again*) — two thousand three hundred and ten.

MIKHAILOV. Thank you. You compute well. I ask you this, then. To make a profit of two thousand rubles would one be willing to give away, as Mikhail Kvassov did yesterday, one hundred and twenty poods in order to shut your mouths? (*Silence.*) I ask you this. Why does the poor peasant and the middle peasant, when they know that the State needs bread in order to strengthen agriculture, sell it at the established price, even when the market has a different price, while the kulak not only hoards his own bread, but, benefactor that he is, overbids the State and buys up all the bread in the village?

OLKHA. You tell us.

MIKHAILOV. Because when winter comes the peasant will have to buy boots. He will have to have clothing. He will have to pay his taxes. He will have to do some repairing. The kulak waits. The kulak waits for the kulak spring. When the market price soars sky-high, the kulak brings his bread to the market.

ROMANOV. Sure! White wagonloads filled with white flour.

MIKHAILOV. What do you think — is this fair? The kulak sells for fifteen rubles, and the peasant for five, six rubles. No — you sell to the State at the same price as everybody else.

VOICES. Correct! Right! Let them sell like everybody else.

(*The crowd moves closer to the platform.*)

GRUNKIN. There are no kulaks in our village!

MIKHAILOV. Fine. Since there are no kulaks here, we'll divide the bread assessment equally among all the peasants. I have a list of names here which I was going to offer for your approval. The situation is this. We need seven thousand poods of bread. Our idea was to exempt eighty per cent of you and to collect the necessary amount from the remaining twenty. And out of these twenty per cent to collect four thousand poods from the richest kulaks — but since there aren't any kulaks here, we'll collect it from the whole village instead.

SHILOV. What do you mean, the whole village?

FIRST PEASANT WOMAN. No, no. That isn't fair!

VOICES. Collect it all from twenty per cent! Let the rich squirm! Eighty per cent to be exempt!

SECOND PEASANT. Let the kulaks be assessed! That's fair, citizens!

VOICES. That's the way to do it! That will be fair! Assess the kulaks!

THIRD PEASANT. Let them sell like everybody else.

OLKHA. Kvassov has a thousand poods — I have only fifty. Should I give ten and he, too, only ten? He repairs his shining little kidskin boots, while I have to piece some rags together for a winter coat.

KVASSOV. You have a short memory. Who helped you out last year?

OLKHA. You helped me out, but you dragged the very soul out of me in payment for the help — and locked it up in your warehouse. (*Laughter.*)

KORITKO. Allow me, citizens.

DYEDOV. Koritko, Ignat! Jump up and take the floor.

(KORITKO *comes forward.*)

KVASSOV (*motions* GRUNKIN). It's time.

GRUNKIN. I'm going. (*Loudly.*) Comrade Mikhailov, may I be allowed to ask a question?

MIKHAILOV. Go on!

GRUNKIN. May I come closer?

MIKHAILOV. Come on. (*The crowd makes way for him.* GRUNKIN *slowly walks forward, winning general attention. When he's at the foot of the platform, he digs his hands into his pockets and brings out two fistfuls of grain.*) Well?

GRUNKIN. My son and I have gone our different ways and have divided our land. I continue to live according to the old ways — my son inaugurates new-fangled ones. Take a look now — here are two grades of wheat — which is the better?

MIKHAILOV (*stretches out both hands, which* GRUNKIN *fills with wheat.* MIKHAILOV *examines the samples attentively. The crowd watches him in silence).* You want to catch me, eh? One is spring wheat, the other winter wheat. (*Laughter.*) You're a practical joker, I see. Well, I've a joke for you, too. (*Puts his hand in his pocket and takes out a handful of grain.*) Come over here, take a look at this grain.

GRUNKIN (*looking*). Oh, Mother in Heaven! Where did you find such grain?

SHILOV. Pass it here! Let us see!

(*The peasants press close, feel the grain, pour it from hand to hand.*)

FIRST PEASANT. Give it to me now!

THIRD PEASANT. Make some room — give another a chance to see.

SECOND PEASANT. Now, that's what I call grain!

OLKHA. What grain! Little Mother in Heaven, what grain! Is it a sample from America?

MIKHAILOV. No, it isn't. I passed the Lenin Collective Farm on my way here and thought I'd bring a sample or two of their grain with me. Not a bad harvest. Eighty in some places, ninety in others.

GRUNKIN. Ninety! They're lying!

MIKHAILOV. Take a trip over there and see for yourself.

OLKHA. And even if they only had eighty — it's not like our harvest.

ROMANOV. Never mind, we too will soon have such a harvest...

KOTIKHIN (*mocks him*). Kolya will lead us to the Kolkhoz, to the collective farm.

SOTIN. He'll not take *you* there, never fear.

AFANASYEV. You'll be turned away from the gates...

OLKHA. Will you take me?

ROMANOV. You'll go yourself... You'll not only go — you'll run.

OLKHA. I will?

KORITKO. Why not? You also. Citizens, I have an idea. This is the idea. When I get up in the morning I spend two hours looking for my boots — and all the time they are standing by the stove, right under my eyes... The State needs bread. You there, Vasily Pavlovich — when you were building your house, you denied yourself everything but the bare necessities for two years. You borrowed from whoever would lend you a kopeck. What, then, do you expect the State to do when they have to build the Five-Year Plan?

OLKHA. That's true.

280

KORITKO. That's just how it is. Except that we both give the State very little and have next to nothing ourselves. In one word, everything is going to ruin.

VOICES. Right! That's true...

KATERINA. How can we help it?

KORITKO. I thought we might do some economic planning, citizens. Now you just reckon this up. We have a thousand or so back yards, houses with all sorts of useless additions — ten versts they take up. Now, if we would only pass the plough over all this land... Eh, brothers? If, let us say, we would only demolish our miserable little huts made of straw, if we would only build one or two large buildings in their stead...

KATERINA. Oy, oy, oy... what nonsense.

THIRD PEASANT. Tsst!

KORITKO. We have some two thousand dogs. Count it up. Every one of them, if you compute in terms of bread, devours a pound's worth a day. In a year — twenty wagonfuls.

SHILOV. Twenty wagonfuls for the dogs!

KORITKO (*inspired by his own new thoughts*). A horse, God forbid, dies. You may as well give up the ghost then. But when there are five hundred horses, all owned in common... Our agricultural economy is a petty one... The land is broken up into tiny lots... Each peasant has to do all the chores by himself, without help from anyone else. But when the farm is large, then there is equal distribution of work. The ant — to take an example from nature — even the ant doesn't carry its piece of straw alone, without help. And the ant, too, is one of God's creatures. That's what I'm thinking, citizens.

KOTIKHIN. We didn't ask you for a speech, Minister of State. Tell us about the bread!

KORITKO. And the bread, citizens, we must sell to the State. Especially those of us who have a surplus. And how much bread we have — that we know.

KVASSOV. You'll have to prove it first.

KORITKO. What everyone knows, Ivan Gerasimovich, needs no proof. Just try to prove that the sun rises in the morning, remains in the heavens the whole day long, but as soon as the day ends — goes down to the land of the Japs. What proof are you talking about?

KOTIKHIN. You, I suppose, have no bread at all. Is that it?

KORITKO. You're right, I have bread. And since you've put the burden on my shoulders, let me see you follow my example. I'll give half of my supply and you give half of yours.

OLKHA. That's justice for you. Give five hundred poods, Kotikhin.

KOTIKHIN (*frightened*). Where do you think I'm going to get a thousand poods from? You'll have a hard time finding even five hundred in my warehouse.

SECOND PEASANT. He fed the other five hundred to the bees. (*Laughter.*)

SOTIN. Let's finish this. Read the list of names.

MIKHAILOV. I don't think, citizens, we need bother the whole meeting with the list. We'll turn it over to the proper Soviet department. Let them decide. What do you think?

SHILOV. Yes, I guess we'd better do it that way.

OLKHA. May we be present when they make their decisions?

MIKHAILOV. The door is open to everyone, except kulaks.

KOTIKHIN. They're trying to split us, brother peasants — to separate us like sheep. Peasants should be divided into two classes only — idlers and hard-working men. Kulaks are an invention of the city...

MIKHAILOV. Kotikhin!

KOTIKHIN. Yes?

MIKHAILOV. What's that you're saying about the city?

KOTIKHIN. I? Nothing at all. Only a few doubts bother me. Permit me to ask for an elucidation.

MIKHAILOV. I know your elucidations. Go ahead.

KOTIKHIN. Why is the peasant burdened with so many loads? Why aren't the city people troubled? Why are the factory workers the favorite sons of the State, while we peasants — we who provide the food for all of Mother Russia — are the step-children?

MIKHAILOV. You think the workers in the factories live better than you do?

VOICES. May God only grant us such a life! Better than we? I should say so! Could we but live like that! They certainly don't suffer the way we do!

OLKHA. We, too, would like to get such treatment. To receive wages.

MIKHAILOV. You want wages! Fine. Dyedov, take a piece of paper and write. We're building a brick factory in our district. We need two thousand additional workers. Anyone who wants to leave his farm, give your name to Dyedov, and we'll transfer you to the city to work in the factory for wages. (*Looks all around. The peasants turn their faces away from him.*) So? There are no volunteers? You only like to make a lot of noise. Well, have you finished now?

OLKHA. Yes, I guess we've finished. Hurry up with the lists.

MIKHAILOV. I have to leave. Comrade Rayevsky will stay here. He'll go over the lists.

DYEDOV. Period!

(*The peasants begin to depart, talking heatedly as they go.*)

MIKHAILOV (*leaves the platform and goes towards* OLGA *and* RAYEVSKY). Well, here we are. No rioting, after all. Olga, two words with you. (RAYEVSKY *moves away.*)

OLGA. Well?

MIKHAILOV. Olka, would you like me to spend a day here?

OLGA. Do what you think best, Mikhailov.

MIKHAILOV. I can leave today, or I can stay here a day. We could both stay at Koritko's.

OLGA. We will not stay together, Mikhailov...

MIKHAILOV (*after a pause*). So that's how things stand... It remains this way, then... In that case, well... I suppose I had better leave right away...

OLGA. As you please...

MIKHAILOV. But how, Olka... There is something wrong... How badly it all came out... No, I guess the sooner I leave the better... Dyedov!

DYEDOV. At your service.

MIKHAILOV. Are the horses ready?

DYEDOV. As you ordered.

MIKHAILOV. So long, comrades.

(MIKHAILOV *leaves hurriedly.* DYEDOV, LOKTEV, ZOTOVA *and the Communist Youths leave with him.*)

RAYEVSKY (*coming towards* OLGA). What did he want to talk to you about?

OLGA. Nothing important. However, the fact remains, Pavel, that he won.

RAYEVSKY. Did you tell him so?

OLGA. Yes.

RAYEVSKY. He saw for himself that we hadn't been able to handle the situation.

OLGA. Not we — you.

RAYEVSKY. Only a few hours before you said — we.

OLGA. But a conference followed during which you became frightened at the possibility of a riot. Both you and Dyedov were worried about shouldering the responsibility. He, however, wasn't afraid to call a meeting right after our ignominious defeat. And he won!

RAYEVSKY. Well — God help the vanquished.

OLGA. I still don't understand what happened. You suddenly lose your head, you behave as if a changeling had been put in your place. You say things that you, of all people, should never say, and you act as if you wanted to spite your real self. This isn't the real Rayevsky. The real Rayevsky is different. How, then, did it all come about? (RAYEVSKY *fidgets with the collar of his shirt.*) What are you doing?

RAYEVSKY. Nothing. My collar is a little too tight. It's constricting my throat. Continue, please.

OLGA. You've probably made the knot in your necktie too tight... Necktie? Maybe your necktie really is the same color as the neckties of all the others... perhaps it is no different from the neckties of the rest of the mob...

A BOY (*running up to* RAYEVSKY). Here's a note for you, uncle. (*Gives him a note and runs away.*)

RAYEVSKY. Who can be sending me a note? (*Reads it and grows excited.*) Stop! Where's that urchin! (*Looks around.*) Dyedov! Ring the tocsin! Call the peasants back to the meeting!

OLGA. What has happened?

RAYEVSKY. Wait... Hey, you, lads, Young Communists! Run! Get everybody back here!

(*The Communist Youths run. The village tocsin is sounded. Frightened and astonished, the peasants begin to gather again. RAYEVSKY ascends the platform alone and stands there, glowering and morose.*)

SHILOV. What have you called us back for?

RAYEVSKY (*pronounces every word distinctly*). I have just received a note. This is what it says. (*Reads.*) 'Delegate: We have scared you off one meeting already. Yet you are still here. Take our advice — begin to save some boards for your coffin. You haven't much longer to live. Your bullet has already been cast. The time has come for you to enter the other world, to plunder bread there. Your hour has struck!' (*In uncontrolled anger.*) That's an expensive note! It's going to cost you two thousand poods of bread! If by morning you don't bring me the author of this note, I shall add two thousand poods to the seven thousand you are already taxed with. And if I receive any more notes — four thousand. (*Pause.*)

OLKHA. How is this now? God only knows who wrote the note, but all of us must suffer for it.

RAYEVSKY. Silence! I'll show you for whom a bullet has been cast.

(*Descends the platform and, without turning, marches right through the crowd, which makes way for him.*)

CURTAIN

ACT IV

SCENE 7

KVASSOV'S *house.* OLGA *is cleaning a revolver.* RAYEVSKY *is at the table, writing.* ZOTOVA *is standing next to him.*

RAYEVSKY (*finishes writing and gives the paper to* ZOTOVA). Here you are. Give this to Dyedov and get everybody together without any loss of time. And get the arms ready. I'll join you in another minute.

OLGA. We'll join you right away.

RAYEVSKY. You had better not take the risk, Olga.

OLGA. Perhaps you think that I shall hide? The Browning is ready.

RAYEVSKY. Let's go. (*To* ZOTOVA.) How are your boys? Dependable lads?

ZOTOVA. They'll do! Loktev has been running from house to house since he found out about the disturbance. He's trying to pacify the peasants.

RAYEVSKY. The coward! Go, Zotova.

ZOTOVA. I'm flying! (*Runs out.*)

RAYEVSKY. And so, a state of war! You're not afraid, Olga?

OLGA. Not at all.

RAYEVSKY. Do you feel the threatening wind? Hasten, hasten with my steed!

OLGA. Will you dash into the enemy's camp?

RAYEVSKY. In the year 1919 I faced a mutinied battalion. There was no one else with me. The soldiers were waiting for their division and getting ready for a battle. I galloped up to them, all alone, and in full view of everybody I shot their leader. Later, this battalion became a unit in our division.

OLGA. You seem to have grown taller.

(MIKHAILOV *comes in, removing his things on the way. He goes up to the door which leads into* KVASSOV'S *room, opens it, and looks in.*)

RAYEVSKY. There is no one in the house. Only the nun.

(MIKHAILOV *shuts the door.*)

MIKHAILOV. What's this mess you've cooked up? Do you want to be tried? Loktev telephoned me at Ryzhovo, and I rushed back.

RAYEVSKY. You needn't have worried.

MIKHAILOV. You know, I suppose, that hell has broken loose in the village. And that there may be a mass attack tonight.

RAYEVSKY. I have taken measures to suppress the revolt.

MIKHAILOV. You have countermanded that order of yours, I assume.

RAYEVSKY. I gave orders to arm the Young Communists.

MIKHAILOV. Have you countermanded your order?

RAYEVSKY. I'm not a coward. That you know well enough.

MIKHAILOV. I command you to rescind this senseless order immediately and to see that every peasant knows about it.

RAYEVSKY. Never.

MIKHAILOV. I could do it myself, but I don't want to make a laughing stock out of you. You, after all, will have to remain here and collect the bread.

RAYEVSKY (*hotly*). I'll not countermand the order. Nor will I allow you to do so. To draw back, to countermand the order merely because we are being threatened with a revolt! That's cowardly and a discredit to the Party...

MIKHAILOV. Calmer, Pavel. The Party can be discredited only by insane orders and unwillingness to correct an error.

RAYEVSKY. You must first prove that an error has been made. You yourself used to impose fines on a city when our soldiers were killed by the inhabitants.

MIKHAILOV. I imposed fines on enemies. Are you, by any chance, among enemies?

RAYEVSKY. Let them give up the kulaks.

MIKHAILOV. You've driven them to unite with the kulaks. You've set the whole village against you. How did you dare make use of the bread collection as an instrument of punishment? Who are you — an English lord visiting one of his colonies? Did you learn this trick abroad?

RAYEVSKY. You think, then, that we ought to allow ourselves to be shot?

MIKHAILOV. Who shoots but the kulak? The kulak who is always shouting at the top of his lungs that we are taking his bread away by force — that we are robbers. You have done everything in your power to help him. That must be corrected. You must show that your order is against the Party line.

RAYEVSKY. How can I continue working after that?

MIKHAILOV. You consider it more important, then, to safeguard your dignity as an individual than to follow a straight Party line?

RAYEVSKY. I will not countermand the order.

MIKHAILOV. You will countermand it.

RAYEVSKY. No.

MIKHAILOV. Countermand the order, Pavel. We have no time to lose. If you don't, I will do it myself and put you under arrest. (RAYEVSKY *grabs his cap and rushes towards the door.*) Put on your coat, it's cold. (RAYEVSKY *puts on a short fur coat and leaves.*)

OLGA. Mikhailov, two words.

MIKHAILOV. I'm listening.

OLGA. Did you rejoice very much when you heard what had happened here? Did your heart begin to beat faster from joy? Did it?

MIKHAILOV. I became very agitated and rushed right over. I was afraid of disturbances.

OLGA. Answer a direct question. Were you happy to hear the news?

MIKHAILOV. Mystification again. Why should I rejoice at the news?

OLGA. Because you could exult once again — because you could once more humiliate Pavel — because you could once again take a base and petty revenge — because he is cleverer than you are, because he is more vital than you are, because he is a thousand times finer than you are...

MIKHAILOV. Do you know, Olga, this is really becoming insulting. What vile things you've been accusing me of lately!

OLGA. You're revenging yourself because of me. Do you hear? I'm not addressing you, the man encased in his armor, but Mikhailov, the inner man, the real Mikhailov. You're revenging yourself because of me. That is why you're here.

MIKHAILOV. How vile, Olga. If you can't understand all that has just taken place here and can only drag it down to the level of a squabble between two rivals — we have nothing to say to each other.

OLGA. Again the Secretary of the Regional Committee is speaking — Mikhailov has hidden himself.

MIKHAILOV. There are no two Mikhailovs, Olga. Drop that nonsense. There is only one man.

OLGA. And that man is the Secretary of the Regional Committee?

288

MIKHAILOV. Yes, that man is the Secretary of the Regional Committee.

OLGA. But you've failed, Mikhailov. You wanted to turn me against him, you wanted to force me to return to you, but you've succeeded in achieving the exact opposite. You will forever — do you hear? forever — remain a stranger to me. I shall go to him — to him who has been humiliated and hunted by you, but who is a real man, the man I love. (*Hastily puts on her coat.*)

MIKHAILOV. Apparently I really didn't know you very well. This, brother, is all so false... But wait a minute, I am also going to the Club... I told Loktev to get together all the peasants he could.

OLGA. I won't go with you. (*Leaves.*)

MIKHAILOV. The free may do as they like... (*Pause.* MIKHAILOV *slowly puts on his things.*) So, Comrade Mikhailov... Two questions. Well? You have nothing in common with Olga, have you? H'm, no ... How does it happen then that you didn't find this out before?... Well... it didn't somehow happen... So far, so good, then... And how do you feel about this stranger now?... You no longer love her? ... Yes, yes, you... (*In a different tone of voice.*) Well, I must go... They must all be there already... No, but answer the question... (*In the same tone of voice.*) Oh, very well, very well... I must go. (*Goes out.*)

MOKRINA (*comes in, looks around*). They've all gone.

KVASSOV (*comes in*). Ekh! (*Sits down.*) How my heart is beating! Death is giving me notice.

MOKRINA. Pray...

KVASSOV. Our prayers aren't agreeable to God — they don't reach His ears...

MOKRINA. Hope...

KVASSOV. I want to. Now you do this, Mother — go to the little cart-shed and knock on the door. Tell them all to come here. Tell them I'm waiting.

(MOKRINA *goes out.* KVASSOV *kneels and prays, making low obeisances.* MOKRINA *returns, followed by* KOTIKHIN, PROSHKIN, ZUBOV, SHILOV, *their sons, and two other peasants. They all cross themselves in front of the ikons and sit down.*)

KOTIKHIN. Ivan Gerasimovich... Well, what? (KVASSOV *doesn't answer. He continues to pray.*) Ivan Gerasimovich! (KVASSOV *prays.*) Ivan Gerasimovich, God's Kingdom is eternal, while we have less than an hour at our disposal. We're all here.

Kvassov (*rises*). I greet you all. Mikhailov is here again.

Zubov. So-o?

Grunkin. Again?

Kotikhin. He's cunning, this Regional Chief, very cunning. And not very good-natured either, not a bit accommodating. He outwitted all of us at the meeting. And now he's here again.

Proshkin. Mikhailov hasn't forgotten Proshkin. But neither has Proshkin forgotten Mikhailov.

Kotikhin. And how did the two of them get along?

Kvassov. Sparks flew between them. The one was burning up more and more — the other trying to put the fire out.

Kotikhin. Couldn't we run a blade through them? Have you given that a thought?

Kvassov. We can't take the time to sharpen the blades. We need an axe now. You always want to play the fox, Vasily Afanasyevich, when we must play the bear.

Kotikhin. The bear has too broad a chest — too good a target for a gun.

Kvassov. Hide behind the logs. Throw oak trees at the hunter. Arouse the beasts in the forest so that even the squirrel begins to throw cones. The forest is large — the hunters small in number.

Kotikhin. If only there were amity among the beasts in the forest. But the hare won't associate with the wolf.

Kvassov. Force the hare to associate with the wolf, scare him into joining the other beasts. (*Addressing everybody.*) We have gathered here, dear guests, in secret. In our own home village we must hide our heads from everybody. We must behave as if we were in the house of a stranger where we didn't belong. Yet who are we? We are the foundation. The belly of Mother Russia is filled with our bread. It is we who clothe Moscow, we who provide shoes for her, we who feed her. But who orders us about? Ragged tramps, beggars, drunkards. And those who live in Moscow? Little have they to worry about. All of Russia is but a field for their experiments. They want to raise a special brand of European herb on it. On that field we are the poisonous weeds — the broom-rape, the wild grass. They've begun to weed us out. By the roots they are weeding us out. They're mowing us down with a scythe. The hour has come when we must either lie down under the scythe or shout so that all Russia should hear us: 'You're wrong, you Moscow agronomists! We're not weeds — we're oaks!' (*Pounds the table with his fist. Pause.*

More quietly.) We will break your scythes. Trusty people have said
— the straw around the village is dry — strike but one match and
it will be devoured by flames. With God's help, we will start the
conflagration.

ZUBOV. Right.

SHILOV. Isn't it too soon?

GRUNKIN. On the contrary! This is the best time. Rayevsky
spoke better than he knew when he said the note will turn out to be
a costly one. Only who will pay the cost...

PROSHKIN. Mikhailov will never leave our village. Our climate
suits him too well.

KVASSOV (*to* KOTIKHIN). And what do you say?

KOTIKHIN. I'll not back out. Only let's make use of our wits,
brother villagers, let's make use of our wits. First of all, we mustn't
forget the little bottle. A little bottle can sometimes accomplish
great deeds. It can turn a rich man into a beggar, and a beggar into
a rich man. Let's give our brother villagers a treat.

GRUNKIN. We must do that... yes, we must do that...

KOTIKHIN. And we mustn't forget God's blessing. Our peasants
are always happier when they know that God's on their side. But
we must do it craftily. Tomorrow's a feast day — the church will be
more crowded than on a week day. We'll tell the Father to announce
a confession hour. And while our dear brother peasant confesses
the sins he has never committed and conceals the ones he has, let
the Father whisper in his ear, 'You must do this and that...' With
God then, and tomorrow we begin.

KVASSOV. Tomorrow will be too late. We must begin today,
brother villagers. We must begin right now.

ZUBOV. How now?

GRUNKIN. What do you mean now?

SHILOV. I'm frightened.

KOTIKHIN. Why the hurry, Ivan Gerasimovich? We'll be more
certain of success if we wait until tomorrow.

KVASSOV. Mikhailov is here to countermand our hero's order.
They won't have time to inform the people today, but tomorrow
the whole village will know about it — tomorrow you'll not be able
to arouse a single peasant... Today's the day.

PROSHKIN (*vengefully*). Mikhailov is mine!

KVASSOV. And now let us pray for the repose of the soul of Mikhailov. (*Crosses himself. Pause.*)

ZUBOV. And the soul of Rayevsky.

KVASSOV. Don't touch that one. With Mikhailov out of the way, our hero will work so much harm, not only our village, the whole district will rise as one man...

ZUBOV. Is Mikhailov in Koritko's house?

KVASSOV. In Koritko's. Now let us send the boys out to gather the peasants. And to ransack the village for arms. We'll all meet in Kotikhin's apiary.

KOTIKHIN. The more trustworthy ones should be called out immediately.

KVASSOV. Get the young lads. May God be with you, dear guests, may God be with you...

SHILOV. Wait a minute...

GRUNKIN. What's the matter, Vasya?

SHILOV. You wait, just you wait a moment... Ivan Gerasimovich, what are you doing?... I can't... I can't... I don't quite understand...

KVASSOV. What don't you understand, Vasily?

SHILOV. That is — we're fighting about the note, aren't we? Because it's not fair to add another two thousand poods... But now ... it seems Mikhailov isn't going to... He understands it isn't just ... And now we... (*Makes a gesture.*) But why? Ivan Gerasimovich ... If he's on our side...

GRUNKIN. You come with me, Vasya. We'll have a drink, and then you'll understand.

SHILOV. No, wait, wait...

KVASSOV. The time has come to act, Vasily... The time for talk has passed. Don't you all leave at once. You mustn't be seen together. To think that we can't show our faces in our own home village! Oh, misery, misery!   (*They leave, one by one.*)

MOKRINA. It's that Kolka, accursèd that he is by God, who's making trouble. Had he not come out of a woman's womb, I would strangle him with my own hands.

KVASSOV. Kolka is only the nail in the horseshoe. We must whip the horse.

SHILOV. Whose horse, Ivan Gerasimovich?

KVASSOV. Go on, Vasily, go on. (GRUNKIN *leads* SHILOV *out.* KVASSOV *shuts the door after them, picks up an axe, kneels, raises one of the boards, and takes out a rifle and a revolver.*) Akh, I'm sorely troubled. Tell me something, Mother.

MOKRINA (*mysteriously, like an incantation*). What shall I tell you, Ivan Gerasimovich? I'll tell you what I saw in the night. I felt oppressed yesterday evening, sleep would not come for a long time. The dogs were whining on the outskirts of the gardens, and behind the stove a cricket chirped ceaselessly — tew-tew. And then — I don't know how sleep finally came to me — but suddenly there was no cricket. Instead, sweet little angels were playing upon strings of a fineness never before seen by the eye of man — strings made out of star-beams. And the little angels barely touched them as they passed the lightest of fingers over them. Then a beautiful garden in full bloom rose before my eyes. Sparkling fountains played in it. Little crystal boats glided upon its clear and limpid lakes. And the flowers reached the sky and floated along the heavenly firmament. Fragrant breezes caressed me. And then a diaphanous table rose before me — a cloth spun out of cloud webs was spread upon it. Around this table sat the shining Host. And in the centre, upon the throne of the radiant sun, sat God, our Lord. I dared not raise my eyes to face our Lord and I threw myself prone upon the ground. And our Lord God said to me: 'Maiden, raise your eyes and gaze.' And I did as I was told. Facing our Lord sat our little Tsar, dressed in vestments white, embroidered all over with diamonds, and a purple halo framing his head. 'Great Tsar,' I asked, 'how much longer is the Kingdom of the Antichrist to last? When will you come back to your flock?' And the Tsar rose from his throne, stretched out his arm, and I...

(PASHA *appears in the doorway. She leans against it and stares at* KVASSOV, *silently.* MOKRINA *looks at her.*)

KVASSOV (*without turning around*). And what did you do? (*Pause.*) But what did you do? (*Turns around, the rifle still in his hand, and sees* PASHA. *Pause.*) A-ah... my dear little daughter. So this is the Club you went to?

PASHA. I witnessed a more interesting performance here.

KVASSOV. Mother, didn't you lock the door?

PASHA. The door was locked. I came in with the peasants. It was dark.

KVASSOV. And what did you expect to find here?

PASHA (*nodding her head at the rifle*). Something different from what you found.

KVASSOV. Spying on your father?

PASHA. I'm curious. I like to know everything.

293

Kvassov (*threateningly*). Pashka!

Pasha. You christened me yourself.

Kvassov. Anger obscures one's memory. I may forget that you're my daughter.

Pasha. If only you would forget, I'd say, 'Many thanks.'

Kvassov. Bitch!

Pasha. The ikons are over your head.

Kvassov. I'll kill you, Pashka!

Pasha. Isn't Mikhailov enough for you?

Kvassov. A-ha! So you heard!

Pasha. I'm not deaf.

Kvassov. Pashenka! What are you going to do?

Pasha. It shall not take place! I'll stop the bloody deed. I'll tell everything.

Kvassov. And send your father to face the firing squad — send your father to his death?

Pasha. Renounce your plan!

Kvassov. You're in my way.

Pasha. You're in *my* way. You've kept me prisoner in this house as in a wooden grave.

Kvassov. This is no time to settle accounts.

Pasha. Are you in a hurry? You'll have time to murder him. I'm going. (*Starts to go.*)

Kvassov. Where to?... Pasha! Stop a minute! Pasha!

Pasha. Didn't you say yourself that I was in your way?

Kvassov. Listen to me, Pashenka. Why are you trying to take your father's life? Is it not for you, Pashenka, that I scrape the soil with my nails? That I tear the bark off the trees with my teeth? Think!

Pasha. I'm not asking you to do it. (*Goes to the door.*)

Kvassov. Pasha! One last word — just one last word — then you can go...

Pasha. Well?

Kvassov. Whom are you going to see? Do they look upon us as human beings even? We're less than insects to them. We're the clay under their feet. Why, for instance, did they deride you?

Pasha. Me! Who was deriding me?

Kvassov. That hero of yours, the one with the medal. And his white-skinned wench.

Pasha. How did they deride me? Speak!

KVASSOV. He was ridiculing you to his wench. 'What a village dolt she is,' he says. 'Fat and snub-nosed... And hangs on to me...' he says, 'as if she had the claws of a cat... And I,' he says, 'invite her to the city with us...'

PASHA (*listens with both hands pressed to her heart and her eyes wide open*). You're lying!

KVASSOV. And his wench laughs: 'Take her along,' she says, 'take her along — we need a cook in the city!'

PASHA (*with tears in her eyes*). A cook...

KVASSOV. And he... 'You'll see,' he says, 'if I so desire, she'll even cook for us...'

PASHA (*with tears, desperately*). You're lying! This couldn't have happened! He couldn't do that to me...

KVASSOV (*solemnly, before the ikons*). I swear it by our Holy Lord — by our most holy Mother of God!

PASHA. You shut up, shut up! Let me collect my thoughts. Ridiculing me to her...

KVASSOV. To her, dear daughter, to her...

PASHA. You shut up! Don't you say another word! So that's the kind of a man you are, my Pavlik! That's the kind! I'm holding on to you, am I? I won't let go! You dolt, Pasha, you painted wooden image! (*Weeps.*)

MOKRINA. Cry, Pashenka, cry! You'll feel better...

PASHA (*in despair and sudden fury*). Tsst, you! I'm not crying. Father, burn everything! Begin... Let them feel the tongues of the flames... Let them not come here again — let the fire devour the dry grass from here to the city, let the flames rage all around them. And we will laugh while the glass windows in their houses crash. Their buildings are tall, but we will demolish them. Aren't we oaks, father? Aren't we oaks?

KVASSOV. Together, dear daughter, we'll begin together. (PASHA *feverishly throws a kerchief over her head and puts on her coat.*) But where are you going?

PASHA. I'm leaving. Don't be afraid. I'll be at the apiary. (*Leaves.*)

(MOKRINA *goes to shut the door after her.* KVASSOV *kneels slowly.*)

KVASSOV. Mother of God, Holy Intercessor, forgive the terrible false oath I swore to my daughter.

CURTAIN

ACT V

SCENE 8

A room in a peasant hut transformed into a communal library. All the benches are pushed to one side. ZOTOVA, ROMANOV, MISHKA AFANASYEV, *Communist Youth boys and girls are in the room. Everybody is smoking.*

ROMANOV. Zotova!
ZOTOVA. Yes?
ROMANOV. Isn't it time to change the guard?
ZOTOVA. We've just sent this one out.
ROMANOV. Akh! If I could only do something!
AFANASYEV. Well, now — here's a nail coming out of the wall — drive it back in with your head.

(*Laughter. Two peasants enter, one of them carrying a rifle, the other a stick with an iron point.*)

FIRST PEASANT. Greetings! Are we going out to raise hell?
SECOND PEASANT. He's mad with rage, the scum!
ROMANOV. Order, order! Sit down.
FIRST COMMUNIST YOUTH. Why doesn't Rayevsky come?
ZOTOVA. He'll be here when the time comes. Keep up your discipline.
FIRST COMMUNIST YOUTH. I'm keeping it up.
ROMANOV. Don't lose it now, be careful. (*Laughter.*)

(SOTIN *enters, carrying a rough club. There is a little boy with him.*)

SOTIN. Comrade Zotova. (*Bows.*) You just let me get at Proshkin. I was one of his poor tenants and I brought this little reed away with me. (*Swings the club.*)
SECOND COMMUNIST YOUTH. Don't swing it so recklessly, Uncle Piotr, or you'll send us all to hell. (*Laughter.*)
SOTIN. Have no fear — I've trained her to hit in only one direction. (*Swings the club to the other side. The young people scream in alarm. Laughter.*)
ROMANOV. Why doesn't the commander come?

(MIKHAILOV, KORITKO, *and* OLKHA *come in.*)

MIKHAILOV. Stand back! What's going on here?

ZOTOVA. Mikhailov!? Marvellous, Maria Dmitryevna! But I saw you leave.

MIKHAILOV. How can one leave you? And you? What are you doing here with a cart shaft?

SOTIN. Why, I'll use it to fight with!

MIKHAILOV. Whom are you going to fight?

SOTIN. Why, whoever is against us.

MIKHAILOV. And you too?

VOICES (*in unison*). And we too!

MIKHAILOV. Go back to your homes! There won't be a sign of disturbance left in another hour. Comrade Rayevsky has countermanded his unfortunate order.

ROMANOV. He has countermanded it?

ZOTOVA. He didn't tell me.

AFANASYEV. That's a clever lad!

MIKHAILOV (*looking around*). Are any of the peasants here? (*To* ROMANOV.) Are these all members of your regiment?

ROMANOV. Yes, of my regiment.

MIKHAILOV. And these are all Communist Youths?

ZOTOVA. Yes.

MIKHAILOV. And is there no one else here? I gave orders to have the peasants called here. What's wrong?

ZOTOVA. Loktev has been running from house to house...

MIKHAILOV. And yet there is no one here. What could have happened? (*To* OLKHA.) What do you think?

OLKHA. There is trouble brewing...

MIKHAILOV (*to a Communist Youth*). Go get Dyedov. (*The boy runs out.*) That's bad, very bad... What's wrong, Ignat Vasilyevich?

KORITKO. The peasants are offended, Dmitri Petrovich. You know how the peasant is. If everything is fair, he may shout his head off a little at first, but in the end he'll do what he's asked. But if you're not fair, then there is hell to pay.

OLKHA. Even I — if I hadn't known you, I wouldn't have come — I tell you frankly. In the days of the Tsar — then perhaps I would have stood for it, but now — no...

ZOTOVA. This is counter-revolutionary!

OLKHA. That I can't say — maybe it's so — you learned all about it in school. But this is my government. I fought for it. Then why

297

should I be oppressed by it? As if, while you're fighting with your right hand, your left one is punching you in the eye.

MIKHAILOV. You know without my telling you that nothing big has ever been accomplished without some blunders...

OLKHA. Yes, that's so... We understand this... only there are so many blunders. So the peasant walks around with a stone in his bosom.

MIKHAILOV. Against whom does he intend to use the stone?

OLKHA. That's just it — he doesn't know. If he knew, he'd throw it.

(DYEDOV *and the* COMMUNIST YOUTH *come in.*)

MIKHAILOV. Have you informed everybody?

DYEDOV. About what?

MIKHAILOV. That the order has been countermanded.

DYEDOV. Not at all — I've received no such instructions.

MIKHAILOV. What do you mean? Hasn't Rayevsky been to see you?

DYEDOV. Not at all. I haven't seen him.

MIKHAILOV. But that's impossible!

DYEDOV. Precisely so.

MIKHAILOV. So that's what you're up to, my friend!

DYEDOV. Guilty.

MIKHAILOV. I'm not blaming you. So that's why the peasants aren't here. Attention, lads! You must go to the village this instant. Knock at every window and make the following announcement: 'The comrade delegate has countermanded his order. Mikhailov is here. Tomorrow all the lists will be checked over and decided upon at the meeting of the Soviet!' Hurry, lads, we must make time...

LOKTEV (*runs in, breathing heavily. His speech is incoherent*). The kulaks have freed Mishka Kvassov. There is a whole mob of them. All drunk. They have rifles and knives.

ZOTOVA. But one of our militiamen was guarding him.

LOKTEV. They killed the militiaman.

MIKHAILOV. We're too late, Dyedov!

DYEDOV (*frightened*). A riot! A riot! I said there would be rioting! What will happen now? Lord! Lord!

MIKHAILOV. Shut up! (*To* SOTIN.) Can you shoot?

SOTIN. I fought in all the wars.

MIKHAILOV. Take the Mauser. Stand by the door. (*Gives him the*

298

rifle. To KORITKO *and* OLKHA.) You see, my friends, what a mess we have on our hands now. I'm going to assign a few boys to both of you and ask you to walk through the village. We must prevent the kulaks from persuading the peasants to join them.

KORITKO. Pick out the lads. We'll go.

OLKHA. What things people are capable of doing...

MIKHAILOV. Zotova, pick out five boys.

ROMANOV. Pick out three for me, too. I'm going to check up on the guard.

MIKHAILOV. Pick out the boys, Zotova.

ZOTOVA (*selecting the boys*). You go, Petya. You, and you....

COMMUNIST YOUTH. I don't want to run through the village. I want to stay here with you.

ZOTOVA. I'll... Ninka, you go.

NINKA. I'm with Romanov.

ZOTOVA. Go with Romanov, go.

KORITKO. So long, Dmitri Petrovich.

MIKHAILOV. All right.   (*The organized groups leave.*)

ZOTOVA. If we could only sound the tocsin...

MIKHAILOV. I'll sound you! Loktev, the arms!

LOKTEV. The arms are in that room, in the Party cell.

MIKHAILOV. How many? (*To the* COMMUNIST YOUTHS.) Don't crowd! Eyes front! Single file!

LOKTEV. Three Berdans, six buckshot rifles, and one Montekrist.

MIKHAILOV. You go with Loktev, Afanasyev. Carry the guns in here! Girls, step out of the line!

FIRST COMMUNIST YOUTH GIRL. We won't leave. We're with the boys.

SECOND COMMUNIST YOUTH GIRL. We want guns, too...

FIRST COMMUNIST YOUTH GIRL. We...

MIKHAILOV. Silence! Zotova! Is this your discipline?

ZOTOVA. Why do you discriminate against us? Why are we worse than the boys? We're going anyway.

FIRST COMMUNIST YOUTH. Better let them come. They'll whine, if you don't.

MIKHAILOV. We'll take care of that later. Distribute the cartridges.

(*The girls go into the adjoining room and drag out cylinders, powder and cartridges.* LOKTEV *and* MISHKA AFANASYEV *bring in the guns and place them on the table.*)

299

DYEDOV. We ought to telephone the city! We ought to telephone the city!

MIKHAILOV. Go ahead — telephone.

DYEDOV. How can I go? The telephone is in the Soviet building. I'll get killed.

MIKHAILOV. Sit down and shut up, then. Have you a revolver?

DYEDOV. Yes.

MIKHAILOV. Give it to me.

DYEDOV. But how can I be left without a revolver?

MIKHAILOV. We'll hide you under the bed. Well! (*Takes his revolver.*) Lads! Get your guns. (*The* YOUNG COMMUNISTS *make a dash for the table.*) Stop! Where are you going? Back! Zotova, pick out the best fighters.

ZOTOVA. Vanka — take a Berdan. (*He leaves the line and takes a rifle.*) Mishka — a Berdan.

MISHKA. I'd rather have a buckshot gun.

ZOTOVA. Take what I tell you. A Berdan hits a thousand paces away.

LOKTEV. A thousand paces?

ZOTOVA. Get out of the way! Stepka — a buckshot gun. Andrei — a Berdan. Vanyechka — a buckshot gun.

LOKTEV (*who is distributing the cartridges*). Fill 'em up tightly, don't begrudge paper.

MIKHAILOV (*to* LOKTEV). Does the liquor agent live right here, next to the store?

LOKTEV. Yes, right here...

MIKHAILOV (*to* AFANASYEV). Go, bring the agent here. (MISHKA *leaves. To* LOKTEV, *in a low voice.*) Is it a large mob?

LOKTEV. It's hard to say.

MIKHAILOV. How do the peasants feel about this? Did you go from house to house?

LOKTEV. They say nothing.

MIKHAILOV. Nothing... That's bad. (MISHKA *comes in with the frightened liquor agent, who is sleepy and has thrown a coat over his night shirt.*) Are you the liquor agent?

THE AGENT. The fourth year now, without a single reprimand.

MIKHAILOV. How was business yesterday and today?

THE AGENT. You'll have nothing to complain about. I may say — without bragging — that I haven't sold as much liquor in half a year as I sold yesterday and today.

MIKHAILOV. Who was buying?

AGENT. Many were buying. Kotikhin alone, Vasily Afanasyevich Kotikhin, took three pailfuls. In order not to lose any business I practically didn't go to bed last night. And this morning I got up before dawn. I do my best...

MIKHAILOV. May the Devil take you with your zeal! Have you any vodka left?

AGENT. Hardly any. How much do you need?

MIKHAILOV. You should enter a contest for fools. Zotova! March over there and pour out all the vodka that is still in the store. See that not a drop is left.

AGENT. What do you mean — pour it out? Just a moment! (*To* ZOTOVA.) Where are you going?

ZOTOVA. Go, kick yourself! (*Leaves.*)

(ROMANOV *runs in. He is accompanied by several peasants who are armed with scythes, pitchforks, and buckshot guns.*)

ROMANOV. I've reconnoitred. They are evidently waiting for more reinforcements. The whole mob is in Kotikhin's apiary. The peasants are following them in good order.

ONE OF THE NEW ARRIVALS. The drones are swarming.

SECOND COMMUNIST YOUTH. Comrade Mikhailov, give those of us who haven't any guns permission to break down the fence and use the boards.

MIKHAILOV. What will you do with the boards?

FOURTH YOUNG COMMUNIST. We'll just carry boards as a starter. If anybody gets shot, we'll take his gun away.

ZOTOVA. Don't you interfere, Mikhailov. Let them all go!

ROMANOV. Curse everything, curse! Eh-eh, what a glorious day! (*To* SOTIN.) Uncle Piotr, let's smack!

SOTIN. Right on the snout!

ROMANOV. Oh, you dear one, my own dear one! (*They kiss.*)

MIKHAILOV. Calm down, bold warrior. Attention! Listen! I'm going to reconnoitre!

ZOTOVA. Do you think we'll let you go out all alone?

LOKTEV. I'll go, Comrade Mikhailov...

MIKHAILOV. Silence! This is no laughing matter. Loktev! Take command of the Red division of the village. If I'm not back within ten minutes, send out another reconnoitring squad and advance towards the enemy. Go in chain formation, maintain complete silence, don't shoot unless it's absolutely unavoidable — and if you must shoot, aim only at the kulaks. Is that clear? (*Goes towards the door.* LOKTEV *follows him.*)

LOKTEV. Comrade Mikhailov, it is more dangerous for you to go out than for any one of us. Let me go. They'll murder you if they catch you.

MIKHAILOV. I'm the one to go. Have you thought about Rayevsky and Olga?

LOKTEV. That's right. Where are they?

MIKHAILOV. That's just it. They're in Kvassov's house. Do you realize what may happen?

LOKTEV. That makes it even more unwise for you to go. How can you go to Kvassov's house?

MIKHAILOV. Unwise? There are, you know, circumstances when reasoned behavior borders on the criminal. (*Smiles.*) A friend once said that to me. Good-bye! (*Presses* LOKTEV's *hand and goes out.*)

CURTAIN

ACT V

Scene 9

EPISODE I: *The outside of* KORITKO'S *hut, a typical village log cabin. A section of the courtyard — cluttered with logs and odds-and-ends of a poor peasant household — is visible, a fence cutting it off on the right from the street, part of which can be seen. It is a pleasant, moonlit night. A group of peasants advances slowly into the courtyard from the left, with* KVASSOV *and* PASHA *in the lead. In the group are all those who conspired at* KVASSOV'S *house and several new recruits.* KVASSOV *carries a rifle,* MIKHAIL *a revolver, and the rest of them also have either firearms or knives; except one of the younger peasants, who is armed with an accordion instead. Except for* KVASSOV *and* KOTIKHIN, *the group is well gone in vodka. They talk in sinister whispers.*

KVASSOV. Tsst... Quiet!

KOTIKHIN (*to* MIKHAIL). See if there is anyone on the street.

MIKHAIL (*goes towards the street and looks*). There is no one.

PROSHKIN. Let me — I have the right...

KVASSOV. Tsst... I'll look through the window. (*Walks to the dark window and peers inside.*)

GRUNKIN. Is he there?

KVASSOV. He's here.

PROSHKIN. Let me.

KVASSOV. Pavel Ivanovich, you stand by the gate.

KOTIKHIN (*carefully tries the door*). The door is latched. I need a knife.

PROSHKIN. I'll open it with this. (*Shows a long, fine blade.*)

KVASSOV. Don't make any noise.

(PROSHKIN *thrusts his knife into the cleft, raises the latch, and opens the door.*)

PROSHKIN. That's how we do things.

KVASSOV. Go with God. You go, Sofron Kuzmich! And you, Mikhail! And you, Piotka!

ZUBOV. Piotka is still very young — don't send him.

KVASSOV. Tsst... I'm sending *my* son, Pavel Ivanovich! Don't hide yours!

PIOTKA. I'll go.

KVASSOV. You'll go. Remember what I told you. Don't shoot. That's only a last resort. Just club him over the head so that he loses consciousness. If he recognizes you — finish him.

GRUNKIN. What's the clubbing for?

KOTIKHIN. For his honeyed speeches. Don't forget, Sofron Kuzmich.

PROSHKIN. I remember.

SHILOV (*staggers drunkenly*). I'm frightened.

KVASSOV. As soon as you open the second door, we'll strike up on the accordion and drown out the screams or the noise in case there's shooting.

MIKHAIL. Play your gayest tune! We're on our way. (*Goes to the door.*)

KVASSOV. Christ save us!

    (*They all cross themselves.* PROSHKIN, MIKHAIL, *and* PIOTKA *enter the house, leaving the door open behind them. Pause.*)

SHILOV (*whining*). I'm frightened...

GRUNKIN (*hilariously drunk*). And I feel happy... so happy...

    (*For a moment there is an ominous silence. Then the creaking of the second door inside the hut being opened can be heard.*)

KVASSOV. Andreika!

    (*The young peasant begins to play the accordion. At first discordant, the song takes form and gathers impetus as it proceeds. It becomes louder, more desperately gay. Two of the peasants begin a drunken dance, stamping heavily with their hobnailed boots.*)

ANDREIKA (*sings*).

> We want no wine, we crave no beer —
> Cock your gun with joy!
> Only vodka our throats will sear —
> Kick up the dust, my boy!

ALL (*sing in chorus*).

> Oh, the lot of the poor is a prisoner's lot:
> A cell that's dark and tight;
> A lonely aspen-tree down in the glen
> And a grave as black as night.

ANDREIKA.

> So drink, men, drink unto the death —
> Cock your gun with joy!
> Soon dank earth will stop your breath —
> Kick up the dust, my boy!

    (*All repeat the refrain. While they are singing,* RAYEVSKY *and* OLGA *run up to the fence. They are not seen from the courtyard and the music proceeds as they talk in agitated whispers.*)

RAYEVSKY. He's in the house. They're murdering him!

OLGA. He can't be in there...

RAYEVSKY. Look! The door is open... He's inside! They're murdering him!

OLGA. No... perhaps... but it can't be, it can't...

ANDREIKA (*sings with ever greater abandon*).

> The crows will croak at break of day —
> Cock your gun with joy!
> A funeral will end your way —
> Kick up the dust, my boy!

RAYEVSKY. Let me go, Olga! I'll attack them single-handedly!

OLGA. Pavel! Don't! They'll kill you too. What can you do all alone?

RAYEVSKY. I must... Don't you understand... they're strangling him! He has a lame leg.

ALL (*in chorus*).

> Oh, the lot of the poor is a prisoner's lot:
> A cell that's dark and tight;
> A lonely aspen-tree down in the glen
> And a grave as black as night.

OLGA (*trying to restrain* RAYEVSKY). I won't let you go! It's mad! Look — they are all armed. The whole village has risen. Let's escape. We can get to the outskirts of the village... We'll hire a wagon and come back here with a military detachment.

RAYEVSKY. I will die together with him. (*Tears himself loose from her.*)

ANDREIKA.

> Drink, men, drink until you're dead —
> Cock your gun with joy!
> The earth will be your final bed —
> Kick up the dust, my boy!

RAYEVSKY. Run away? That's how *he* would act, but I can't. (*Pushes* OLGA *away and, revolver in hand, leaps over the fence. The music is broken for a few moments.*) What are you doing, you scoundrels?

KOTIKHIN. There are no scoundrels here, only peasants.

(*They surround* RAYEVSKY; *the music and singing is quickly resumed.*)

RAYEVSKY. Where is Mikhailov?

KVASSOV. We're not Mikhailov's keepers. But what are you worrying about? (*Suddenly strikes* RAYEVSKY'S *arm with the butt-end of his rifle, knocking the revolver out of his hand. The younger peasants hit* RAYEVSKY *on the head with clubs from behind and grab him.* OLGA *screams and falls unconscious.*) Tie his hands. (RAYEVSKY *is carefully tied.*)

KOTIKHIN. Here, shove a rag in his mouth.

KVASSOV. Put him over there, near the fence. Beat him, lads, beat him harder. (*The trussed-up* RAYEVSKY *is carried to the fence and thrown against it.*)

ALL (*singing*).

> Oh, the lot of the poor is a prisoner's lot:
> A cell that's dark and tight;
> A lonely aspen-tree down in the glen
> And a grave as dark as night.

(*The stage revolves slowly, until the interior of the hut faces the audience. The singing dies down as the second episode begins.*)

EPISODE 2: *It is pitch dark. The accordion music and the singing outside the hut can be heard; also the squeak of the door being opened and careful steps.*

MIKHAIL. Shut the door, or he'll get away.

PROSHKIN. He won't get away. I'll see to that.

PIOTKA. Where shall I go?

MIKHAIL. Shut up!

PROSHKIN. I'll go to the bed. How about striking a match?

PIOTKA. Better not.

MIKHAILOV'S VOICE. Would you like a light, lads? (*Pause.*) I'm asking you if you would like me to give you a light?

PROSHKIN. Many thanks! We'll find you without one.

MIKHAILOV. Oh-ho! So it's you, Proshkin? Why so late?

PROSHKIN. So you've recognized me?

MIKHAILOV. Of course! Well, what's new?

PROSHKIN. We've brought you two thousand poods of bread. Take them with our compliments.

MIKHAILOV. That's fine. And I thought you were bringing me a second note.

MIKHAIL. We haven't settled accounts for the first one yet.

306

PROSHKIN (*infuriated*). We'll settle them. Where are you? (*Walks, stumbles over a bench, which falls with a crash.*) God damn you!

MIKHAILOV. Be careful! You needn't be in such a hurry! You have plenty of time to cut my throat! Why do you want to kill me, lads? (*Pause.*) I'm asking you — why?

PROSHKIN. Because...

MIKHAILOV. Still...

PROSHKIN. I want to hear your soul fly out.

MIKHAILOV. Won't you spare me? I'm too young to die!

PROSHKIN. That's enough from you, Mikhailov! Go in, Mishka! You had better not shoot, Mikhailov. If you behave, we'll make it easy for you. If you shoot — we'll make it difficult. I mean what I say.

MIKHAILOV. Oh, no! Why should I shoot? But I'd better give you a light. (*Scratches a match and lights a candle.*)

(*The house is lit up. Along the walls, in all the corners of the room, next to MIKHAILOV at the table, everywhere are peasants and YOUNG COMMUNISTS — all aiming their guns at the intruders. In the ensuing silence the music and singing behind the scenes becomes more distinct.*)

MIKHAIL. Damn you! (*Lowers his gun.*)

MIKHAILOV. Take them!

(*The intruders are surrounded and disarmed. SOTIN walks up to PROSHKIN and grabs him around the chest with both arms.*)

SOTIN. I've been waiting for you a long time, Sofron Kuzmich. (*Shakes him, at first gently, then harder, more and more harshly, more and more implacably.*)

(*The house revolves slowly, and the third episode begins.*)

EPISODE 3: *Outside the hut again. The singing is just ending. The kulaks crowd around the door.*

SHILOV. Good Lord, what's going on there?

KVASSOV. They're slow.

ZUBOV. Not a sound.

A YOUNG PEASANT (*looking through a crack*). They've lit a candle.

GRUNKIN. What's going on there?

(*They crowd around the window trying to see.*)

A YOUNG PEASANT. Oy, little mothers! Ivan Gerasimovich, the whole Communist Youth League is in there! Our men are trapped!

SHILOV. Run, brothers!

(*The crowd rushes away from the window.*)

KVASSOV. Wait! Where to? From whom are you running away? Stop!

KOTIKHIN. We must do something. He's cunning, very cunning, that Regional Chief!

KVASSOV. No more cunning than we are. Get ready, fellow villagers. No one is going to leave this house. Pick up the logs, pile them up against the door, against all the windows.

(*The kulaks quickly pile logs as instructed, and those inside the hut begin to pound on the doors and windows.*)

PASHA. Ah-ha! Go on, knock! You wanted to burn them, well, go ahead, burn them!

KVASSOV. I'll burn them! You'll not outwit me, Mikhailov! Pour the kerosene!

(*One of the young peasants runs up and pours kerosene on the logs. The tocsin is sounded in the distance. The clink of broken glass is heard. Kulaks hold the logs in place, against the pressure from within.*)

MOKRINA. Burn them, brother Christians, flay them with tongues of fire! Let them writhe in pain, accursèd that they are by God!

KVASSOV. Faster, faster! Don't you hear? The alarm is ringing.

KOTIKHIN. Ivan Gerasimovich, your son's in there...

KVASSOV (*suddenly remembering*). In there...

PASHA. Well, father, you wanted to start a conflagration, didn't you? Afraid now?

(*Those inside the house are trying to break the shutters. The kulaks press against the logs.*)

ZUBOV (*looks down the street*). What's going on there? The people are running towards the tocsin.

KVASSOV. Holy Mother of God! Set the house on fire! Light the logs! Burn them! Quick!

SHILOV. Wait a minute, Ivan Gerasimovich? How burn people who are alive?

GRUNKIN. Citizens, citizens! What are we doing?

FIRST PEASANT. Stop!

SECOND PEASANT. What are we doing, we peasants?

MOKRINA. Burn them! Burn them! Burn them!

GRUNKIN. Wait a minute, citizens! I'm sobering up.

KVASSOV (*to* GRUNKIN). I'll kill you like a dog! Tsst!

THIRD PEASANT. What's it all about, fellow villagers?

ZUBOV. They're coming here. Kolka Romanov is leading them.

KVASSOV. Burn them! Light the logs!

SECOND PEASANT. Don't you dare!

GRUNKIN. Ivan Gerasimovich, I bow to you gratefully for the vodka. But I won't let you set fire to this house!

KVASSOV. You won't let me!

(*Some of the peasants fall on* KVASSOV. *Others form a ring around him, to protect him.*)

SECOND PEASANT. Hold him, he'll kill someone!

(KVASSOV *hits* GRUNKIN *in the face and knocks him down, and a confused free-for-all battle is on. The shutters are broken down and* MIKHAILOV *appears in one window with a Mauser in his hands.* SOTIN *is at another window with a club.* ROMANOV *jumps over the fence with a revolver in his hand. His 'regiment' and sundry peasants pour in after him. The fence falls. The* YOUNG COMMUNISTS *spring out of the house and join the fighting throng. The kulak group is getting the worst of it.*)

MIKHAILOV. Bind all of them.

(*The kulaks are bound.* SOTIN *twists and tightens the rope with which he's binding* KVASSOV.)

SOTIN (*gloating*). Is it too uncomfortable? You tell me, Ivan Gerasimovich, and I'll loosen up.

KVASSOV (*through clenched teeth*). It's fine. Thank you.

OLGA (*reviving*). Where is Rayevsky?

MIKHAILOV. I haven't found him.

(Pause. Commotion in the crowd.)

GRUNKIN. Oh, he? There he is.

(ROMANOV and a Communist Youth untie RAYEVSKY.)

ROMANOV (*to the bruised* RAYEVSKY). Dear one! What are you lying down there for, little dove!

MIKHAILOV (*loudly*). Why didn't you countermand the order?

RAYEVSKY. We'll talk about that later.

MIKHAILOV. Yes, we'll certainly have a talk. You're recalled. Leave for the Regional Office immediately.

OLGA. He went to certain death to save you, all alone he went. Just for you he attacked the whole mob... and you, is that all you have to say to him?

MIKHAILOV. Thank you, Pavel! But you'll have to stand trial. (*Sharply.*) I'm sorry, Olga, I haven't time to talk to you now.

OLKHA (*approaching* KVASSOV). Well, citizens, this is what we got... You and I shouted our heads off, and Kvassov, Ivan Gerasimovich here, wanted to burn the Soviet Government — (*pointing to* MIKHAILOV) — here...

SHILOV. You're right, Vasil Pavlovich, you're right...

OLKHA. And we? Are we to stand aside? That's not right — no, it's not right... We ought to say a word or two for ourselves. I tax myself with thirty poods of bread. I'll put them on the wagon this very minute. And I ask all of you to follow my example.

SHILOV. That's right, Vasya... I said to him, citizens... 'What are you trying to do, Ivan Gerasimovich...' I gave fifty poods!

GRUNKIN. Villagers... Citizens... I have bread. Kvassov, Ivan Gerasimovich, stored it in my place. 'Tell them it's yours,' he says. And if it's mine, then I give it to the Government... A hundred poods I give...

SHILOV. Let's leave immediately — we can make the city by morning.

ROMANOV. To the city, damn it! On to the city! Ah, what a life! What a beautiful life! Mikhailov, what shall we do with the kulaks?

MIKHAILOV. Drag them away!

KVASSOV. Aren't you celebrating too early? It's all one — either you or we must disappear from the face of the earth. There isn't room enough for both of us in this world.

MIKHAILOV. I'm afraid it will be you. You made a mistake in your reckoning, Ivan Gerasimovich. You wanted to kill Mikhailov, but you made a mistake in your reckoning. You thought there was only one Mikhailov — but there are so many Mikhailovs they can't be counted. Look at all the Mikhailovs! (*Points all around him; then points at the audience.*) And here are some more Mikhailovs! You can't destroy us by fire!

CURTAIN

INGA

A Play in Four Acts and Thirteen Scenes

By ANATOLE GLEBOV

Translated from the Russian
By Charles Malamuth

You want me to remain the same as ever —
  Obedient and tender, meek and prim?
But what if year by year the wild waves sever
  Our vanished days, and tear them limb from limb...
And what if I — with you shoulder to shoulder —
  In battle and in work your mate, your peer —
Meet hostile fate with mien increasing bolder
  And mete out death... and yield to love, my dear?

Nadezhda Pavlovitch

INTRODUCTION

Anatole Glebov states the theme of his play *Inga* as follows: 'The Soviet woman: the old in the new and the new in the old.' Incidentally it touches upon the problems of the new family, love, everyday domestic existence in a collective society.

Glebov has brought together in one factory and in one community house attached to it a group of women combining in varying proportions the old, pre-revolutionary psychology and the new Soviet attitudes. The capable, intellectual Inga — strong-willed and in fact the equal or superior of any man around her — is contrasted with the clinging, softer character of Glafeera. Mera, who outwardly at least seems committed to a sexual anarchy carried over from the chaotic civil-war days, is at one extreme; and Nastya, an old-fashioned wife who still accepts old-fashioned beatings from her husband as the appointed scheme of God's world, is at the other.

The relations of these women to one another and to their men provide the substance for a very human and revealing story, unfolded against a background of the Five-Year Plan in a clothing factory. It is the transformation of Glafeera — her emancipation from the kitchen and her development into a self-reliant woman — that dominates the play. Inga is childless by choice and by physical necessity. She is a little too 'manly' to be sympathetic, even to Soviet partisans of sex equality. Glafeera, in whom the mother instinct remains fresh and natural even after she is politically emancipated, is a closer approach to the author's, and to the Soviet, ideal of a woman who is man's equal without sacrificing the distinctive qualities of her femininity.

Inga was written in 1928 and had its première at the Moscow Theatre of Revolution in March, 1929. It had two hundred and fifty performances in that theatre and is still widely played in all parts of the Soviet Union. It was produced in Piskator's Theatre, Berlin, under the title *Frau in Front*.

Glebov was born in 1899 and began earning his own living at fifteen as proof-reader on a newspaper. He fought as a Red Guard in the Revolution and thereafter held responsible posts in Communist Party, government, trade-union, military, journalistic, and diplomatic work. But more and more he concentrated his efforts in the field of theatre, both as a playwright and as a political organizer. Already he has sixteen plays to his credit, among them *Zagmuk*, *Growth*, *Inga*, *Power*, and *Gold and Brain*. He was the first secretary of the Theatre Section of RAPP (the Russian Association of Proletarian Writers); one of the heads of the society 'Proletarian Theatre' between 1928 and 1931; and is now a member of the Presidium of the International Society of Revolutionary Theatre. Although a prolific writer, he is among the most active figures on the organizational side of literary life in the new Russia — on the 'literary front' of the Soviet Revolution.

CHARACTERS

Inga Martinovna Rizzer: thirty, a tall, strong, handsome, capable woman, neatly dressed; a Communist intellectual; manager of the clothing factory.

Dmitri Gretchaninov: thirty-five, well-built, handsome, nervous and abrupt in manner; a Communist worker and chairman of the Factory Committee.

Glafeera: thirty-two, his wife, a seamstress; a wholesome peasant type.

Mera Gurvitch: thirty-five, dark, slender, nervously mobile; a Russian-Jewish radical intellectual of the type that neglects even feminine vanity for the sake of the Revolution; organizer of the Women's Section.

Somov, Gregory Danilyitch: sixty, slender and wiry; an old-time Communist worker; secretary of the local Communist Party collective.

Ryzhov, Ignat Ivanovitch: forty, stocky, substantially built, dignified in a lumbering way; cocky; a bristling red moustache, ill-fitting foreign clothes; a Communist worker; assistant manager of the factory.

Nemtsevitch, Roman Frantsevitch: forty-five, an elegant military gentleman with an appreciative eye for feminine charm; a college-trained engineer.

Veronica: thirty-five, his wife; a fading woman, addicted to the abuse of cosmetics.

Boltikov, Sofron: fifty, short, stocky, morose; bushy eyebrows, the purplish bulbous nose of an alcoholic; an old-fashioned worker; foreman of the women's apparel shop.

Nastya: forty, his wife; shrewish but kind.

Savvushkin: sixty-five; a neat, clean-shaven old worker.

Men and women factory workers

Place: One of the larger industrial towns in the Union of Soviet Socialist Republics.

Time: The era of the first Five-Year Plan.

ACT I

SCENE 1

The clubroom of this large clothing factory is decorated with bunting, streamers, posters; portraits of Lenin and Stalin, one of each, hang side by side centrally on the back wall. One of the posters shows a model crusade against the house fly — in twelve pictures; another reads: '2 plus 2 equals 5: the Five-Year Plan in four years!' Red streamers with white letters: 'For Socialist Competition!'; 'Every Factory is a Fortress of Militant Socialism'; 'Clear the Road for the Shock-Brigaders!'; and a huge pennant: 'Down with Double-Dealers — Opportunists — Right-Left Deviators!'; 'For the Construction of Socialism in Our Country! For the General Line of the Party! Long Live Lenin's Best Disciple — Comrade Stalin!'

On the frosted pane in the upper part of the door (right) in reversed Russian letters the word CLUB appears in black; another door (left) leads to the refreshment stand; the massive double door (centre) is below the portraits of Lenin and Stalin and directly behind the small platform, somewhat to the left. On the platform are a table and three chairs. Before the platform are rows of chairs, occupied by an audience of factory workers. At the Chairman's table sit SOMOV, the Chairman, and beside him a woman factory worker who keeps the minutes. In the audience of factory workers are RYZHOV and SAVVUSHKIN.

INGA is discovered on the platform, gathering her notes and statistical charts as she concludes her report on the state of the factory.

INGA. And let me remind you, comrades, that the dry figures of my report contain the blood and sweat of the fight for Socialism in our own little sector. This annual report records a year of twelve months, of three hundred and sixty-five days of stubborn struggle — day by day, hour by hour. Every worker, every Party member, every union activist, every one of us has made his contribution to it. We have fought as one unit — as one collective — for greater labor efficiency, for genuine Socialist standards of production, for discipline, for quality, for a concrete bit of the Socialist mode of life... These are not merely the dry figures of a bookkeeper's report — nor is all this represented even by the finished product of our factory which is distributed throughout the land... This report is first of all about *Man*. It concerns, above all, the human being — that new Socialist being which, in our everyday struggle, we forge out of the old mutilated material that for the most part is alien to us. It is this drama of free Socialist labor which we, our Party, our various organizations, have been able to elevate, to manifest, to help bring into being!... This, comrades, is what is important in the work we have done! This is what we must concentrate on in the future! (*Applause.*)

RYZHOV (*from the floor*). Vulgar idealism! We must face facts! There is no sense in all this preaching!

(*There is commotion in the hall.*)

INGA. Comrade Ryzhov, I have already spoken enough about you. You are a shining example of how much of the old, of the alien, there is still in us.

RYZHOV (*dishevelled, angry, jumps on the platform*). In *us!* And how about *you?* How about *you*, Comrade Manager?

INGA (*snapping her brief-case shut and about to leave the platform*). I don't set myself up as a model. I am just like everyone else, with the same shortcomings.

RYZHOV. Then what are you fussing about? Tell me that! Why do you shame me before everybody — me, a Party member, a responsible comrade? What do you think I am?... Petrushka?... A clown? You have to blame somebody for everything, I suppose, so you've tacked all the deviations onto me — made a monkey out of me!

(*The Chairman rings the bell for order.* RYZHOV *pays no attention.* SOMOV *comes up to him and rings the bell close to his ear.*)

SOMOV. Comrade Ryzhov, I have not given you the privilege of the floor. Besides, such a tone to Party comrades in a public meeting cannot be tolerated! You know better than that! (RYZHOV *is stopped short.*)

INGA. I spoke of your shortcomings because they have cost us seven thousand rubles in *valuta*. And that is everyone's business, Comrade Ryzhov, that is *not* a personal matter, but a matter of public concern.

SAVVUSHKIN (*unseen, for he is in the back of the hall, but shouting lustily offstage*). Danilyitch! Comrade Somov!

SOMOV (*looking in the direction of the voice*). Who's that? You should have spoken before. The discussion is closed.

(*The general commotion continues.*)

SAVVUSHKIN (*still unseen, but his voice louder, as he is approaching*). I have something to say. May I?

SOMOV (*shouts back*). But we've already had the concluding re-marks... (*His voice is lost in the noise.*) All right, all right! Comrade Savvushkin has the floor on a personal matter.

(SOMOV, *furious, goes to the chair, ringing the bell continually until the audience subsides and he sits down.* INGA *continues to stand on the platform; so does* RYZHOV. SAVVUSHKIN, *the veteran worker, is excited as he ascends the platform, casting angry glances at* RYZHOV.)

SAVVUSHKIN. It's not about a personal matter I want to speak, but about a public matter! Who cares about personal matters? Personal matters have no interest for us unless they concern us as a whole. (*Turns to the Chairman.*) Here, Comrade Somov, is what I want to say: the working class can judge about this — that is, we, the non-partisans... (*The audience applauds and he shouts back.*) Stop it! Maybe I'll be a Party member myself tomorrow! (*Applause.*) In a word, I'll put it this way, Comrade Ryzhov: if you can't stand a little criticism, if the truth upsets you and you begin to sweat, then why don't you go back to Germany, dear comrade, where we sent you to get the machines? And you can stay there for good! (*Laughter, applause.*) There you can find the right kind of company for yourself — all kinds of Social-Democrats! They will talk with you very politely, and you'll get drunk together. But as far as we are concerned, Comrade Ryzhov, don't try to lure us into those deviations. We have had enough of them. So if you want to be with us, don't get on your high horse, but pay attention when the masses criticize you for your own good! (*Applause.*)

INGA. Right, Savvushkin! Bravo!

(*Applause.* RYZHOV *looks at* SAVVUSHKIN, *at* INGA, *at the audience, and suddenly bursts out.*)

RYZHOV. Oh, you all go to... with such self-criticism!

(RYZHOV *runs out. There is general excitement.*)

CURTAIN

ACT I

SCENE 2

The refreshment stand at the club. Posters on the wall. Several small tables and chairs, a large samovar, sandwiches, pastry, fruit, candy, cigarettes. The woman behind the counter is reading. She is bored. RYZHOV runs in, excited, wiping the perspiration off his brow.

RYZHOV. Well, she certainly gave me hell! What a pest! There's a woman for you — that Inga! She sticks to me like a leech! (*Wipes his forehead.*) So I should go abroad again! I'll be damned!

(*Enter NEMTSEVITCH.*)

NEMTSEVITCH. Ignat Ivanitch, have you calmed down yet?

RYZHOV. What do you mean, 'calmed down' — when she makes a monkey out of me before the whole factory? What do you mean, 'calmed down'?

NEMTSEVITCH. Come on, cool off! Will you have some soda water — or tea?

RYZHOV (*in the same indignant tone — to the woman at the refreshment stand*). Give me a sausage sandwich. (*Goes to the table.*) Calm down!

NEMTSEVITCH (*setting his tea and sandwiches down on the table*). But who is to blame? Why did you buy the wrong things? What will we do with all those machines? (*Both sit down.*) They're no good to us. Do you expect us to throw them away?

RYZHOV. Roman Frantsevitch, that's not the point, my friend. I admit all that. That was *my* mistake. But please tell me what my silk underwear has to do with it? What has my... well... getting drunk in Hamburg to do with it? Why did they have to drag that in? (*Bites the sandwich savagely.*) I did certain things there... well ... (*swallows hard*) in a physiological way... But to drag all that into the conference on production! (*Bangs the table and the tea spills.*) I am a responsible Party member. The assistant manager... making a monkey out of me before the whole factory! Cracking jokes about it!

NEMTSEVITCH (*laughing quietly and sipping his tea*). Hormones! Everywhere and anywhere — hormones!

RYZHOV (*not understanding the allusion, but pretending to*). Aha! You see!... My dear friend, I understand everything! It's like this: kick me out and put Dmitri in my place! On the face of it, it seems that it makes no difference whether it's he or I. Yes, I am a simple man — I am what I am. Here — (*slaps himself*) — pants, coat, vest — all here! But *he's* putting on airs, you see!

NEMTSEVITCH (*munching his sandwich*). Just what I've been saying — hormones!

(DMITRI *enters quickly from the left on his way to the clubroom. He carries letters and documents.*)

DMITRI (*stopping for a moment*). So you finally got what was coming to you.

RYZHOV. We'll see what *you'll* get! You're next!

DMITRI. What can they do to me? I haven't been degenerating abroad. I don't suffer from Right deviation, and (*ironically*) I'm not a — 'business man'!

RYZHOV (*rising from the table*). Who do you think you're talking to? Look out! You think that just because you're chairman of the Factory Committee you can say anything you like! You look out! I'm no Inga. (*Coming ominously close to* DMITRI.) You'll gather a few bumps with me...

DMITRI. What has Inga to do with it?

RYZHOV. Just that.

NEMTSEVITCH. Comrades, less passion!

DMITRI. No! (*To* RYZHOV.) You've started something — and you've got to finish it. Just what are you talking about?

RYZHOV. About the intimacy between the chairman of the Factory Committee and the Administration... Understand?

DMITRI. Comrade Ryzhov, for such words I'll...

RYZHOV. Well? Well? What *are* you going to do to me for such words? What, eh?

DMITRI. You don't imagine I'll handle you with kid gloves, do you?... I'll give it to you straight from the shoulder...

(*Enter* INGA *from the right.*)

INGA. What's all the noise about? (*General confusion.*) What's happened?

RYZHOV. We'll see whether it'll be straight or crooked! I'll show you what kind of an opportunist I am! (*Exit at the left.*)

INGA. What's the matter, Dmitri?

NEMTSEVITCH. It's just like Spain! You might think we've had a change of climate! There's never been such passion before!

(*He looks out of the corner of his eye at* DMITRI, *goes to one side, sits down, and resumes drinking his tea.*)

DMITRI. Oh, to the Devil with him, Inga!

INGA. Have you the report?

DMITRI. I have. Just a moment... I must see you for just a moment. (*He leads her toward the footlights.*)

INGA. Well, what is it? Hurry!

DMITRI (*admiring her*). I love you — that's what!

INGA (*sharply*). Dmitri! It's simply disgusting!... This is neither the time nor the place.

DMITRI. Now, don't get mad. (*Holds her back.*) Just one second ... You are like... fireworks today! A rocket! Do you remember them during the war? Like... the Devil knows what!

INGA. Dimka, I can't stand this slush! They're voting already. Let me go!

(*She suddenly pulls away her hand, which he is trying to kiss.* NEMTSEVITCH, *sitting a little way off, and* RYZHOV, *who re-enters from the left, witness this scene.* INGA *runs to the right — to the clubroom.* DMITRI *follows her.*)

RYZHOV. Did you see that, Roman Frantsevitch? Did you? You see... I am not even allowed to drink! But the woman manager and the chairman of the Factory Committee may make love in broad daylight! I suppose you think that's fair?

NEMTSEVITCH. Well, what can you do about it? The implacable laws of physiology. You Marxists do not appreciate Freud. Strictly speaking, if you look at it objectively, is it your Marx that rules the world?

RYZHOV. What do you mean?

NEMTSEVITCH. Freud, friend, Freud! Not *class*, but *sex!*

RYZHOV. You can go to the Devil with your bourgeois deviation! They've put a woman over us — that's why it's Freud!

CURTAIN

ACT I

SCENE 3

Factory assembly hall. A meeting has just adjourned. Men and women workers crowd around the large committee table, which is covered with a red cloth. In the centre of a group is SOMOV, *still holding the bell.* SAVVUSHKIN, BOLTIKOV, *and* MERA *are also in the crowd.*

BOLTIKOV (*gesticulating excitedly*). No, Gregory Danilyitch! No! To make a woman a brigade-leader... Well... that's not exactly the thing to do!

SOMOV. What's your objection? Doesn't she know her business? Or isn't she a human being at all?

SAVVUSHKIN. Hear! Hear!...

BOLTIKOV. How shall I put it?... (*Morosely.*) Of course, I'm not the boss here. The factory is yours; you are responsible. Only, as a foreman, I will say one thing from experience: a woman is a woman, and all her imagination — how shall I say it? — is turned backwards!

SOMOV. You Asiatic! You reactionary! (*To* MERA.) Do you see this? (*Points at* BOLTIKOV.) My friends, this is a stone wall... Try to break through it!

MERA. Don't worry, old man! We'll break through it! We'll get after him! Not like today. We'll make it real hot for him!

BOLTIKOV. What's the point?

MERA. The point is that you beat your wife.

SAVVUSHKIN. Right!

BOLTIKOV. What of it? Can't I beat my own wife?... If you let a woman have her way, you become a woman yourself.

SOMOV. Here's a type for you! A perfect reactionary!

MERA. I'll arrange a trial to make an example of him.

BOLTIKOV. A trial? Why a trial?

SOMOV. Because you are corrupting our entire factory, like a rotten tooth in the mouth. You reek with decay!

BOLTIKOV. Oh, go away!

(BOLTIKOV *turns away;* SOMOV *swings him back. There is a pause as they measure each other.*)

SOMOV. Well?

323

BOLTIKOV. What do you mean — well? You've put women all over the factory. Decent people can't live! I'll go to Moscow! Then you can look for a foreman that wears a skirt!

SAVVUSHKIN. We'll *throw* you out, if you behave like this!

BOLTIKOV. That's how I *will* behave!

SAVVUSHKIN. And we'll throw you out!

SOMOV. And as for me, I'll never put up with it, Sofron. As far as I'm concerned, a fellow like you — a woman-hater — and that's just what you are — is just as bad as a Jew-hater... A fellow like you in our midst should be the first to get kicked out! I'll iron these things out of you!

BOLTIKOV. Oh, you can all go to...

MERA. Comrade Boltikov, no profanity, if you please!

(*Enter* RYZHOV. BOLTIKOV *waves his hand in disgust and turns to the incoming* RYZHOV. SOMOV *is surrounded by the crowd, which hides him from view.*)

BOLTIKOV. Well, friend Ignat Ivanovitch, they gave us plenty! It seems that we are the most conspicuous counter-revolutionists in the whole factory! Oh-ho-ho! God's ways, I suppose! (*He goes out.*)

(RYZHOV *shrugs. He is too disgusted to speak. The crowd now moves aside and reveals* SOMOV'S *group.*)

SAVVUSHKIN. Well, Danilyitch, how about the rates now?

ELDERLY WOMAN WORKER. Will we have the nurseries?

YOUNG GIRL COMMUNIST. Comrade Somov, what about the departmental bureau?

SOMOV (*covering his ears*). Oh, you... magpies! (*Smiles distractedly.*) I can't understand a thing! (*To the* YOUNG COMMUNISTS.) Say, youngsters, suppose you see me tomorrow — in the morning? My head is like a boiler!... My God!... (*The workers smile sympathetically.*) After all, I'm sixty years old! Rushing around all day ... just as if I were on a motorcycle! By evening something snaps. (*Takes the* ELDERLY WOMAN WORKER *by her shoulders.*) We'll do all we can, my dear. We'll talk over everything — explain it forty times... (*The workers depart, talking and gesticulating as they go out.* SOMOV, *seeing* RYZHOV, *comes up to him and leads him to the footlights.*) Well, I must tell you, Ignat Ivanovitch... They ought to write a strict reprimand into your Party ticket for such a performance. You certainly distinguished yourself! To start such a rumpus at the general meeting! What do you mean by that?

RYZHOV. I'm sorry. But do you take me for a clown? Didn't I slave in the factory for twenty-six years? Didn't I shoulder a gun for *four* years?... Not like some others, such as...

SOMOV. I know all that... I know your record... What of it?

RYZHOV. Just this: I'll go myself to the Control Commission. I won't spare *myself* — but I'll show *them* up, too!

SOMOV. Who do you mean by 'them'?

RYZHOV. Who? The rotten intellectuals! I won't permit every... *female*... to make a monkey out of me!

SOMOV. And do you know what I'm going to tell *you?* You yourself are touched with rot. Yes! And see to it that I don't hear any more talk like this in *my* collective!

RYZHOV. So! That's it! Shutting me up! Maybe you'll even tack a deviation onto me!

SOMOV. It doesn't have to be tacked! It's there already! You must learn from Inga and stop making trouble. Inga is a worker. I fight with her myself at times. There is something to her... At times she tries to bite off more than she can chew. Then I have to stop her. But she is a mass-worker — a revolutionary. Look how she's made this factory hum! And how she has stirred the masses! Eh? This is not just talk, my friend... Firmness! Clarity! Knowledge! She has all of that! And we should appreciate it!

RYZHOV. Well, of course... She may fail in some things, but she certainly can get things stirred up... But it's too much for me!

CURTAIN

ACT I

Scene 4

Factory manager's office. A desk. On it, among other objects, a modest little vase with a few flowers. On the walls are architectural projects of the proposed new buildings, sketches of new costumes, blueprints, and diagrams.

INGA *enters, followed by several men and women workers,* NEMT-SEVITCH, MERA, DMITRI, *and* SAVVUSHKIN. SOMOV *and* RYZHOV *enter later.*

YOUNG WOMAN COMMUNIST. So you *will* support us, Comrade Rizzer?

INGA. Go ahead, girls! Start in. The Young Communist brigades get our first attention. And, Mera, don't you forget about this in the wall newspaper. I'll include it in tomorrow's orders.

MERA. You can depend on the wall newspaper.

(*The* YOUNG COMMUNISTS *group around* INGA *and crowd her into the background. She talks to them.*)

SAVVUSHKIN. We're having trouble with the light, Comrade Rizzer. If we had light, it would have been a different story.

INGA. This week we shall make windows in the rear wall. You'll have light!

ELDERLY WOMAN WORKER. Don't forget about the nurseries.

INGA. We'll have the nurseries before the third shift goes to work. You have my word for it.

YOUNG WOMAN WORKER. And how about the smoke? It's really terrible!

INGA (*quickly, to* DMITRI). Chairman of the Factory Committee, how about this business?

DMITRI (*confused because of all the glances turned upon him*). I have already reported to you... Don't you remember?... Labor protection?

(*Somebody in the crowd snickers. There is a slight confusion.*)

INGA. Oh, yes! Roman Frantsevitch, you must speed that up.

NEMTSEVITCH. All right.

(NEMTSEVITCH *jots in his notebook. The workers go out in groups and pairs.* SOMOV *and* INGA *talk. What they say is not heard until* SOMOV *screams.*)

326

Somov. Must, must!... You know, this is more important than new styles. (*He jerks his head toward the sketches on the wall.*)

Inga. Again the styles? I think you're lagging behind, old man! In politics, in economics, you lead all of us, but you're weak in æsthetics!

Somov. And is æsthetics the most important?

Inga. No one says that. The most important are the new forms of labor: shock-brigades, Socialist competition, mass participation in the development of the factory...

Somov. Well?

Inga. The most important — is our construction, these new buildings into which we will move in seven months... full of light ... hygienic... with up-to-date machinery... (*Points to the architectural sketches.*)

Somov. Right!

Inga. The most important — more production... cheaper... and better in quality...

Somov. Right again! That's just what I...

Inga. And better — means not only stronger, but also more beautiful. More beautiful in a new way. It's time to reconstruct not only the methods of production, but also the goods we produce. We must introduce art into production. This problem demands our attention. Our masses are growing up. We can afford it.

Mera (*slightly ironic*). The Five-Year Plan of good taste?

Inga. Why not? This is real!

Dmitri. That's right, Inga! Shake! (*He offers his hand, but she is too busy to respond.*)

Inga. Why is it that in politics, in economics, we seek new ways, but in everyday life we must inevitably imitate Europe? Why are we afraid to say that our life ought to be better than theirs — more rational, more beautiful? When we call in an artist, why should we follow only European standards, when for the same price we can produce Soviet models that are so much better? What can we lose by that?

Ryzhov (*sarcastically*). Why, of course! Only fools live in Europe! They've thought and thought — and haven't thought up a thing!

Mera. You'd better keep still about Europe, you European!

Ryzhov. What I am is neither here nor there. Now this is what I say: you've got pants, coat, vest... well, wear them! You're going crazy! You ought to concern yourself with mechanization instead.

INGA. The way you do?

NEMTSEVITCH. By the way, Inga Martinovna... what shall we do with those machines that Ignat Ivanovitch brought back?

INGA. What *can* we do? Write them off on his personal account!

NEMTSEVITCH. Very well.

RYZHOV. What do you mean — my personal account?

INGA. It's very simple. You'll drink less and waste less. By the end of the Five-Year Plan you will have paid for them.

RYZHOV. Let me tell *you* something, Comrade Rizzer. You can make a fool of yourself if you want to, but not at the expense of anyone else!

INGA. In business matters I never make a fool of myself. You'll read about it in tomorrow's orders.

RYZHOV. Do you mean it?

INGA. No, I'm joking. (*Sharply.*) You think you can waste money and the Government will stand the expense?

RYZHOV. So that's what you're aiming at!... So that's what it is! You want to disgrace me — finish me! Is that what you mean to do? And you, Gregory Danilyitch, you, the Party leader, you side with her?... You're silent, eh?

SOMOV. I think she's right.

RYZHOV. Right? And is it right that she's been sent here to build up the factory, to do real work, and then she...

INGA. What?

RYZHOV. She... she puts flowers everywhere!

SOMOV. What nonsense!

MERA. He means to say something else, but he's afraid.

RYZHOV. Afraid? Then I'll say it openly! Standing around with young fellows in dark corners! Making love! That's what it is! (DMITRI *springs toward him.* INGA *is dumbfounded.*) I saw it myself! Is *that* right, eh?

INGA. With whom?... Where?... How dare you!

DMITRI. Danilyitch! On my word of honor!...

SOMOV. Get away! Don't mix into this!

DMITRI. What do you mean, don't mix in? He throws mud, and I...

INGA. What have *you* to do with it, Dmitri? I don't need anyone's protection. I can take care of myself.

RYZHOV (*crowing over* DMITRI). He answered all right! He's given himself away!

DMITRI. Comrade Ryzhov, think what you are saying!

RYZHOV. Don't you teach me what to think! (*They clinch.*)

SOMOV. Enough! (*Runs to them, bell in hand.*) This is a fine place to settle personal accounts! You can't fight here! (*Places himself between them.*) To your places! I'll settle this myself tomorrow. That'll do!

INGA. No, I don't want to leave it like this! (*Comes up to* RYZHOV.) Ignat, do you realize what you have said? I will make you prove what you say with facts — or you will be responsible for libel. I demand — do you hear? — I demand that you lodge a formal accusation with the Control Commission. Then we'll see who is right. We'll discuss it there.

RYZHOV. Oh, well, you're a funny person! I talk to you in a simple way, in a proletarian way...

INGA. You have to answer only one question: Will you lodge a complaint with the Control Commission?

RYZHOV. Stop pestering me!

INGA. Ignat, don't try to wriggle out of it! I am asking you.

RYZHOV. What the Devil do I want to complain for? Why the Control Commission?

INGA. Ah, you don't dare! You're afraid! That means that you've been lying!

RYZHOV. Let me alone!

DMITRI. No! Say it!

SOMOV. That's no way, that's no way, Ignat Ivanovitch!

RYZHOV. Well, maybe I *was* mistaken. Maybe it wasn't you... Oh, you all go to... God! Why don't you let a fellow alone? You know I have weak nerves! (*Goes toward the exit.*)

MERA. Oh, you... 'business man'!

SOMOV. Ignat! Where are you going? You start something and then you run away! Stop! We're talking to you. (*Rushes after him.*)

MERA. Things are certainly humming! Let's go home now, comrades... We've dragged it out long enough. And I have to spend the night over the wall newspaper! Oh! (*Stretches.*) Inga, let's go home! (INGA *doesn't answer her and goes to the side. It is apparently difficult for her to overcome the depressed mood evoked by the unexpected scene.* MERA *pursues.*) Come on, what's the matter? What are you moping about?

INGA. Why don't they regard men in the same way? *They* can do anything! But as for us... they're always putting us under the magnifying-glass! (*Tosses her head.*) Oh, to hell with it! Let's go!

NEMTSEVITCH. Inga Martinovna, just a second!... These papers must be signed — for tomorrow morning...

DMITRI (*to* INGA). Will you be ready soon?

INGA (*to* DMITRI). I have to see you about something important. Don't go away.

MERA. Well, all right. I'm off!

DMITRI (*to* INGA). I'll see you later. (*Goes away with* MERA.)

NEMTSEVITCH. Well, well, well... Ignat Ivanovitch! I didn't expect such temperament from *you*.

INGA. Did you want to see me about something?

NEMTSEVITCH. But, oh, Inga Martinovna, you amaze me! You're inimitable! To cut him short like that!

INGA. Roman Frantsevitch, I have a frightful headache... What can I do for you?

NEMTSEVITCH (*playfully*). I wish I could tell you! I am simply — how shall I put it?... (*He studies her face keenly.*) To me, you're like... a window opening onto a beautiful, fragrant garden...

INGA. Comrade Nemtsevitch, haven't you ever noticed that when engineers wax poetical, they're invariably trite and funny?

NEMTSEVITCH (*reddening*). You think so?

INGA. I do. And I beg you earnestly: let us keep within the bound of business. It will be better for both of us.

NEMTSEVITCH. You're astonishing! On my word of honor! After such a hellish day you're still formal!

INGA. Comrade Nemtsevitch, I shall not repeat it to you ten times. If you have nothing to say, I am going. (*She turns brusquely.*)

NEMTSEVITCH. I beg your pardon. I've finished, I've finished! Here you are.

(*He gets the papers, puts them on the table, and gives her the fountain pen. She glances at them and signs them, bending over the table.*)

INGA. I won't sign this one.

NEMTSEVITCH. What! Why not?

INGA. It hasn't been approved by the chairman of the Factory Committee.

NEMTSEVITCH. Again the chairman of the Factory Committee? Have mercy! This is a purely administrative matter.

INGA. You're working in a Soviet factory.

NEMTSEVITCH. I don't doubt it.

INGA. Whenever the interests of the workers are involved, it is necessary first of all to obtain the opinion of the union.

NEMTSEVITCH. But look here! That's absolutely insufferable! It binds us hand and foot.

INGA. Anyone who finds it 'insufferable' need not work here.

NEMTSEVITCH (*bowing, but with an injured air*). Thank you!

CURTAIN

ACT I

Scene 5

A landing in a co-operative apartment house. Two doors — on one of them a neat door-plate with the name 'Nemtsevitch'; the other, without a name-plate, leads to Inga's *apartment.* Nemtsevitch *and* Inga, *both in street attire, are standing at* Inga's *door.* Inga *is fumbling with the key, ready to enter.*

Nemtsevitch (*raising his hat*). Good night, Inga Martinovna. But just the same, I insist that you evidently misunderstood me.

Inga. Roman Frantsevitch, enough! I don't care to discuss it any more. Until tomorrow...

(*She is about to enter her room. At this moment the door of* Nemtsevitch's *apartment opens and* Veronica *peeks out. She is dressed in a bright kimono and her hair is pretentiously arranged.*)

Veronica. Romulka, why are you so late? We can't start the card game without you. Oh, Inga Martinovna, how do you do? How do you do, my dear? You were brilliant tonight! Divine! Marvellous! But why did you treat Ignat Ivanovitch so cruelly? You're driving him to suicide!

Nemtsevitch. No, he'll just get drunk.

Veronica (*to* Inga). If I were a man, I'd hate you! You're avenging us women — as a sex! And you're quite right. One has to be inhuman with them. Oh, how I envy you! You are so talented, so energetic! And most important of all, how you burn with your work! How I would love to catch fire with something like that! (*To her husband.*) Or with somebody! But are there any real men left now? Or any real beauty?... Nothing! There's literally nothing left! Just commonplaces! Stark materialism!

Nemtsevitch. My love... Aren't you afraid you'll catch cold?

Veronica (*turning her back to him*). You refuse to believe that I want to work! Well, to be a chairman somewhere... to appear in public... I aspire! I shout: Give me something to do! Give me... how do you say it?... burdens to bear! But, in the first place, where could anyone go with a husband on her hands?... A family?... all this nonsense? And then, darling... as an intelligent person, you must admit... do we have a real society now, real glamour? I understand the French Revolution. They had everything there, absolutely everything... salons, carnivals... But what do *we* have? Factories, factories, factories!... An economic régime!... Ha-ha!... Reconstruction conferences!... Indus — my God, I never can say that word all at once! — industri — onization... There! How can one catch fire from a thing like that?

INGA (*unable to stand it any longer*). Excuse me... I am very tired.

(*She starts to enter her apartment.* NEMTSEVITCH *is entering his.*)

NEMTSEVITCH. My angel, are you coming, or are you staying on the stairs?

VERONICA. Please don't dictate to me how I should behave!... Of course, I'm coming... What irrational questions! Good night, Inga Martinovna. (INGA *goes into her apartment.* VERONICA *turns to* NEMTSEVITCH.) What's the matter? I explain myself beautifully. It's only you who think I'm an idiot.

NEMTSEVITCH. No, that's not exactly what I think.

VERONICA. What, then?

NEMTSEVITCH. I think that I'm a needle and that you're a thread...

VERONICA. What do you mean — I'm a thread?

NEMTSEVITCH. The whole evening... at the club... at the conference... and now on the stairway... it's enough to drive a person crazy!

VERONICA. You're a scoundrelly egotist! You only want a cook ... a slave! When I want to become a social worker, you insult me! ... Thread! The impudence of it! I'll make you eat your words!

NEMTSEVITCH. Gladly! You are *not* a thread! You're a rope with which I shall hang myself one of these days! (*He goes in.*)

CURTAIN

ACT I

SCENE 6

INGA's *room. It is modestly furnished: an iron bed, a small chest of drawers, a writing-table, but no dressing-table; three stiff chairs and a baby-grand piano; bookshelves. The only touches of beauty are a few expensive engravings, copies of Renaissance masters and photographs of sculpture — classical and modern. Over the grand piano is a portrait of Beethoven in a simple black frame. On the piano are a vase of flowers, sheet music, and a couple of books.*

INGA *sits at the piano, motionless, weary, thinking.* MERA *looks in through the door.*

MERA. Inga, are you alone? (*Peering into* INGA's *face.*) What's wrong with you?

INGA. I don't know... I feel... as if I had been spat on... or as if someone had poured something smelly over me... something sticky ... All the strength that I give, all the nerves, all my personality — all this can be wiped out with one dirty lie! All — just because I'm a woman!

MERA. Stop stewing over it! It's nothing new. 'It's hard to be a woman!' Catch me worrying about some insignificant Ryzhov! And then, don't you see... how can I put it more delicately... you've been seen 'spooning' with him.

INGA. 'Spooning'? With whom?

MERA. Well, really... You don't expect me to get lyrical, I hope. With Dmitri, of course.

INGA. Do you actually think me capable of 'spooning' with him in public?

MERA. No... But generally speaking...

INGA. Generally speaking!... If you care to know, I *am* in love with him — with every drop of my blood, with all of my being!... And after all, why not? What am I? A nun? A convent girl? Why can't I love? Young girl Communists can fall in love to their hearts' content. And women workers also. But the manager! How dare she! What a violation of the proprieties! Does love clash with industrialization? Is that it?... Yes, I love him! I am in bloom —

334

because of this love... I sense it everywhere — in everything... I hear so many sounds, see so many shades of color... How fragrant the rain is! Did you know that the rain is fragrant? There is fragrance in the earth — in the leaves — in the air... Can you hear the buds unfold?

MERA. Buds? What are you talking about? Oh... on the trees! ... I've heard about it in my time.

INGA. All this astonishes me, intoxicates me. It's as if I were seeing life through a magnifying-glass. I didn't know how beautiful it was. And I too want to be beautiful! I want to... my God! How silly and how simple it all is! And just because it's so simple, it's so silly. But I feel that I am growing in every way, that something within me is becoming stronger! All these years I have been like a soldier in the ranks. I had nothing of my own. Everything was for the Party. Do you know what I mean? As if I had been put into a travelling-bag and shipped wherever they found it necessary to send me. But now, it's so different — as if another side had opened — as if something that had been crushed or cramped began to stretch, to live again! I have become richer! I have become stronger! I feel as if I were — you may laugh — a girl... a sixteen-year-old girl! I'm so happy with him! What right have they... how *dare* they lash me with their sneers? Have I forfeited the right to love?

MERA. That's not the point. Love to your heart's content... But, you see, you do everything so strangely. (*Looks around sceptically.*) These engravings... Beethoven... But no Marx! 'Colors,' 'fragrance,' the Devil knows what! I may not know anything about fragrance and color, but I *have* been married — seven times. Be more simple, Inga, and forget all this romanticism — these phantasies. To my way of thinking you're still sitting in the swamp — you know, the good old swamp of lyricism.

INGA. Why do you call it a swamp?... When a person opens up — unfolds completely — when she wants to do twice as much work, when she is impelled to create, to fight... Oh!... You call *that* a swamp? Is it a swamp — to believe in a man, to find a real friend in him — the great friend who understands you completely? Is it — to go with him hand in hand, shoulder to shoulder?...

MERA. But suppose you get stuck?... Or suppose you have to pay for it with your heart's blood? All this, you know — how shall I put it? — it's the... the refuse left in all of us. And this refuse has to be burned, discarded. We mustn't give it a chance to grow again...

335

Do you know what I am going to tell you?... If you and I had children — girls — they would do everything in an entirely new, a different way. And they will! You and I, you know, are somewhat like the last of the Mohicans. We've grown up with the old, and we're old ourselves. But the Young Communist League is something entirely different... Frankly, I want to live as they do — as if I were my own daughter!

INGA. I don't know... I entered the Revolution when I was a child — because of my father. He was a Bolshevik. He called me into the world, he gave me knowledge. That's unfortunate. It stands in the way of my being entirely new. But what can I do? I don't know any life outside the Revolution. I give myself up to it entirely. Perhaps someone else could do it better. But I can't. I give all I can — and it's not enough...

(INGA'S *voice breaks. There is a silence.* MERA *hesitates, then speaks.*)

MERA. After all, what's holding you back?

INGA. He has a wife... You know that, of course.

MERA. Who pays any attention to such trifles?

INGA. But a child?

MERA. Who hasn't a child nowadays?

INGA. I don't know whether you're pretending or making fun of me. It's so painful, so complicated — when you come face to face with it!

MERA. Don't be silly! You're moping again!... (*Sighs and shakes her head.*) Tell me: when all is said and done, is all this tragedy necessary?

INGA. How is one to avoid it?

MERA. Live all together — the three of you — that's how!

INGA (*taken by surprise*). Well, you know... You certainly don't share your toothbrush with everybody!...

MERA. Oh, oh! That reminds me: I've just lost mine. Thanks for reminding me.

INGA. Have you no fastidiousness at all?

MERA. Fastidiousness is a bourgeois prejudice.

INGA. To me — fastidiousness is that minimum of elementary culture which you have evidently lost.

MERA. You don't say!... It sounds awfully important. But, to put it plainly, you're jealous — just like any other female. You don't want to share the boy.

336

INGA. No, I don't! I can't stand this tawdriness. I don't want any small share — casual relationships, the indifference of one person to another. I demand the same crystal purity that I bring to him.

MERA (*ironically*). Mother! Mother! Hold me!

INGA. Mera, I beg of you... Stop it! I don't like your tone.

MERA. The activist! The factory manager!

INGA. Mera!

MERA. Oh, go to hell! What's the matter with you?... You live as you like, and I'll live in my own way. We'll see who'll get more hard knocks. (*Enter* DMITRI.) Ah!... Here he is, the hero of the novel! Come over here, come! Why do you torture the woman, eh? You deserve a good thrashing. Do you hear? Love and kisses! And you can both go straight to the Devil! I've missed my supper because of you. And I am so sleepy I could die! I'll take a nap first — and work on the wall newspaper later. (*She yawns loudly and walks out.*)

DMITRI. He got it this time all right! You should have seen how infuriated the old man was. Henpecked him to death! On my word of honor! I even felt sorry for that scoundrel, so help me!... Well... well... why are you so sad? (*Pause.*) Inga!... Forget it!

INGA (*her face twisted with pain*). We must forget everything, Dmitri.

DMITRI. What?

INGA. All that binds us.

DMITRI (*taken aback*). What do you mean?

INGA. I can't go on like this... Do you understand? I can't! If we hadn't been working together, it wouldn't have mattered. But now it hurts my standing as an activist as well. (*Desperately.*) I can't go on like this! We must find a solution. Either we are one — or we are nothing to each other. We must decide once and for all.

DMITRI. Right now?

INGA. When, then? When?

DMITRI. Inga!... Do you think I would hesitate?... To me you are ... you know... how have I lived until now? As in prison — as in a dank cellar. Did I know what life meant? What love meant? Did I know that any woman could be what you are? Not a cook, not a laundress, not a senseless thing, not a piece of flesh, but a person, a real person, strong, finer than I am, finer than everyone! I could drink you up like dew from the palm of my hand!

INGA. Dmitri, I didn't call you for that. What do these phrases mean — if you haven't been able to make a choice between Glafeera and me by this time?

DMITRI. It's not Glafeera. It's the little one that I'm worried about... My daughter!... Is it because I'm growing old that I feel this attachment to her? I don't know.

INGA. And for the sake of your daughter, you're prepared to go on like this — dissatisfied, stunted in mental development — you who are so gifted? There is so much to you! But now... you are growing rusty... I hate to talk about it... I hope you do take it all personally. Dimka, do you believe me? Do you believe that I am speaking, not as a woman, not as a mistress, but as a comrade, as a member of the Party?

DMITRI. It's hard for me, Inga... Working, fighting — I am at home, I know what to do. Never have I slowed down — lost the tempo — on the job. But with this sort of thing... I am in the woods. I can't think of anything... What shall I do? To whom shall I turn? My head is splitting in two. At the beginning of the Revolution I dropped everything — Glafeera, Piotka — grabbed a gun and marched off. I did it in 1919 and I did it in 1920... I'd come from the front, get well, take care of my wounds a bit, and again — to horse and away. Little Piotka died of typhus... He wasn't three years old yet. But what of it? I gnashed my teeth! All right!... But now it's a different story! Now I must think.

INGA. Think, Dmitri, think! But be quick about it. These days we can't afford to give so much to personal matters. You must decide and act. There is no time to lose. We at least should not be sunk in the morass of personal affairs. We at least should not lose strength and shed tears over such trifles. You see: we are surrounded by battles. The class war is raging on every front — all over the world. How many lives, more valuable than ours, are rotting in prison at this very moment! How many comrades are dying in the fight! Brace up! Be strong! Be as you always are in work! Be as I love you! You have no right to vacillate like this... Dimka, you are my falcon! You have no place in a hen-coop.

DMITRI. Inga, what shall I do?

INGA. Only one thing: stop tormenting me. Don't drive me mad. I can't endure it any longer! I can't stand it! *You* must find a solution, or I shall find it myself...

DMITRI. You know what?... Inga! I've got it! As God is my

witness, I've got it! Let us go away for a week... into the country, if you like... or to Moscow!...

INGA. And then what?

DMITRI. Oh, what does it matter? Something will come of it... or it will adjust itself somehow...

INGA. Something will come of it!... It will adjust itself!... No! That solution is not for me! The knot has to be untied. If it cannot be untied, it must be cut. Either way. At any cost. (*She walks away from* DMITRI. *There is a long pause.*)

DMITRI. Inga...

INGA (*in a low voice as if talking to herself*). Why should it be I? Why is it necessary for me to sacrifice myself?... Is it just because *she* is a mother? Is it a greater thing to give birth to a child than to go through what I have gone through? — denying myself everything to which I have an inalienable right as a person, giving everything to others? Don't I have an equal right to a bit of happiness — to friendship, to warmth?

DMITRI (*decisively*). Inga! Very well. (*A pause.* INGA *walks toward him.*) No... I can't leave them like this! Do you understand? I cannot defy the entire collective! Something holds me back!

INGA. Oh, this is ridiculous... and insulting to me!... What are we talking about? As if I were trying to persuade you!... I don't want any sacrifices! If you haven't decided yourself which way is the best... why all these tragedies? Let's put a cross on all of it and everything will be finished. I don't intend in the least to persuade you... I don't want anything!... Nothing! Nothing! (*She looks around with unseeing eyes.* DMITRI *wants to say something. She stops him with a gesture.*) Dimka, I have no strength left... Go!

(DMITRI *starts to go to her, then changes his mind, and, turning abruptly, goes out.* INGA *stands with her back to him.*)

CURTAIN

ACT II

Scene 7

The Gretchaninov one-room apartment in a new co-operative house. Two large square windows. The sparse assortment of furniture is typical of a worker's family: a bed, a chest of drawers, a kitchen table, four kitchen chairs, a small kerosene cooking-range on one side of the sink. A small washtub, kitchen utensils, dishes, towels, a hunk of rye bread, a head of cabbage. The tea-kettle is simmering. There are diapers on three lines across the room, in one corner a crib. It is the evening of the same day.

GLAFEERA is pretty, despite the tired look on her face. She is ironing. The board rests on the backs of two chairs. Her hair is dishevelled; it strays from under her white headkerchief. Her simple dress — blouse, skirt, cotton stockings, shoddy slippers — is in disarray from the strain of working. She looks dowdy, even according to the prevailing Soviet standards of women's dress.

GLAFEERA listens, puts the iron down, goes to the crib, and, lifting the top, looks in. The baby is asleep.

GLAFEERA. Sleep, baby girl, sleep! (*She rocks the crib.*) Oh, Valka, Valenka! (*Almost in a whisper.*) If you only knew how I love you! My little button!... I'd give anything... Oh, what a fool your father is, what a fool!

(*GLAFEERA wipes away her tears with the back of her hand and returns to the ironing-board. Sniffling, she takes up her husband's heavy blouse and irons it. The iron catches on something. She stops, puzzled, pulls the pocket out. A crumpled note falls out. She picks it up from the floor and opens it. Her breathing becomes jerky as she reads. She is shaken by sobs. The note falls from her hand. GLAFEERA sinks to her knees and drops her head on the ironing-board.*

NASTYA looks in at the door, then enters. GLAFEERA lifts her head from the board and stifles a sob. She rises, picks out a rag from the pile of unironed laundry, and blows her nose. NASTYA looks dour and belligerently sympathetic.)

NASTYA. Hasn't he come home yet?

GLAFEERA. No...

NASTYA. Well, mine has! Mother of God!... (*She looks askance at* GLAFEERA, *who is calming down.*) He's a regular sabotager, that's what he is. He got what was coming to him, all right. You see, they frightened him at the production conference because he's opposed to women. Of course, you can't expect anything else of him. But if you let him, he'll treat all women as he treats me... We've been married only sixteen years, and look what he's done with me! I am no longer a human being — am I? At my age, others strut about like peacocks! There was a time when I looked in the mirror once in a while. But now I've given that up. It's frightful! (GLAFEERA *stands motionless, staring into space; her shoulders begin to shake.*) Come on! What's the matter with you? What is it, Glashenka? (GLAFEERA's *sobs increase; she hides her face in her apron.*) Stop it! ... He'll come all right. Maybe he's detained somewhere.

GLAFEERA. I know where he is... That's where! (*Gives* NASTYA *the note.*)

NASTYA (*takes the note and turns it helplessly in her hands*). What's it all about? I can't make it out... I took a few lessons last year when they were liquidating illiteracy, but now I've forgotten everything. You can't read very much — with my Sofron around!

GLAFEERA (*wipes away her tears and reads the note*). 'Dimka, I will be home at ten. Come without fail...' (*She gasps and pronounces the last word with difficulty.*) '... Inga.'

NASTYA (*listening with bated breath*). From herself! From *her!* Where did you find it? Oh, Mother of God, what a rascally woman! She must have cast a spell over him! To run away from such a wife! Eh? And how happy you were together! A shining example for everyone! What is the world coming to? Men lived, knew their business, some were tailors, some something else, and everything was all right. But now — it's as if somebody had started twisting their tails, the damned dogs! They don't know what they want themselves!

GLAFEERA (*falls across the ironing-board*). Oh, Nastenka!... I have no strength left!

NASTYA. They want the educated ones!... And where shall we go — we, with the children? Eh? God knows what's going on these days!

GLAFEERA. I expected it right along. My heart told me. Since All Saints' Day he's been like a stranger... He used to be so tender ... I could talk with him about anything... laugh... we had everything in common. But now everything is in silence. He looks at me

341

as if I were a strange woman. I don't even know how to come to him any more. Words freeze on my tongue. I want to say one thing — and I say something else... (*Sobs.*) Sometimes I think to myself: What is it, really? Am I such a fool that I cannot say a word? (*Sobs more violently.*) And I am afraid of him! Of Mitya! He's not mine now — not mine!

NASTYA. And how you used to be! God! Heart to heart!

GLAFEERA. I never heard an unkind word. All his thoughts were about home. He didn't complain about anything... nothing at all! He was glad of everything. But this week he complained about the soup... and the meat was not fresh... and the tea was not right... Everything is topsy-turvy! When he goes to sleep, he puts his clothes under his pillow. (*She looks disconsolately at the note.*) And now — this!

NASTYA. What does he see in her?

GLAFEERA. I don't know. (*Begins to sob again.*) I don't know anything. My head is whirling. I can't live without Mitya. I won't give him up to anybody! I'll either poison them or... (*Her gaze rests on the crib; she rushes to it.*) Valenka! Valenka!

NASTYA. Stop it.... God be with you!...

GLAFEERA (*appealing to the absent* DMITRI). Why punish the baby?... She may be better than I — better-looking — but why should Valka suffer? That I shall never forgive him! My own grievances I can forgive, but this — my flesh and blood.... this little chick! — I will never forgive for her sake.

NASTYA (*looking in the corners of the room*). You live without an ikon. That's the real trouble. You ought to pray, put a candle before the image of the Holy Virgin. Perhaps everything will be all right then, and your man will come to his senses. Or you might go to a fortune-teller. There is one in the neighborhood.

GLAFEERA. I have no faith. I have no faith in anything now!

NASTYA. What do you mean?

GLAFEERA (*pulls out a drawer from the chest of drawers*). Here is a little ikon... my mother's. I've hidden it from Mitya — I put it away here.

NASTYA. Well, that's splendid! Now pray, pray, darling.

GLAFEERA (*at first hesitates, then raises the ikon to her lips*). My God, what is all this punishment for? (*In despair.*) No! He won't hear me! I won't believe in anything any more! (*She throws down the ikon.*)

NASTYA. How dare you. Holy Mother! (*She rushes to pick up the ikon.*)

GLAFEERA (*despairingly*). Why doesn't He answer? Why doesn't He? (*Weeping.*) Perhaps Mitya grew cold to me because of that! He must have seen me praying. Oh, Nastenka, I am in a fog! I'm all tired out! (NASTYA *reverently dusts the ikon with her apron, puts it up on the chest of drawers, and crosses herself.*) I can understand nothing! Only one thing I know: he has become a stranger. He's not mine any more! She has him in a net! He's bewitched! The snake. You would think she'd take pity on someone else's children. She had no children; she was never tied down by marriage. She has neither fruit nor root. These shameless women! They will go with any man! He just has to whistle! But why are they smashing my life? What for?

(GLAFEERA *sobs hysterically.* NASTYA *looks distractedly at her, then begins to rush around without much sense; seizes first one thing and then another, makes a sign of the cross over the water prepared for the ironing and sprinkles it over* GLAFEERA, *making the sign of the cross over her.*)

NASTYA. Enough of that! Enough! Stop it!

(GLAFEERA *calms down. She lifts her head and looks long and indifferently before her. A pause.*)

GLAFEERA. Tomorrow my vacation is over. I have to get back to the factory. How can I go, feeling like this? I can't even finish my own ironing.

NASTYA. I'll finish it for you. (GLAFEERA *hugs her gratefully.*) Don't mention it. Aren't we all human?... Everybody will understand your situation. Don't worry about that!... I'll iron and look after everything for you.

GLAFEERA. Don't do anything. Leave it as it is. Never mind. (*Drops her head again in utter prostration.*) But the baby...

NASTYA. Sit down, sit down. I'll look after her.

GLAFEERA. No, let me! I want to do it myself!

(GLAFEERA *jumps up and runs to the crib. The baby begins to cry. She quiets it.* NASTYA *prays on her knees before the ikon.*)

(BOLTIKOV *enters noisily. He is drunk and disorderly.*)

NASTYA. Holy Father! My man is here! (*Rises hastily.*)

(BOLTIKOV *looks at* NASTYA, *at the ikon, waves his arms, and yells.*)

343

BOLTIKOV. We don't pray to the Lord God! There is no God in the Republic!

NASTYA. Ugh! You shark! Sabotager!

BOLTIKOV (*regards* NASTYA *haughtily*). The proletarians are fighting Him so that the bourgeoisie will not rule!

NASTYA. Pickled again! It's Heaven only when you're not home! The minute you appear, everything goes topsy-turvy!

BOLTIKOV. I'll smash you with this iron!... Why aren't you at home? Do I have to set up the samovar myself? Is that it? Am I a dog to you, or am I your husband?

NASTYA. Quiet! Quiet! Don't yell!

(NASTYA *looks uneasily at* GLAFEERA, *who stands near the crib, rocking the baby to sleep. The baby has stopped crying.* GLAFEERA *seems utterly indifferent — in a stupor.*)

BOLTIKOV. Your business is to stay at home and look after *me!*... But what are you up to instead? The samovar is cold — and you are here! Chattering away! Wagging your tongue! Is that the way? I'll fix you!

(BOLTIKOV *swings at her.* NASTYA *retreats. He advances, stumbles over a chair. The chair falls.*)

NASTYA. Quiet. Quiet! Don't threaten me! You're not at home. You damned heretic!

BOLTIKOV. You vermin have been given freedom! (*Spits violently.*) Tfui! The whole factory is full of your kind! All sorts of women's departments! For forty years I have been working quietly without trouble. But *they* won't let a fellow be! They've started shock-brigades, Socialist competition... (*Spits again.*) Tfui! I, an experienced master operator, have to compete! Think of it! Has anybody ever heard the like! And *who* is the brigade-leader? A wo-man. Who is the manager? A wo-man! A manager with a skirt on; Eh? And what kind of a skirt? What kind of a skirt, eh? (*Indicates above his knees.*) Up to there! Eh? What do you call that? What have we come to?... Shaming me at the conferences; Threatening a trial! (*Spits.*) Tfui! A nightmare. What *is* this? When will this rule by women be overthrown? They've bound me hand and foot, damn them. (*He weeps drunkenly.* NASTYA *tries timidly to approach him. He jumps at her.*) Ugh! Anathema! (BOLTIKOV *stamps his feet, slams the chairs against the floor.*)

NASTYA. Be quiet, you! You're not in your own house! Have

344

you no decency? You're shameless! When did you have the time to get so plastered? *Makhaon!*

BOLTIKOV (*blinking*). Don't call me that! Don't you dare call me that. Do you hear? You can call me anything you like, only so I can understand you! But that word I cannot understand!

NASTYA. Cool off, blockhead!

BOLTIKOV. I won't be ruled by women! I don't want to! I don't want to be a shock-brigader! Let those who want to submit! But I will go on beating my woman as I have done in the past! If I want to, I'll twist her head off: If I want to, I'll ride on her! I'll do whatever I like with you!

(NASTYA *runs away from him as he pursues her, and upsets the ironing-board, the laundry, and the iron. The crash wakens the baby, who begins to cry again.*)

NASTYA. Oh, Mother! Oh, Holy Virgin!

(GLAFEERA *is not yet shaken out of her stupor. She ignores the baby and merely looks with wide eyes at the scene enacted before her.* BOLTIKOV *chases* NASTYA.)

BOLTIKOV. I'll kill you! I'll tear you to pieces!

NASTYA (*hiding behind* GLAFEERA). Oh! I'm so frightened!

(*Enter* VERONICA, *dressed as before.* BOLTIKOV *stares at her in amazement, stops in his traces.* NASTYA *quiets down the baby.*)

VERONICA. What's going on here? I... I simply don't understand. Do you think that just because this is a factory home, you have the right to smash the ceilings?... The plaster is coming off in our place! Have you no shame? After all, you're supposed to be cultured proletarians!

(NASTYA, *although still apprehensive of* BOLTIKOV, *ventures to walk toward him as she speaks to* VERONICA.)

NASTYA. You be quiet!... This is not your *private* home! We have the same share in it as you. 'Shame'?... You're wearing expensive silks, painting your finger nails — while *he* had to work all day long! And it's been that way all his life... Always the same thing! Anybody would take to drink!

VERONICA. Don't you think *we* work?... Amazing! (*Looks around with disgust.*) Hanging diapers! That's why it's so damp in the corner! How can one live in such an odor?

(GLAFEERA *comes to life suddenly and takes a step toward* VERONICA.)

345

GLAFEERA. Get out of here! Go away!

BOLTIKOV. Women *up*stairs, women *down*stairs! Women here, women there! Everywhere around us, women!

(BOLTIKOV *seizes his head in his hands and runs out, bellowing imprecations. In the doorway he bumps into* DMITRI, *who enters, silent and sullen and pale.*)

DMITRI. What's going on here? Why the uproar?

GLAFEERA (*in a scarcely audible voice*). Mitya!

NASTYA (*looking at them, then at the door*). Sofron has been cutting up here. No end of trouble! When he gets drunk, the only thing to do is to run away from home!

DMITRI. Haven't you got enough room in your own place? The Devil knows what kind of people you are!

(DMITRI *lifts the chair.* GLAFEERA *hurries to pick up the iron, the laundry, and the board.* NASTYA *helps her set the room in order.*)

VERONICA. Comrade Gretchaninov, you, as chairman of the house committee, ought to see about this disgraceful conduct! We have guests. Roman Frantsevitch came home *so* tired... He spent the whole evening at the construction conference... and then here — trak-trak-trak! They won't let him rest! If we had known, we would never have left the old apartment! After all, you ought to consider the Party instructions!

DMITRI. What do you mean — instructions?

VERONICA. About making normal conditions for us honest specialists.

DMITRI. Listen — whatever you call it — 'honest specialist'! I'm in no condition to speak to you now. I need rest, too.

VERONICA. Then don't throw chairs and irons on the floor. Cad! (*Exit.*)

(*On first impulse,* DMITRI *turns after her, then, waving his hand contemptuously, goes to the opposite side of the room.*)

NASTYA. That's the way they all are... educated ones! The good-looking ones! (*She looks significantly at* DMITRI *and then goes out.*)

GLAFEERA. Mitenka, shall I get supper ready?

DMITRI. I don't want any.

GLAFEERA. Tea, perhaps?

DMITRI. I don't want anything! I told you plainly!... Dirt everywhere! Dust! Just like a pigsty! You didn't have time to sweep up, eh? (*He is irritated, scratches his ear. Suddenly he puts his hand in his pocket with embarrassment, and, taking out a handkerchief, begins to wipe his hand surreptitiously.*)

GLAFEERA (*laughing nervously*). Using perfume! Very good perfume! What are you wiping it off for? (*Suddenly loses control of herself.*) Mitka! You're a fool! You don't know what it's all about! You'll make an end of us all! And that'll be your own finish, too!

DMITRI. What's the matter with you? Have you suddenly gone mad today? (*Sees the ikon.*) And what's this? Something new! Starting in with the gods! (*Sweeps the ikon off the chest of drawers.*)

GLAFEERA (*falling to the floor*). Mityushka! Light of my life! My bitter happiness! (*Clutches at his legs.*)

DMITRI. Let me alone! Let me be quiet!... All day long stewing and sweating, and then — here! (*Raises her from the floor.*) Did you wash yourself today? You reek of borshtch!

GLAFEERA. So I'm repulsive to you! Repulsive, am I? I see that I'm repulsive to you! Say it! Don't try to fool me! Don't make fun of me!

DMITRI. That I have never done, Glafeera. What's the matter with you anyway?

GLAFEERA (*showing him the note*). You haven't done that, either, have you? You have no conscience! (*Breathless.*) You're a skunk!

(DMITRI *takes the note, slowly folds it, and puts it away. A long pause.*)

DMITRI. Well, so be it! (*Smiles wryly.*) If so, let it be the end.

GLAFEERA. The end?

DMITRI. Why prolong the agony? Don't you see it yourself? You and I are strangers.

GLAFEERA. Strangers? And what about the eleven years? What about our Piotka?

DMITRI. True... But now everything is different. Times have changed.

GLAFEERA. And what about Valka?

DMITRI. I shall not abandon Valka. No matter where I am, I shall remain her father. (*Takes her hand.*) Glasha, you *must* understand: I have grown up; I've changed. What was I before? I was paid on pay-day, bought a chain for my watch, or a new kerchief for you. We'd go out once a month to visit, or to the cinema, or to the fair on holidays. That's all. The house and the diapers! But now my life has opened up before me. I want to grasp it all, so that none

347

of it will escape me... But I can't even expect you to understand! It's as if we were talking different languages.

GLAFEERA. Different languages! And what language did you speak then, when you came to me wounded, sick with typhus, when I spent nights over you, nursing you, when you were living on a scholarship, when you were spending night and day over your books, studying at the workers' school while I was bending over a sewing machine, when you were dying of fever?... What language did we speak then? Oh, Mitka, you have no conscience!

DMITRI. What has that to do with it? I'm talking about the present.

GLAFEERA. And I — about the past... about the years I have given you. You remember about yourself all right. But how was *I* living? How was *I* struggling? You're not interested in that! While you were in the army, do you think I was doing nothing? And who nursed your son Petyushka?

DMITRI. Well, Petyushka is dead. What's the use of talking about it now?

GLAFEERA. Yes, dead! Because there was no strength left in me! Dead of hunger! I did everything to save him — everything except cut off a piece of my own flesh! Do you think those were easy years? The house so cold that even wolves would have frozen in it! I — sick with typhus! Piotka — sick with typhus!... Hunger! ... Not a crust in the house! It may be easy to talk about it, but to live through it all was harder than your battles at the front!

DMITRI (*coldly*). Have you anything else to say?

GLAFEERA. All of my life... all of my life I have given and given and given — to you... and you don't even see it!

DMITRI. What have you given me? You mend my socks. You cook! Why, I can get Nastya to do it for me for twenty rubles!

GLAFEERA. Nastya?... But my tenderness? My love? How do you price that? Did it ever occur to you that when I mend your shirt, I sew my soul into it with each stitch?

DMITRI. Stop talking nonsense!... What do I want with your soul, when I am tied hand and foot by you? I have no way out! I tried to talk to you, read newspapers to you, dragged you out to meetings... But would you take any interest? You!... When you do say a word, you make a fool of yourself! I'm ashamed of you before strangers! I tell you: *we* have become strangers. Well, you may grow, and get polished, but at the same time, I'll be forging *far* ahead — farther and farther ahead of you. Do you expect me to lag behind for the whole of the Five-Year Plan, waiting for you? Or to drag you along like a dead weight, hopping on one foot?

GLAFEERA (*hanging her head*). Oh, Mityenka! (*Weeps.*)

DMITRI. There! Reproaches and tears! A fine kind of a life this is!

GLAFEERA (*straightening up*). True! Your Inga is not like this!

DMITRI. If she were, I would not love her.

GLAFEERA. *That's* the point — not all this talk about 'no way out,' 'hopping on one foot'! That woman has caught you in her net! That's the whole thing! The rest is only make-believe!

DMITRI. You have understood nothing. It's no use!

GLAFEERA. You said yourself that you love her.

DMITRI. Yes, I do! I love her as I have never loved anyone before! I had no idea... I didn't know it was possible to love so much! I've left you *so* far behind that if we go on like this... it'll be the end of both Inga and me!

GLAFEERA. The end of *you?* And what about *me?* I'm already finished! I don't know where I will find the strength to drag out this existence. But you're not interested in that, are you? Oh, Dmitri! (*She begins to cry.*) Mitya! My Mitenka! My beloved! I love you so much! So much! (*She tries to embrace him.*)

DMITRI (*repulses her in disgust*). Stop it! Why must you do that? It's useless! (GLAFEERA *bends over the baby's crib, where she continues to weep.* DMITRI *loses his temper, stamps his foot.*) Shut up, I tell you!

GLAFEERA. My baby! Valenka! If anything should happen to me, what will become of you? You'll be fatherless! Homeless...

DMITRI. Oh, what a rope around my neck! (*Turns angrily to stop her, but forthwith changes his mind.*) No! It's no use!... It's too painful... (*Pause.*) Is the laundry ready?

GLAFEERA (*through tears*). No, not quite.

DMITRI. Give me the basket.

GLAFEERA. Which one?

DMITRI (*picks up a basket*). This one — all right?

GLAFEERA (*breaking into tragic sobs*). It's for the baby's clothes! Take anything else you like, but I won't give you that!

DMITRI. Oh, what does it matter? I'll put it in a newspaper. (*Picks out his laundry.*) Don't you want to finish it?

GLAFEERA (*taken by surprise*). Well, Dmitri, you... that's going

349

too far! (*Angrily.*) Get it ironed over there... where you're going! I'm through working for you... Enough!

DMITRI (*embarrassed*). I just meant... (*He takes the laundry, crumples it hastily, and wraps it in a newspaper; it falls apart.*) Oh, well, let it go. I'll take everything tomorrow. Good-bye, Glafeera.

(*He goes out quickly. GLAFEERA follows him with her eyes, standing motionless, as if petrified. After a few moments, the scared face of NASTYA appears. She is dishevelled, her clothes are torn, and she displays a black eye. She enters.*)

NASTYA. Well, what?... (*She looks around distractedly and comes closer to GLAFEERA.*) How is it?

GLAFEERA. He's gone away... to her!...

NASTYA. Gone? (*She sees the ikon on the floor.*) Lord! The Holy Virgin has been thrown to the floor twice in one and the same day! (*She picks it up.*) Dear, dear! What's the meaning of this? Oh, these damned men! Just give them a taste of honey, and they turn their noses up at our borshtch — our cabbage soup! They have no use for the likes of us! (*She points to herself.*) See how my savage has decorated me? (*Sighs — almost fondly.*) He threw the samovar at me! Well, that's how it goes!... This is not the *first* time. All my life it's been like that!... Glafeerushka, do you want me to make you some tea?

GLAFEERA (*looking at her, dazed*). I don't want anything. Not anything! Everything tastes like grass. I'm frightened, Nastenka! Everything is whirling! I'm so helpless! Nastya! (*She suddenly rushes to the window and grabs a bottle of acid.*)

NASTYA (*runs to her and seizes her hand*). Glafeera! What are you trying to do! Are you mad? (*There is a short struggle. GLAFEERA succeeds in swallowing some of the acid. NASTYA knocks the bottle from her hand.*) How could you think of a thing like that? This is a sin against God!... And who will take care of your baby?

GLAFEERA (*pressing her hands to her breast and looking at the crib*). Valichka! Darling! My baby! (*Sobbing, GLAFEERA throws herself across the crib. The baby cries fitfully.*)

NASTYA. Lord! What shall we do now? I don't know where to begin!

(*GLAFEERA is writhing with pain; with NASTYA'S aid she attempts to rise.*)

GLAFEERA. Valenka! Valka! Everything is burning inside me! (*She falls and then writhes on the floor.*) Oh, my darlings!... Oh, how

350

it burns! What have I done? My little daughter! Darling! Everything is so twisted! O Lord! What will become of us now?
(NASTYA, *completely lost, stands over her — tremulous, white-lipped, and makes the sign of the cross.*)
NASTYA. Mother of God! Holy Virgin!

CURTAIN

ACT II

SCENE 8

The Gretchaninov apartment, as in the preceding scene. A sunny morning several days later. GLAFEERA *is in bed. At the bedside is a little table with medicines. There is a pause.*

(*Enter* SOMOV.)

SOMOV. Well, self-wrecker, how are you? Getting better? Little by little? (GLAFEERA *hides her face in the pillow.*) What's that? Tears again? Glafeerushka! (*He comes up close to her and strokes her hair.*) Oh, you scatterbrain!... It seems we have discussed everything with you, and you're up to your old tricks again! Aren't you ashamed of yourself?

GLAFEERA (*sobbing*). I'm sorry for Mitya!

SOMOV. Mitya! Mitya! What has Mitya to do with it? Aren't you a human being yourself?

GLAFEERA. That's just the point — I am! And he treated me like a dog... and worse — like a piece of wood! All my suffering, all my love... and he spat on me! Is that the way a Communist should act? He wrung me out and threw me away like a rag! He says he's grown! He puts on airs! But on whose back did he climb? Whose neck has he bent? Who helped him grow? Oh... you Communists!

SOMOV. I'm not defending him. He has done a nasty thing. It's bad! (*Hastily.*) Of course, you can't lock up the heart. We don't intend to restore serfdom. That's true, too. But all the same, in his particular case, something's wrong! Bad! He couldn't lift you up with him — that's what's bad. Everyone in the factory condemns him for this. (*A pause.*) And you... though you reproach him, you still pity him!

GLAFEERA. Eleven years! That's no laughing matter. I loved him, and I love him now. He is Valka's father!

SOMOV. Yes, it's mighty hard. (*With determination.*) But you tear it out! Tear it out by the roots, Glasha! Tear it out and start anew... on your own! Did you read the book I gave you the other day?

GLAFEERA. I've finished it... I've thought a lot about it.

SOMOV. Well?

GLAFEERA. I don't know if I'll have enough strength, Gregory Danilyitch. I'm all alone... I'm weak. And there is Valka...

SOMOV. Valka will go to the nursery. And strength will come. You won't notice it, but it will come. Have more faith in yourself, Glafeerushka. Move everything inside of yourself, rebuild it. We live in such a stirring day. Everything old goes into the melting-pot. They're even accusing *me* now... they say that I'm lagging behind. Never mind. Even *I* can still put up a good fight. And you're young! You have only to live and breathe deeply! You *are* silly — shedding tears! Work! Study! Start a new life! What is there to cry about? Before you had only Mitya to love you and defend you, but now the whole world is yours! And the whole collective is for you!... Do you think you're all alone? We'll all back you up so that your life will get on the right track. Do you hear? And what's more: I'll take you under my personal wing!

GLAFEERA (*smiling with embarrassment*). You're so good, Gregory Danilyitch! So kind!

SOMOV. Well... not to everybody.

GLAFEERA. I feel ashamed of myself. You have so much on your hands, and yet you find the time to bother about me!

SOMOV. I must. I must, Glafeerushka! Every life matters now. All of you here are my army. I am responsible to the Party for you, for the whole factory. The fight is raging. Every factory is a trench in the Five-Year Plan. A trench of the new life. If something is wrong in the army, something threatening the life within — *who* is responsible?

GLAFEERA (*laughing*). Well, all right. You're a fighter, Danilyitch! A commander of men!

SOMOV. Wrong! An organizer!

GLAFEERA (*lifting herself up*). If that's so, we must follow you! Everybody! It's fun! I *will* get well, Danilyitch. I'll do anything to get well. (*She tries to rise.* SOMOV *smiles and puts her back in bed, quiets her. She, too weak to contend against him, smiles back brightly.*)

SOMOV. We'll do everything! That's because we are Bolsheviks, Glafeerushka, Bolsheviks!...

CURTAIN

ACT III

Scene 9

A corner of the factory's sewing department. It is as busy as a bee-hive. Two rows of sewing machines going at full blast. Parallel to them a long, narrow table, on both sides of which, next to the machines, sit youthful seamstresses, mostly members of the Young Communist League. Long lamps suspended on cords hang down from the ceiling. Between the end cords is a rope from which hangs a red banner with the sign in white block letters: 'LET US SURPASS THE AUGMENTED PLAN FOR THE THIRD YEAR OF THE FIVE-YEAR PLAN!' Piles of materials move quickly across the table from hand to hand. Two women workers at both sides of the table bring new work and take away the finished product. The second one of these women is GLAFEERA. She has changed amazingly — has become infected with the general tempo of this shock-brigade work. Her clothes are neat, although as simple as before. She wears her red kerchief at a dashing angle; she has bobbed her hair; and seems prettier, self-assured.

GLAFEERA. You certainly are shock-brigaders!

FIRST YOUNG COMMUNIST. What? Getting swamped?

GLAFEERA (*tossing her head gaily*). I'll pull through!

SECOND YOUNG COMMUNIST. She'll pull through if anyone will!

GLAFEERA. If someone were to say to me today: leave the fifth table and go work with — let's say, those old women — I wouldn't do it for anything!

FIRST YOUNG COMMUNIST. Our table is famous! (*Triumphantly.*) The first Young Communist Brigade of the third year of the Five-Year Plan! Girls, let's sing!

THIRD YOUNG COMMUNIST. All right! But keep your eyes on your work!

FIRST YOUNG COMMUNIST (*leading the singing*).

> If the KIM [1] is in your heart,
> Stand up bravely, have no fear...

(*Gradually the whole table joins in the singing. The work goes more rhythmically. GLAFEERA, too, is drawn into the singing.*)

[1] KIM: Young Communist International.

(*Enter* BOLTIKOV. *He passes by, stops, listens. The girls wink at each other and sing still louder. He spits with indignation.*)

BOLTIKOV. Tfui! Are you supposed to sing here, or to work?

FIRST YOUNG COMMUNIST. I wish *you'd* work as we do!

BOLTIKOV. I work as I always work.

SECOND YOUNG COMMUNIST. But we do it in the new way. (*Reciting.*) 'Labor is an affair of honor — of valor...'

FIRST YOUNG COMMUNIST. And the result — a hundred and twelve per cent of the Plan! And our unit is ahead of everybody!

GLAFEERA (*to* BOLTIKOV). Try to beat that!

SECOND YOUNG COMMUNIST. Like fun!

BOLTIKOV (*sputtering*). Damn you!... Turning all life upside down!... Oh, if I only had my way...

FIRST YOUNG COMMUNIST. Enough of this chatter! Get to work — or we'll report you for loafing! (*She sings again.*) 'If the KIM is in your heart...'

> (*The others catch on,* GLAFEERA *too.* BOLTIKOV *angrily shakes his fist at her; she laughs.*)

(*Enter* INGA, SOMOV, *and* NEMTSEVITCH, *walking rapidly.* SOMOV *catches* BOLTIKOV'S *arm.*)

SOMOV. Comrade Boltikov, are you crazy? During working hours! That's a fine example to set for young people! You'd better watch out, old man! I'm warning you. I'm going to have a serious talk with you. Get to work!

> (BOLTIKOV *flashes an angry look at the smiling* YOUNG COMMU-NISTS, *and leaves.* GLAFEERA, *seeing* INGA, *turns white, com-presses her lips, shrinks, and bends over her work.* INGA *pays no attention to her.*)

INGA. No 'buts,' Roman Frantsevitch. By the new year the conveyor must be working. Do you see what's happening?

> (*She points to a pile of materials that has accumulated at the end of the table because* GLAFEERA *has lost her speed for a moment.* GLAFEERA *hastens to correct it. The work goes on at full blast.*)

NEMTSEVITCH. We must have the machinery.

SOMOV. Must? Then we'll have it! That's clear. By the new year we'll mechanize the unit. (*To the workers.*) Is that right?

VOICES. Correct!... It's high time!... Delays and delays!

INGA. The matter is settled. And with the conveyor, what percentage shall we put out?

FIRST YOUNG COMMUNIST. Two hundred! Our table sets its task at two hundred!

(*A penetrating, continuous ringing of the bell. Everybody jumps up gaily.*)

VOICES. Lunch time!... That much is done!...

(*Everyone is hustling around. Loud voices. The song begins again: 'If the KIM is in your heart...'*)

CURTAIN

ACT III

Scene 10

Office of the factory local of the Communist Party, a few moments later. Offstage rings the same lunch bell as at the end of the preceding scene and there is the noise of voices. A table, a bench, and several chairs.

Mera *is writing at the table.* Ryzhov *stands beside her.*

Ryzhov (*looking at his watch*). Lunch time. Let's go eat.

Mera. Haven't time.

Ryzhov. Forget it! (Ryzhov *sits on the edge of the table, plays with his watch chain.*)

Mera. Ignat, you're getting on my nerves!

Ryzhov. Which nerves in particular?

Mera. Don't be vulgar! Get out! Let me work.

Ryzhov. This is lunch time... not work time... And, anyway, you know where your work really is?

Mera. Well? Where?

Ryzhov. You won't throw something at me?... You seem to be out of sorts today.

Mera. My head is splitting. I'm sick and tired to death of everybody, and of you most of all!

Ryzhov. Oho! Why such a change?

Mera. You're all beasts — you men! And you're the worst of all!

Ryzhov. Well, well, well — aren't you pleasant today!

Mera. One comes to you men as to comrades, but you have just one thing on your mind — dirt! You all aim at one point. I am as sick of you as I am of gruel! I'm going to sit here alone and not say a word to anyone!

Ryzhov. Petty bourgeois idealism!

Mera. You're an animal! You can't even understand what the relations between men and women ought to be.

Ryzhov. Well, well... you don't say!

Mera. You're petty, shallow, and lecherous! Do you understand? Petty and lecherous!

RYZHOV (*jumping off the table*). Stop all this high-falutin' talk! From the physiological point of view, we're all alike. And you women like to drag things out... You want the moon, the boat... Maybe you want me to sing you a ballad! Is that it? Get on my knees? (*Mockingly.*) Oh, my darling, oh, my precious! (*Spits.*) Tfui! Never in my life have I wasted my valuable time on such red tape! Love is naked passion and mutual accommodation — that's all! What are you looking at? A bedbug? (*Looks over his shoulder.*)

MERA. I'm looking at you. (*She shrugs her shoulders.*) Reptile! Give me a cigarette and get the hell out of here... (*She rises, lights the cigarette.*) Get out!

RYZHOV. Quiet! Quiet! You're a husky one, but I'll take care of you! (*He begins to struggle with her.*)

(SOMOV *enters from the left, looks at them over his glasses.*)

SOMOV. Getting playful... Couldn't find a better place, eh?

RYZHOV. We're resting. There was a bell just now.

SOMOV. Inga isn't docking your pay for nothing! You deserve it!

RYZHOV (*his expression changing suddenly*). Docked again?

SOMOV. Again. I just saw the pay schedule.

RYZOV. Gregory Danilyitch, what is this? Taunting a fellow? (*His voice rises.*) All right, you may dock me once, you may dock me twice, for appearances' sake. I understand discipline. If that's the way the Bureau has decided, it's all right with me. But if she does it every time... What is it? Prison labor? What do you think I am? A slave? A laughing-stock for all of you?

SOMOV. Don't yell. First of all, don't yell.

RYZHOV. Gregory Danilyitch, I know just what I am. I may drink and... well, many things. I admit I have sins. I'm not denying that.

SOMOV. Well, go on.

RYZHOV. How can I help all that, Gregory Danilyitch, if I've been kicked around and bossed for over — thirty years? You must understand that. Now, of course, I have — how shall I put it? — an important job. You should have seen me when I was first made a commissar! You should have seen me then! In comparison, this is nothing!

SOMOV. An important job! Really? Isn't it about time to make you a bit less important?

RYZHOV. You're the best judge of that. I will say only one thing:

I may have a deviation, but even that's a proletarian one. (*To the sceptical* MERA, *who snorts.*) Sure it is! What are you neighing about? But your Inga! She has a bourgeois deviation! You want to expel me. But I will say one thing anywhere — even at the Central Executive Committee: the likes of her should be cleared out, despite her father and all such things!

SOMOV. Stop it, Ignat Ivanitch! Workers of her kind should be appreciated... It's true... sometimes she is not quite right... not in our way... Take this case, for instance.

MERA. Again about Glafeera? Do you mean that Inga had no right to fall in love?

SOMOV. Love! Love! You're talking like a magpie! One must not love at the expense of someone else. We loved, too, in our time. But we didn't disregard the rights of other people.

MERA. I don't think that either Inga or Dmitri can be blamed for this.

SOMOV. You don't think so, but *I* do! And the whole factory blames them. I hear of nothing else but that!

MERA (*ironically*). Of course... If we let the petty bourgeoisie dictate to us...

SOMOV. No, it's not the petty bourgeoisie, but the true class instinct.

RYZHOV. Right! I, too...

SOMOV. You shut up! You have no such instinct at all! (RYZHOV, *offended, walks away.*) Mera, tell me directly, honestly: do we need the family or not?

MERA. Pots? Diapers? Jealousy?... To hell with it!

SOMOV. Not pots, not jealousy!... But an entirely new, different family... *our* kind of family. We need it, don't we? And the working class knows it and is building it and will attain it. But he who does not see this new thing, who considers that we do not need the family at all — 'in general' — understands everything just as little as those who shout that we 'in general' do not need force, 'in general' do not need power, and so forth! All this, to put it bluntly, is counter-revolution — a blow at that family which the working class is building, without which it will not be able to draw one-half of humanity into the Revolution!

MERA. Ho-ho-ho! A quaint little ideal! No, comrade. You're getting old. You're a romanticist!

SOMOV. As far as your Nemtsevitches are concerned, or these

matches — (*waves the extinguished match before her*) — of course I am a romanticist! But I have suffered in prison for this romanticism. I haven't very long to wait for this — how is it? — well, to the grave... to the crematorium! Even now I sometimes wake up in a perspiration, all shaky!... What do you think? I see myself like this (*stretches out his hand to show how small*) and... my father is beating my mother. I remember it all right! I've remembered it all my life. And to me it is not a 'quaint little ideal' that the dark, savage, illiterate beings should begin to live like human beings. To me such a union, when both are equal, friendly, free, is the ideal for which I have been struggling for forty-five years. One can chatter about anything. But just you try to abolish all law, give freedom to such types as this... (*points to* RYZHOV).

RYZHOV. Now I'm lost!

SOMOV. Ask yourself, what would happen then? You don't know? Well, I'll tell you: there will be abortions, there will be infanticides, another hundred thousand homeless children! And as a result, such specimens — (*points again to* RYZHOV) — and we have plenty of them — will push woman back along the entire line. That is what will happen! One has to be realistic... I admire Inga. I like her decisiveness, her firmness. She lives audaciously, strongly. But, after all, she is — how shall I put it? — a laboratory product. She had to have a father exiled abroad — a remarkable Bolshevik! — she had to grow up abroad. But the millions? The millions are praying to God... the millions are suffocating in kitchen stench, and carry bruises from their beatings! You won't find many like Inga. That's what you have to understand. The millions have other problems. They need the family. It's you, the intellectual women of ripe age, who dream about various kinds of free love. But *they*... my God!... There are so many other things of much greater importance!

RYZHOV. That's right, Danilyitch! That's it! Hit the bourgeois deviation!

(*Enter* INGA *and* NEMTSEVITCH.)

NEMTSEVITCH (*from the doorway*). May a non-Party person enter? (*Enters.*)

INGA (*to* RYZHOV). Again about me? Or my models?

RYZHOV (*challengingly*). Again!... And you docked me again!

INGA (*mimicking his tone*). Again! The models will be ready in a month. And by that time you will have made up another two hundred rubles!

RYZHOV. Gregory Danilyitch! Really! What do you say to that, eh?

INGA. There's no use talking about it, Ignat. I won't give in to you. In the first place, because I am right; in the second place, because you don't need to think that I am afraid of your blackmail! You couldn't discredit me! You haven't a thing on me; so, now you want to discredit my experiments. All right — go ahead! Here's your opportunity. Prove that my models are worse than those we are putting out now! If you can prove that, I'll agree with you.

RYZHOV. What is there to prove? We don't want your bourgeois beauty — even if you paid us for it! Venuses! What do you think of that? Even I could be a Venus if I had a hundred women slaves!

NEMTSEVITCH. Not less? Oho!

RYZHOV. What we want is working-class beauty — something serious. This is just a lot of dialectics — that's what it is!

NEMTSEVITCH. I understand! The face exhausted by socially indispensable labor?

RYZHOV. Yes, yes! You caught my idea at once, in spite of the fact that you're not a Marxian!

NEMTSEVITCH. With deep wrinkles...

RYZHOV (*hesitating*). Well, yes... rather...

NEMTSEVITCH. ... arms like ropes...

RYZHOV. Correct!

NEMTSEVITCH. ... breasts...

INGA. Roman Frantsevitch, that will do!

(MERA *bursts out laughing.* NEMTSEVITCH, *also laughing in* RYZHOV's *face, puts his hand on his shoulder. General laughter.* RYZHOV, *not understanding that the joke is on him, also begins to laugh.*)

MERA. Oh, you!... Dialectics!

RYZHOV (*suddenly turning serious, and then morose*). So that's how you are, Roman Frantsevitch! You're all alike. Well, well! I'll remind you of it some day! (*He goes toward the exit.*)

NEMTSEVITCH. Ignat, we're only joking! Ignat Ivanitch! (*He follows him out.*)

INGA. Danilyitch, congratulations are in order. The trust just telephoned. We're getting the machines! And now I'm going after the licenses.

SOMOV. Really? You got the permission?

INGA. How I battled for it! But still I managed to wrench it out of them!

SOMOV. You're a wonder! That's really splendid! (*Pats her shoulder.*) I take off my hat to you!

MERA. Isn't it fine? And you've been scolding her!

SOMOV. She deserves some scolding, too... But for this — only praise!... Go to it, Inga! Go to it, friend! (*Exit.*)

MERA. And how are things on the family front? A cloudless Paradise? Still swimming in delight? Aren't you going to drown?

INGA. I am very happy. I seem to have everything I desired... (*She suddenly stops.*)

MERA. But...

INGA. But?... Yes, there are some buts. That's right. Much of what I did not expect at all.

MERA. What do you mean? What in particular?

INGA. I'll tell you sometime... later.

(*She walks toward the exit.* MERA *whistles significantly.* NEMTSE-VITCH *looks through the door.*)

NEMTSEVITCH. Inga Martinovna, are you coming?

INGA. Yes.

NEMTSEVITCH. How he attacked me! All because of your models!

INGA. It's perfectly senseless — to have to prove that beauty is not counter-revolutionary! Believe me, this work requires exceedingly strong nerves.

(*Enter* DMITRI. *He is sullen and irritated.*)

NEMTSEVITCH. I have always considered you a heroine.

INGA. Of a novel?

NEMTSEVITCH. No... opera. Let us say, Brunhilde.

INGA. And yourself? Gunther?

NEMTSEVITCH. Oh, no! Rather Siegfried.

INGA. Aren't you afraid?

NEMTSEVITCH (*playfully*). How is one to know?

DMITRI. Listen, you two... enough of that twisting around! You're making a fine spectacle of yourselves as it is! You can't improve on it any more!

(*A pause.* INGA *raises her eyebrows in surprise.*)

MERA. What's the matter with you, Mitka?

INGA (*abruptly*). Let's go, Roman Frantsevitch.

DMITRI (*to* INGA). I want to see you.

INGA. Not now. I'm going to the trust.

DMITRI. Inga!

INGA. What's the matter?

DMITRI. Can't you spare a *minute* for me? You manage to find even a half-hour — for others...

INGA. Others talk to me in a different tone.

DMITRI. What tone should I use with you? After all, what do you expect of me? I am not a college man. When you lived abroad with your father, my father was exiled in Siberia. I have been homeless since I was seven years old. For five years I lived at the Thieves' Market. I had no time to learn 'different' tones!

NEMTSEVITCH. Inga Martinovna, I'll wait for you in my office. (NEMTSEVITCH *departs with studied dignity, ignoring* DMITRI.)

INGA. Mera... if you please... leave us alone for a moment.

MERA (*in a huff*). Oh, go to the Devil! The same old mess! (*She follows* NEMTSEVITCH *out.*)

INGA. What is it, Dmitri? Why such idiotic scenes? Jealousy again? You can't stand my talking to someone else?

DMITRI. You don't talk to him as you talk to everyone else!

INGA. Shame on you! I value in him an experienced worker, an educated man, that's all. How can you see anything wrong in that?

DMITRI. Of course, I'm not so educated. I didn't have such advantages...

INGA. Dimka! Why all this? Don't you know that what I love in you is exactly what is lacking in him?

DMITRI. And in him, exactly what is lacking in me!

INGA. Dmitri, this is rotten of you... vile!

DMITRI (*regarding her intently*). Do you know... Glafeera never tormented me like this!

INGA. I am not Glafeera. I have been and I am going to be — free!

DMITRI. And I... understand this once and for all... I cannot reconcile myself to the idea that you may... with someone else! I know you will call me savage, possessive, but... I cannot! I love you too much!

INGA. You think *that* is love?... It's barbarous! I want purity more than you do. I came to you myself... to be with you... but you want to bind me with a rope!

DMITRI. But if...

INGA. If what?

DMITRI. If you should want to leave me...

INGA. If I should want to leave you, I shall. And I *will* want to, Dimka, if you persist in behaving in this insane fashion! (INGA *goes out*. DMITRI *stands, thunderstruck*.)

(*Enter* SOMOV.)

SOMOV. Ah, Dmitri! Hello! Well, how are things going in the Third Department's Trade-Union Bureau? Getting down to work?

DMITRI. It's going badly, Danilyitch... Everything's wrong!

SOMOV (*apprehensively*). What's wrong?

DMITRI. Inga and I... Everything's going to pieces.

SOMOV. Tfui! Don't scare me like that! You're just like a woodpecker — hitting the same spot all the time! Can't you think of anything but your personal affairs? When are you going to sober up? (DMITRI *makes a move to leave*.) Wait a minute! Didn't I tell you it would be like this? Didn't I? You see, I know you inside out... how you lived with Glafeera, and everything... You got along all right, didn't you?

DMITRI. What's the use of bringing that up? I got along well enough.

SOMOV. You're a liar!

DMITRI. What do you mean — a liar?

SOMOV. You got along badly! You didn't get along at all!

DMITRI. What do you mean by that?

SOMOV. Just that! Did you take an interest in her? Did you really know how she lived? Did you try to help her? Did you try to raise her to your own level?

DMITRI. I feel as if everything in my head were topsy-turvy! Would you believe it, Danilyitch... never in my life, neither in the war nor on the job, was I ever up against anything like this! Never! You know yourself, I have lost myself completely in Inga.

SOMOV. Yes... yes... But what about Glafeera?

DMITRI. That's the whole trouble. Eleven years... you can't scratch that away with a finger nail! I suppose I got used to her, or something like that... And then there's Valka. That finished everything. And yet, to remain with them meant... what? To bury myself? To sink into the swamp?

SOMOV. You're trying to squirm out of it, Dmitri! I can see that you're trying to squirm out of it! You know that you're lying, that

you didn't do everything in your power to raise her to your level!
My friend, the easiest thing in the world is to place the blame for
your own faults on somebody else. (*Mockingly.*) I must grow, don't
you see, and you're standing in my way!...

DMITRI. And suppose it *was* like that?

SOMOV. But it was *not!* You're lying! You know yourself it
wasn't. My friend, don't try to cover up your weaknesses with
talk about revolutionary necessity!

DMITRI. What weaknesses?

SOMOV. Don't pull the wool over my eyes! I see right through
you! Love of honor! Ambition!... A halo!... Fiddlesticks!...
You're flattered. A famous father!... Education!... Glamour!...
Glitter!... Europe!... That's what attracted you!

DMITRI. Will you stop, Danilyitch! What has ambition to do
with it? What do you think I value in her? She is a comrade to me.
She understands every word, every thought. There are some things
which one cannot express in speech. You have to understand them.
But Glafeera? Oh! (*He shrugs his shoulders.*)

SOMOV. Glafeera! Glafeera! We're not talking about Glafeera
now. You've finished with Glafeera. But you, you yourself, what
are you headed for, eh? How are you working now? Is it a good
thing that you, chairman of the Factory Committee, are making a
spectacle of yourself with your personal affairs? Friendship is one
thing, but work, my friend, is quite another matter. And what have
you been doing? You let her have her way about the rates. You
let her have her way about the ventilators. That business has been
hanging fire for five months. But where are the ventilators? And
the entire business of labor protection? Is that the way to work?
Are you following in Ryzhov's footsteps?

DMITRI (*depressed*). Let me alone, Danilyitch. Let me alone.

SOMOV. What do you mean — let you alone? I'm talking sense
to you, and you listen!

(DMITRI *turns away abruptly and goes toward the exit as* GLA-
FEERA *and* NASTYA *enter through the same door.*)

GLAFEERA. Comrade Gurvitch!... Isn't she here?

SOMOV. Aha! There she is! Speak of the Devil! Well, how is
everything with my ward today? (*To* DMITRI.) Isn't she fine?
What do you say? In another year she'll be a delegate to the Soviet!

(DMITRI *does not answer. He looks eagerly and with pleasure at*
GLAFEERA.)

365

GLAFEERA. You like to tease, Gregory Danilyitch, my guardian! And how about your membership dues? You call yourself a Friend of the Children, and then you forget to pay your dues!

SOMOV (*jokingly*). Oh, misery! Do you expect me to keep everything in my head? How much is it? For half a year is it, or... Holy Father! (*He fumbles in his pockets.*) Is it possible that I owe for the entire year? Shame on you, Gregory Danilyitch! Shame on you, Old Guard! It's scandalous!

GLAFEERA. Hello, Mitya! Why do you run away from me? This is the first time in three months that I've seen you face to face. I only see you at the meetings. Are you afraid that I'm going to ask for alimony? I told you that even if you beg me, I won't take it. Valyushka and I live pretty well without it... Well, how are things going with you?

DMITRI. Why do you talk like that?

GLAFEERA. Oh, well, all right... Mitya, how nervous you've become!... I won't, I won't! All right! (*To* SOMOV.) I've come on Nastasya's business. Do you know what I mean, Gregory Danilyitch? Sofron is storming. Can't pacify him with anything.

SOMOV. Drinking and beating her?

NASTYA. With whatever he lays his hands on! The samovar... the chair... I'm black and blue all over! It's a wonder to me that I can still walk!

GLAFEERA. Every night! Every single night! He goes to the beer-hall after work, and when he gets home at about ten o'clock (*waves her hand*), you might as well call the fire department!

NASTYA. It's a wonder that the house doesn't fall down!

SOMOV. Why do you stand for it? (*Testily.*) Oh... you dummies! — Drag him into court, and that's all there is to it!

GLAFEERA. We'll drag him in here today. That ought to take the starch out of him!

SOMOV. Bring him before the Woman's Committee. That's the thing! Mera will put a bridle on him.

GLAFEERA. You bet that's the thing to do! Yield an inch and they'll take a mile!

SOMOV (*rubbing his hands*). Oh-ho, Mitenka! Do you hear? Do you see what kind of women delegates we are raising? (*He takes* GLAFEERA *by the shoulders and shakes her affectionately.*) Correct, Glafeera Trofimovna! Don't give 'em an inch! Fight for the rights of women! (*To* DMITRI.) My friend, do you see how the millions are rising? Without glamour, without hullabaloo! But the real strength is in them! Well, now, Nastasya Petrovna, shall we do it, eh? Let's go into the corridor and look for Mera. Hurry! Come on!

NASTYA. All right. (*Hesitates — to* GLAFEERA.) I'll wait outside.

(SOMOV *and* NASTYA *leave.*)

DMITRI. How... different you are now!...

GLAFEERA. What's different about me? I'm just as I always was — working, collecting dues... That isn't much — a trifle! But I have also become proud. Yes, proud.

DMITRI. And your eyes... they're not quite the same, it seems.

GLAFEERA. Anything else? You have quite an imagination!

DMITRI. And your mouth... somehow... it's firmer...

GLAFEERA. Oh, stop it, Mitka! What are you trying to do anyway — look me over as if I were a statue? Eyes! Mouth! Why don't you ask about Valka? You haven't seen her for three months! Aren't you interested?

DMITRI. I spend sleepless nights over Valka. Do you know that?

GLAFEERA. Well, I declare! And yet, you went away! Why did you do that?

DMITRI. If I had known that it was going to turn out like this... maybe... I wouldn't have gone.

GLAFEERA (*taking his hand*). It's hard for you, Mitenka, isn't it?

DMITRI (*after a short pause*). It was easier with you.

GLAFEERA. What are you talking about? Poor boy! I thought you were all right... happy... living a new life! But just look at you!

DMITRI. Valka is preying on my mind. It's just as if she had caught me with a fish-hook!

GLAFEERA. Shall I tell you something, Mitya? Before, I used to look up to you. You seemed so strong, so big! I was afraid of you! I mean it! What a fool I was! And now you've suddenly become small. I feel sorry for you. I could press you to my bosom like Valka and sing you to sleep!

DMITRI (*smiling*). You've grown up, all right! That's why you feel like that...

GLAFEERA. Grown up? And why don't *you* go on growing? You must grow, Mitya. Do you remember you said that I wouldn't catch up with you, that you'd have to drag me after you like a dead weight?... No, Mitenka, I *will* catch up with you! And if you don't look out, I'll leave you behind! I've come to understand about life, Mitya. And not only to understand... but also to feel how it is bursting everywhere, what it smells like... well... I haven't learned to talk yet. (*Laughs curtly.*) I can't tell you about it in words that hang together. But give me time, Mityushka. We'll not only catch up with your Ingas, but we'll outdistance them! Little by little, with little stitches, we'll sew everything up tight! You know, we have more backbone than they, and more strength. And you know our blood is a bit warmer... (*She wants to embrace him, but he shrinks from her laughingly.*) I am bold now! I'll tell the truth to anyone... whatever I think!

DMITRI. By God!... I look at you, Glasha — is it you, or isn't it?

GLAFEERA. It's I, all right, Mitenka, I myself!

DMITRI. But no! It can't be! It's just as if it were not you at all!

GLAFEERA. No, it's I. Or perhaps you're right... I'm not quite the same.

DMITRI. Glashenka! (*He moves toward her, stretching out his hands.*)

(INGA *appears in the doorway, where she stops short. There is a silent scene.*)

INGA. Isn't Mera here? (*She enters slowly, measuring* GLAFEERA *with a glance.* GLAFEERA *shrinks a bit, but is ready to stand her ground; she also measures* INGA.) How do you do?

GLAFEERA. How do you do, Comrade Rizzer? (*She offers her hand to* INGA. INGA *hesitates, then shakes hands with her.*)

INGA. You know, we have abolished hand-shaking.

GLAFEERA. I beg your pardon... There is no notice about it here.

INGA. Why aren't you working?

DMITRI. This is lunch time.

INGA (*slightly embarrassed*). I seem to be in the way...

DMITRI (*abruptly*). Why does it seem so to you?

INGA. You were talking with such animation...

DMITRI. Well, what of it? Let's all talk together... the three of us. Enough of this running away from each other... this jealousy!

INGA. Jealousy?

DMITRI. What a tone!

INGA. Now it's *my* tone! Don't be ridiculous, Dmitri. This is no topic for conversation before strangers.

GLAFEERA. Please don't mind me. I'll go away. (*Starts to go.*)

DMITRI. Wait, Glasha...

(DMITRI *restrains her with his hand on her arm.* GLAFEERA *turns and suddenly blurts out.*)

GLAFEERA. Which of us *is* more of a stranger to him? I don't know if anyone can give Mitya as much as I gave him! (*She blushes.*)

INGA. Everyone gives what he can.

DMITRI. What a knot! Three lives bound together!... Inga... Why haven't we the courage to do things in a new way? Tell me... why should we pay for our happiness with her misfortune?

GLAFEERA. Mitenka, don't go into that! Do you hear?

DMITRI. Inga, you're a new woman! You are essentially one of us. Why should we break up three lives? What for? Who gets the benefit from it? You? She? What is it all for?

INGA. Dmitri, what do you want? To live all together... the three of us? *You* cannot bear to share me with anyone, but it's all right for us women to share you! Man's eternal logic!

GLAFEERA. And I, too, Mitya — to be the chief cook for the comrade manager? No, thank you!

INGA. You must stop dreaming! It's unthinkable to go on like this!

GLAFEERA. It's better to settle it once and for all, Mityusha. One way or the other! You're tormenting yourself, too.

INGA (*petulantly, to* DMITRI). Go away from me! Go away! Do you hear? I don't want any more of this!

DMITRI (*almost with hatred*). I won't go away! You know I won't! You have bewitched me! (*He runs out.*)

GLAFEERA (*pale, in a low voice*). How he's torturing himself!

INGA. I didn't know he was so weak.

GLAFEERA. He wasn't weak when he was with me! He was a fighter then...

INGA. He misses his little girl very much.

GLAFEERA. The girl is not his — she's mine! He left us, so why should he miss her? And it doesn't take so dreadfully long to get another one.

INGA (*looks at her long*). I cannot have any children.

GLAFEERA. You can't! (GLAFEERA'S *satisfaction changes suddenly to sympathy, almost commiseration. For a moment it appears that a new warm feeling springs up between the two women, but this fades at once. Both shut themselves up again.*) Well, everyone has his own troubles... and everyone his own joy.

(*The* FIRST YOUNG COMMUNIST *runs in.*)

FIRST YOUNG COMMUNIST. Glasha, are you here? (*With some embarrassment.*) Comrade Rizzer, won't you come too?

INGA. What's going on?

FIRST YOUNG COMMUNIST. We're going to take the starch out of Boltikov!

GLAFEERA. Good-bye, Comrade Manager. (*She goes out, firm and proud.*)

FIRST YOUNG COMMUNIST. Will you come?

INGA. Yes, for a minute. (*The* FIRST YOUNG COMMUNIST *runs out.* INGA *looking into space long and contemplatively.*) No... it's impossible this way... It interferes with work...

CURTAIN

ACT III

SCENE 11

Cultural 'red corner' of the factory sewing department. Two black-boards, one framed in red, the other in black. Posters, slogans of the Five-Year Plan, a chart of indicators of Socialist competition, loud-speakers, bookshelves, a magazine-rack, tables and chairs.

MERA *is seated at a small table. The crowd of women workers has surrounded* BOLTIKOV *and* NASTYA, *who are being questioned by* MERA *in the capacity of presiding judge.*

BOLTIKOV. What do you want with me? I told you I won't go. I have nothing to do there.

MERA. You don't have to do anything. We'll just talk.

BOLTIKOV. I haven't any use for you and your talk! I have business to attend to. Please don't delay me. The lunch period is only a half-hour — not the whole day.

(*Enter* GLAFEERA, *followed a little later by* INGA. GLAFEERA *comes up to* NASTYA *and puts her hand on* NASTYA'S *shoulder.* NASTYA *nestles closer to her; she is frightened.*)

GLAFEERA. Your business! Is it in the beer-hall?

INGA. What's it all about, Mera?

MERA. Trial and justice — in the rough.

BOLTIKOV. What do you mean — trial? Who are *you* to try *me?* You pass judgment on me and I... Who ever heard of such a thing? I can't beat my wife, eh? What do you think — am I master in my own house, or am I not? I have always beaten her, and now all of a sudden you say I can't!... Oh, I could tell you a thing or two! And to the point!

MERA. All right, all right... We'll question you to the point ourselves. Don't bristle!

BOLTIKOV. And suppose I won't even talk to you? What judges! Petticoats!

INGA. Mera, I'm going to the trust and I may be detained. Please put my report about the women's activities second on the list. Don't forget.

MERA (*intently regards her and* GLAFEERA, *then nods*). All right...

(*Angrily.*) They have nothing better to do, so they just torment each other!

VOICES FROM THE CROWD. She's busy!... Stealing other women's husbands!... She remembers her models all right!... It'd be a good thing if she remembered her conscience that way!

(INGA *flares up, stops, looks for the ones that spoke. A strained silence.*)

MERA. Well, go, go!

(INGA *goes out, followed by hostile looks from the crowd. When she disappears behind the door, the atmosphere becomes more informal.*)

VOICES FROM THE CROWD. They're good talkers, all right!... Activists — that's what they are!

MERA. All right. We have work to do. (*She sits down on the edge of the table.*) Let's begin at the beginning... He drinks... Everybody knows that.

VOICE FROM THE CROWD. Well, what of it? He's a man, isn't he?

NASTYA (*prodded by* GLAFEERA). He drinks without stopping, comrades women! Without stopping! Others come home from work, but my *Makhaon* goes straight to the beer-hall. After swilling like a hog, he feels that the ocean itself is knee-deep to him! Judge him, darlings! And... that's all!

GLAFEERA. He raises thunder up and down the stairway. He pays no attention to anything or to anybody. Some are sick... some are sleeping... some have small children — it's all the same to him! Yelling and shouting... What do you yell about, eh?

BOLTIKOV (*awed by the seriousness of the occasion*). I don't yell... I sing.

NASTYA. What songs! Just plain curses! (*Suddenly becoming frightened of her own voice, she hides behind* GLAFEERA.)

BOLTIKOV. Oh, you...

OLD WOMAN WORKER. Well, what of it? He may drink, and he may beat her, but he hasn't left his wife!

BOLTIKOV. That's a fact, citizens! I may drink, and I may fight...

NASTYA (*weeping*). You're nothing but a hooligan!

BOLTIKOV. That's right. But I don't do *that* kind of monkey business. What are you keeping me here for?

MERA. Here, here! You're not at home!

GLAFEERA. Where do you think you are — in a beer-hall?

BOLTIKOV. Why are you reproaching me with a beer-hall? I've been drinking ever since I was seven. Is anything else possible in our kind of work? If you don't drink, what are you going to do? Am I drinking at your expense? I spend my own money! What are you barking for? Comrades! If you only knew my life! I fought in three wars, carried all kinds of rifles — Russian, German, and Japanese! A machine-gun drilled right through me! I was probably the best fighter against Tsarism and the bourgeoisie! And now all kinds of insignificant creatures... worthless women... have come into administrative posts, pretending to be various kinds of shock-brigaders! But Sofron is still bending his back over the irons and measures, bathed in his sweat the year around! And all for others! While I'm without shoes and in rags... (*His voice breaks.* NASTYA *looks at him pityingly and begins to cry.*) And on top of it, all the riff-raff throws it up to you! Drunkard! You beat your wife! Oh, you... Is this what I fought for — for women to hold the upper hand? Did I suffer for that? Can a man help getting sore about it? (*He looks around, seeking sympathy.*) Tfui! Not a human being among you. Only women!

MERA. All this is quite beside the point. Why do you torment your wife?

BOLTIKOV. Torment her! Who told you that?... She?

GLAFEERA. Well, isn't it so?

BOLTIKOV. Torment her?... I?... Never in my life!

GLAFEERA. What do you mean — never?

BOLTIKOV. Beat her — yes! I do! How can you help beating such a louse! But torment! What do you think I am — a savage — or a fool?

NASTYA. This... Yes, comrades, that's right.

(GLAFEERA *nudges* NASTYA *with her elbow to keep quiet.*)

BOLTIKOV. Oh, you shameless one! Do I torment you? Do I?

NASTYA. No, Sofron Nikititch... You beat me, that's all.

MERA. But what's the difference? We'll write it down like that. (*She writes in her notebook.*)

BOLTIKOV. What are you writing?

MERA. Never mind. We'll show you. Then you'll know that your wife is just as much of a human being as you are.

BOLTIKOV (*suddenly angry*). I'll take this human being and drag her home by her hair, and show her with a belt... so she won't stick her nose where she's not supposed to! She'll learn to denounce her husband... to hobnob with the women's departments! (*To* NASTYA.) Go home! Quick!

NASTYA. Sofron Nikititch...

BOLTIKOV. Go, I say! For sixteen years you were as silent as a table. Then all of a sudden you begin to baa like a sheep! I'll twist your head for such talk!

MERA. Quiet! Shut up! Stop it!

GLAFEERA. Women!... Well, look! There he stands!

BOLTIKOV. Nastasya Petrovna! Will you go, or must I ask you again?

GLAFEERA. Don't go, Nastya. I won't ever speak to you if you give in!

BOLTIKOV. So that's how it is!

NASTYA. Nikititch...

GLAFEERA. Nastasya, don't be a fool!

NASTYA (*pleading with the assembled women*). Darlings... four children...

BOLTIKOV. So, then, it's to be the court! You'll lodge a complaint!

GLAFEERA. I will! (*Slightly embarrassed.*) *She* will!

BOLTIKOV. Don't butt in! It's none of your business!

MERA. She'll speak for herself.

GLAFEERA. Well, Nastya?

BOLTIKOV. What? Have you bitten your tongue off?

NASTYA. Holy Father! Sofron Nikititch! I won't do anything about it! Forgive me!... These women turned my head!

GLAFEERA. Nastasya! What are you talking about?

MERA. What a chance one has to work with you! You're not women... you're the Devil knows what! Just like flies on fly-paper!

NASTYA. Glafeerushka, don't be angry with me! I encouraged you for nothing. I thought something would come of it... You can see for yourselves... I can't cope with him — the shark! He bends me like a straw! He's squeezed everything out of me as it is. It's worse than a sentence of hard labor to live with him! But where shall I go, alone, with the kids? You young ones are free. If you're not here, you're there. But I... it seems I'll die like this under the flatiron! (*She weeps.*)

MERA. Oh, you're silly! We'll show him...

GLAFEERA (*interrupting*). We... (*Suddenly embarrassed.*) We'll singe the wings off all of them! We'll put our whole heart into it!

BOLTIKOV. Enough of that!... Singe!... You were licked, weren't you?

MERA. So you're getting arrogant again? Do you realize where you live?

BOLTIKOV. What do you mean — where? Everybody knows that. In Apartment 5!

MERA. In what country? Eh? Whom are you trying to impress? You're entirely too impudent.

FIRST YOUNG COMMUNIST. I say he's a sabotager!

VOICES. Down with him!... Out with him! Out!... He spoils everything!... He hurts Socialist competition!... The Devil's mushroom! Toadstool!

SECOND YOUNG COMMUNIST. Blacklist him!

VOICES. Blacklist! Blacklist!

FIRST YOUNG COMMUNIST. Done! (*She writes the name of* BOLTIKOV *on the black-framed blackboard.*)

MERA. I'll teach him a lesson in court, you may be sure of that! The meeting is adjourned.

    (*She collects her papers and goes out. The women workers surround* BOLTIKOV *and crowd him into the corner.*)

GLAFEERA (*to* BOLTIKOV). Why are you laughing at us women? ... What is it about? What are you grinning at? You've guzzled up a human life, and now you're boasting about it! Evidently you have nothing else to boast about! Licked! We're not licked yet! We're worse than old socks to you! At least you take care of an old sock. But a woman may poison herself or tear herself in two — that's none of your business! Listen, women! I am speaking to you in particular: The road is clear before us. Am I talking sense, women? We'll fight against everything that stands in the way of a better life. Against pots — and washtubs, and against men such as this idiot! We'll sweep you all out! Everything that is written in the books, everything that the law speaks about — we'll fight for it! We've become hard enough for that. You won't drive us back into our corners! (*The bell rings. Everybody rises. The women yell and hiss at* BOLTIKOV, *who runs out, followed by them. The women workers take their places.*) Men like you are living your last days! Each day, each stitch on the machine, is death to you. You're doomed! And by the time the Five-Year Plan is finished, it will be all finished with you!

    (*Noise, songs, applause, shouts. The department gets back to work.*)

CURTAIN

ACT IV

SCENE 12

Office of the factory's assistant manager, Comrade RYZHOV. *It is very simple and business-like; a file, desk, chairs, charts, portraits. Near a small table, with its back to the audience and to the door on the left, sits the figure of a woman-mannikin draped in a new model dress. There is no one in the room.*

VERONICA *sticks her head through the door.*

VERONICA. May I come in? (*She enters.*) Nobody here! (*Sees the figure.*) Pardon me, will you tell me where I can find Comrade Ryzhov? (*A pause.*) I beg your pardon. (*After a pause she carefully approaches the mannikin.*) Miss, you... (*She touches its shoulder.*) Oh!... (*She looks into the face and jumps back.*) My God, how that frightened me! (*She puts her finger to her lips coyly and listens. Then she quickly sits in the chair at the other end of the table and assumes a rigid pose. Heavy steps are heard.* RYZHOV *enters, gloomy and rumpled. Seeing two elegant women's figures, he stops for a moment. Evidently interested, he approaches them and looks into the face of the mannikin. Petrified with astonishment, he angrily twists the head of the mannikin around, and without any warning, takes a step toward* VERONICA *and tries to twist her head similarly.*) Oh, what impudence!

RYZHOV. Oh, pardon me... It's you!

VERONICA. Ignat Ivanitch, what's the matter with you? (*She sees the reversed head of the mannikin.*) My God, what have you done to her?

RYZHOV. Who brought this stuff in here? Who? That's Inga's tricks, the Devil take her! (*He rings the bell viciously.*) I took you for a doll, too.

VERONICA. Thank you!... You're simply remarkable!... So this is the famous model! (*She examines and feels the dress on the mannikin.*) I just came to ask you if I might be present at the examination of the model... You know, to my mind, this lacks the real old culture. And where could that come from? Who wants a real dress now? Where would one wear it? Who is going to appreciate it? (*Dreamily.*) France! God!... There were salons there, carnivals, fireworks, cafés de fois... that's what I call real revolution! But what do we have? Everything is so grey, so threadbare! No burning moments, no burning men!

RYZHOV. Excuse me... You know, I... I didn't sleep all night... I was working. (*He sits down at his desk and rummages in his papers.*)

VERONICA. Don't worry. I'm going. (*She examines the model again.*) You know, after all, this line is very pretty. But here I would have done something a little different. (*Indicating.*) I would have led it up to here... and here...

RYZHOV (*raising his head*). What's that?

VERONICA. Look... this way... and...

RYZHOV. Oh, no! They would have done it entirely different abroad.

VERONICA. How? (*She comes coquettishly closer to him.*)

RYZHOV. For example... Well, from here, and... (*He indicates on* VERONICA'S *dress.*)

VERONICA. Oh, oh, oh! Ignat Ivanitch! I'm terribly ticklish! Stop! You're not at home!

RYZHOV. Oh, I'm not doing anything. I just wanted to show you.

VERONICA. You're terrible! You know, I'm peculiarly excited over the fact that you're proletarian. Well, you may show me... From where?... Only, don't tickle me!

(NEMTSEVITCH *enters and observes what is going on.* RYZHOV *indicates suggestively.*)

RYZHOV. From... here...

VERONICA. Yes? And?

RYZHOV. And...

VERONICA. And?... Well, go on, go on...

RYZHOV. And...

NEMTSEVITCH. And to where? (*Silence.*)

VERONICA. Oh, here I am, Romotchka! (*With a silly grin, she comes up to* NEMTSEVITCH; *he pays no attention to her.*)

NEMTSEVITCH. Well, I must say, Ignat Ivanovitch...

RYZHOV. Roman Frantsevitch...

NEMTSEVITCH. I'm astonished!... Upon my word of honor! Of course, Veronica Vasilyevna is not so young...

VERONICA. What impudence! Rom...

NEMTSEVITCH (*still talking to* RYZHOV). Where are your ideals of proletarian beauty? Any way you take it, neither her feet nor her hands smell of any labor except the labor of a manicurist...

RYZHOV. Roman Frantsevitch...

NEMTSEVITCH. But there are not so many wrinkles, comparatively speaking...

VERONICA (*stamps her foot*). You cynic! You downright scoundrel! You reptile! I hate you! Do you hear? I shall be unfaithful to you! I will!

NEMTSEVITCH. It has been at least ten years since I stopped worrying about your infidelities.

RYZHOV. Roman Frantsevitch, as God is my witness, you misunderstood!

VERONICA. What right have you to treat your legal wife in this way? Any passing stranger may insult me, make indecent proposals, rape me...

RYZHOV. Veronica Vasilyevna, that is going too far!

NEMTSEVITCH. Veronica, go away. I have a lot to do.

VERONICA. No, don't you dare brush me aside! Don't you dare treat me like this! Why don't you give me some social work to do? Why? Am I more stupid than your Inga? Ha-ha! I'm as good a member of society as she is! A woman of the same sex! I'm going to buy myself a political primer! I'll learn it by heart! I'll memorize all your hocus-pocus, and I'll be just like Inga! I will! I will! I will! Then you'll be running after me, you wretch!

NEMTSEVITCH. Listen, my angel. I beg of you... go home!

VERONICA. There! Always the same! The same always! Don't you boss me! I know when to go myself! (*She walks toward the exit; from the threshold she shouts.*) Imbecile! (*To* RYZHOV.) And you are dull... inane... And, anyway, I despise you! (*She goes out.*)

NEMTSEVITCH. Ignat Ivanovitch, I want to have a serious talk with you.

RYZHOV. Roman Frantsevitch, I... I... Do you understand? I give you my word!

NEMTSEVITCH. I must know, clearly and definitely... Have you any matches?

RYZHOV. Please... here you are! Won't you have a cigar? (*He gets out a box of German cigars.*) Best quality... 'Alhambra'! Try one!

NEMTSEVITCH (*lighting a cigar*). I'm tired of this.

RYZHOV. I give you my word of honor...

NEMTSEVITCH. We must decide finally... When are we going to put in the conveyor?

RYZHOV. Conveyor! And I thought you were talking about your wife!

NEMTSEVITCH (*putting down the cigar*). What trash you brought back with you! You don't know how to buy anything!... About my wife... Well, you know, we've got so on each other's nerves that ... And, anyway, it's her own affair... Listen, this is what I want to talk to you about... you see, Inga is making me work out the project all over again! Everything's in a mess! Such things as nurseries, restaurants, check-rooms... the Devil knows what else! I can't make head or tail of it! If you want me to build Socialism, then don't hold me back, the Devil take you all! Give me a chance to open up in a real Socialist way!

RYZHOV. Roman Frantsevitch, you don't need to propagandize me. I understand you. You might say that I myself am an engineer at heart. Oh, if I only had your learning! I'd create... oh, the Devil knows what!

NEMTSEVITCH. Let's trade. Give me your proletarian origin and Party card, and you can take my training! And Veronica along with it, if you like.

RYZHOV. And Veronica! Well, you know, that's plain sabotage!

CURTAIN

ACT IV

SCENE 13

Factory manager's office, as in Scene 4. INGA is sitting at her desk, on a corner of which MERA is perched. NEMTSEVITCH, very formal, stands near-by.

INGA. Roman Frantsevitch, how are the corrections to the project getting along? I asked you to give them to me today.

NEMTSEVITCH. You see...

INGA. What! You haven't made them yet? You know, I asked you!

NEMTSEVITCH. Inga Martinovna, I ask *you* to understand the substance of my arguments.

INGA. I've been all over that. Your arguments don't convince me.

NEMTSEVITCH. But, pardon me, there is actually no room for the nurseries. And besides that, you want something — I don't know what — some dove cotes!

INGA. Don't be absurd! Nothing was said about dove cotes! But there must be and *will* be nurseries!

NEMTSEVITCH. But you must admit that you can't disrupt the entire plan of the conveyor in order to please Comrade Gurvitch!

INGA. You can!

MERA. Right!

NEMTSEVITCH. Inga Martinovna... You belong to the class of paradoxical women. If you will excuse me, paradoxes are very well after working hours, but during work...

INGA. Comrade Nemtsevitch, please don't trouble yourself to teach me how and when I should behave! I know it without your assistance.

NEMTSEVITCH. But do you realize that there will be no place for the machines? After all, this is a factory and not an establishment for the protection of mothers and babies!

MERA. This is a Soviet factory where the workers are the masters. That's difficult to understand, isn't it?

INGA. *I* will find a place for the machines! And that's that!

NEMTSEVITCH. Then, pardon me... Perhaps my presence here is superfluous.

INGA. Comrade Nemtsevitch, don't make an ass of yourself! Just because you don't want to work over a new variation of the project, I can't deprive the women workers of what is absolutely necessary for them. I have already made an appropriation for the nurseries.

NEMTSEVITCH. I understand nothing! I confess my petty bourgeois limitations. Until you show me yourself where the conveyor can be put, I will not start planning.

INGA. I've shown you a dozen times. Enough talk! Let's get to work!

MERA. You won't get away with it, Comrade Nemtsevitch! You're playing a losing game. If necessary, I'll bite your head off to get those nurseries!

NEMTSEVITCH. My God! But, after all, you have no children of your own!

MERA. Not yet. (*She starts to leave and bumps into* RYZHOV *in the doorway. The telephone rings.*)

INGA (*at the telephone*). Yes... Hello, Dubov... Quarterly accounts?... Ready... For the third shift we need at least a thousand workers... Where will we find them? True, there are no unemployed ... We'll have to use some of the office workers. Well, typists... We'll find them. What can we do?... Of course... By the first of May we must start the seven-hour day, at no matter what cost... I'll be at the Regional Committee... All right. (*During the telephone conversation a messenger enters with a dossier. All this time* NEMTSEVITCH *is winking significantly at* RYZHOV, *who nods in reply.* INGA *puts down the receiver, takes the dossier from the messenger, and signs the papers.*) Please send someone here from the Third Department. (*The messenger nods and goes out.*) Roman Frantsevitch, you see how they drive me? I'm asking you for the last time to give me all your estimates within two days. I will not tolerate any more delays.

NEMTSEVITCH. Ignat Ivanovitch also has some objections.

RYZHOV. I think it's fantastic!

INGA. What do you mean — fantastic?

RYZHOV. Certainly! We'll spend a lot of money on nurseries, ventilation, and then we'll have to cut down on the principal construction.

INGA. The principal construction has to be linked up with the interests of the workers.

RYZHOV. Oh, that's how it is! Of course, I understand...

INGA. What do you understand?

RYZHOV. Just that! What all tongues are wagging about.

INGA. Ignat, I ask you to speak without insinuations. I am sick of this!

RYZHOV. It's perfectly clear... If I had been the chairman of the Factory Committee, and Gretchaninov were in my place, everything would have been exactly the opposite!

(*He lights a cigarette and angrily snaps the imported cigarette-case shut.* DMITRI *enters, stops, and listens.* NEMTSEVITCH *tries to rush away.*)

NEMTSEVITCH. Well, you decide... I'll look in later. (NEMTSEVITCH *goes out quickly, looking at* INGA *over his shoulder.*)

DMITRI. What are you talking about? The same thing again?

RYZHOV (*to* DMITRI). Well, well! (*To* INGA.) I bent my back for the bosses! You might think it's something unusual — to have no air and no nurseries! But we used to work without light!

INGA. I'll throw you out of here if you dare once again...

RYZHOV. Oh-ho-ho! See that you don't get thrown out yourself!

INGA. You're a petty bourgeois! It's disgusting to be in the same room with you! You've degenerated altogether!

RYZHOV. Degenerated! We'll see what the Control Commission will have to say about you! So I have degenerated, have I?

(SOMOV *enters.*)

SOMOV. Ignat, what did that painted fool talk about in the office?

RYZHOV. Which one?

SOMOV. Veronica. She's yelling at the top of her lungs that you raped her in your office... or something to that effect.▪

RYZHOV. I?... Her?... I?... Well! Oh, Gregory Danilyitch, I can't find words for such... what shall I say?... Well, cross my heart... before God! (*He crosses himself vehemently.* SOMOV *regards him quizzically, and he, embarrassed, stops.*)

▪ SOMOV. I'll get to the bottom of this, Ignat! You bet I will! I've been watching you for a long time; you'll end badly.

RYZHOV (*pointing to* DMITRI *and* INGA). Look at them! It's obvious. No good will come of it! (*He goes out.*)

SOMOV. What's the matter?

INGA. I'm putting the question point-blank: it's either he or I! I am sick and tired of these squabbles!

SOMOV. The same old thing... I understand... Well, while we're on the subject, Inga, I'll say this: neither he nor you should be here any more — and that's that!

DMITRI. How can you compare them? Any way you take him, he's a reptile, while this is a personal matter.

SOMOV. There are no personal matters! Everything has social significance to us. We are constantly watched by the masses. We set the example for them. Thousands of eyes are watching us. What do you mean by personal?

INGA. There is nothing personal. You're right.

SOMOV. I'm glad to hear it. You are not Ryzhov. You know what you are saying. (*He goes out.*)

DMITRI. Do you agree with him?

INGA. And you? Don't you?

DMITRI. Let's drop the subject. It will lead us too far.

INGA. Let's leave it until evening. Do you see how personal affairs interfere with matters of social significance?

DMITRI. Let's stop it, and forget that we are man and wife.

INGA. What do you want to see me about?

DMITRI. When are we going to repair the ventilators?

INGA. I told you that I'm going to look over the estimates.

DMITRI. And in the pants department, the temperature is twenty-five degrees Centigrade. The workers are sweating. It means the grippe... loss of time! Do you know how many infirmary orders we write every day? I don't intend waiting any longer! The boys are already getting after me. And they're right! It's high time to transfer this whole mess to the labor session. *You're* tired of being frowned on. Don't you think that *I* am tired of having our love affair thrown up to me constantly?

INGA. You're talking about personal affairs again!

DMITRI. The Devil alone can tell what's personal and what isn't!

INGA. We shall repair the ventilation within the next three months. That is my final decision.

DMITRI. Impossible!

INGA. For personal reasons?

DMITRI. No, it's *you* who have personal reasons!

INGA. That's not true!

DMITRI. I declare objectively, without any personal reasons, that I cannot give in. What is all this fuss about? What have personal reasons to do with it? We are Communists!

INGA. Certainly. And also objectively and without any personal reasons, I say that the question is settled. You may lodge a complaint with the Bureau.

DMITRI. Inga! You're mocking me!

INGA. No. But I am tired of all this eternal ambiguity. We are discrediting each other and all the things which are bigger than both of us. I am putting the question finally as an ultimatum: either you stop interfering with my work, drop your whims and moods, or...

DMITRI. Or what?

INGA. Or it's the end of everything. I will not permit anyone to bind my will! I will upset everything if you continue doing that... You won't break me with any ultimatums!

DMITRI. Inga! (*He attempts to take her hand.*)

INGA. Dmitri, this is no time for sentiment. I'm speaking seriously. There is a limit to all whims.

DMITRI. I cannot give in to you!

INGA. What do you expect me to do — sacrifice my duty as I understand it, my work? What are you talking about?

DMITRI. What does this mean, then? The end?

INGA. If you put it that way, I can do only one thing: go. I cannot choose between my work and you.

DMITRI. Is this your final answer?

INGA. I shall do as I have said.

(DMITRI *covers his face with his hands. She comes to him, touches his hair. He, too weak to speak, brushes her hand aside.*)

DMITRI. So this is how you love me!

INGA. I doubt if you know how much I love you, and what I am losing in leaving you.

DMITRI. Leaving...

INGA. Yes. One must be able to recognize one's mistakes. I was mistaken when I took you away from Glafeera. I had no right, no moral right to do that. I should not have lost control of my heart and let it rule my reason.

DMITRI. Inga, this damned knot! Why is it so? Why are you... such... No! What am I saying? I fell in love with you because you are you.

INGA. Dimka... let it end like this... It's better this way than to reach the stage of rancor, of bitterness. You need a friend, a wife. And I... no matter how dear you are to me... I can only be a comrade. I am a person... not a wife... not a second fiddle... not a 'friend.' I struggled just as you did. I have killed. I am a fighter, just as you are... It is difficult for me when you approach me otherwise. Try to understand. (*He squeezes her hand.*) Get up. If anybody should come in, you'd feel embarrassed. (*He does not let go of her hands. She suddenly leans over him.*) You cannot change this ... Pull yourself together... (*There is a knock on the door.*) Who's there? (*Enter* GLAFEERA.) What do you want?

GLAFEERA (*looking at them distractedly*). You sent for... I'm from the Third Department...

INGA. Oh, yes... Take this down there. (INGA *goes to her desk, gives* GLAFEERA *some papers.*)

GLAFEERA. Very well, Comrade Rizzer. (*She takes the papers, but does not move.* INGA *takes other papers from the table and goes out. A pause.*) What's the matter with you, Mitenka?

DMITRI. It's as if something has been torn loose inside of me... We're not together any more.

GLAFEERA (*catching her breath excitedly*). Not together?

DMITRI. It's too stifling with her. She oppresses me.

GLAFEERA. Still, you love her...

DMITRI. And with all that, I can't stand it. You couldn't find a mate for her... a woman like that... Oh, I wish I could pull it out by the roots, and that everything would be as it used to be!

GLAFEERA. As it used to be, Mitya, it will never be again.

DMITRI. Now *you're* lecturing me, too!

GLAFEERA. Well, what do you think I am? A complete fool? No, Comrade Mityusha. I used to be a zero without a digit. But now... now it's a different story. A river doesn't flow backwards, and I won't ever be the same as I used to be. Shall I tell you the truth? I used to hope and hope that you would come back to me. I thought only of that. (*She drops her eyes.*) All those nights, Mitya, I was with you... Perhaps I went on living just for that, and took up all this hard work for the same reason. And now that time has gone — and I don't know whether I am glad! It's like this: if you are with me, it's all right; if you are not — well, what of it? I have my own road to travel. And I shall not permit anyone... not even you... to stand in my way!

DMITRI. Perhaps... you have found someone else...

GLAFEERA. And suppose I have? What of it? Look at you! You want to have everything in the same old way. No, Mitya! Some women may welcome such opportunities, but I... perhaps I am stupid, not sufficiently grown up to your standard... but to mix up with men in that way — I cannot! I have no heart for it.

(*Enter* INGA, *inwardly agitated but outwardly calm.* MERA *is with her.*)

INGA. You are still here? I told you...

GLAFEERA. Comrade Rizzer... Excuse me... I have only a word to say to you... If you happen to think that I had anything to do with Mitenka's...

INGA. Enough! This is no place for such talk!

GLAFEERA. Excuse me. (*She goes toward the door.*)

INGA. I have much to tell you, Comrade Gretchaninov. (*She suddenly goes quickly to* GLAFEERA.) Just two words now... Do not consider me your enemy. It is exceedingly painful to me... that I have brought unhappiness to you.

GLAFEERA. Comrade Rizzer, I don't regret my tears. I saw life through them. Of course, it was painful. There is no doubt about that... You see my grey temples? (*She shows them.*) But now... if you could look into my heart, you'd find no feeling against you there.

(*She comes up to* INGA, *extending her hand. There is a moment of hesitation. Looking into her eyes,* INGA *suddenly grasps her hand. Impulsively they embrace and kiss.*)

MERA. You're both fools, that's all! Think of it! One might think you were solving the world's problems! You could have all lived together...

INGA. Mera, can't you be tactful at this moment?

GLAFEERA. You may live like that if you want to, but *we* will blaze our own trail! (*She goes out.*)

MERA. You bet I'm going to live my own way! I'm not going to ask you!

INGA. Mera!

MERA. Oh, go to hell!

DMITRI. Everything is going wrong! What's it all about?

INGA. You've not learned anything.

DMITRI. I *have* learned. Do you understand, Mera? I've been everywhere, I fought the foreign interventionists... Makhno... the Poles... I went through the workers' faculties... did some... colossal work. Everything went all right. But here, they've finished me ... completely... The Devil take all you women! (*He goes out.*)

(*There is a long pause.* INGA *stands, silently looking before her.*)

INGA. One more scar!

MERA. Serves you right. Don't build castles in the air!

INGA. Mera, can't you understand?... I'm not only a fighter... I want to take *everything* from life!

MERA (*whistling*). Utopia!

INGA. It hurts... But after all, Mera, the old man was right. If you only knew how easy everything has become, how good I feel because again I belong only to myself! Utterly free — for the Party, for the good fight! (*She seizes the telephone.*) Give me Somov... Old man, is that you? Congratulate me! Your instructions have been carried out... Do you understand? You are wise... Everything which stands in the way of reconstruction... everything external, internal, personal, general, has to be swept away... Sentiments are mobilized, too! Oh, you know that this is not easy! But however it may be, the personal life of Inga Rizzer will give you no more trouble!

CURTAIN

FEAR

A Play in Four Acts and Nine Scenes

By ALEXANDER AFINOGENYEV

Translated from the Russian
By CHARLES MALAMUTH

INTRODUCTION

THE relation between the intellectuals and the proletarian régime in the Soviet Union provides the theme for Alexander Afinogenyev's most successful play, *Fear*. Dealing specifically with intellectuals in abstract scientific pursuits, it applies with no less force to the 'intelligentsia' as a whole.

Science, according to Afinogenyev and Communists generally, cannot remain apolitical. It is an instrument of the class struggle, of the Revolution, and must be approached in that spirit. The process whereby an honest but old-fashioned and individualistic scientist, Professor Borodin, learns this Communist lesson makes the subject-matter of the play. Desiring to establish eternal, classless, apolitical laws of science, the professor finds himself a tool in the hands of anti-Soviet elements; only after he is convinced of his error by his own suffering is he reconciled to the new surroundings.

The theme is one which has stimulated a great many Soviet novelists and playwrights, if only because many of them, being intellectuals themselves, must solve the problem in their own lives. Afinogenyev has handled the touchy subject with more daring than most, exposing not only the mistakes but the genuine grievances of the old educated classes called on to serve new masters.

The play was written in 1931, and the date is significant. The first Five-Year Plan was by that time well under way. There had been time for the education of a new generation of all-Soviet scientific and technical leaders, so that the revolutionary régime was no longer as completely dependent on the old 'intelligentsia' as in the early years. The hope of a capitalist restoration which animated some old intellectuals in the initial years, the hope of a capitalist-socialist compromise which consoled them during the period of the New Economic Policy, were now dead. They must accept the new order, or perish. These changes enabled Afinogenyev to pose and resolve his problems more sharply and effectively than he could have done earlier.

Because it is encouraged by the powers-that-be as politically wholesome dramatic fare, and because of its intrinsic power, *Fear* is one of the most popular and widely produced plays in the Soviet

Union. The author states that it has already been staged in three hundred and ninety Soviet theatres, professional and amateur, and is on the regular repertory of the Moscow Art Theatre, the Leningrad Academic Theatre of Drama (where it had its première in 1931), and the theatres of Kharkov, Tiflis, Ulianovsk, and perhaps a score of other cities.

Afinogenyev, born in 1904, was only thirteen when the Revolution came. His mother was a village school-teacher, his father a writer. He began writing at the age of fifteen and before he was twenty had published three books of poetry and verse. But, as he records himself, 'being disillusioned in his poetic talents, he went over to prose.' From the first he was drawn into active work in revolutionary political and literary undertakings. In 1920, he indicates, he held sixteen different jobs simultaneously: military censor, editor of a newspaper, etc.

While attending the Institute of Journalism in Moscow in 1923, Afinogenyev wrote his first play, *Robert Tim*, and had it accepted by 'Proletkult,' a proletarian dramatic group. The same group accepted other of his plays and soon other theatres began to produce his works. He wrote about ten plays in the next few years and a few of them can still be met with in the provincial theatres.

With the production of *Chudak* (*The Eccentric*) by the Second Moscow Art Theatre in November, 1929, Afinogenyev was definitely established as among the leading playwrights. *Fear*, put on in Leningrad in 1931 and by the Moscow Art Theatre a year later, consolidated his position. At thirty, a tall, gangling, straw-haired fellow, he gives every promise of surpassing his own achievements.

CHARACTERS

BORODIN, IVAN ILYITCH: professor, Scientific Director of the Institute of Physiological Stimuli, aged sixty.

VALENTINA (VALYA): his daughter, a sculptress, aged twenty-three.

BOBROV, NIKOLAI KASYANOVITCH: professor, Director of the Experimental Section of the Institute, her husband, aged thirty-eight.

ZAKHAROV, VISARION ZAKHAROVITCH: professor of the History of Ancient Oriental Religions, aged sixty.

KASTALSKY, HERMAN VITOLDOVITCH: favorite pupil of Borodin, graduate student of the Institute, aged twenty-eight.

VARGASOV, SEMYON SEMYONOVITCH: Executive Secretary of the Institute.

AMALIA, AMALIA KARLOVNA: a very old lady.

ELENA (ELENA MIKHAILOVNA MAKAROVA): Communist, research assistant at the Institute, aged thirty.

TSEKHOVOI, NIKOLAI PETROVITCH: Communist, graduate student at the Institute, her husband, aged thirty-three.

NATASHA: Tsekhovoi's daughter by his first marriage, aged ten.

KLARA (KLAVDYA VASILYEVNA SPASOVA): Communist, factory worker, member of the Control Commission of the Communist Party, aged sixty.

KIMBAYEV, HUSSAIN: Kazak, Communist, graduate student, 'vydveezhenyets' (a worker or peasant who is advanced by the Soviet Shop or Party organization to higher duties in the fields of research or public administration.)

NEVSKY, BORIS NAUMOVITCH: Communist, Managing Director of the Institute.

TACITURN MEMBER OF THE PRÆSIDIUM.

WOMAN INVESTIGATOR.

Time: The present.
Place: Moscow, U.S.S.R.

ACT I

Scene i

The living-room in Professor BORODIN'S apartment. The late-Victorian furnishings are crowded by the addition of bookcases for which there was no room in the professor's study. At the left is a pedestal covered with a wet sheet, hiding a large angular clay figure — the work of the professor's daughter, VALENTINA, a sculptress. Before the curtain rises, we hear KASTALSKY singing to his own accompaniment on the piano. He enunciates his words softly, romantically, and only the second verse is sung in full voice. When the curtain rises, we discover VALENTINA near the pedestal and Professors BOBROV and BORODIN seated beside each other on a settee, listening to KASTALSKY'S music. Professor BORODIN is a scientist of the pre-Revolutionary stamp, an old 'intellectual.' He is a thick-set, pleasant-looking old man, intense and excitable; his clothes are old but neat and his beard well cared for. His daughter is pretty, with a distinct leaning towards feminine fripperies. Her husband, young Professor BOBROV, is an earnest scholar who is deeply attached to his wife. Young KASTALSKY, favorite pupil of Professor BORODIN, seems a little too carefully dressed, a little too romantic for the new Soviet era; he has been reared in the older tradition.

KASTALSKY (*singing*).

> Years pass... Their ruthless tempest lashing
> Across my dreams — my faith, in truth —
> Has stilled your tender voice in crashing,
> And dimmed the radiance of your youth.

> Now, Heart, with hope and longing beating,
> Bring back to life the wasted years,
> The heavenly ardor of first meeting,
> The startled touch, the kiss, the tears...

BORODIN. Fine, isn't it? What songs people sing about love! But nothing can be done about it. It's the eternal unconditioned stimulus. Since the very first dawn of the earliest human specimens on earth to the last sunset of the human race, always — love, hun-

395

ger, rage, fear... Well, what kind of trip did you have, Nikolai Kasyanovitch?... Nikolasha?

BOBROV. An excellent trip, excellent... An excellent song...

BORODIN. Sure, it's excellent. But why?... Because it comes from an unconditioned stimulus. All human behavior rests on four whales. People love, fear, rage, and hunger. And everything else is derived from these. Yes, yes. And the artist must always keep this in mind. Take Valentina, for example. She has applied my theory of stimuli to sculpture and she has created a most excellent piece. By my beard, I'll wager that she will draw the first prize in the contest. The Contest Committee will be here presently and you will see for yourself. (*Proudly.*) She is more talented than any of them — my Valya!

KASTALSKY. I'm sure you will get the prize, Valya.

VALENTINA. My husband doesn't think so. He doesn't like it.

BOBROV. I can't make up my mind whether Valya's work is good enough for the *first* prize.

VALENTINA. But suppose you were a member of the jury?

BOBROV. Naturally I would give my wife the prize.

KASTALSKY. Nikolai Kasyanovitch can no longer make up his mind about people and things. That is the result of his trip to the provinces.

VALENTINA. He is very solicitous about protecting his refined individuality from petty thoughts. (*Turns to* BOBROV.) But, as a matter of fact, you are merely listless and — if anything — lacking in individuality. You are growing stupid, Nikolai — like the rabbits you work with.

BORODIN. Valya!

BOBROV. I suppose it really is so...

BORODIN. Really! (*To* VALENTINA.) You haven't seen your husband for a month — and the very first evening... Bad temper, bad temper... Yes... Why don't you follow *his* example? (*Points to* KASTALSKY.) There is a meeting in session to decide his fate, but he sits here singing love songs and having a good time. But, of course, he's a Kastalsky. The whole family is like that. All of them sturdy oaks — professors, members of the Academy, senators...

KASTALSKY. That's the point. Senators! The son of a member of the Academy and a senator cannot become an assistant. But a metal worker's daughter, Elena Makarova, will become your assistant — and she will be sent abroad, too.

VALENTINA. Herman Vitoldovitch is a paragon of self-control!

KASTALSKY. At the preliminary session the decision was definitely against me.

BORODIN. But we have made an issue of it before the highest authority. It is my inalienable right to choose my own assistants. Now the highest authority is in session and we are represented there by Semyon Semyonovitch. Don't worry, Herman. You are a man of unusual talent, a worthy successor to us. Besides, I know that Semyon Semyonovitch had telephoned Efrem Efremovitch and had a conference about it with Alexander Gregorevitch. They promised their support.

KASTALSKY. Did they promise anything definite?

BORODIN. Tst... tst... Secret... Conspiracy...

KASTALSKY. In that case I am prepared to... hope for the best.

VALENTINA. You're a lucky fellow, Herman. You're lucky at everything. (*The doorbell rings.*) Must be the art commission.

KASTALSKY. I dare say it's Semyon Semyonovitch. (*They wait expectantly.*)

(*Enter Professor* ZAKHAROV. *He is a moth-eaten old man, evidently in bad circumstances; vague, mystical, and out of place in the new, hard Soviet society.*)

BORODIN. Visarion Zakharovitch, you're a rare guest. I'm awfully glad to see you. Sit down, my dear fellow, sit down. We have good news for you. Herman will become my assistant and will go to Berlin for his research, and Valentina's statue will be placed on Red Square right in front of the Kremlin. Everything is turning out fine. Yes, indeed. I have a graduate student by the name of Elena Makarova. She's a Communist. Think of it: this same Makarova proposes to organize a laboratory to investigate *human* behavior. 'You have studied the behavior of rabbits long enough,' she says. 'It's high time to transfer your investigations to human beings.' Well, what do you think of that? Our young people are certainly in a hurry... What do you say?

BOBROV. Human behavior is the concern of politicians. You and I are physiologists, Ivan Ilyitch.

KASTALSKY. Physiology will crowd out politics. The fate of men should not be decided in executive committees and in Communist locals, but rather in the Institute of Physiological Stimuli.

BOBROV. *Makarova* doesn't say so.

397

KASTALSKY. But *I* say so.

BOBROV (*to* KASTALSKY). I have seen quite a lot during my month's journey. I became acquainted with politics. I am still convinced that the methods for managing human beings are considerably more complex and varied than the management of rabbits.

BORODIN. It's not so simple, my dear fellow, to manage people.

VALENTINA. But it must be fascinating to treat people like rabbits! Scratch your husband behind the ear and he'll become good. (*The doorbell rings. Enter* VARGASOV.) Semyon Semyonovitch! (KASTALSKY *runs up to* VARGASOV.)

KASTALSKY. Victory? (*A pause.*)

VALENTINA. Are congratulations in order?

VARGASOV. Failure!

BORODIN. You're joking, Semyon Semyonovitch. You're joking!

VARGASOV. I'm not joking, Ivan Ilyitch. We have failed.

BORODIN. But then what about Efrem Efremitch and Alexander Gregorovitch?

VARGASOV. They lost courage. (*Silence.*)

BOBROV. So Makarova was appointed research assistant?

VARGASOV. Yes, Elena Mikhailovna Makarova.

VALENTINA. And who is going to Berlin?

VARGASOV. She, of course — in the spring... If you'll allow me... (*Sits.*)

BORODIN (*cries out*). I won't let them! Scoundrels! Good-for-nothings! (VARGASOV *jumps up.*)

VALENTINA. Papa!

BORODIN. I'll resign. The loafers! (*He runs agitatedly up and down the room.*) Give me some paper. I'll put it down in writing. I'm going to London. They've been begging me to come. I will not work with Makarova. She's a blockhead. Her head is made of wood. (*Raps on the table.*) Cork! Cotton! Wood-shavings! Yes!

VALENTINA. Quiet, papa, quiet! Your heart...

BORODIN. I don't care! I don't care if I have a stroke! I want everybody to know how scientists are treated in our country. Vydveezhentsy![1] The upstarts! The idea of promoting someone from a workers' school to a responsible scientific position! She doesn't know where to place her commas! She doesn't know any languages. A fine assistant she would make! It's disgraceful!

[1] Workers or peasants drawn from the ranks and promoted to positions of trust or given higher training in preparation for such positions.

ZAKHAROV (*mysteriously*). An indifferent sphere.

BORODIN. What?

ZAKHAROV. Ours is an indifferent sphere, I say. We must wait. Krishna taught: 'Do not cease being calm during the succession of grief and joy. Sever your feelings from your taste for them.'

BORODIN. Try to sever them — to separate one from the other! (*He paces back and forth.*)

VALENTINA. Poor Herman! Do you feel very bad about it?

KASTALSKY. Not at all. (*Sarcastically.*) I'm fortunate. Everything I undertake succeeds. The world looks bright to me. Ugh! How lucky I am! No, my dear teacher, you have worked with rabbits too long; it is high time to study the behavior of the vydveezhentsy. That, too, is founded on unconditioned stimuli. They are afraid of us, my dear teacher; they are afraid of us and they don't trust us. They crawl into scientific work like rats into Hatto's tower — in armies of hundreds of thousands, and when they finally take possession of science, they will destroy us.

BOBROV. I am very glad. (*Everyone turns to him.*) I'm very glad that you are not going to Berlin.

BORODIN. That's nonsense about the rats. You're wrong about that, my dear fellow. We can't take that attitude. These vydveezhentsy respect me. I matter to them. I might even say that they treasure me. And who would you say treasures me — the rats? No, we can't take that attitude. I disagree with you.

KASTALSKY. I'm very sorry, my dear teacher; my generation is paying for the sins of the past that it does not even remember. I know that Barbarossa had a red beard, France was ruled by the Henris and the Louis, and I remember nothing else about the past, and I need nothing else. I curse my father. Do you hear? I curse him!

BORODIN. Don't you dare! Your father was a member of the Academy, while you are a mere boy, a weakling...

VALENTINA. You must study, Herman — twice — three times as hard as before. Develop yourself, outshine the others, write a scientific work and become famous. You must become famous without fail.

BORODIN. Yes, yes. It is absolutely necessary for you to study. I'll help you. Select a subject and go to work.

KASTALSKY. Very well. I'll burn the midnight oil. I'll give up shaving and singing until I become a famous scientist. I will avenge all those who like myself have been crushed by the weight of their social origin.

BOBROV. I think you had better shave, at any rate.

VALENTINA. Don't trust my husband, Herman. He doesn't understand you any more than he understands me — no more than he understands life, or the world. He knows nothing, except rabbits and dogs. Work, Herman! And become famous in spite of them. (*Exit.*)

KASTALSKY. Nikolai Kasyanovitch, you were Kotomin's favorite pupil. Is that the way he helped you when you were in difficulties?

BORODIN. Yes. Kotomin let no one hurt his pupils. I'll write to Kotomin. I'll complain to him. Yes, I think I'll complain to him... What?

VARGASOV. Professor Kotomin was arrested last night.

BOBROV. Kotomin arrested?

BORODIN. It doesn't get any easier from hour to hour. A fine man like that! He wouldn't hurt a fly. And suddenly... What's happening to people? What's going on?

BOBROV. People are waging a class struggle. That is what politicians say, at any rate.

ZAKHAROV. I, too... Ivan Ilyitch... I too was — expelled.

BORODIN. You're joking, Visarion Zakharovitch, joking!

ZAKHAROV. After a lecture of mine on the History of Eastern Religions a young man with protruding cheekbones and in round spectacles came to me and said, 'You have no Marxian basis.'

BORODIN. And what did you answer him?

ZAKHAROV. The brave word died in my throat. I remembered Dejuro, the patron of the hunt, who was wont to laugh at simpletons who believe in universal happiness... I walked away in silence, Ivan Ilyitch, and came to you for advice and help.

(*Enter* KIMBAYEV, *a young Kazak workman. He is at once awkward and self-confident, with the mongoloid features and the distinctive accent of his race.*)

KIMBAYEV. All these fine books! Professor Bobrov? (*Shakes hands with the astonished* BORODIN.) I am Hussain Kimbayev, a graduate student — a vydveezhenyets. How do you do, comrade? Here are my papers.

400

BORODIN. I'm not Bobrov... You must be mad! On my word!

BOBROV. I'm Bobrov.

KIMBAYEV. Excuse me. (*Presents his documents.*) I've just arrived by train from Kzyl-Orda. I studied at the Workers' Faculties, was promoted, will now attend the Institute, and I will work hard... (*In naïve admiration.*) O-bai-ai! What a lot of books! And all of them must be read! I did nothing until I was twenty years old. Now I must catch up. The people of Kazakstan are a backward lot. I must catch up. I've come here to study. I came as soon as I could. We have no books. We have no trained men.

BORODIN. You might have come to the Institute tomorrow instead of breaking your way into the home of strangers at night.

KIMBAYEV. You don't call this night, do you? It's only eight o'clock. We must not waste an evening. Bobrov will give me a book, and I'll spend the evening reading it. Look, comrade, there's dust on your books! Don't you ever read them? Your books are going to waste! Books should not go to waste.

BOBROV. Come with me, Hussain Kimbayev. (*Exit* BOBROV *and* KIMBAYEV.)

ZAKHAROV. I was fired by a fellow just like this one — with protruding cheekbones.

BORODIN. These wild men from Kirghisia, bursting in on us — making a lot of noise — catching up with someone — I'll show them! Semyon Semyonovitch, I wish you'd talk matters over with Zakharov and place him as a librarian at the Institute. I'll show them a Marxist basis! Will you take the job, Visarion Zakharovitch?

ZAKHAROV. Gladly.

VARGASOV. You may depend on me. I'll see to it. But we'll date the application before your dismissal, so that it will appear to be a voluntary transfer.

ZAKHAROV. I bow to the ground before the wise old man. (*He falls to his knees, and* BORODIN *is taken aback.*)

BORODIN. Lift him up! You mustn't do that! A scholar mustn't humiliate himself like that! No! No!

VARGASOV (*goes to the door, stops, and turns to* KASTALSKY). You may depend on me. I am in sympathy with everything you have said. I'll help you to the best of my ability. I expect nothing in return.

KASTALSKY. So Kotomin was arrested!

VARGASOV. That's right.

(KASTALSKY, VARGASOV, *and* ZAKHAROV *go out.* BORODIN *sits down. He is thoughtful. He is alone now. A thin, tall woman, shabbily dressed, enters as if she were stealing her way in. This is* AMALIA.)

AMALIA. Good God, how you have aged!

BORODIN (*turns around, frightened*). Whom do you want? I can't do anything for you.

AMALIA. Only the eyes are the same as ever... No wonder — all these years...

BORODIN. I've never seen you before!

AMALIA. How much time has passed!... Ivan Ilyitch, do you remember Tatiana's Day — the student festival — the lights in the Hall of Columns — the student celebration — a young student on the stage — he's reciting a poem in prose — do you remember?

> How good, how fresh were the roses!

BORODIN (*rubs his forehead*). Yes, I remember. It was I who recited that. (*He is thoughtful again.*) 'How good, how fresh were the roses!' Wait! And then...

> Winter — the window-panes are frosted.
> A single candle glows in the dark room.

I remember... Of course, I remember.

AMALIA. It was in the winter-time, and I brought you a bouquet of real roses.

BORODIN. Wait! (*He jumps up, paces up and down.*) Amalia Karlovna... Mollie! Wait! A seventeen-year-old girl in a white, flimsy gown... Incredible! I was in love with you — madly in love! Ever since that day, Tatiana's Day... Amazing!

AMALIA. And you were a handsome young student. You had light, wavy hair.

BORODIN. And you were an admiral's daughter. You married a military prosecutor and you forgot the young student.

AMALIA. That isn't true. I never forgot you — never!

BORODIN. Enough! It's funny that we should remember and protest our love now. Don't say anything. It's funny, but it's interesting. Don't you think it's... amusing? (*Blows his nose.*)

AMALIA. My husband died in the Crimea.

BORODIN. Have you any children? Are they living?

AMALIA. My son works in your Institute. (*Seeing the professor's*

402

astonished face.) But quiet — for God's sake, quiet! Don't say a word about it to anyone. He has disowned me. He denies that he's my son. He has begun to live a new life. I don't want to interfere with him. I only want to find out about him. What is he like now?

BORODIN. You are saying terrible words! Disowned you! Forsook you! Your son has disowned you!

AMALIA. Mine was the wrong social origin for him. You won't give me away, will you? I trust you, so I am frank with you.

BORODIN. Monstrous!

(*Enter* KASTALSKY.)

KASTALSKY (*to* BORODIN). A member of the Art Commission. (*He goes to* VALENTINA'S *room.*)

BORODIN (*to* AMALIA). Come with me. We must do something about it. What horrible times we live in! (*Exit* AMALIA *and* BORODIN.)

(*Enter through the opposite door* KLARA *and* NATASHA. KLARA *is a vigorous, self-reliant woman, forthright in her manners — the type of the Old Bolshevik. The ten-year-old* NATASHA *wears a red neckerchief, symbol of the Pioneers, the children's Communist organization. The little girl is immediately attracted to some boudoir dolls.*)

NATASHA. My, how many dolls!

(*Enter* BOBROV *and* KIMBAYEV.)

KIMBAYEV. Thank you, Comrade Bobrov, thank you very, very much. I'll read all night.

BOBROV. No, don't go in for reading at night. It's harmful.

KIMBAYEV. I must hurry. (*Exit.*)

NATASHA. Whose dolls are these — your daughter's?

BOBROV. No, my wife's.

NATASHA. In our Pioneer division even little girls don't play with dolls. Not to speak of a wife! It's funny.

(*Enter* VALENTINA, *followed by* KASTALSKY.)

VALENTINA. But where are the other members of the Commission?

KLARA. They've postponed coming here until tomorrow, but I can't come tomorrow because I must attend the plenary session of the Control Commission, so I decided to come now; and this little girl is the daughter of Nikolai Tsekhovoi.

VALENTINA. Nikolai Petrovitch's daughter?

KLARA. Yes. I live with them — in the same apartment. Their little girl insisted on coming with me to look at art... Well, pull off the sheet and show us what you've done.

VALENTINA. This statue is called 'The Proletarian.' It does not represent the idea of a single personality, but rather the fundamental idea of our epoch — Collectivism under the stimuli of rage, love, suffering, and victory.

NATASHA. Is it true that you play with dolls?

VALENTINA. No, my dear girl. I don't play with dolls.

NATASHA. Why, then, do you have dolls around here?

VALENTINA. For you to play with.

NATASHA. I don't want to. I am a Pioneer. (*She sits down beside the dolls on the settee.*)

(KASTALSKY *takes off the sheet from the larger statue and reveals a huge impressionistic mound of muscles, bodies, and faces.*)

VALENTINA. There it is.

KLARA. That?... Uh-huh.

(*Silence,* KLARA *walks around the statue — once, then again, looks at it through her fist, walks away.* NATASHA *breaks the general silence.*)

NATASHA. Auntie Klara, what is this — a camel?

KLARA. Natasha!

(BOBROV *bursts out laughing and hurries out of the room.*)

NATASHA. But it has little humps.

VALENTINA. Those are muscles, little girl.

KLARA. So... (*She begins to pace up and down rapidly and then stops before* VALENTINA.) Where did you study?

VALENTINA. I graduated from the Government Shops. Only twelve of us graduated.

KLARA. Your name is Valya, isn't it? Listen, Valya. I don't know very much about the art of sculpture...

KASTALSKY. Then you can't judge...

KLARA (*to* KASTALSKY). Did you ever wear, instead of trousers, an idea about trousers in general? What you might call trousers without material? Have you ever tried that? This is exactly what Valya has been trying to do. She has worked out an idea about trousers — and now look at the mess!

KASTALKSY. So far Socialism is also only a dress without material. Nevertheless, we are building it.

404

KLARA. Where did you learn such principles in politics?

KASTALSKY (*bitterly*). I learned that from my ration book.

KLARA. The ration book is very serious literature. Do you read it at the rate of one coupon per day — or more?... (*Turns to* VALENTINA.) The main thing in art, Valya, is to convey simplicity. Did you ever go out into the fields on a summer evening? The grass is fresh — dewy. The clouds look as if they had just been washed. The mist rises from the river. The earth is warm. Time passes quietly. Everything is simple. The birch trees — the meadow — the clearings in the forest — the fields of rye. And this simplicity makes the thoughts and the feelings cleaner and deeper, more profound. And that's the point, Valya. You have made a statue for our Workers' Palace. The statue must rouse feelings and thoughts. But instead of thoughts, I am merely astonished for five minutes. I suggest, Valya, that you forget this hunch-backed uncle here and start all over again... Come on, Natasha, let's go.

NATASHA (*preoccupied with the dolls*). Auntie Klara, why don't you talk some more?

KLARA. Let's go.

NATASHA (*rises, with a sigh*). All right, then, let's go. I have a lot of work to do myself. I must rewrite the report of the Sanitary Commission.

(*Exit* KLARA *and* NATASHA. VALENTINA *looks crushed and pathetic. Enter* BOBROV.)

BOBROV. Forgive me, Valya.

VALENTINA. Don't come near me!

BOBROV. I'm sorry — I didn't mean it. On my word of honor, I didn't mean it at all.

VALENTINA. Don't come near me! You can laugh at me now. They didn't pass my piece of sculpture. (*Enter* BORODIN.) It's all because of your silly stimuli.

BOBROV. Valya, please!

VALENTINA. Please — what? You're laughing at me — secretly. You funny little professor! Laugh openly at me — go on, laugh at me! (*She runs out.*)

BORODIN. What has come over people? I want to know what has come over people!

KASTALSKY. People are carrying on a class struggle, Professor.

BORODIN. Silence! You understand nothing and I understand nothing. Kirghisians with protruding cheekbones expel scholars,

405

professors are put in jail, graduate students become professors, talented graduate students are crowded out by vydveezhentsy... What has come over people, I ask you?... Silence! You don't understand anything! Sons deny their mothers and make a secret of their past! Daughters denounce their fathers! My first love has just become my housekeeper! What has come over people, I ask you?

KASTALSKY. Save the Russian intellectuals!

BORODIN. Nonsense! Everyone has gone mad!

KASTALSKY. I suggest that you accept Makarova's proposal to organize a laboratory for the study of human behavior. We've had enough of rabbits. We must discover the real stimuli of human madness.

BORODIN. Ah, ah, ah! (*Strikes his forehead.*) Excellent! Remarkable! The thought of a genius, my dear fellow! Yes, indeed! We're done with doubts! We will organize a laboratory for the study of human behavior — immediately! We shall test thousands of individuals — strictly scientifically, objectively, without any bias. The laboratory will prove that our life is going to the Devil — that we are heading straight for the abyss. The country should be managed by scientists, not by vydveezhentsy. Yes, I will prove that scientifically.

KASTALSKY. Our laboratory of human behavior will prove that the Soviet system of governing people is good for nothing. Am I right?

BORODIN. Of course you are!

BOBROV. That will never be, Herman Vitoldovitch.

KASTALSKY. It will be, Nikolai Kasyanovitch.

CURTAIN

ACT I

Scene 2

The living-room in ELENA'S *apartment. Its furnishings are simple, almost severe, consisting of bare necessities.* ELENA *is a rough-hewn proletarian young woman, vital, energetic, and handsome in an unadorned style. Her husband,* TSEKHOVOI, *is a tall, attractive person, a suggestion of his old-régime breeding discernible under his proletarian clothes and manners.* NATASHA, *his daughter by his first marriage, is at the table preoccupied with newspaper cuttings.* ELENA *pulls* KLARA *out of her room and almost throws her onto the couch.* TSEKHOVOI *is in high spirits.*

KLARA. I'm busy— I'm busy— I'm busy!

ELENA. Victory— complete victory!

TSEKHOVOI. We are winning the Institute! The Behavior Laboratory has been organized. Elena Makarova— my wife!— is in charge. But that Bobrov... what do you think of him? That apparently quiet fellow took the floor and, as if nothing of importance had happened, said: 'I am in charge of the Experimental Department, and in that capacity I protest against the organization of a laboratory for the study of human behavior.'

ELENA. Borodin was so surprised that he began to sneeze. I've always said that Bobrov was a trained flea. He's always either silent or agreeing with Borodin. But it seems that even trained fleas can bite.

NATASHA. Papa! Elena! Don't make so much noise! You don't let me think.

TSEKHOVOI. Better get used to thinking among people, my daughter.

NATASHA. I am getting used to it, little by little.

ELENA (*runs up and swings* NATASHA *around*). Give up your newspaper clippings and take a rest.

NATASHA (*imitating* KLARA). I'm busy — I'm busy — I'm busy!

KLARA. Natasha, stop teasing me!... And so you say that Borodin has organized a laboratory for the study of human behavior — the very thing Elena has been fighting for for such a long time? And you say that Bobrov is opposed to it?

ELENA. He'll never dare to oppose it actively. *We* are laying the

407

plans, *we* are organizing the investigation brigades, and *we* won't let Bobrov stick his nose in this business... Why don't you tell us that we are good, Klara? Haven't we done a marvellous piece of work? What do you say?

TSEKHOVOI. Elena is devilishly lucky. I have been preoccupied with the stimuli of rabbits for three years, and I am still only an insignificant graduate student. But she became interested in social studies a year ago, and she's already not only a research assistant but has a laboratory of her own.

ELENA. Look out for me! Before long I will replace Bobrov and be in charge of Bobrov's department. Then you will be *my* graduate student.

TSEKHOVOI. You never can tell...

ELENA. But the main point is, that everybody laughed at me. No one believed I could do it. They said that politics cannot lay down their own laws of physiology. But we will show them that it can. Our politics is to transform people. Feelings that were considered innate are now dying out. Envy, jealousy, anger, fear are disappearing. Collectivity, enthusiasm, the joy of life are growing. And we will help these new stimuli to grow!

KLARA. In other words, the time has come to manufacture behavior in laboratories! That's a tall order. In the old days we learned behavior in prisons, in exile, or in party activity. But now you young people can do everything.

ELENA. The laboratory will become the Party local.

(*Enter* VALENTINA.)

KLARA. Valya's here! Hello, Valya!

VALENTINA. I thought a lot about what you said last time, Comrade Klara. I want to get a job in a factory. I want to transform myself into another person — into a new human being. I want to create that — *make* it — just as machines are made. Help me! Be my engineer!

KLARA. And then *you* will be the tractor, is that it?... Well, we'll talk about it — we'll talk about it, all right. My tractor's lips seem to be rather too red, the face looks damaged — and you have naturally a beautiful face... Still, come on... (*Exit* VALENTINA *and* KLARA.)

TSEKHOVOI (*after a pause*). Yes, she has a pretty face... Is she a good sculptress?

408

ELENA. She is the professor's daughter; and so she demolishes clay because she has nothing else to do.

TSEKHOVOI. I have seen her work... But after all, she's going to the factory to remake herself.

ELENA. At least she thinks she is.

TSEKHOVOI. Don't you believe that the factory transforms people?

ELENA. Transforming a person is not like repairing a tractor. A nobleman who works at a machinist's bench is not yet a proletarian.

TSEKHOVOI. What do you expect — that he should come to your laboratory to have proletarian glands grafted on? That's a lot of academic nonsense. The factory is the school of Communism.

ELENA. That's a very fat slogan — very significant. It makes my head spin.

TSEKHOVOI. Why don't you accuse me of a Left deviation? Go on!

NATASHA. Papa, which is the greater menace — a Left deviation or a Right deviation?

TSEKHOVOI. Never mind.

NATASHA. I think that double-dealing is the greatest menace.

TSEKHOVOI. Never mind, I say.

(*Enter* BOBROV. *He wears an overcoat and holds his cap in his hand.*)

NATASHA. I am writing a report about it, and you keep on saying, 'Never mind.'

BOBROV. I saw Valentina's fur coat in your hall.

ELENA. Your wife is visiting Klara Spasova. You may go there.

BOBROV. I have come to see you, Elena Makarova. I say again, don't hurry with the laboratory. Consider every question carefully. Weigh it pro and con. Think over every proposal of Borodin's attentively. Don't rush with conclusions. In a case like this, hurry is not permissible.

ELENA. How many years are we to go on investigating?

BOBROV. I am not interested in predictions.

ELENA. But I *am* interested in predictions, and I predict that we who are Marxists and Bolshevists will accomplish in one month what it takes you, an idealist, an entire year to do.

TSEKHOVOI. In politics, slow tempos are called 'opportunism.'

BOBROV. I am not concerned with politics.

TSEKHOVOI. Do you mean to say that science is beyond politics? We happen to know what sort of people advance this slogan. You don't like Kastalsky's declaration that the laboratory has been created to aid politics?

BOBROV. Kastalsky is really carrying on his own policy — that of discrediting us.

TSEKHOVOI. Well, Nikolai Kasyanovitch, if we're going to talk about deception, you had better look after your wife.

BOBROV. That's a rude and unjustified insinuation!

TSEKHOVOI. Forgive me. This is the working-class way.

ELENA. Nikolai, this is silly!

NATASHA. Papa, is six times seven thirty-seven or forty-eight?

TSEKHOVOI. Ask Elena. She is smart, while your father is only a graduate student. (*He raps on* KLARA'S *door.*) May I come in? (*Exit.*)

ELENA. There you are!... (*To* NATASHA.) Six times seven is forty-two. (*To* BOBROV.) Why do you stand there like a monument?

BOBROV. I am never at ease in other people's apartments... And so you reject my proposal? May I go home?

ELENA. Nikolai Kasyanovitch, you have spent a month travelling through the country; and so, if you are still opposed to closer co-operation between science and politics, I take it that you have seen nothing and have understood nothing.

BOBROV. On the contrary, I have seen a lot, and right along I have been thinking seriously of what I have seen. The country is governed by politicians; but, you see, while the politician lives in the present only, the man of science must think on the scale of centuries. Even the very best of politics compels one to waste time, like money, on details. Take yourself, for example: you know that the State farm 'The Giant' was the first to finish sowing, that the Red Putilov factory will fulfil the financial plan. You have in mind that tomorrow there will be elections for the local committee, that barley is being issued as a ration, that yesterday was your day of rest. But you have forgotten who was the author of *Faust*.

ELENA. I haven't seen that opera.

BOBROV. May I inform you that *Faust* should be read, not heard? You cannot tell the difference between a piece of Sèvres china and a Saxon cup.

ELENA. I drink tea out of a glass.

BOBROV. History has raised us from a herd of monkeys to select cultivated individualities, while you are smashing the differentiations in the collective mortar of politics.

ELENA. We are making history. If you were to participate in real life for a little while, you would understand that we are not concerned merely with the smashing of differences. (*Doorbell rings.*) Excuse me. I'll be right back. (*Exit.*)

NATASHA (*who has been studying* BOBROV). Have you many rabbits? I'll bet you have a hundred.

BOBROV. Why don't you come over and see them for yourself? I have some fine rabbits.

NATASHA. I am burdened with too many duties. I have no time. Right now I am busy with a report of the Five-Year Plan. (*She notices that* BOBROV *is smiling.*) Don't laugh! That's much harder work than making a camel out of clay.

BOBROV. Where are you going to read your report, little girl?

NATASHA. At my club. I am the official school reporter.

BOBROV. Do you have a gay time at your club?

NATASHA. Come with me. I'll take you there. It's very interesting. I've asked Papa and Elena, but I can't make them come, because they are burdened with so many duties. It's very gay there. We have just learned a new song. Sing with me.

(*She sings a Pioneer march.* VALENTINA'S *head appears in the doorway of* KLARA'S *room.* VALENTINA *speaks to* BOBROV.)

VALENTINA. Kolya, will you wait for me? (*Head disappears.*)

BOBROV. Very good.

NATASHA. What do you mean — good? How about going to the club with me?

BOBROV. I'm sorry, but I can't.

NATASHA. There you go! If only you could get interested in real life!

(*A burst of laughter comes through the closed door.*)

BOBROV. All right, I'll come with you, little girl.

NATASHA. Hurrah! (*Pulls him by the sleeve.*) Hurry, hurry, or you might change your mind! (*Runs out.*)

(*Enter* ELENA.)

ELENA. Kastalsky has just telephoned. They have formed six investigation brigades. The creaky wagon of the Institute has finally been started on its way. The little Scientific Institute is assuming

411

war-time proportions — and two years from now we will move from this small house to a six-story building — into the Institute of Social Behavior!... Oh!

BOBROV. Elena Mikhailovna, family ethics do not permit me to tell you what I know about the Institute of Human Behavior, but again and again I must warn you to be careful. We are being involved in a suspicious enterprise. (*Begins to take his leave.*)

ELENA. See you later!

(*Enter* NATASHA, *dressed in her street attire. She is carrying* BOBROV'S *overshoes.*)

NATASHA. Come on, I'm waiting for you.

                        (BOBROV *goes out with* NATASHA.)

ELENA. I wonder why he is so set against us? What 'family ethics' was he referring to? What does he mean by it? (*She comes closer to* KLARA'S *room; her hand is on the handle of the door, but she hears* TSEKHOVOI'S *ringing laughter,* VALENTINA'S *voice, changes her mind, goes to the table, and begins to empty the contents of her brief-case.*) Again I missed my study-circle of current politics... You'll get it in the neck in your party local, Makarova... *Sie reisen nach Deutschland?*... Are you going to Germany?... *Es stimmt... Ich reise nach Berlin... Haben Sie schon Ihren Auslandspass? Natürlich... Und mit allen Visa?... Hier ist mein Pass.*

(*Enter* TSEKHOVOI, KLARA, *and* VALENTINA.)

VALENTINA. Nikolai Petrovitch, you would make an excellent model for the sculptural group 'The Proletarian in Science.' Everything about you comes from the factory. Your self-assurance, your carriage, your voice... At one time the Greeks boiled their Venuses in olive oil, which made the marble warm and alive. But we must boil our statues in *machine* oil! We must saturate them with the sweat and smoke of chimneys. Then they too will come to life.

KLARA. We are trying to arrange showers for those who are sweaty and greasy, because we want them to be clean...

VALENTINA. Let's hurry to the factory. I want to see everything, touch it with my hands, find new spatial forms. I must transform myself to the very roots of my being... But where is my husband?

ELENA. Your husband went to the club with Natasha... *Ich reise nach Berlin — und mit allen Visa.*

VALENTINA. Who will see me home then?

TSEKHOVOI. I'm afraid the hereditary proletarian will have to do it.

VALENTINA (*offering her hand*). Good-bye.

ELENA (*abruptly*). See you later... *Sie reisen nach Deutschland?... Es stimmt.*

TSEKHOVOI (*escorts* VALENTINA *out, then returns*). You might have been more courteous.

ELENA. Excuse me. That's the working-class way.

TSEKHOVOI. A letter for you. (*Throws letter on the table.*) There it is! (*Exit.*)

KLARA. You don't like her, do you? But I think she's all right. I'm taking her to the factory as a cultural worker.

ELENA. You're always busy with all sorts of nonsense.

KLARA. You young people see out of only one eye. You look at the world out of your laboratory. But we don't ignore people. Not on your life!

ELENA (*finishing her reading*). You know... Bobrov is a pupil of that Kotomin who was arrested.

KLARA. Well, what about it?

ELENA. What do you mean — what about it? He — the pupil of a sabotager — is in our Institute!

KLARA. But that doesn't make *him* a sabotager.

ELENA. Oh, let me alone, please! (*She is worried; she paces up and down.*)

KLARA. Why should I let you alone? You got up on the wrong side this morning, my dear girl. Don't wave your arms around like a windmill. What frightened you? That anonymous letter you just received?... Think of it!

ELENA (*to herself*). Highly cultivated individuality!... Sèvres china! The scale of centuries!... Very well... (*defiantly.*) If *you* are against the laboratory, then I'm sure that the laboratory is indispensable!

CURTAIN

ACT II

SCENE 3

The library of the Institute. The door on the left leads to Professor BORODIN'S *study. The door on the right, to the apartment for workers of the Institute.*

When the curtain rises, ZAKHAROV *is discovered writing on the blackboard. He is drawing mystic triangles and making calculations.*

KIMBAYEV *is browsing among the books.*

KIMBAYEV. So silly to waste one's life on sleeping and eating! I'm glad I didn't sleep another night last night... So I read another book. I'm now reading three books at one time. *War and Peace, The Development of Capitalism, The Function of the Brain.* Let me have Kotomin's books. I want to write a paper about that sabotager's book. Let me have Kotomin.

(Enter KASTALSKY.)

ZAKHAROV. All right. (*He looks for the book on the shelf.*)

KIMBAYEV. Feels like sand in my eyes. I've kept vigil night after night. Strong tea helps to keep one awake.

ZAKHAROV. The philosopher Bodhi-Dhama cut off his eyelashes in order to keep awake, and out of these eyelashes the tea plant grew. That is why tea keeps us awake now.

KIMBAYEV. That's a fairy tale... I have a headache...

KASTALSKY. Night was made for sleep, Kimbayev. (*Sarcastically.*) It was all right for *us* not to sleep for months when we studied, but *you* mustn't do it. You represent one of the most backward nationalities. It is harmful for you.

KIMBAYEV. You mean to say it's harmful for us but not harmful for you? You are a great people; we are a little people. A little people, like a little boy, must go early to bed. In the past we slept a lot, Comrade Kastalsky; but it's different now. Whatever you can do, I can do twice as well. If you don't sleep *one* month, I can go without sleep for *two* months. I'm determined to catch up with the graduate student Kastalsky.

KASTALSKY. Go on catching up, Kimbayev, go on! You really must hurry...

KIMBAYEV. I know that well enough without asking you about it.

(*Enter* BORODIN *and* ELENA.)

ELENA. Our Laboratory of Human Behavior is investigating milk-women, expelled bookkeepers, and even paupers. I don't see why we should study the behavior of such social categories.

BORODIN. I study people, not social categories.

ELENA. There are many more people in the factories.

BORODIN. From the point of view of science, a milk-woman is just as interesting as a factory mechanic.

ELENA. For our purposes, the factory mechanic is more interesting.

BORODIN. I don't know anything about your purposes. You young people have a distaste for facts. You're concerned only with bare purpose. And science doesn't like these 'bare purposes.'

ELENA. It's necessary to know *why* to collect facts. Now we are working with our eyes shut — blindly.

BORODIN. All of us are more or less blind.

ELENA. I don't approve of this method.

BORODIN. In that case, give up your place to Kastalsky. To him, *I* am the method.

KIMBAYEV. And what about self-criticism, Comrade Borodin?

BORODIN. Indulge in your self-criticism as much as you like, but don't touch me.

KIMBAYEV. Why shouldn't we touch you? Anything may be touched, even things as breakable as glass dishes.

(*Enter* NATASHA.)

BORODIN. Whose little girl is this? What do you want, little girl?

NATASHA. I've brought my class for an excursion. We want to look at the rabbits.

BORODIN. I won't permit any excursions here... Herman! (*He goes into his study, followed by* KASTALSKY.)

ELENA. What's the big idea, Natasha? This isn't a museum.

NATASHA. It was Uncle Bobrov's idea... First he invites me, and then all this trouble...

KIMBAYEV. The rabbits won't die of it. Take your class inside, Natasha.

ELENA. Since when are you the director of the Institute?

KIMBAYEV. They offered me the job, but I turned them down. You ask Bobrov. Sit down, Natasha. (*To* ZAKHAROV.) Have you found Kotomin?

ZAKHAROV (*takes the cover off a book, reads slowly, closes the book*). We haven't any books by Kotomin at the Institute.

KIMBAYEV. You may not have any today. But you *must* have it by tomorrow. I need it, do you understand? (*Exit.*)

NATASHA. Elena, I'll write a note about the old man for the wall paper.

ELENA. What? Oh, yes, yes. War is war, Professor Borodin. We'll discuss the issue in the press. (*She sits at the table and writes.*)

NATASHA. Give me a pencil, too. (*Writes.*)

(*Enter* AMALIA.)

AMALIA (*to* ZAKHAROV). I've brought lunch for Ivan Ilyitch, and a bite for you, too.

ZAKHAROV. Kwannon was the goddess of charity. I have a button with her image that I will give you.

AMALIA. Who is this woman?

ZAKHAROV. This is Nikolai Petrovitch's wife.

AMALIA. Oh, yes, of course. The research assistant. (*She walks up to* ELENA, *studies her, meets* ELENA'S *gaze, and walks away.*) Have they any children?

ZAKHAROV. Nikolai Petrovitch has a child by his first marriage.

AMALIA. Natasha?

NATASHA. Here!

AMALIA. Oh! (*Turns around, looking frightened.*) Oh! Do you want some candy, Natasha? (*She rummages in her pocket and offers a piece of candy to* NATASHA.)

NATASHA. I don't want it. It's dirty. What are you chewing all the time?

ELENA. Natasha! Stop!

NATASHA. Why do you always interfere with me? I can see that she's chewing gum. At school Sergei was always doing it, too. I'm going back to the children. (*Exit.*)

AMALIA. Natasha... Oh... (*Mutters to herself.*)

(*Enter* KASTALSKY.)

ZAKHAROV (*to* AMALIA). Go into his study. (*He goes to* KASTAL-

416

SKY *with a book in his hand and says sotto voce.*) I refrained from issuing this book because the author's signature is on it.

KASTALSKY (*takes the book and reads*). You did the right thing. This inscription might get Nikolai Kasyanovitch into trouble. It's compromising, to say the least.

(*Enter* VARGASOV *on his way to the study.*)

KASTALSKY. Take a look at this, Semyon Semyonovitch, and hide it so nobody will ever see it. (*Gives the book to* VARGASOV, *who reads the inscription and goes out hastily with the book.* KASTALSKY *walks up to* ELENA.) When I was five years old, I found a diamond earring in the garden. Since then I have been called lucky. And since then I have been only halfway lucky. The second earring was always missing... I thought I might find it in Berlin, but it is *you* who's going to Germany, not I. You were born with a silver spoon in your mouth, because you happen to be a proletarian.

ELENA. Why are you so eager to go abroad?

KASTALSKY. To hear the songs of Maurice Chevalier, and to take a look at three hundred naked chorus girls in a revue.

(*Enter* KIMBAYEV *and* BOBROV.)

KIMBAYEV. Go on, Comrade Bobrov, talk to her.

BOBROV (*to* ELENA). Kimbayev has just told me about your argument with Borodin. They have blindfolded you, and they are leading you by the hand. You argue, you object, but you continue to stumble along the same road. It is high time, Elena Mikhailovna, that you should draw the inevitable conclusion of this argument.

KASTALSKY. In other words, you expect Makarova to work according to *your* plans? The non-partisan professor is giving partisan instructions.

KIMBAYEV. Kastalsky is afraid that the Kazak might catch up with him. He says, 'Don't read at night, play in the daytime.' Listen to what Bobrov tells you, Elena. Bobrov is telling you the right thing. Bobrov is a good teacher.

KASTALSKY. Quite right. Nikolai Kasyanovitch is a pupil of Kotomin himself, and all of Kotomin's pupils are excellent teachers.

KIMBAYEV. You have the tongue of a serpent, Kastalsky.

BOBROV (*to* ELENA). Why don't you say something? I can see that you don't trust me. Everyone in the Institute avoids me. They don't speak to me, they don't even look at me when we meet.

Instead of meeting me eye to eye, they lower their eyes as if they were looking for footprints, the footprints of a sabotager. People whisper and titter behind my back. It's very hard to work under those conditions, Elena Mikhailovna. Hussian Kimbayev is the only one who has faith and who gives me courage. If it were not for him...

ELENA. Why don't you say something definite about the *purposes* of Borodin's laboratory? What does he expect to prove with the results of his investigation? Why are you silent about that? Are you afraid? 'Family ethics'! You haven't taken a definite stand against Kotomin, either. Not yet. You walk around the Institute like a retired monarch, mumble your complaints, and offer advice. Before you can go around instructing others, you must publicly set yourself apart from a sabotager. (*She goes toward the exit.*)

KIMBAYEV. Elena! You're talking nonsense! Bobrov has given me a definite assignment — to expose Kotomin! I'm trying to get that last book of Kotomin's — to write my report.

ELENA. That doesn't alter matters.

KIMBAYEV. Why not? It very *definitely* alters matters. You've no grounds for your suspicions against Bobrov. We must unite in our opposition to Borodin. (*Exeunt* KIMBAYEV *in conversation with* ELENA.)

KASTALSKY. Hurry, run for a droshky, and to the newspaper office!... Write your letter to the editor! Renounce your teacher! Spit at his beard! You need not be afraid — he is behind the bars now! And they will hail you as a great man. Why don't you do it?

BOBROV (*shouts*). Keep still!

BORODIN (*running in*). Nikolasha, your lips are trembling.

BOBROV. Tell your favorite to stop.

KASTALSKY. Nikolai Kasyanovitch is in a hurry to renounce Kotomin in order to win the favor of Elena Mikhailovna.

BOBROV. I have disagreed with Kotomin's views for a long time.

BORODIN. But surely this is not the time to protest your differences — when he is in prison!

BOBROV. It may be a little late, but better late than never. I don't want Kastalsky to take advantage of my being a weakling about it.

BORODIN (*exclaims*). Nikolai! Nikolai! Nikolai Kasyanovitch!

BOBROV. I'm going to the newspaper office at once.

BORODIN. Professor Bobrov, you are mature enough to know what you are doing — what you find necessary to do.

KASTALSKY. And advantageous as well as necessary...

BORODIN. But I want you to know that our friendship is less secure than ever.

BOBROV. To me, principles are more important than friendships.

(*Enter* NATASHA.)

NATASHA. Uncle Bobrov, we have written a notice about the old man here.

BOBROV. What? Oh, yes, yes. I'll take a look at it right away. (*Exit.*)

BORODIN. Yes, show her your rabbits, Bobrov.

NATASHA (*to* BORODIN). That's different. Maybe we won't publish that notice about you.

BORODIN. Thanks. (*Exit* NATASHA, *following* BOBROV.) Think of it! A child like that writing political notices about men of my standing!

KASTALSKY. I think it's worse that Bobrov should be writing to the newspapers renouncing his teacher Kotomin forever and aye... The time will come when he will renounce you, too.

BORODIN. Yes, I know. People are becoming petty. There are no large principles to guide them. Before long we won't be able to tell the difference between a professor and some vydveezhenyets. I'm sorry about Nikolai. It's a great pity. He's heading straight for the abyss. But after all, that's his own affair. I suggest that you get better acquainted with Nikolai Petrovitch — a very interesting person. I have been observing him scientifically, studying him as I used to study the rabbits.

ZAKHAROV. Nikolai Petrovitch is guided by the stars: Venus, Mars, and the Moon. Mars invests him with noble manliness; the Moon gives him limitless power; and Venus — great love.

(NEVSKY, *the harassed, overworked Managing Director, runs in, swinging his brief-case in the air.*)

NEVSKY. Ivan Ilyitch, hurry about filling up your library. Our appropriations have been cut down.

BORODIN. I never see you around the Institute, in spite of the fact that you are the director.

NEVSKY. I must confess that I'm running around in circles. I have dragged the budget of the Institute through twelve Government departments, and now I'm stuck in the thirteenth. They've cut it to the bone, but I won't surrender. We'll get what we're after. Nevsky never loses in a case like this. Let me show you the budget. (*Exit with* BORODIN *into* BORODIN'S *study.* KASTALSKY *also goes out of the library.*)

(*Enter* VARGASOV. ZAKHAROV *addresses him.*)

ZAKHAROV. Bobrov is writing a letter to the newspapers — renouncing Kotomin.

VARGASOV. That won't save him. It's all set now. Don't forget, Visarion Zakharovitch, under what circumstances you came here. It will be to your advantage to stick with me and tell me everything.

ZAKHAROV. Pentogram.

VARGASOV. What?

ZAKHAROV (*points to a triangle on the blackboard*). The pentogram will not tolerate lies, forbids to lie. Either say nothing, or speak the truth. I say nothing, in their presence, but to you I tell the truth.

(VARGASOV *goes toward the study, and on the threshold meets* AMALIA, *who is just coming out of the study.* AMALIA *crosses the library, opens the door, and suddenly runs back.*)

AMALIA. Hide me! Hide me! I must not meet him!

ZAKHAROV. Whom?

AMALIA. I'll tell you later. Hurry, Visarion Zakharovitch, hide me!

ZAKHAROV. Wait there.

(ZAKHAROV *opens a small door behind one of the bookcases, and* AMALIA *disappears through it.*)

(*Enter* TSEKHOVOI *and* ELENA. TSEKHOVOI *knocks on the door of* BORODIN'S *study, from which* VARGASOV *emerges.*)

TSEKHOVOI. Please tell Nevsky that I am here. I want to see him on important business. (*To* ELENA.) I know as well as you that Borodin is not a Marxist, but the problems of human behavior as solved by Borodin will benefit our country greatly, and thus an idealistic professor will aid the building of Socialism. Such is the dialectic!

ELENA. I'm fed up with such dialectics! Borodin is talking all sorts of heresy about human blindness. We're investigating the Devil only knows what. Kastalsky does with us what he likes. I write a paper, and he won't let me publish it.

TSEKHOVOI. You're indulging in an academic argument, forgetting politics. That is why politically your article against Borodin will play right into the hands of the sabotagers.

ELENA. You've lost your mind!

TSEKHOVOI. Bobrov will be the only one to support you in your present stand, and don't forget that he was always opposed to the laboratory, and that he is in agreement with Kotomin.

ELENA. The fact that he's Kotomin's pupil doesn't necessarily mean that he's in agreement with him.

TSEKHOVOI. You think so? (*Enter* NEVSKY.) Listen to this, Comrade Nevsky. (*Reads the inscription on the book.*) 'To one who shares my views, my friend Nikolai Bobrov — Pavel Kotomin.' Inscribed in his own hand on his own book. And this sabotager who has not yet been exposed is still in charge of a department. To me it seems evident that the management is guilty of opportunism.

NEVSKY (*laughs*). Och!

TSEKHOVOI. This is no laughing matter, Nevsky.

NEVSKY. No matter what you do, you can't avoid a deviation, it seems. For Heaven's sake, tell me what to do. Borodin won't let me touch Bobrov's head.

TSEKHOVOI. We must meet the issue squarely. It seems to me that Borodin will not protest so strenuously any more against Bobrov's dismissal. They're not as thick as they used to be.

NEVSKY. That being the case, we can attack the matter decisively. But who will take Bobrov's place? What about Makarova? Are you willing, Elena?

ELENA. Not Bobrov — not Bobrov, comrades. Borodin and Kastalsky — these are the real enemies.

TSEKHOVOI. Have you ever seen the like? Not Bobrov! She's trying to smooth matters over. Elena is lacking in decisiveness. We must be firm about this.

NEVSKY. In that case, it's your job, Tsekhovoi. There's no one else to do it.

ELENA. We mustn't do things that way, comrade. We can't put a graduate student in the place of a professor, and especially a graduate student from another department. It's a great responsibility.

TSEKHOVOI. I'm amazed at your strange lack of faith in a member of the Communist Party who, moreover, is your husband.

NEVSKY. The important thing is to be able to manage in general and as a whole. I was put in charge of the Institute and was taken directly from the Leather Trust. The only thing I know about rabbits is rabbit skins. And yet I'm the Managing Director of the Institute of Physiological Stimuli. Such is the dialectic!

ELENA. Now you, too, are talking dialectics — dialectics!

NEVSKY. That's true! It *is* a convenient word. Everybody's using it. Well, how about it, Nikolai? Do you agree? We will remove Bobrov and put you in charge and make you chairman of the department.

TSEKHOVOI. And member of the Præsidium?

NEVSKY. Naturally. That goes without saying. One calls for the other.

ELENA. And the problem as to who should be investigated at the laboratory — the question of Borodin's method...

TSEKHOVOI. Is not to be touched in the press.

(*Exit* NEVSKY, ELENA, *and* TSEKHOVOI. ZAKHAROV *goes to the door of* BORODIN'S *study, raps on it.* VARGASOV *comes out.* ZAKHAROV *beckons to him and they both stop before the blackboard.* ZAKHAROV *is sketching.*)

ZAKHAROV. The height — this peak — is the little girl. Her father is Nikolai Petrovitch Tsekhovoi. (*He puts a dot to the left and draws a line through the dot.*) Amalia Karlovna knows the little girl. (*Draws a line on the right.*) There is some cabalistic connection between Amalia Karlovna and Nikolai Petrovitch. (*He connects the lower dots, thus forming a triangle.*) Pentogram. Would you like to know what is the nature of the connection between them? (*He opens the door behind the shelf, through which* AMALIA *had passed.*) Go in there.

VARGASOV (*speechless*). What?... Tsekhovoi!... Amalia!...

CURTAIN

ACT II

SCENE 4

ELENA'S *apartment, the living-room as in Scene 2.* KIMBAYEV *is reading a book which he neglects from time to time in order to speak to* KLARA *or* ELENA.

ELENA. I don't understand. It's quite beyond me. Borodin told the truth. I have the forehead of a mouse. With a forehead like that, there is no place for me in scientific work.

KIMBAYEV. You're all wrong, Elena. My head is fit for scientific work. My heavy head. My Kazak head — which you can hit with a stone without cracking it. I stay awake nights and read thick books and after each book I grow so much... (*indicates with his hand*). Before long I'll break through the ceiling. We must always go forward, Elena.

ELENA. I'm beginning to fear this Laboratory of Human Behavior. Borodin is setting a trap for us. He's collecting questionnaires from all people who have been hurt by the Soviet Government — and we cannot oppose this.

KLARA. You fool! Fool! There is no other name for you. How does it come that you talk such nonsense? Your father was a genuine proletarian. You yourself have worked in a factory for quite a while; and now — just look at you! A Hamlet in skirts! Afraid of the laboratory! Running into the bushes like a frightened hare! We'll pull you out from the bushes by your ears. We'll put you at a table — and we'll force you to think about it sanely.

KIMBAYEV. Bobrov spoke of it long ago. But Bobrov was fired — Bobrov walks around very sad. He went away from Borodin, but he did not come to us. Call Bobrov, Elena. We will work together.

ELENA. I don't want to call anyone.

KIMBAYEV. Now Nikolai, your husband, is in charge of the department. Your husband — and a member of the Communist Party... But he did not treat Bobrov right.

ELENA. Nikolai thinks that I am too panicky. We no longer have dinner together. We quarrel so bitterly on the street-car that the passengers gloat with pleasure. But he's very happy with this

423

manner of living and with his new appointment. I think I'll become a chauffeur.

KLARA. If you do, we'll expel you from the Party. It really is amazing! The moment you step away from your class, immediately you are possessed by all sorts of cosmic doubts. I suppose you think that's the result of thinking, but I tell you that it comes from lack of will, from non-partisan scholarship. Stop contemplating your navel!

KIMBAYEV. What did you say? I never heard of that before.

KLARA. Her navel has become the centre of the universe, and the Party is way behind — something in the nature of a tail. If I had my way about it, I would turn all of you over my knee and spank you.

ELENA. It's easy enough to spank. You might help us.

KLARA. You don't expect *me* to go into the Institute! I'm too old for study.

KIMBAYEV (*jumps to his feet*). Who expects you to study? We don't want you to study. Why don't you become a patron of the Institute? Have the entire factory become a patron of the Institute! The factory will help us to straighten out our line of conduct. Our present line is bad — bad. Hussain has a smart head. He has thought of all this himself! (*Seizes his head.*) I have a headache. At night the sheep run in all directions. The words and letters scatter in all directions. It's hard to catch them.

(*Enter* TSEKHOVOI *and* VALENTINA.)

KLARA. Where do you come from — beaming so?

VALENTINA. I've again taken up modelling, and Nikolai Petrovitch here is now my model. The new statue is 'The Proletarian in Science' — a marvellous theme, and a rare model! Look at his head! It's made for marble! The arms and shoulders — they already look sculptured!

TSEKHOVOI. Valentina Ivanovna, you positively embarrass me.

KLARA. I hope, Valya, that you haven't forgotten already what street-car takes you to the factory.

VALENTINA. Oh, Klavdya Vasilyevna! It's so dusty and noisy there. A kind of machine hysteria. I suffer from migraine every day. No one pays any attention to me, I don't seem to understand anything, and — I stopped modelling. I can't stand it any more.

KLARA. Another one running off into the bushes... In your case I don't care so much. Do what you like. Go ahead — rouge your

424

lips, model your golden proletarian, and be happy in your own way. Come on, Hussain, we'll arrange about the patronage for the Institute.

KIMBAYEV. You are still young, Klara. You're a spry one — *argamak!* (*Exit with* KLARA *into her room.*)

VALENTINA. She's hurt.

TSEKHOVOI. The old woman is stubborn. Don't pay any attention to her. Forget it!

ELENA. That's putting it strong.

VALENTINA. And you... wouldn't you like to pose for me?

ELENA. We have no time for nonsense.

TSEKHOVOI. Not we, but you... Art does not exist as far as Elena is concerned. To her, Venus is simply some naked woman, and a picture of the Crucifixion — religious opium. And she is a scientific worker — an assistant; the brain is alive, but feelings and sensitiveness have dried up.

ELENA. Nikolai!

TSEKHOVOI. Look at this room! Bare windows, crumpled newspapers, stains on the wallpaper, crumbs on the tablecloth, cigarette stubs, dirty dishes, an empty tin can — and it makes no difference to you! You don't even notice these things!

ELENA. There was a time when *you* didn't notice them, either.

TSEKHOVOI. At that time I was a simple graduate student.

ELENA. Excuse me. I hadn't attached any importance to the change. You are now an important official!

TSEKHOVOI. It doesn't hurt to live in a civilized manner — and especially these days.

ELENA. That's so. I'll set things in order right away.

TSEKHOVOI. Any fool can set the room in order. The important thing is to sense the situation.

VALENTINA. I'm going. I've something to talk about with Klara. I'm sorry I hurt her feelings... (*She raps on the door.* KLARA's *voice is heard saying 'Come in' and* VALENTINA *goes into* KLARA's *room.*)

ELENA. You made me blush before that girl.

TSEKHOVOI. You might learn manners from that girl.

ELENA. Her manners have already had their effect on you. Feeling, sensitiveness... Of course, I am thirty. She is only twenty-three. She's young — fresh.

TSEKHOVOI. You were born like that. It is a mistake of nature that you are a woman.

ELENA. That didn't prevent you from living with me for five years.

TSEKHOVOI. Man can get used to anything... (*Slaps the folded newspaper against the wall.*)... Even to fleas...

ELENA (*seizes the empty tin can and throws it at* TSEKHOVOI). You skunk! (*She is about to throw a brush at him when* VALENTINA *enters. There is a painful pause.*)

TSEKHOVOI. I'll see you home, Valya.

VALENTINA. No, no! I'll go alone.

TSEKHOVOI. Let me see you home, Valya.

VALENTINA. Good-bye, Elena Mikhailovna.

ELENA (*takes* VALENTINA'S *hand*). Valentina Ivanovna, there is no reason why you should hide with him in your studio, whisper in corners... (*Squeezes her hand.*) There's no use hiding and deceiving...

VALENTINA. Let go of me! (*Cries out in pain.*)

ELENA. Louder! Louder! Shout with full voice — and love with full voice!

VALENTINA. I love no one! Let go of me! Your hands are cold! (VALENTINA *wrenches herself loose and runs away.* TSEKHOVOI *runs after* VALENTINA.)

TSEKHOVOI. Enough! I shan't live any longer with a jealous Philistine!

ELENA (*shouts after him*). I am not jealous! I am not jealous! I am not jealous! (*She sits and weeps.*)

(*Enter* KLARA.)

KLARA. Why are you yelling? Have you a toothache?

ELENA. I'm not living with Nikolai.

KLARA. When did you have time to decide that, my dear girl? Here you've been billing and cooing — and all of a sudden you've taken a trip on a motorcycle, and it's all over. Let me see your eyes — come on, let me see your eyes, little girl. (*Lifts* ELENA'S *face.*) Don't cry so much! Don't cry! Dry your tears! (*Offers her a handkerchief.*) Women are always the first to weep. Are you definitely separated, or is this only a temporary spat?

ELENA. We've separated for good.

KLARA. Did he go away with Valentina?... Beautiful girl!

ELENA. She's a nasty doll! She's a coward!

KLARA. Jealousy is all over your face.

ELENA. I am not jealous!

KLARA. That's the spirit!

ELENA. She has the advantage over me because she is younger.

KLARA. And you are an old lady, I suppose. When I was your age, I twisted life around as if it were a ball in my hands. What if a man did leave you? The world doesn't come to an end with him. Forget him! I'll help you find another fellow. There are thousands of them in our factory. I'll have ten of them come up to see you by Party orders. Choose the one you like best. Or, better yet, come with me today to the opening of the factory restaurant. There will be a celebration there. You won't have any time to think. They'll make you forget your troubles.

(Enter KIMBAYEV.*)*

KIMBAYEV. Here's more work for you — plans for the patronage, Klara... What's the matter, Elena? Why are your eyes red? Are they tired? My eyes hurt very often. There's sand in them. Your husband, Elena, is a smart husband. You, Elena, are a smart wife. I too will be a smart husband. So find me a smart wife, Elena.

KLARA. Marry Elena. She has divorced Nikolai.

KIMBAYEV. Ai, ai, ai! Divorced! Divorced! Nikolai is a big fool to have let you divorce him. I would take my wife to the steppes. I would beat my wife. I wouldn't let her divorce me. O-bai-ai-ai!

ELENA. Nikolai and I had our work in common. We helped each other. We thought the same things — worked for the same goals — ever since we met as undergraduates. But now he no longer needs my help. He is a big official himself.

(Enter NATASHA. *She places a goldfish bowl on the table.)*

NATASHA. Klara, look! Elena, look! An aquarium! Uncle Bobrov made this aquarium for our class at school. He comes often to our club, and in the spring he promised to make us a rabbit hutch. Come, look at it! Klara! Elena! Hussain!

KIMBAYEV. You must have a talk with Bobrov, Elena. Bobrov is a good comrade. He needs your help — and his advice can be of use to you.

ELENA. I don't want to. That little non-partisan saint will make fun of me — will crow over me. 'I told you so,' he'll say. 'I warned you.' No, I prefer to live and fight alone!

KLARA. I'm afraid you're sick. I don't like the way you're be-having. It can't go on like this.

NATASHA. Come, Klara! Come, Elena! Come, Hussain! Look at my little fishes!

ELENA. They are lovely. But you are even lovelier. Why aren't you my own daughter?

NATASHA. Why do you say that?

ELENA. Then we would live together — would never part.

NATASHA. But we *are* living together, and there's no reason why we should part. I love you very much, Elena, but you are always busy.

(TSEKHOVOI *enters the room and crosses it in silence.*)

NATASHA. Papa! Look at my aquarium! Papa!

TSEKHOVOI. Let me alone. (*Exit.*)

NATASHA. What's wrong? It's funny.

ELENA. It *is* funny.

(*A moment of silence.* NATASHA, *preoccupied with the goldfish bowl, is telling of her school experiences as if thinking aloud.*)

NATASHA. Syeryozhka was expelled from our group... His father was a priest, you know, but he said that he was the son of a clerk... The leader said if Syeryozhka has deceived the group, he can deceive the working class, and, after all, Auntie Klara, it's bad to deceive the working class...

KLARA. Must be bad, if your leader says so.

NATASHA. I bet you don't know who is the most important leader. Do you? But I know. The most important leader is — the Party... (*Watching the fish.*) Just look at that fish dive!

ELENA. Oh, Natasha! Klara, I want the little girl with me... Why haven't I a daughter of my own? I would sing songs to her in the evenings, and I would never be tired of doing that.

KLARA. Stop it, Elenka. Always asking why — why? You have still plenty of time ahead of you. Get your things together. We'll go to the opening of the restaurant.

ELENA. You're right, Klara. I must pull myself together. Forgive me. Let's go.

KIMBAYEV. Take me along. I don't want to be away from Elena even for a moment. Elena must not be alone, must not go around alone. I have three street-car tickets for us. Let's go.

(KLARA, ELENA, KIMBAYEV *go out.* NATASHA *is alone.*)

NATASHA. I'm glad. I'm all alone. No one to bother me. I'm going to feed the fish. I'm glad I'm alone! (*Sings.*)

How glad we are, how glad!
We are glad of the golden fish — ish — ish.
How glad we are, how glad!
Glad of the golden fish!

(*Enter* KASTALSKY.)

KASTALSKY. Please call your father.

NATASHA. Won't you sit down? (*Runs out.*)

(KASTALSKY *waits. Enter* TSEKHOVOI *and* NATASHA.)

TSEKHOVOI. Go to bed, Natasha.

NATASHA. I want to play with the fish.

TSEKHOVOI. Go to bed, darling.

NATASHA. Don't let anybody touch my fish. (*Exit.*)

KASTALSKY. I came to ask you, Nikolai Petrovitch, whether you believe in God.

TSEKHOVOI. An absurd question!

KASTALSKY. So you don't. In that case you, of course, don't believe in the Devil, and you don't believe in the kinship of souls.

TSEKHOVOI. Are you mad, or are you trying to pull my leg?

KASTALSKY. But I'm sure that you believe in *class* kinship, Nikolai Petrovitch. You believe in what one might call social homogeneity, or uniformity. Tell me... please answer my question ... I'm speaking quite seriously... Do you believe that it is possible to be class brothers?

TSEKHOVOI. Of course.

KASTALSKY. And brothers by virtue of the same social origin? Because if you do believe that, then we are brothers, Nikolai Petrovitch.

TSEKHOVOI (*increasingly worried*). What nonsense are you talking about?

KASTALSKY. Of course we're not brothers by virtue of having the same father. My father was a senator. Yours was a petty post-office clerk. He took no part in the Revolution, on either side, and the mail was regularly delivered no matter who was in control of the government. It was your privilege to write that in your documents.

TSEKHOVOI. I refuse to discuss the matter with you.

KASTALSKY. In your Party records you have stated that your father was a petty postal clerk. That's all. Rather, that was not all you said. You also stated that your mother was a townswoman and that she died of starvation in Samara in the year '21. So? And in

429

1922 you got a job in a factory. You worked there till 1925, and then you joined the Party. You were assigned to the University, and from there as a graduate student you came to our Institute. So? As you see, I am rather well-informed. (*Slowly, emphatically.*) But all of this is quite beside the point, most respected son of a military prosecutor!

TSEKHOVOI. Talk to the point, the Devil take you!

KASTALSKY. Momus burst with envy because he could find no flaws in Aphrodite. I wanted to follow the example of Momus, and so I decided to read your Party record. But one little flaw saved me from following in the footsteps of Momus. Nikolai Petrovitch, that flaw... Your mother is alive!

TSEKHOVOI. What!

KASTALSKY. This is no time for expressions of astonishment... Now I hope you understand just how you and I are brothers. We come from the same environment. One and the same *milieu* gave birth to us. We differ, however, in the way we carry the burden of our social origin. You, being the older and wiser brother — this is no compliment, it's a fact — you have simply stricken out of the record of your life the military prosecutor and the admiral's daughter, while I — a failure, and my name is Herman — I did not know how to take advantage of such a possibility — I am a fatalist, and I believe if it has been decreed at your birth that you should go through life with one earring, then to the very moment of your death you will not find the other earring. I've already become reconciled to the thought that Elena Mikhailovna will be sent abroad and that I shall remain here indefinitely as merely a graduate student. But you, on the other hand, how will you feel now?

TSEKHOVOI (*jumps up*). I have actually worked in a factory! I have become a proletarian! I have been a member of the Party for over five years. You cannot frighten me with my mother!

KASTALSKY. God bless you! This is not why I have come here. I merely wanted to warn you, as one brother would naturally warn another. Do something about it, Nikolai Petrovitch. Hiding your true social origin when you enter the Party is punishable by expulsion from the Party. Be careful! And forgive the interference of a meddlesome bystander. I will never again bother you with any reference to the subject. You may sleep in peace. (*Exit. The door bangs after him.*)

TSEKHOVOI (*alone; in a panicky frame of mind*). He is lying! He

430

is lying!... And yet — I have worked in a factory for three years, and five years in the Party... Five years in the Party!... Three years as a factory worker!... I'll go to the Control Commission and make a clean breast of it all — tell them just what happened and how it happened — let them pass judgment on me. They will understand. They will forgive me. They might demote me, but that's all right... (*Begins to dress hastily.*) I'll come and make a clean breast of it... Three years in the factory... Five years in the Party... My mother's alive... Nobody can frighten me!... I'll make a clean breast of everything! Three years at a bench in the factory. Five years in the Party! That is the thing! That's what tells the whole story!

(*He goes out. The door bangs shut. The room is empty. Then NA-TASHA sticks her head out of the door of her room and looks around. She has been listening.*)

NATASHA (*cries in fright*). Papa! (*Louder.*) Papa! (*Almost hysterical.*) Papa! Where have you gone? Where are you? You have deceived the working class! You have deceived the leader! My papa... (*Weeps.*)

CURTAIN

ACT III

Scene 5

Conference room. This is represented by a large conference table slanting centrally from the back down toward the footlights, and a row of chairs on one side.

At the conference table are Borodin, Nevsky, Tsekhovoi, Elena, Bobrov, *and the* Taciturn Member of the Præsidium, *who throughout the scene drinks tea and eats sandwiches.*

In the side chairs sit Kastalsky, Kimbayev, *and* Vargasov, *who sits next to the telephone and acts as secretary.*

Nevsky *is the Chairman.*

Nevsky. Comrade Makarova has the floor.

Borodin. We have been at it for three hours. (*Telephone rings.* Vargasov *answers it.*) There's no sense to this.

Vargasov. Nevsky, you're wanted at the telephone.

Nevsky. Go ahead, Makarova. (*Goes to the telephone.*) I'm listening.

Elena. As I was saying, on the surface it seems to be all right. We are in the Laboratory of Human Behavior — investigating, writing reports, filling out questionnaires, measuring blood pressure — six brigades of us — from morning until night, all day long. But then... then all of this material accumulated by us... the professor takes with him into his private study, where he locks himself in and works on it all by himself. We scientific workers are in the position of slaves who deliver the raw material to some mysterious factory ... (*She bangs the table.*) But we want to know now what is being manufactured in that factory — whether it's boots or wax candles, or poison gas...

Kastalsky. Whom do you mean by 'we'?

Elena. Party members... and members of scientific brigades...

Kastalsky. I, too, am a worker in such a brigade. I protest against your attack as unrepresentative. I declare categorically that as far as my brigade...

Elena. I'm speaking in the name of a conference of the brigadiers of the laboratory. Nevsky, are you the Chairman?

NEVSKY (*at the telephone*). Wait a minute... wait a minute! This is about the budget... (*Hangs up the receiver.*) Any questions? (*Returns to his seat at the table.*)

ELENA. I haven't finished yet, Nevsky. I insist that the professor must open his study and tell all of us just how he's handling the material furnished by the laboratory.

BORODIN. Do you expect me to give everybody a piece of it — to divide it up? I have been accumulating ideas on this subject for twenty years! Now you want to fritter it all away — steal it! What will you do with it when you have it? Put it back into circulation? I won't stand for it! You cannot dispossess us as you did the kulaks; you cannot expropriate us. (*Strikes his forehead.*) All my wealth is here!

KIMBAYEV. The Institute doesn't belong to Borodin. The Institute belongs to the State.

BORODIN. Everything that I have ever done belongs to the State. But bear in mind that all this that belongs to the State was made by me. Bear that in mind, young man with prominent cheekbones!

KIMBAYEV. The cheekbones are mine, and the blood is mine. It's the blood of a poor peasant, Professor Borodin!

KASTALSKY. I'm sure the State will be satisfied with our work.

BOBROV. That remains to be seen.

KASTALSKY. But anybody can see already that the State is not satisfied with Professor Bobrov — (*ironically*) — the responsible member of the Præsidium — minister without portfolio!...

ELENA. We demand that the Præsidium of the Institute...

BORODIN. I won't let you 'demand'! (*He snatches the Chairman's bell from* NEVSKY'S *hand and dashes it to the floor.*) — First learn where to place your commas, and then we'll let you make demands. Go ahead, copy the materials... use them any way you like... Discover your own laws of nature — with the Bobrovs and the rest of them — and then we'll see whose conclusions are better. But don't go into other people's pockets, or I'll tell the policeman on the corner — the militiaman...

(NEVSKY *patiently picks up the Chairman's bell from the floor.*)

BOBROV. I've already made my conclusions.

KASTALSKY. Then sit at home with them.

KIMBAYEV. No one gave you the floor. Shut up!

ELENA (*screams*). Nevsky! Conduct the session, the Devil take you!

433

BORODIN. You might at least refrain from swearing in an executive session of the Institute.

NEVSKY (*rings the bell frantically*). Comrades! I call you to order! Try to get along with one another. (*The telephone rings again.*) Proceed with the order of the day...

VARGASOV. Nevsky, you're wanted at the telephone.

NEVSKY (*goes to the telephone*). Go ahead, comrades, I'll be with you in a minute.

BORODIN (*to* BOBROV). Tell us your conclusions, Professor Bobrov.

BOBROV. I have kept quiet for a long time. If anything, I have been altogether too patient. I've kept my peace too long. The prestige of Ivan Ilyitch, my personal relations with him, family ethics, family loyalty... It is not easy for me to raise my hand against Professor Borodin... But Ivan Ilyitch is committing a grave scientific error. He is intent on explaining the behavior of people by the simplest animal stimuli. This error is the result of his political views. It is against this that I must take my stand.

KASTALSKY. Go on, you disciple of a sabotager!

KIMBAYEV. What did you say? Repeat what you said!

BOBROV (*to* KASTALSKY). Have you read my letter about Kotomin?

TSEKHOVOI. That's a belated confession.

ELENA. We are discussing the laboratory, and any reference to Kotomin is beside the point — quite irrelevant. We protest against Borodin's attitude. You are concerned with the behavior of man in general, irrespective of his class connections. You are interested only in classless eternal stimuli. From that point of view the Revolution may appear to be the result of rage, Socialist competition may be explained by sexual activity, and shock-brigading as the result of hunger. But this is to us a theory utterly foreign and politically harmful.

BORODIN. You cannot possibly know what conclusions will be reached — because I don't know them yet myself...

BOBROV. The conclusions have been suggested by Kastalsky. He wants to discredit the present system of governing people.

KASTALSKY. Shut up, you scoundrel! The nerve of him, libelling me so shamelessly! A jealous husband — a camouflaged sabotager! And so he takes his revenge against a defenceless graduate student...

ELENA. Shut up, you diamond earring!

KASTALSKY. Chairman! I want you to arrest Bobrov on the

charge of criminal libel! I insist that it be entered in the minutes. He's persecuting me, and I demand...

KIMBAYEV. And I demand, I demand... He called Bobrov a sabotager!... I'll take Kastalsky direct to the prosecutor...

BORODIN. I want to help the Government. I want people to learn to behave better. But you won't let me. You're interfering with me.

KASTALSKY. Bobrov and Makarova envy you.

BORODIN. Yes, of course they envy me! They figure this way: the professor is altogether too smart for us... let's get him rattled! That is why I am being kept at these endless sessions... losing a lot of time and energy in shouting... and the end is accomplished: instead of thoughts, I have confusion in my head. You call me your enemy. And yet, all of you ask to be in the enemy's department. Why do you? Tell me! Why?

KASTALSKY. In order to expose you, Professor.

ELENA. Of course! If our suppositions are justified, we *will* expose you.

(*There is a silence — broken only by* NEVSKY's *voice at the telephone.*)

NEVSKY. Put a lot of pressure on Guylees. I've talked to him about it... The roof in the rabbit hutch is leaking.

(BORODIN *runs up to* NEVSKY, *snatches the telephone receiver, pulls it out of the socket, and throws it on the floor.*)

BORODIN. To hell with the rabbit hutch! And to hell with Guylees! Here is my final word: the Institute will have to choose between Makarova and me. Make your choice.

KIMBAYEV (*jumps up on his chair*). No threats, no threats! We put people like you against the wall in 1920!

BORODIN. Scoundrels! (BORODIN *goes out, banging the door.* VARGASOV *runs after him.*)

NEVSKY. Comrade Kimbayev, I ask you to leave the session immediately.

KIMBAYEV. I have a question about the matter of patronage. Is the plan ready?

NEVSKY. We're not interested in your patronage idea. It's all nonsense. Leave the session immediately, find Borodin, and at once apologize to him.

KIMBAYEV. You go on, apologize yourself. Elena is a fine fellow. Bobrov is a fine fellow. They talk sense, but you have no faith.

NEVSKY (*shouts*). I'll throw you out of here!

(KIMBAYEV *swears in Kazak fashion and leaves the room.*)

BOBROV. I declare again: the laboratory was organized for a political purpose foreign to us.

KASTALSKY. *You* may insist on that purpose, but not the Soviet Government.

BOBROV. The Soviet Government does not need to be defended by the Kastalskys.

KASTALSKY. And even less does it need the support of the Bobrovs!

ELENA. The laboratory must be reorganized. We will compel Borodin to lay his cards on the table.

NEVSKY. After all the money we have spent, you want to reorganize! I won't let you do it! They'll fry me alive at the Workers' and Peasants' Inspection. I won't let you!

TSEKHOVOI. Declare a recess. We'll have a session of the Party fraction.

NEVSKY (*relieved*). Right! I declare a recess.

(NEVSKY, TSEKHOVOI, *and* ELENA *are going out together.* TSEKHOVOI *speaks to* NEVSKY.)

TSEKHOVOI. Makarova and Bobrov — what an unprincipled combination! (*Exeunt.*)

TACITURN MEMBER (*rises*). The tea is gone. The sandwiches are gone. Now I can go home. Should the voting begin... I vote 'Yes.' (*Exit.*)

(KASTALSKY *and* BOBROV *pace up and down.*)

(*Enter* VALENTINA.)

VALENTINA. I have a ticket to *Lohengrin* for Nikolai Petrovitch. Will you give it to him, please, and tell him that I've already started?

BOBROV (*in anger*). Give it to him yourself.

VALENTINA. So you're still angry. Suit yourself. Herman Vitoldovitch, will you give it to him?

KASTALSKY. With pleasure.

BOBROV (*loses his self-control, lifts a chair to strike* KASTALSKY *and screams*). Get away from here! I'll knock your head off!

KASTALSKY. Well, well... (*Saunters toward the door.*) Well.

(*Exit.*)

VALENTINA. My husband expresses his jealousy with a chair!

436

Ha-ha-ha! (*Ironically.*) You — the terrible Moor, Nikolai Kasyanovitch!

BOBROV. Valentina Ivanovna!

VALENTINA. Yes, my patronymic *is* Ivanovna, and your patronymic is Kasyanovitch. Kasyan occurs four times during the year. With such a patronymic, you should not be jealous. If you had been a Spaniard... Ventura García Calderón... then I could forgive you even the chair.

BOBROV. Keep still, you silly woman! You're not even on my mind right now.

VALENTINA. That's very amusing — the fact that I'm not even on your mind. (*Laughs.*) Even your jealousy is petty. There is such a thing as beautiful jealousy, and it is like beautiful food. At the factory I visit, we fight to have our food beautifully served. A clean dining-room increases productivity. That's a fact. But you — you express your jealousy with a chair!

(*Enter* KASTALSKY, BORODIN, *and* VARGASOV.)

BORODIN. Listen, Valentina! Your husband has become a timeserver. He's burying your father alive. Before long he will become a people's commissar — and he won't even shake hands with me when he meets me. That being the case, I rather think I should refuse to shake hands with him *now*.

VALENTINA. I am not concerned with strangers.

BORODIN. Is he then a stranger to you now?

BOBROV. Professor Borodin, my aloneness is coming to an end. Yours will soon begin — and you will find it terrifying...

(*Enter* TSEKHOVOI, NEVSKY, ELENA. VALENTINA *goes aside, unobserved by the others.* KIMBAYEV *appears in the doorway.*)

NEVSKY. Please take your places. The fraction of the Præsidium has considered the situation, comrades. We have decided on several recommendations. Let me read them to you:

'One: Because of her lack of faith in the work of the laboratory on the basis of an unprincipled bloc with reactionary elements in the Institute, Comrade Makarova is to be relieved of the office of Manager of the Laboratory.

'Two: The chairman of the department, Comrade Tsekhovoi, is

to take over concurrently the direction of the laboratory and proceed to establish shock-brigade tempos of work and the competition of brigades.

'Three: In view of the fact that the management is besieged by requests for qualified workers, and because there is a sharp need for scientific workers who are also members of the Party in the provinces, Comrade Makarova is to be sent to Saratov University in the capacity of an instructor.

'Four: In connection with this decision the assignment to go abroad is to be transferred to Kastalsky, and this matter is to be taken up by the proper authorities...'

The report also contains Makarova's dissenting views.

BORODIN. Excellent! My respects, Nikolai Petrovitch! Boris Naumovitch, I thank you! Now we'll show them. My respects!

KIMBAYEV (*distressed*). What are they doing? What are they doing? O-bai-ai! I have a headache!

NEVSKY. Any questions? I'm taking a vote. Who is in favor of the first proposition? (*Five arms go up.*) Who is in favor of the second proposition? (*Five arms go up.*) Who is in favor of the third? (*Five arms go up.*) Who is in favor of the fourth? (*Four arms go up.* BOBROV *is not voting.*) The session is closed.

(*All present rise and proceed to go out.* KASTALSKY *approaches* TSEKHOVOI.)

KASTALSKY. Thank you, brother.

TSEKHOVOI. Let me alone.

KASTALSKY. Valentina Ivanovna is waiting for you.

BORODIN (*to* ELENA). Good-bye, Elena Mikhailovna. Write to me from Saratov.

(VALENTINA *goes out with* TSEKHOVOI. *They are followed by others until only* ELENA, BOBROV, *and* KIMBAYEV *remain. There is a pause.*)

ELENA. They've licked us to a frazzle. (*Walks up to* BOBROV *and presses his hand.*) Well, you 'reactionary element,' either they will throw me out of the Party — or you and I together will expose Borodin.

KIMBAYEV (*in the fervently banal monosyllables characteristic of him*). You must not leave the Party! You must join the Party. Go to it! Have the Party step in. If the Fraction fails, appeal to the Regional Committee. If the Regional Committee fails, go to the

District. If the District fails, go to the Central Committee. I would go to Stalin himself.

ELENA. We have no time to lose. We will attack Borodin from new positions. We will raise the issue in the press. We will carry the fight outside the walls of the Institute. I am going away. We must discuss a number of things before my departure. Let's go.

BOBROV. At any rate, I'm glad that my aloneness has come to an end.

KIMBAYEV. It has come to an end, Comrade Bobrov. You will go with us. Don't look back! There's no way out in back of you.

(BOBROV, KIMBAYEV, *and* ELENA *go out. The stage is empty for a little while. Then* VARGASOV *enters, followed by* KASTALSKY.)

KASTALSKY. You helped me defeat Bobrov. You helped me work in the laboratory. You discovered Tsekhovoi's secret and told me about it. I am at a loss to understand your solicitude on behalf of a lonely intellectual, hurt by life.

VARGASOV. I'll get you some *valuta* money for the trip. You may also depend on me for your visas and your passport.

KASTALSKY. You are a sincere and altruistic friend of the intellectuals.

VARGASOV. I, too, was an intellectual... I used to write for scientific journals... articles... about racing-horses... I had some very fine racing-horses. Now it is only a dream! I used to take them to the Tsar...

KASTALSKY. I don't know how I can ever repay your kindness.

VARGASOV. There is a way... there is a way... (*Whispers.*) I have a message for you to take abroad.

KASTALSKY (*frightened*). No, no, no! I will not join any organizations!

VARGASOV. Don't get up on your hind legs, Herman Vitoldovitch. You live, at best, indifferently. You work alone. But we included you in our little plan long ago.

KASTALSKY. What little plan?

VARGASOV. We, too, must have our successors. The question of qualified successors is a crucial one. And so we observe the dissatisfied fellows who like to talk... and so, in a word, come over in the evening... We'll have lots of time to discuss the matter in detail.

KASTALSKY. This is very dangerous. I only want to live...

VARGASOV. But I have no intention to die myself. So far everything has gone well. With God's help we won't have any trouble in the future. (*Bows in farewell.*) And so this is the end of *your* aloneness, Kastalsky...

CURTAIN

ACT III

Scene 6

BORODIN'S *living-room.* BORODIN *is pacing in great excitement, newspaper in hand, reading to* KASTALSKY.

BORODIN. 'They crawl into scientific work like rats into Hatto's tower — in armies of hundreds of thousands...' My daughter's former husband is taking advantage of the confidence placed in him! Professor Bobrov has reported a family conversation to the newspapers, so as to prevent your going abroad. (*Brandishes the paper.*) People decompose before our very eyes! Their corpses pollute the air!

KASTALSKY. A newspaper reporter has already called at the office of the Institute. He waited for Vargasov, but Vargasov has been gone since morning.

BORODIN. You can't trust anyone. Even friends betray. (*Shakes the paper.*) Kotomin is on trial. He was a member of a party of sabotagers. Such a fine man — but even he proved to be a traitor!

KASTALSKY. The world is waiting for the final accusing words of Science.

BORODIN. I work day and night in order to finish sooner. In three months I shall publish my conclusions.

KASTALSKY. No Soviet journal will print your work.

BORODIN. I'll send it to London.

KASTALSKY. They will confiscate your manuscript at the border.

BORODIN. Then I'll go out on the public square and shout!

KASTALSKY. In the public square you will split your throat.

BORODIN. Then I'll shout in a building. (*Strikes his forehead.*) I'll make a report — the Devil take it! — A report about the stimuli of contemporary behavior. We will have stenographers and foreign correspondents there. It's a brilliant idea, Herman! The only trouble is that I may be arrested. What?

KASTALSKY. Friends abroad will publish protests against the persecution of scientific thought — and then they will not dare to touch you! The protests will be signed by the foremost representatives of science and culture. They will raise you like a banner, my teacher!

BORODIN. I have very few friends — and there's no one who could write a protest.

KASTALSKY. But it is already written. Tst! (*He runs to the door, then to the other door, listens at them and comes back.*) Look! (*Takes out a manuscript and unfolds it.*) 'To all cultured people': Read it! (BORODIN *reads.*) The Russian names will be kept secret.

BORODIN. 'Professor Borodin is in prison.' — But I am still at liberty.

KASTALSKY. This document will be printed after your lecture.

BORODIN. Do you mean to say that I will be arrested — after all?

KASTALSKY. We will liberate you. Read on!

BORODIN. H'm, h'm. 'They will not let science take a breath.' But our Institute first began to live with the Revolution...

KASTALSKY. Read on!

(VARGASOV *runs in.* KASTALSKY *quickly snatches the paper.*)

VARGASOV. Ugh! (*Sits down.*) Bad!

KASTALSKY. What is bad? What's wrong?

VARGASOV. You're bad at hiding the document. It's very noticeable.

BORODIN. Running around in circles, Semyon Semyonovitch?

VARGASOV. It's a lot of trouble. However, we have the passport. You'll get it tomorrow at twelve. The visa will follow. And here is the *valuta.* (*Takes out money.*)

KASTALSKY. Bravo, Semyon Semyonovitch, bravo!

BORODIN. Tell us — tell us how you managed it.

VARGASOV. Later, Ivan Ilyitch. I've no time now. It's high time for Herman Vitoldovitch to go away. So long as there's even a mere notice in the paper, the victory is only half won. But as soon as that notice goes from the newspaper to... other places, it will be too bad. Bobrov has certainly done a thorough job of it. Yes, indeed. Here — read this. A friend has brought us proofs — an article by Makarova — straight against Ivan Ilyitch... (*Offers the proofs.*)

KASTALSKY (*takes the proofs*). 'Caste Exclusiveness as the Manœuvre of the Class Enemy.' That's not a title — that's a drum.

BORODIN. Let me see it! (*Snatches the proofs.*) They have decided to stone the old man — as a parting shot.

442

VARGASOV. The magazine will be issued late. It will appear a month after it should appear.

KASTALSKY. That means that a month from now Borodin will not be permitted to deliver any lecture.

VARGASOV. I've had a telephone call from an acquaintance — a man I know. At the conference of the graduate students Kimbayev will deliver a derogatory lecture about Ivan Ilyitch.

KASTALSKY. Your days are numbered. You are being attacked on all sides.

BORODIN (*throws the proofs to the floor*). They have made a class enemy out of me! Thank you very much! Look at me, brothers! A living example of a class enemy! (*Enter* BOBROV *and* KIMBAYEV. BORODIN *blocks* BOBROV's *path*.) Ah-ha! Professor Bobrov! I am silent. One must not talk aloud in your presence — or you will have it all reported in the newspapers.

BOBROV. Speak aloud — but learn to assume responsibility for what you say.

BORODIN. Even before intimates — even in the presence of intimate friends?

BOBROV. Even in the presence of yourself...

BORODIN. When will you move out of my home?

BOBROV. Not before I find a room elsewhere.

KASTALSKY (*to* BOBROV). You are not only persecuting me, you have sicked this Kirghiz at Borodin. Why did you ever accept a professorship in biology? You should give instead a course in spying and shadowing.

KIMBAYEV. You lie, you traitor! Bobrov is one of us — a real teacher. He teaches us to look far. My eyes have become different eyes. I look with them now — I see little balls and blood — I see planets in the sky — I see other lands — I see my own land. The land is growing. My Kazakstan is growing. Once there was a steppe, and in the steppe a salt-marsh. But now in the same steppe there is copper. In the same steppe — the Turksib, the Turkestan–Siberian Railroad. Cities grow — and in the cities are books and teachers. Kazakstan has gone to school. At one time I knew only two hundred words — now I cannot count the number of words I can say. I'll go to Kazakstan, I'll go into the steppe, and I will cry out in the steppe about the books I have read — about the world I have discovered. There was a shepherd — and on his shoulders he had a noodle. But now the noodle is gone — and in its place is a

443

head! And not only *one* head on his shoulders, but a hundred heads! (*Runs up to the books, seizes one of them.*) *This* head is sitting inside of *my* head. (*Takes up another book.*) And this head is also sitting inside of *my* head. All of these heads! But you — you throw sand into the eyes. You make my head hazy... foggy... You should be shot, you sabotager! (KIMBAYEV *flings himself at* KASTALSKY. BOBROV *holds him back.*)

BOBROV. Quiet, Kimbayev! Calm yourself!

KIMBAYEV. He's a sabotager — and he's going abroad! Shoot him, Comrade Bobrov! (BOBROV *leads* KIMBAYEV *away.*)

KASTALSKY. Madmen — refuting the theories of their masters.

BORODIN. Excellent! This clouded brain is a new link in the chain of my observations. Excellent! Last week I drove a rabbit to madness... Yes, I did. A mad rabbit — and a mad vydveezhenyets! And at the basis of the madness is the very same stimulus! Amazing!

(*Enter* TSEKHOVOI, NATASHA, *and* VALENTINA.)

VARGASOV. It is high time for me to run along. Herman Vitoldovitch, take good care of the document! Keep it like the apple of your eye.

VALENTINA. Papa, meet my new husband!

BORODIN. What! Now I am really beginning to lose my own mind...

VALENTINA. I will move over to his apartment... Natasha, this is your new grandfather.

NATASHA. I have no grandfather. (*She nestles in a corner of the settee.*)

VALENTINA. Won't you say hello to my husband, Papa? His name is also Nikolai. You won't have to get used to a new name. (BORODIN *is silent.*)

KASTALSKY. Congratulations to the newlyweds!... Valentina Ivanovna! (*Kisses her hand.*) My dream! My lost dream! Nikolai Petrovitch! (*He offers his hand;* TSEKHOVOI *hesitates.*) Permit me to congratulate you, Nikolai Petrovitch! (TSEKHOVOI *finally shakes hands.*) Let me sing you a song by Maurice Chevalier. Listen!

(KASTALSKY, *at the piano, sings a song in French. The others listen. When he finishes,* VALENTINA *speaks.*)

VALENTINA. I must get my laundry together... (*Exit.*)

BORODIN (*goes to* TSEKHOVOI). Well, my dear son-in-law, I might

444

as well say hello to you. Your predecessor, Nikolai Bobrov, has declared war against me. I expect that as a kinsman you will have to come to my defence.

TSEKHOVOI. We will expel Bobrov from the Institute.

KASTALSKY. And Valentina's predecessor is not far behind. Look around — the class enemy is everywhere.

TSEKHOVOI. We will expel Makarova from the Party.

KASTALSKY. The epileptic Kimbayev is getting ready to attack the professor in a lecture.

TSEKHOVOI. We will send Kimbayev to an insane asylum. Down with sentimentalism! Down with this slobbering! We will sweep the demagogues and the brawlers away with an iron broom. The country needs Borodin's work. You may work in peace, Ivan Ilyitch!

KASTALSKY. Soon, very soon, my teacher will deliver a public lecture about the results of his investigation.

TSEKHOVOI. That will be the best answer to all the panic-mongers. I dare say, Professor, that we are on the threshold of a tremendous revolution in the science of human behavior — and I am proud that to this revolution I, too, have contributed my widow's mite.

BORODIN. You are an interesting person, Nikolai! Who could have ever thought that you, Nikolai Tsekhovoi, son... pardon me, husband of my daughter... Thank you from the bottom of my heart for your compliment.

(*Enter* VALENTINA.)

VALENTINA. Well, have you had a nice talk?

TSEKHOVOI. We have talked of everything.

KASTALSKY. I think I had better run away from this family reunion... Good-bye!

BORODIN. Herman! (*Takes him aside.*) I know that you are defending me and that you wrote this document. It's very noble of you, but I'd rather you wouldn't. I don't like the idea. There's no reason why we should drag London into our affairs. I don't like it.

KASTALSKY. It is too late now to retreat to Moscow. He who hesitates is lost. (*Exit.*)

BORODIN (*after seeing* KASTALSKY *to the door*). I wish you would tell me how this miracle has occurred, my dear friends. I don't understand it.

445

VALENTINA. Poor old fellow! You're getting too old to understand anything. But I assure you that it has all occurred in agreement with natural laws. I work in a factory. Inside of me a new human being is growing. I am becoming a new person — and we new people are no longer concerned with the shape of the nose or the curve of the hip. We are interested rather in social content. And so, I have fallen in love with a regular proletarian who has come to science directly from a worker's bench.

BORODIN. H'm, h'm! So! (*To* NATASHA.) Well, my serious little Pioneer, now you cannot write any more notices against your *grandfather*... I am a kinsman of yours.

VALENTINA. Don't frown, Natasha! I shall be your new mamma.

NATASHA. Live and learn...

VALENTINA. I wish you would smile at least once — or play with the dolls. They are yours now.

NATASHA. I don't want to.

VALENTINA. Why are you angry with me?

TSEKHOVOI. Let her alone. She is a capricious, mean, little girl — just like her mother.

NATASHA. I'm glad I'm not like you, you double-dealer!

TSEKHOVOI (*shouts*). Shut up, you trash!

VALENTINA. Nikolai! You can't say such things to a child.

(*Enter* BOBROV *and* KIMBAYEV. BOBROV *is seeing* KIMBAYEV *out to the door.*)

KIMBAYEV. Forgive me, dear comrade. I'm sorry I made all that noise. Very bad, ai, very bad. I'm ashamed of myself. Do you think I should apologize to Borodin? Tell me.

BOBROV. Don't worry. Go home. This can happen with anyone. (*Exeunt* BOBROV *and* KIMBAYEV.)

VALENTINA. I never want to see him again. Let's go.

(*All except* NATASHA *proceed toward the door.*)

BORODIN. You have a brilliant future ahead of you, Nikolai Petrovitch. Mark my words: Borodin is never mistaken about people.

(VALENTINA, TSEKHOVOI, *and* BORODIN *go out.* NATASHA *remains alone.*)

NATASHA. Why do I want to cry?... Pioneers don't cry... Pioneers are always happy. (*She weeps, hiding her face in the pillow on the settee.*)

(*Enter* BOBROV.)

BOBROV. Natasha! My dear little girl! You're all alone! (*Takes her hand.*)

NATASHA. I can't stand it any more! I wanted to tell Auntie Klara, but I'm sorry for my papa, and so I say nothing — nothing. I'm silent. But my heart is heavy with silence.

BOBROV. Has your father hurt you?

NATASHA. He hasn't hurt me, but he has deceived everybody. Ai, Uncle Kolya, why do I want to cry so much? I will tell you everything about Papa's mother. All right? You and I are friends, aren't we?

BOBROV. Of course you can tell me everything. I am your friend — and I'll understand.

(*Enter* AMALIA.)

AMALIA. Valentinotchka! Natasha, my little one!... Want some candy?

NATASHA. Uncle Kolya, let's go!

BOBROV. All right, let's go. (*He picks her up in his arms and carries her out.*)

AMALIA. That isn't the kind of daughter I wish Nikolai would have... (*Calls.*) Valentina, my child, the laundry is ready... Where are you?

(*She goes to the door. The door opens, and* TSEKHOVOI *comes out. * AMALIA *takes a step back, in fear and amazement, and in a voice scarcely audible she falters his name.*)

AMALIA. Nikolai!

TSEKHOVOI. You! (*Closes the door.*) How did you manage to remain alive? I was certain that you...

AMALIA. It was a miracle, Nikolai, a miracle... God, how handsome you are!

TSEKHOVOI. Let me alone! The time will come when I will acknowledge you as my mother, but in the meanwhile you must forget your son.

AMALIA. But the time *will* come, Nikolai?

TSEKHOVOI. Yes — after we finish this work in the laboratory. After the professor's lecture, everyone will see that I alone made it possible for Borodin to do his work in peace. I am sure I'll take the place of Nevsky as Managing Director of the Institute. He has nothing in his head except the budget. He doesn't realize what im-

447

portant problems confront the scientific worker. Surrounded by general confidence and fame, I shall then come before the Control Commission, I shall take my stand before its red table, and I shall say: 'Here I am. I am guilty. I have deceived the Party. Pass your judgment against me — with all the severity of Party laws.' And when they discover the nature of my crime, they will smile and say: 'Go thou, and work, and sin no more.' I will return to the Institute as a director, and to my mother as her son.

AMALIA. Och! You speak as beautifully as your late father.

(*Enter* BORODIN. *There is a pause.*)

BORODIN. Don't let me disturb you. Go on and talk. I'm no stranger.

TSEKHOVOI. Do you... know... anything?

BORODIN. Everything.

TSEKHOVOI (*to* AMALIA). Ah! An old woman's tongue must wag.

BORODIN. Tell me, my dear son-in-law, frankly, are you afraid? You are a warrior in a cuirasse, but under the cuirasse your heart writhes in pain, because you are afraid. Am I right?

TSEKHOVOI. Nonsense! Do you hear me? That's all nonsense!

BORODIN. You are a man of our kind. You are no vydveezhen-yets. You can become a great political figure. It is in your blood.

(*Enter* VALENTINA.)

AMALIA. Valentinotchka, my dear child, I've been looking for you.

VALENTINA. We must be going now.

BORODIN. Well, Valyushka, try to be happy.

VALENTINA. I'll try, Papa.

TSEKHOVOI. Good-bye, Ivan Ilyitch, remember my words — nonsense!

(*Exeunt* VALENTINA *and* TSEKHOVOI.)

AMALIA. Why did you have to worry him?

BORODIN. It is not nonsense, Nikolai Petrovitch! It is the truth. The simon-pure truth. You are afraid. You will go far, but you, too, are afraid. My little chain is coming together. Ivan Borodin will deliver his lecture, not three months from now, but in three weeks. Yes, yes! 'The years ahead of us are buried in the mist, but I see my lot inscribed on a clear forehead...' I see the lot of all men; the fate of the entire country do I see... I will tell everything

— everything... This madness will come to an end. People will understand — and they will listen. It is a pity that Valya has gone away. She has fallen in love and has gone away. Children do not bring back youth to their fathers. Old age is always lonely. Amalia Karlovna, I try to be strong. I work like a beaver, but my back is already bending under the burden of my experiences. I am drawing closer to the fireside. It is difficult to rise in the morning.

(*Enter* ZAKHAROV.)

ZAKHAROV. Youth has activity. Old age has wisdom.

BORODIN. But when you realize in your old age that you have lived badly, foolishly, no amount of wisdom will save you, Visarion Zakharovitch... Here we are — three old people. Which one of us has lived right? Which one?

AMALIA. Do you remember?... Tatiana's Day... the lights in the Hall of Columns... and on the stage a young student, not very tall, a handsome young student...

BORODIN. 'How good, how fresh were the roses!' (*Strikes the keys of the piano.*) I will deliver that lecture, in spite of all! (*He continues to play the piano as the curtain falls.*)

CURTAIN

ACT III

Scene 7

Lecture Room of the Institute. At the rostrum stands Borodin. *At the table behind him sit* Nevsky, Tsekhovoi, *and the* Taciturn Member of the Præsidium. Borodin *faces the footlights, addressing the audience in the theatre.*

Borodin. I'm coming now to the end of my lecture. You have seen in the case of the rabbits that at the basis of their behavior are the stimuli that rouse them. Whenever we succeed in discovering a certain stimulus, we are able to alter behavior by influencing that particular stimulus. Analogously, we are able to discover the ruling stimulus of a social environment and thus forecast the path of development of social behavior. The time is coming when this science will take the place of politics. We have decided to bring as much good as we can to our country and to analyze what stimuli lie at the base of the behavior of contemporary man. Together with comrades who are members of the Communist Party — and among them I want to note especially the energetic co-operation of Nikolai Petrovitch Tsekhovoi — we have managed to make a survey — an objective survey — of several hundred individuals of various social strata... I will not touch upon the methods and the results of this investigation. Those who are interested may study the material at their leisure. I should like to point out, however, that the common stimulus of the behavior of eighty per cent of all those investigated was — fear.

Voice in Audience. What?

Borodin. Fear!

(From this point on to the very end of the lecture, a constant stream of notes from all parts of the lecture room is being relayed to the chairman.)

The work of Thorndike, Watson, Lashley, and others leads us to the conclusion that the unconditioned stimulus which calls forth fear is either — a loud noise or loss of support. Eighty per cent of those who have been studied live under the constant fear of an outcry, or the fear of losing social security. The milk-woman is afraid that her cow will be confiscated; the peasant is afraid of compulsory collectivization; the Soviet worker is afraid of the endless purgings; the Party worker is afraid that he will be accused of deviations; the scientific worker is afraid that he will be accused of idealism; the technical worker is afraid that he will be accused of sabotage. We live in an epoch of great fear. Fear compels talented intellectuals to renounce their mothers, to fake their social origin, to wangle their way into high positions. Yes, yes. In high places the fear of exposure is not so great. But fear stalks everyone. Man becomes suspicious — shut in — dishonest — careless — and unprincipled. Fear gives rise to absences from work, to the lateness of trains, to breakdowns in industry, to general poverty and hunger. No one attempts anything without an outcry, without having his name inscribed on a blackboard, without the threat of arrest or exile. The rabbit who has seen a boa constrictor is unable to move from the spot. His muscles petrify. He waits, submissively, until the rings of the boa constrictor squeeze him and crush him. All of us are rabbits... In view of this, can we work creatively? Of course not! The other twenty per cent of those who are investigated are the vydveezhentsy. They have nothing to fear. They are the masters of the country. They walk into institutions and into science with a proud face, clattering their boots, laughing lustily, talking sonorously. But their *brain* is afraid for them. The brain of people accustomed to physical labor is afraid to carry too great a burden, and there develops a persecution mania. They are always striving to catch up and to outstrip everyone; and, choking in this endless race, this brain either goes insane or slowly degenerates. Destroy fear — destroy everything that occasions fear — and you will see with what a rich creative life our country will blossom forth! With your permission, I shall stop here. (*He walks back from the rostrum.*)

Tsekhovoi. That's cutting the throat without a knife! (*Wipes the perspiration off his forehead.*)

Nevsky (*walks up to the rostrum*). More than a hundred comrades have expressed the desire to comment on Professor Borodin's lecture. Please don't submit any more notes. The first one to have the floor is Comrade Spasova from the factory Red Rolling Mill. She will be followed by Professor Bobrov. (*Sits down.*)

Klara (*rises*). I represent the factory which wanted to assume patronage over the Institute. But the Institute was too busy to be concerned with such unimportant things as patronage.

451

NEVSKY. We are discussing a scientific lecture. The question of patronage is beside the point.

KLARA. If our factory had patronized the Institute, we wouldn't have permitted such 'scientific lectures.'

A VOICE. Correct!

KLARA. We live in the epoch of great fear. You and I, Professor, are old enough to know that fear has lived on earth for many hundreds and thousands of years. Ever since the earth has known a world of slavery and oppression, fear has existed as a mighty weapon for the suppression of man by man. To frighten, to paralyze the will, to break the opposition of those who are oppressed, to transform people into obedient rabbits — this is what the boa constrictors of all times and all peoples have striven for. To frighten! That is why melted lead was poured down the throat of Bolotin; that is why the Stenka Rahzins were broken on the wheel; that is why Pugatchov's head was cut off; that is why entire villages of rebellious serfs were whipped; and that is why the vanguards of the working-class district of Moscow were executed, and that is why the bellies of the partisans of Siberia were slit. The priests threatened us with heavenly punishment for resisting the Tsarist Government; the professors told us from their rostrums that man conditioned to physical labor had no talent for science and for government. They tried to frighten us. But the oppressed are not rabbits, Professor Borodin. They fought in the detachment of Spartacus; they shouted about freedom from the pyres of the Inquisition. They spat in the faces of their executioners. They called to the good fight from the platform of the scaffold. They were driven to hard labor in Srednekolymsk, walking on foot for thousands of miles. Do you happen to know, Professor, how long it took to walk to Srednekolymsk? Eight years! To Yakutsk it took two and a half years. That's not the same as the case of your milk-women. They were driven to hard labor — imprisoned — but they ran away from there in order to continue the struggle.

It was thus that fear gave birth to fearlessness! The fearlessness of the oppressed who have nothing to lose, the fearlessness of proletarians — of revolutionists — of Bolsheviks. And is it us you want to frighten with the lateness of trains? You can't get away with it, Professor! You can't get away with it! You say that in high places the danger of being exposed is not so terrifying. But do you know how many people in high places our Party *has* exposed? Today a man is great; tomorrow he is nothing — nobody — if he betrays the trust of the working class which has advanced him to the high place. You, too, are a great man, Professor, and you, too, will be exposed pitilessly, because you are defending — not the Soviet worker, but the bureaucrat; not the Party member, but the fellow who has wormed his way into the Party; not the technical worker, but the sabotager; not the peasant, but the kulak. This fear stalks behind the man — yes, it stalks behind those who deceive us, who wait for the return of the old order. It stalks behind you, contemptible and petty little people, behind *you* stalks the fear of the proletarian dictatorship. But when the ragged and hungry Red Army men in torn footwear and rags were taking Perekop, what fear was stalking behind *their* backs? What fear, I ask you? Know then, Professor, be guided by it in the future: we are fearless in the class struggle — and merciless with the class enemy. (*Pause.*) In 1917 they hanged my son. Twenty years later in the Museum of the Revolution I found the bill of the executioner. Since then whenever my old bones ache, I read that bill and draw fresh strength from it. Here it is: 'The ring — three ten kopeck pieces; the rope — half a ruble; the sack over his head — a ruble.' They put a sack over his head so as not to see his face. They were afraid of the face of the hanged man. They were afraid to read therein their own verdict! They would like to throw a sack over the head of all of us. They would gladly pay for that rope — not half a ruble, but a million! But they cannot compel us to forge rings of death — in order to throw us into such seas of blood and fear the like of which the world has never seen before. We will not cover your heads with sacks, gentlemen capitalists, when the hour of our last meeting comes. (*Pause.*) When we break the resistance of the last oppressor on earth, then our children will look for the explanation of the word 'fear' in a dictionary. But until then, temper yourself in the fearlessness of the class struggle! Prepare yourself for the new advances of the enemy, and strike with all the might of which the strong arms of the working class are capable!

CURTAIN

ACT IV
Scene 8

Investigator's Office at the O.G.P.U. (Secret Service) Headquarters. A large, high room. The doors themselves seem to preserve the silence. They open soundlessly. BORODIN enters the room, carrying a bundle of newspapers. The door closes behind him. He walks to the table at which the WOMAN INVESTIGATOR sits writing. She is a calm, business-like person.

BORODIN. I knew that I would be arrested. Will you please be kind enough to telephone my home and ask them to send me my bedroom slippers? (*The* WOMAN INVESTIGATOR *with a gesture invites* BORODIN *to sit down, and continues writing.*) This is very kind of you. (*Sits down, places the newspapers in his lap.*) Still... you *are* afraid of science... You refute scientific conclusions by arresting me. That, my dear woman, is power, but it is not proof... You will not frighten me with imprisonment. I have lived my life, and it is a matter of indifference to me whether I die in my own bed or on a prison cot... But my ideas will live on. And my students will continue to develop them... Of course, I'll admit that that old Bolshevik woman made a very good reply... Wrathfully. Most wrathfully. I must confess that I became thoughtful about certain things she said. After the lecture I did not sleep all night. I was thinking about that old woman. She and I are the same age, but our old age is different. Quite different. And we see the world differently. I even began to write her a letter, but I did not finish it. And yet, the letter didn't turn out so bad. Yes. Thirty years ago everything seemed much clearer to me... I've brought some newspapers... saw what they wrote about me. (*Pause.*) Well, go ahead with your investigation. (*The* WOMAN INVESTIGATOR *rises, gathers certain papers, and goes out.* BORODIN *is alone.*) So... (*He is silent for a while, then he opens a newspaper and reads.*) 'The Class Enemy in the Rôle of Professor.' That's all about me. So... (*Reads on.*) That's putting it strong, all right, pretty strong. (*Takes up another paper.*) 'Borodin's Theory Must be Exposed.' Articles, letters, resolutions... Professors, students, metal workers, textile workers

454

... all are, for some reason, indignant. (*Takes a third newspaper.*) 'More Daring with the Advancement of Proletarians into Science.'

(*Quietly the frightened ZAKHAROV enters.*)

ZAKHAROV. Ivan Ilyitch...

BORODIN (*pointing to a passage in the newspaper*). Look here, Visarion Zakharovitch... Here is a picture of the former servant Nastya. Now she is a textile worker, a shock-brigader. Under her picture is a short article... Nastya wrote that short article about me. Nastya writes! Think of it: until recently she was hardly literate! ... How people have changed!

ZAKHAROV. I have other things to worry me besides Nastya, Ivan Ilyitch.

BORODIN. Ah, yes, yes, of course. (*Looks around.*) How do you happen to be here?

ZAKHAROV. God only knows. I worked quietly, didn't hurt anyone... It is very strange, Ivan Ilyitch.

BORODIN. Never mind, never mind. Appeal to Krishna to help you. 'Sever your feelings from your taste for them. Rise above human squabbles.'

ZAKHAROV. Try and do it.

(*Enter the WOMAN INVESTIGATOR, followed by KIMBAYEV, who is speaking to her.*)

KIMBAYEV. Look, comrade, at the kind of books Zakharov was buying for the Institute. For physiologists he bought *Occult Intelligence, The Cross and the Pentograms, A Medium's Handbook, Mysticism as the Basis of the World.* There is still another pile of them. Sabotage! What do you say, comrade?

WOMAN INVESTIGATOR. What will *you* say to that, Ivan Ilyitch?

ZAKHAROV. Occultism is the most perfect science of human behavior. And in view of the fact that we are studying human behavior...

BORODIN. Once upon a time, Visarion Zakharovitch, you were a professor, weren't you?

KIMBAYEV (*to the WOMAN INVESTIGATOR*). Well, good-bye, comrade, I'll leave it to you. I must go back to the Institute. We have important things to do there. (*Exit.*)

ZAKHAROV. So it's because of the books... For a bad selection. That's fair enough. Is there anything else? May I go now?

WOMAN INVESTIGATOR. Anything else?

ZAKHAROV. Why? I swear... oh, no, nothing. (*Pause.*) Nothing. I did sign an appeal to all civilized people... But I swear... I didn't get a kopeck for it. They promised to pay me a hundred rubles a month if I would sign this appeal, but they didn't pay me a kopeck...

WOMAN INVESTIGATOR. Who promised?

ZAKHAROV (*very much confused*). What? (*Points to* BORODIN.) He.

BORODIN (*astonished*). I?!

ZAKHAROV (*indicating* BORODIN). He did. I wanted to buy a telescope with the money, and show the stars to people on the boulevards... I...

WOMAN INVESTIGATOR. Who wrote the appeal?

ZAKHAROV (*indicating* BORODIN). He did.

WOMAN INVESTIGATOR (*reading*). 'Professor Borodin has been arrested.' But it isn't true, Ivan Ilyitch.

BORODIN. I told him not to do it...

WOMAN INVESTIGATOR. Whom did you tell that?

BORODIN. What? That's not it. I didn't write the appeal.

WOMAN INVESTIGATOR. Who did it then?

BORODIN. I don't know...

ZAKHAROV. It was he... he... he...

WOMAN INVESTIGATOR. Go! (ZAKHAROV, *walking backward and stumbling, goes out. The* WOMAN INVESTIGATOR *presses a button, and* VARGASOV *enters.*) What do you know about Borodin?

VARGASOV. I did everything under his instructions. I collected signatures for the appeal by his orders. Then he ordered me to send the appeal abroad. He said that this was the program of our scientific party. But what kind of program it was and who took part in it and why, I don't know. I was not initiated into these mysteries.

WOMAN INVESTIGATOR. Go!

VARGASOV. I want to add, however, that Professor Borodin held me in awful fear, like a rabbit. That is why I did not report him. I was afraid of him — afraid...

WOMAN INVESTIGATOR. Go! (*Exit* VARGASOV.)

BORODIN. Evidently we are not going to discuss my lecture?

WOMAN INVESTIGATOR. Read this. (*She gives him a paper.* BORODIN *reads.*)

BORODIN. I never incited anyone... I didn't organize the laboratory for a struggle against the vydveezhentsy... I did not write any appeals... I don't know anything about any scientific party... (*The* WOMAN INVESTIGATOR *presses a button, and* KASTALSKY *enters.*) Herman! Tell her everything, Herman, everything!... This is my pupil, my student. He's my witness. We worked together over the lecture. He knows everything. Say what you know, Herman.

KASTALSKY. Must I repeat my deposition? (*The* WOMAN INVESTIGATOR *nods her head.*) Very well, then, I shall repeat it. I was detained at the border and brought here. I was confronted with a number of accusations, but it is Professor Borodin who is guilty of all my crimes.

BORODIN. I?

KASTALSKY. Professor Borodin was my teacher and my mentor. I believed in his theory. I bowed before his erudition. He enslaved me with his sincerity and his authority, his eminence. Professor Borodin instilled in me hatred against the vydveezhentsy. He taught me that science should fight them. He said to me: 'Study twice as hard as before. Don't let these vydveezhentsy catch up with you. Prove to everybody that it is not they but we who must rule the State.' He taught me to see everywhere only fear, hunger, and insanity. 'There is no difference between a dog-fight and a workers' rebellion,' Borodin would say. 'In either case it is hunger. Dogs fight over a bone; workers fight for a crust of bread. The class struggle is an invention of idle politicians.' Oh, Borodin was a good politician. He preached — he incited — but he himself remained on the sidelines — away from the struggle, while I, like a pathetic pawn — I was young — I wanted to defend justice that had been violated. I knew that the theory of fear might become the banner of a counter-revolutionary political movement.

BORODIN. Monstrous!

KASTALSKY. Yes, monstrous! Borodin worked on the plane of pure science, while I did the dirty work, and placed my shoulder under the yoke of conspiracy and all sorts of dark deeds. I sank up to my neck in darkness and dirt, so that a professor might quietly prepare his so-called scientific lecture. But now I denounce him. You must judge him ten times as strictly as you would judge me.

WOMAN INVESTIGATOR. Go, Citizen Kastalsky.

KASTALSKY. Why did you do that to me, Ivan Ilyitch? (*Exit.*)

WOMAN INVESTIGATOR (*walks back and forth, stops before* BORODIN, *reads a stenographic report which she holds in her hand*). 'We are all

457

of us rabbits. Is it possible, then, for us to do creative work? Of course not.' Well, and what about these people, Ivan Ilyitch? Are they rabbits, or are they boa constrictors? Don't you see the ring in which they have squeezed you? Will you say that, too, was done because of fear of life? However, they overcame that fear when they decided to join a counter-revolutionary gang... The class war, Ivan Ilyitch, is stronger than any fear. Well... What have you to say to their accusations?

BORODIN. I can say nothing. This is all... not so... not as it should be... Monstrous!

CURTAIN

ACT IV

SCENE 9

Early morning in the living-room of ELENA'S *apartment. The room is in disorder. It seems vacant and everything in it transient. On* ELENA'S *table are pots and pans. In one corner is a wicker trunk with* AMALIA'S *belongings. Now everywhere are boxes, bottles, vials, and other truck. The furniture has been shoved hither and thither.*

On NATASHA'S *table by the window is a small bit of sculpture just begun.* VALENTINA *is standing by it, trying to model.*

AMALIA *quietly dodges out of one door and into another, always carrying something, chewing, and muttering.* VALENTINA *throws the clay down, wipes her fingers, and stands in thought.* AMALIA *comes up to* VALENTINA *and whispers.*

AMALIA. Kolenka is up. He will want an omelet for breakfast. You don't love him enough. You annoy him often. You don't look out for him properly. I thought that you would be a much better daughter-in-law.

VALENTINA. You're a rat... Yes, yes! A rat — in a vacant apartment. You crawl along the floor and gnaw at the furniture.

(*Enter* NATASHA *with a bundle.*)

NATASHA (*to* AMALIA). You're not a little girl. You should pick things up after yourself. You left all that dirt in the kitchen. We'll have to organize a cleaning expedition.

AMALIA. I will tell Nikolai everything — everything! (*Exit.*)

VALENTINA. Dirt! All around us — dirt... Cigarette butts...

(*Enter* KLARA, *who goes toward her room.*)

KLARA. You have forgotten me altogether, Natasha. You come home only to sleep.

NATASHA. I'd like your advice, Auntie Klara.

KLARA. All right, what is it?

NATASHA. My father drinks and drinks. Yesterday we quarrelled. I tell him I will not live with a drunken father, and he tells me in that case to get out. I will gather all my things together and will

459

get out. I want to live with Uncle Bobrov. And then I will go to my Pioneer detachment and I will live with the detachment.

VALENTINA. This place is empty and dusty. No one ever comes here... He lies in bed — careless and coarse — all day long... He sputters and scolds us — me, and my father, and all of us. I've entirely lost my bearings, Klavdya Vasilyevna.

NATASHA. Let's go together, Valya. I'll teach him to disobey his own daughter! Will you take your things with you? No? Well, don't bother — I have a towel...

KLARA. Well, my girls, what shall I do with you? I might give you some tea in my room, and over the tea we might discuss everything.

NATASHA. I will put the tea-kettle on — and we'll have our talk.

(*Enter* TSEKHOVOI.)

TSEKHOVOI (*to all those present*). Valentina called my mother a rat! (*To* VALENTINA.) Rats can give birth only to little rats. Do you mean to say then that I am a little rat? Is that it? Is that what you wanted to say?

VALENTINA. And to think that it was in your love that I sought the strength to help me transform my life!

TSEKHOVOI. 'The transformation of man is not the same thing as the repair of a tractor.' Who said that? I don't remember. I don't remember anything. No — I do remember. I was expelled from the Party, and I was expelled from the Institute — that I do remember. It was this old woman who expelled me from the Party. I forbid you to speak to her. Do you understand — I forbid it!

NATASHA. You cannot forbid self-criticism.

TSEKHOVOI. Shut up!

KLARA (*to* VALENTINA *and* NATASHA). Come along with me.

TSEKHOVOI. Valentina! Stand back! Natasha, march into your room!

KLARA. Let us pass!

TSEKHOVOI. No!

KLARA (*masterfully and firmly*). Let me pass immediately! (*She advances upon him.*)

(*Enter* ELENA.)

ELENA. Who will not let whom pass?

NATASHA. Lenna is here! Lennotchka! (*Runs to her.*)

KLARA. At last!

(*Enter* KIMBAYEV *with a suitcase. He is followed by* BOBROV.)

KIMBAYEV. Klara — we have a guest. A dear guest is here. (*Puts down the suitcase.*)

BOBROV. The new director of the Institute was met at the train by the secretary of the Party cell (*points to* KIMBAYEV, *who is just leaving the room*) and by his assistant (*points to himself*) with fitting solemnity.

NATASHA. Have you come for good, Elena?

ELENA. For good, my little girl, for good. How do you do, Valya? Nikolai, hello! You're unshaven and dishevelled. Don't you ever wash?

VALENTINA. He hasn't had time to sober up. (*Exit.*)

NATASHA. Let me carry my things into your room.

ELENA. Do carry them. We'll live together.

NATASHA. We'll have tea right away in Auntie Klara's room. (*Runs out into* KLARA'S *room.*)

KLARA. And you, my dear, have begun to dress up. A new suit of clothes, I see.

ELENA. I'm a professor now! And, generally speaking, it doesn't hurt to live in a more civilized manner, as Nikolai used to say... Believe it or not, I've acquired new habits. I've suddenly acquired a taste for good music. I'm always at the concerts... That's me. I'm talking about myself!

(NATASHA *enters with a tea-kettle.*)

KIMBAYEV. Are you alone, these days, or what?

ELENA. So far I am alone, Hussain.

KIMBAYEV. That's good... (*Waxing tender in his crude way.*) See, Klara, how young and beautiful and healthy and wise is our dear guest Elena... (*Panicky with embarrassment.*) Where do you keep the water here, Natasha? (*Goes out with* NATASHA.)

BOBROV. I am afraid that the secretary of the Party local has succumbed to the influence of our new managing director.

ELENA. Fine chap... On the way over he told me all the news twice... Why is there so much truck here? You've turned a perfectly good room into an attic.

KLARA. This room has now become something of a front-line trench. Tsekhovoi and I are carrying on a civil war. I have expelled him from the Party, and he's trying to expel me from the apartment, and so we are carrying on the fight.

ELENA. Aren't you ashamed of yourself, Nikolai? (TSEKHOVOI *is silent. Enter* KIMBAYEV *and* NATASHA.) Hussain, come on, let's set things in order.

KIMBAYEV. Let's, Elena...

(NATASHA *brings the hot water in a tea-kettle.* ELENA *and* KIM-BAYEV *are busy setting the room in order.*)

ELENA. We have plans enough for three Five-Year Plans.

BOBROV. The Institute will be considerably expanded, Elena Mikhailovna.

KIMBAYEV (*barging in*). We have eighteen new graduate students. Ten of them are Party members. We have organized a strong Party local.

BOBROV. Just because you're the secretary of the Party local is no reason for interrupting me.

KIMBAYEV. Please excuse me, my friend... I'm very excited. Go on, talk.

BOBROV. The Institute will work on a new type of man.

ELENA. And that, Klara, is no clay model of some 'Proletarian in Science.' This one is borne by life itself.

BOBROV. A new breed of man is being created. In fifteen — twenty years from now we will be hopelessly old-fashioned specimens.

ELENA. Don't be afraid, Nikolai Kasyanovitch, you too are growing. Don't you think, Klara, that his reply to Borodin was excellent? I read about it in the papers.

KLARA. He made a political speech. He found simple words — convincing words.

KIMBAYEV. Have you heard, Elena? She said 'a political speech.' It was I who taught him the elements of politics. If you don't believe me, ask him.

BOBROV. It's true.

KIMBAYEV. I have a good pupil, Elena. Look at the books he's reading. (*Takes a book out of* BOBROV's *brief-case.*) *The Dialectic of Nature.* What do you think of that, Elena? (*To* BOBROV.) Study — study.

ELENA. A scientist cannot go into politics without hurting himself. You may lose the scale of centuries.

BOBROV. Learn to think on a scale of centuries from this remarkable woman.

ELENA. And what about Sèvres china?

BOBROV. Elena Mikhailovna!

ELENA. But *Faust* is after all a remarkable piece. I read it while I was in Saratov. Take this bucket into the kitchen and throw the dirty water out. Rinse it and bring me some fresh water. (BOBROV *takes the bucket and goes out.*) Open the window, Hussain. Spring and sunshine are in the streets. And you sit here in this poison-gas refuge! (KIMBAYEV *opens a window.*) On the front entrance of our new building we will carve the inscription 'Institute of the Diamond Fund.' And under it will be the slogan: 'People decorated with the order of the Red Banner, the advance men of the collectivist columns, workers of shock-brigades, you are the Diamond Fund of humanity.' Like it? I thought of it on the train.

KIMBAYEV. Diamond is a hard rock. It cuts glass, resists fire, and shines. You are a diamond, Elena.

KLARA. Is your head all right, Hussain?

(*Enter* AMALIA.)

KIMBAYEV. I inspected the library, I exposed Zakharov, my head is all right. But I did get a little dizzy when I saw her... Where shall I put this wicker trunk, Elena?

AMALIA. This is my trunk. Don't you touch my trunk. Nikolai! Tell him, Nikolai!

TSEKHOVOI. Let go!

KIMBAYEV. Take it, old woman. Take it to the dust-heap. (AMALIA *drags her trunk out.*) Ai-bai-ai, she's a funny old woman.

TSEKHOVOI. Ach! (*Waves his arms and goes to the door.*)

ELENA. Nikolai! (*Exit* TSEKHOVOI.)

KIMBAYEV. Let him go! I'm not sorry for him.

ELENA. Yes, neither am I sorry... Like a tooth that was pulled out.

KLARA. That tooth is rotten at the root.

(*Enter* NATASHA.)

NATASHA. Oh, fresh air! I wanted to open the window long ago, but the old woman wouldn't let me. The tea is ready, comrades, the tea is ready!

ELENA. As soon as we wash our hands, Natasha...

KLARA. Well, Lennka, let me see your forehead. (*Kisses* ELENA *on her forehead.*) 'With such a forehead one must not go in for science.'... 'A Hamlet in skirts!' (*She goes out with* NATASHA.)

463

KIMBAYEV (*going toward the kitchen*). Listen, Elena, now you are smarter than I am. You stand above me. But I'll catch up with you. And when we become equals, then I'll have something serious to tell you — something important.

(*Enter* BOBROV *with a bucket of water.*)

KIMBAYEV. Let's go wash our hands, Elena.

ELENA (*to* BOBROV). Tea is served, Nikolai Kasyanovitch.

(ELENA *and* KIMBAYEV *go out to the kitchen.* BOBROV *places the bucket near the table on which the statue rests.*)

(*Enter* VALENTINA *with a suitcase. There is an embarrassing pause.* VALENTINA *walks up to the sculpture, picks up a paperweight, and smashes the statue, which falls to pieces.*)

BOBROV. Why did you do that?

VALENTINA. The whim of a woman of genius. 'A Proletarian in Science'! Proletarian! I'm not yet able to express anything new, but I am sure that I can well afford to break this thing without regret. Everything is disgusting and meaningless. You, on the other hand, you have changed a lot, Nikolai Kasyanovitch.

BOBROV. Really? Do you think so? I rather think you are right. We always regarded ourselves as teachers of life, and we taught others. Now we sit in the preparatory class and learn everything from the beginning. But we haven't yet rid ourselves of the tendency to moralize. It's difficult... At any rate, the road ahead of me is clear.

VALENTINA. You have found yourself. But even working in the factory did not help me.

(*Enter* ELENA *and* KIMBAYEV.)

ELENA (*noticing the suitcase*). Valentina Ivanovna! I will not live here very long. There is no reason why you should go away. Even today I can...

VALENTINA. I'm going away for good. I will never come back to Nikolai.

KIMBAYEV. Oh, Nikolai — another wife running away from you! Valya, why don't you first have tea with us before you go?

(VALENTINA *is silent.* ELENA *quietly leads* KIMBAYEV *away.*)

BOBROV. You — you are going away?

VALENTINA. Look — clay and grey dust on the floor... That is all there is left of me, too — only grey dust... And it was my father who broke me... Yes, yes, yes! He taught me to look everywhere only for unconditioned stimuli... I fell in love with Tsekhovoi ... Love is everywhere an unconditioned stimulus... and that love was to have made me a new person. But now I'm going away into emptiness — to no one... My father has smashed me into shards and broken bits, and he has smashed himself. Now I could say very many cruel words to my father.

(*Enter* BORODIN, *bent and aged. In his hand is a bouquet of snowdrops. Behind him like a shadow comes* AMALIA.)

BORODIN. Well, speak!

VALENTINA. Papa! Papa has come!

BOBROV. Ivan Ilyitch! Sit down, Ivan Ilyitch!

BORODIN. Speak, Valyusha! Say everything!

VALENTINA. No! What are you saying! I'm silly, Papa. I don't know what's happened to me.

BORODIN. I, too, am only an old clay shard. I have neither friends nor students nor a daughter. I am as lonely as a mangy cur.

VALENTINA. I can't bear to listen to him. I don't want to listen to him. I'll burst into tears in a minute! (*Runs out.*)

BOBROV. Well, there you are! (*Starts to run after her, then turns to* BORODIN, *then again goes after* VALENTINA.) Ivan Ilyitch, I'll be back in a minute.

(BOBROV *runs after* VALENTINA. NATASHA *comes out of* KLARA'S *room.*)

AMALIA. There you are! You shouldn't have come — you shouldn't have.

BORODIN. Let me alone! I can't even recognize my own daughter. Thirty-five years ago everything seemed much clearer to me.

AMALIA. Do you remember, Ivan Ilyitch... thirty-five years ago ... Tatiana's Day... the lights in the Hall of Columns... and a little student on the stage...

BORODIN. Go away with your student — to the Devil's own grandmother!... There is nothing to you except the memory of that little student. Get away, or I will beat you up... (AMALIA *runs out of the room.*) And to think that once upon a time I was in love with that old ash-tray! I can't understand even myself. Now I'm all alone. In airless space.

NATASHA. I am here too. I'm standing.

465

BORODIN. Is that you, you little Pioneer?

NATASHA. But she was always dirty, that old woman, and she's always chewing and chewing. I'm even surprised...

BORODIN. I've never noticed it before, but it is true. She is always chewing.

NATASHA. And thirty-five years ago the power was in the hands of the Tsar and the landlords. And there were policemen. I swear by my honor as a Pioneer they would skin three hides from every workman. Lyoshka told me about it. Do you know, his father had actually seen a living policeman... On my word as a Pioneer!

BORODIN. I have just come from the Institute. Just to have a look — that's why I went. The corridors were noisy. There were many faces of strangers to me — young graduate students. My study is still under lock and key. They stood there in argument before my door. They argued very warmly. Someone proposed to break the lock. The proposal was rejected. I stood behind a closet and listened to them criticize me.

NATASHA. Why didn't you open it?

BORODIN (*looks at* NATASHA *and becomes thoughtful*). I wanted to, but then... I was ashamed to come out from behind the closet.

NATASHA. What if you *were* ashamed? In school I once broke a window and kept quiet about it. They were asking to find out who did it, and I was still quiet. I was ashamed to tell them. But after a while I did tell them, and I felt much easier then.

BORODIN. Perhaps — perhaps... Perhaps you are right. I am all alone, my dear Pioneer girl. I have no one to go to for advice.

NATASHA. You know what? Why don't you come to our Pioneer detachment for the discussions? Why don't you consult with us?

BORODIN. I am too old, my girl — too old.

NATASHA. Yes, that is true. We accept members only up to the age of fourteen. Do you know what? Sit here for a while. I'll be right back.

(NATASHA *goes into* KLARA'S *room.* BORODIN, *alone, gazes at the small bouquet of flowers in his hand.*)

BORODIN. They were selling snowdrops in the street. People passed by, bought them, laughed... How is it I hadn't noticed?... Yes. If I were only fourteen years old now...

(BORODIN *smells the bouquet of flowers as* ELENA *and* KIMBAYEV *come in.*)

ELENA. How do you do, Ivan Ilyitch?

BORODIN. Elena Mikhailovna... You... You see, I... I have brought you the keys to my study. (*Gives her the keys.*) Take them and open it, and...

ELENA. You'll open it yourself, and you will take charge of the new graduate students. We are waiting for you to tell us when you will be ready to resume your work, Ivan Ilyitch.

KIMBAYEV. Come on, Comrade Borodin, come on. It's as clear as day. We'll work together. We will look for diamonds.

BORODIN. I am no longer of any use to science or to you, Elena Mikhailovna. I have been too seriously mistaken in people and in my conclusions. I cannot step across those mistakes.

ELENA. That isn't so, Ivan Ilyitch. You will step across them. You can, if you only want to.

BORODIN. I'd like to.

KIMBAYEV. It's hard to do it alone. We will help you.

ELENA. You studied life sitting at the window of your study, which was just like studying the sea in a glass of water. But the glass does not have the tides or the swells or storms, but only salt crystals and infusoria. Well... Here you tried to explain the tides of the sea by the indignation of the infusoria. Confess that it was so, Ivan Ilyitch!

BORODIN. What do you mean?

ELENA. Come out in the open, publicly, with a criticism of your own lecture.

BORODIN. Ah, so that's it...

(*The door bursts open and* TSEKHOVOI *enters.*)

TSEKHOVOI. Go on, Mother, don't be afraid! Go on! Come here — all of you!

(AMALIA *enters, and out of the other rooms* KLARA *with* NATASHA *and* BOBROV *with* VALENTINA.)

TSEKHOVOI. Here! All of you who haven't seen yet, look, here she is! The mother of Nikolai Tsekhovoi — of a proletarian from the worker's bench... I have the honor to present myself: the son of a military prosecutor...

KLARA. We have known it right along.

TSEKHOVOI. I want to know who told you!... What traitor betrayed me? I am asking all of you!

KIMBAYEV. Go to sleep, you sheep's tail.

TSEKHOVOI. What scoundrel denounced me?

BOBROV. I told them about your past.

TSEKHOVOI. So it was you... with Valentina... In that case let us go away, Mother. Natashka, come here! We'll take our place on the boulevard. We'll stretch out our hands. We'll become beggars. We'll ask them to take pity on us who have been expelled from everywhere. You, too, have been expelled, Mother, and Natashka will be expelled as soon as they discover whose daughter she is.

NATASHA (*tears herself out of his grasp*). You're lying! There's no reason why they should expel me. Klara, is there any reason?

KLARA. Don't listen to him, Natasha.

ELENA. You're a filthy little fellow, Nikolai.

TSEKHOVOI. But then you are a proletarian — a Red Director — a famous person — ha! (*Laughs.*) Shall I bow to you? Come on, old woman, let's go... Your son has acknowledged you before all the people. Are you glad now? (*To* BORODIN.) Come on, old man, come with us. We belong to the same tribe. We are a famous company. You, too, are no longer good for anything. You're an old overshoe. You — forecaster of fate!

(TSEKHOVOI *goes out. He is followed by the muttering* AMALIA.)

KLARA (*comes up to* BORODIN). You can trust me, Ivan Ilyitch. I am an old woman, but I am sure that you and I can still be useful. It's too soon to throw us away on the ash-heap. Of course, they might retire us on a pension...

BORODIN. No, no! Why pension me off? I want to work, Klavdya Vasilyevna. I want to work with Elena Mikhailovna, with Kimbayev... But not with those others — no! Let them — let them say what they like. Let them titter behind my back and say that the old man was frightened out of his wits, scared out of his convictions. Then I will tell the whole world how I protected the rabbits and how the rabbits proved to be boa constrictors. I was afraid of Makarova. I closed my study to keep her out. I led her along the wrong road. And I opened the door to Herman. I will tell about that, too. I will tell how I joyously greeted every manifestation of fear and how I failed to notice fearlessness. I welcomed the madness of Kimbayev, and I overlooked the growth of his reason... I lived a phantom life. I created it in my home and in my study. I did not understand real life. And life penalizes those who shun it — with loneliness... That is really a frightful vengeance! I think I'm weeping, but I'm not ashamed... because now I will go to those who masterfully demand the keys to all the studies and I will give them all of my keys. I accept your condition, my new director. (*Then to* KLARA.) You and I can still be useful. I'll show him how to call me an old overshoe!

CURTAIN